An Introduction to Religious and Theological Studies

An Introduction to Religious and Theological Studies

CYRIL ORJI

RESOURCE *Publications* · Eugene, Oregon

AN INTRODUCTION TO RELIGIOUS AND THEOLOGICAL STUDIES

Resource Publications
An Imprint of Wipf and Stock Publishers
199 W. 8th Ave., Suite 3
Eugene, OR 97401

www.wipfandstock.com

ISBN 13: 978-1-4982-2146-7

Manufactured in the U.S.A.   08/06/2015

Dedicated to Luke Orji, my brother

Contents

Acknowledgments | xi

1 **The Complex Matter of Religion** | 1
   What Is Religion?
   The Matter of Religion Reconsidered
   Is Religion Different From theology?
   Study Guide

2 **Creation Accounts of the Abrahamic Religions** | 26
   Judeo-Christian Accounts
   Creation Accounts in the Quran
   Proliferation of Sin
   Christian Application of Creation Story
   Study Guide

3 **Judaism** | 46
   Sojourn in Egypt
   The Covenant
   Exodus A Creation Story?
   Prophecy and the Prophetic Books
   Prophecy in the Ancient Near-East and Israel
   Prophetic Books
   Isaiah the Prophet
   Study Guide

4 **The Canon of the Hebrew Bible and the Christian Old Testament** | 80
   Ancient Civilization and Israelite History
   Nature of the Bible
   The Christian Old Testament
   Catholic and Protestant Canons
   Pentateuch and Historical-Critical Method
   Study Guide

5   **The Christian New Testament** | 95
The Gospels
The Centrality of Mark
Critical Reconstruction of the Life of Jesus
The Stages In-Setting of the Gospels
The Four Senses of Scripture
Hermeneutics and the New Testament
Characteristics of Catholic Exegesis
Study Guide

6   **Two Great Influences** | 128
Aurelius Augustine (354–430)
Conclusion
The Middle Ages and Christianity
Thomas Aquinas (1224/5–1274)
Revival of theomism
Critique of Thomas Aquinas
Study Guide

7   **The Church, Christology, and Salvation** | 152
The Problem of Evil
The Church
Christology
Catholic and Catholicism
Study Guide

8   **Development of Christian Doctrine and Spritiuality** | 169
Christian Communities in Asia Minor
The First Ministerial Position: the Diaconate
Church Leadership and Organization
Origin and Rise of Monasticism
Early Ecumenical Councils
Christianity in Africa

9   **Schism and Reformation** | 191
The Great Schism and Conciliar Movement
Social Changes in Europe
The Catholic Reform

10 **Islam** | 220
Pre-Islamic Arabian Peninsula
Al Qur'an
The Five Pillars of Faith

11 **Religious Rapprochement and African Traditional Religions** | 249
World Religions: Common themes
Tribal Religions
African Traditional Religions
Nine Core Set of Beliefs
ATRs in Post-Colonial Africa

Bibliography | 275
Index | 283

Acknowledgments

THIS BOOK HAS BEEN years in the making. My thanks to all the good people who made this book possible. I must mention particularly the students I taught in my graduate student days at Marquette University and the University of Dayton undergraduate students. Together they shaped my teaching identity and raised the critical questions that set the wheel of this book in motion. Special thanks also to Prof. Bradford Hinze and Dr. Christine Firer Hinze, who believed in me and created the environment that gave me my first opportunity to engage in what I like best—teach.

1

The Complex Matter of Religion

THE PHENOMENON THAT GOES under the umbrella term "religion" is one of the many ways individuals and communities engage in human search for meaning. From the beginning of human origins religion has served as a unique response to the fundamental human question, "Who am I?" At a recent conference on the Environment and Economic Sustainability in Copenhagen, Denmark, a young man from Brazil gave a fascinating account of their primary school curriculum. According to this young man, at a very early age all Brazilian children are exposed to three different cultures: the cultures of the indigenous peoples of Brazil, African cultures, and Portuguese culture. The first African slaves arrived in Brazil in the sixteenth century to replace the indigenous labor. At this time Brazil was occupied by the Portuguese crown. Modern Brazilians believe that they all hail from at least one or two of these cultures that have mixed over time. What they are trying to find out in essence is their roots—who they are as Brazilians. We all confront the same dilemma as humans: Who are we? Where do we come from? And why are we here? For some, this is a question about the mystery of life.

Questions about the mysteries of life are much more common during times of distress, war, famine, earthquake, or other disasters. On January 12, 2010, a 7.0 earthquake left about 230,000 Haitians dead and about 1.3 million others homeless. A 9.0 earthquake hit Japan the following year in March, triggering a tsunami that left hundreds of people dead. The tsunami also hit parts of Japan where their radiation plants were located, setting off a radiation crisis in the region. The impact of this calamitous event was felt

1

beyond Japan. For example, the tsunami brought about 1.5 million tons of debris from Japan to the west coast of the United States, fueling further fears of radiation crisis and irregular climate patterns. Natural disasters and wars in general produce calamities and destruction. The instability they produce can and does raise serious questions about the human person, the world, and our place in it.

The question "Who am I?" is ultimately related to the matter of our place in the world—the question of human agency. The question of human agency is a fundamental "religious" question: How are we related to the earth or planet? In 1991 what used to be known as Yugoslavia collapsed. The collapse led to a series of armed conflicts from 1991 to 2001 (the Balkan War) between then Yugoslavia's multiethnic groups—Serbs, Bosnians, Croats, etc. As the country disintegrated the world saw grotesque pictures of massacred innocent people, particularly women and children. The International Court of Justice called the massacre of Bosnian Muslims at Srebrenica in 1995 an act of genocide. By the time the war was over more than 200,000 people had lost their lives and a thousand others had been displaced from their homeland. The end result was a divided Yugoslavia federation that split along ethnic lines: Serbia, Slovenia, Bosnia, Croatia, Kosovo, and Macedonia. In situations such as these, when people are faced with questions that touch the core of their existence, they turn to religion for answers. We return to our question of human agency that religion addresses: How are we related to one another? How are we related to the planet? What does our relationship to the planet and to others say about who we are—question of personal identity?

The way Western cultures conceive personal identity is somewhat different from the way non-Western cultures conceive it. Although those of us in the West acknowledge that there are many factors (family, school, environment, etc.) that shape who we are, we still think of personal identity as a rather personal thing to be resolved by the individual. The individual self is often conceived as an independent and autonomous entity. But that is not so in non-Western cultures where the emphasis is on community—personal identity is a rather communal thing. We should keep in mind that the difference between the Western conception of personal identity and the non-Western conception of personal identity invariably affects the respective definitions or conceptions of the activity we call "religion."

WHAT IS RELIGION?

The activity we call religion is an ancient human phenomenon that predates Western culture itself. Before Christianity and Islam, indigenous peoples all over the world were always religious, although they may not have had a word to capture that religious activity. Indigenous peoples lived their lives in the particularities of their culture, community, and language, and expressed their belief in divine realities in the context of these. Religion, for them (if we may use the term), was not limited to worship of deity, but was rather for them a way of responding to the challenges posed by the harshness of their environment and the world at large. Religion and culture were, for them, one and the same reality, and participation in religious practices was considered part of what it means to be a member of the community. What we call "religion," in a nutshell, was for them a way of being human and a way of answering questions concerning the mystery of human life. In other words, they confronted questions posed by the mysteries of life in the larger context of what it means to be human: Why are we here? Who made us? Who or what is God? Do angels or spiritual beings exist? Why do we suffer? What is the meaning of suffering? Why is evil in the world? Do our actions here on earth have eternal consequences? Is there a life after death? They transmitted their answers to these questions orally from generation to generation, often embedding them in folklore, rituals, songs, dances, proverbs, customs, and ethical codes.

In its technical sense, the term "religion" is a Western concept. The term has a history—it was used at a particular time in human history to capture practices and ideas that are considered religious. What is technically called "religion" is an attempt to answer the same questions indigenous peoples have grappled with: What is humanity? What is the meaning of human life? Why are we here? Why suffering? Does suffering have a purpose? Why death? "What, finally, is that ultimate inexpressible mystery which encompasses our existence: whence do we come, and where are we going?"[1] All people, in some sense, answer these questions, but they do so somewhat differently. Some answer them categorically, while others answer them unconsciously.

---

1. See Vatican II, "Nostra Aetate."

Important Terms for Understanding the Meaning of Religion		
Term	**Meaning**	**Examples of Persons/Cultures**
Syncretism	Religions, like cultures, sometimes come in contact with each other. When this happens blending takes place. The blending that takes place when two cultures come in contact is known as acculturation. The blending that takes place when two religions come in contact is known as syncretism. Syncretism seems unavoidable in religion, the same way acculturation is unavoidable in culture.	Hinduism began as an intermingling of Aryan and Harappan cultural and religious traditions. The Harappan people lived in the Indus Valley region (modern-day India) around 200, 000 BCE, before they were invaded by the Aryans. The intermingling of their religions resulted in Hinduism. Judaism borrowed aspects of Canaanite religion. The Canaanites called their gods or shrine *El*, and Jews would call God *El-ohim*. Christianity borrowed aspects of Judaism, e.g., Jewish Scripture.
Theism	Belief in a personal deity or god	Judaism, Christianity, Islam, Zoroastrianism, Hinduism, African Traditional Religions (ATRs), and Native American religions
Atheism	The idea that there is no deity or god	Contemporary atheists like Richard Dawkins and Christopher Hitchens Some self-proclaimed atheists in the US protest against Christian or religious holidays. They also want the words "in God we trust" removed from US currency.
Agnosticism	The idea that, since we do not know for sure whether God exists, we should doubt it	Some Hollywood celebrities and TV stars claim to be agnostics.
Deism	The idea that God created the world and absconded; that God does not actively engage in the world	Some of the US founding fathers, like Thomas Jefferson and Benjamin Franklin, espoused deist views.
Monotheism	Belief in one God	The three Abrahamic monotheistic religions: Judaism, Christianity, and Islam Two non-Abrahamic monotheistic religions: Zoroastrianism and Egyptian (during the reign of Akhenaton)

Polytheism	Belief in the existence of multiple deities or gods	Hinduism, which has about 333 million gods Greek and Roman religions
Pantheon	Belief in the existence of multiple gods, hierarchically structured	In the Greek Pantheon the gods live on Mount Olympus, and Zeus is the head.
Scientism	The idea that only what can be proven by science is correct and that disbelief in God is a scientific hypothesis that can be rationally demonstrated	The New Atheists, such as English evolutionary biologist Richard Dawkins, Anglo-American literary critic Christopher Hitchens, and American philosopher and neuro-scientist Sam Harris
Rationalism	The idea that only what can be proven by reason is valid and that faith is not a form of knowledge	Philosophers like David Hume and Bertrand Russell, and also the New Atheists

Unconscious Religiousness

Whenever human existence is threatened, as in war, famine, or violence, religious and non-religious people alike look for answers. Religious people look up to the heavens for answers because they believe God is the origin and end of human life and therefore God must have an answer. Non-religious people, for their part, may look to the heavens but in a slightly different way, perhaps somewhat "unconsciously," if we may borrow the use of that term from the Auschwitz survivor and psychologist Viktor Frankl (1905–1997). Whenever I teach a class on religion I get two or three students who tell me off the bat that they are not "religious" or that they don't believe in any deity. But when I ask how many people in the class have done volunteer work to help the needy some of these same people who are not "religious" tend to be in the forefront. When I ask them why they volunteer or give their time to help others they often tell me they do it because it is the right thing to do. Frankl says this kind of activity is motivated by one's "spiritual unconscious" or "unconscious religiousness." According to him, life does not mean something vague, but something real and concrete, and because of this questions about the meaning of life cannot be answered by sweeping statements.[2]

2. Frankl, *Man's Search for Meaning*, 98.

Viktor E. Frankl (1905–1997)

Viktor Frankl was an Austrian psychiatrist and holocaust survivor. He was born into a Jewish family in Vienna, Austria, in 1905. As a student Frankl was fascinated by the works of the Austrian neurologist who later became known as the father of modern psychoanalysis, Sigmund Freud (1856–1939), and his student Alfred Adler (1870–1937). Frankl built on their works and went beyond them.

He studied medicine at the University of Vienna and later concentrated in neurology. He was particularly interested in matters pertaining to depression and suicide. While studying neurology in Vienna, Frankl was part of a team that worked in a "suicide pavilion" that treated over 30,000 women who suffered from depression and were near suicide. Frankl always put to his patients who suffered such torment the question, "Why do you not commit suicide?" From their answers he discovered that there is always a deep or fundamental reason why suicide was not an option—that "hunger, humiliation, fear and deep anger at injustice are rendered tolerable by closely guarded images of beloved person, by religion, by a grim sense of humor, and even by glimpses of the healing beauties of nature." From this Frankl derived what he called "logotherapy," an existential analysis whose central theme is "to live is to suffer, to survive is to find meaning in the suffering. If there is purpose in life at all, there must be a purpose in suffering and dying. But no man can tell another what this purpose is. Each must find out for himself, and must accept the responsibility that his answer prescribes."

When the Nazis took over Austria in 1938 Frankl was prevented from treating any Aryan patients because he was a Jew. In September 1942 Frankl and his wife, Tilly, together with his parents and his brother and sister, were deported to the Theresienstadt Ghetto by the Nazis. In October 1944 he and his wife were sent to the concentration camp in Auschwitz, where he spent five months working as both a slave laborer and physician. In Auschwitz he was separated from his wife, who was sent to a nearby concentration camp, Bergen-Belsen, where she died. His mother, Elsa, died in the gas chambers of Auschwitz. His father and brother also died in a concentration camp. In total Frankl spent about three years in different concentration camps. During that time Frankl discovered the importance of finding meaning in life. He returned to Vienna in 1945 after the American troops liberated Auschwitz, and then continued his work as a psychiatrist. In 1959 he wrote his famous book *Man's Search for Meaning*, in which he described his experiences in the concentration camps. The book was his way "to convey to the reader by way of a concrete example that life holds a potential meaning under any conditions, even the most miserable ones."

In Frankl's analysis of the human condition, everyone (religious and non-religious alike) has an "unconscious religiousness." It is this unconscious religiousness that makes us go beyond ourselves (transcendence) and reach out to others (actualize ourselves in freedom). Human existence, according to Frankl, insofar as it has not been neurotically distorted, is always directed at something or someone other than oneself. This reaching to something other than oneself he calls "self-actualization" or "self-transcendence." According to Frankl, self-actualization is not easy to attain. Like success, self-actualization can be elusive; the more one strives for it the more one misses it. "Don't aim at success," writes Frankl, "the more you aim at it and make it a target, the more you are going to miss it. For success, like happiness, cannot be pursued; it must ensue, and it only does so as the unintended side-effect of one's personal dedication to a cause greater than oneself or as the by-product of one's surrender to a person other than oneself."[3]

Self-actualization is implicit in the notion of religion. Many people who consider themselves "religious" can relate to Frankl's idea that the more one forgets oneself by giving oneself to a cause greater than oneself the more one fully actualizes oneself. Religious people think that self-actualization is fully realized only when one has found or discovered God—that this is what makes a person fully human. This is not to say that people who do not believe in God or who do not consider themselves "religious" are not fully human, but rather that to be religious is to be human in a unique way. One theologian who described this very well was twentieth-century German Jesuit theologian Karl Rahner (1904–1984). Rahner raised the question regarding whether a human person can know God, and answered in the affirmative. According to Rahner, we know God in our reflections on the meaning of life and existence. As human beings we experience our limitations when we face difficult situations such as natural disasters or human tragedy. It is when we experience our limitations that we begin to experience that which is beyond us. In such experience we begin to grasp the mystery of human existence and life in general. As we go through this experience we not only begin to go beyond (transcend) ourselves, we also begin to know ourselves as "mystery." Rahner calls this process of self-discovery "transcendental experience." It is in transcendental experience that we also experience God. When we start to speak of our experience of God, it is then that we begin to come to knowledge of who we really are in the true sense of the word. The God that we experience is mediated to us through religion.[4] The prison experience of Viktor Frankl may be a good example of a transcendental experience. Frankl suffered a great deal in Auschwitz. There he saw the highest level of human degradation and brutality. But rather than despair, he turned his experience into something positive. His prison experiences made him come to terms with himself as an authentic human person who is capable of enduring suffering. More than enduring suffering, an authentic human person is one who has learned to surrender him- or herself through a "religious" experience.[5] This then leads us to the question: What is religion?

---

3. Ibid., 17.

4. Rahner, *Foundations of Christian Faith*, 44–71.

5. Lonergan, *Method in Theology*, 104.

Other Important Terms for Understanding the Meaning of Religion		
Term	Meaning	Examples of Persons/Cultures
Animism	The idea that spirits inhabit everything	Shinto is an ancient religion of Japan that was founded around 1000 BCE. Shintoists believe that spirits, which they call *kami*, live everywhere.
Pantheism	The belief that God is in everything	In the Hindu philosophical text the Upanishads, there is the idea that although Brahman is the foundation of all reality, God is everything and everything is God.
Henotheism	The belief that there are several gods but some are more important than others	This idea is found in religions like Hinduism and Greek and Hellenistic religions.
Monolatry	The idea that one may acknowledge and choose to worship one deity while not denying the existence of other deities	Egypt during the time of Akhenaton (1360–1344 BCE) advocated worship of Aton, one of the several deities in Egypt.
Morphology	The study of the changing forms or structure of religion	Hinduism is a good example of a religion that has gone through several changes. It has assumed new forms in different phases.
Anthropomorphism	The idea of depicting God in human form and assigning human characteristics to God	Christianity, Judaism, and Islam often speak of God as if God were human. In both the Bible and the Quran God is described as "walking in the garden," "speaking to Abraham," and being disappointed with Adam and Eve. These are human characteristics ascribed to God.
Theriomorphism	The depiction of gods in animal forms	Polytheistic religions like Hinduism and ancient Egyptian religions have animal gods.

THE MATTER OF RELIGION RECONSIDERED

Raimon Panikkar (1918–2010), the Spanish-born Roman Catholic priest who had a Spaniard Catholic mother and an Indian Hindu Father, argued long ago against the idea of a universal theory of religion. His reason was that any universal theory of religion will be "loaded with political overtones"[6]

6. Panikkar, "The Invisible Harmony," 136.

and will inevitably be derived from the particular culture of those provid-ing the theory.[7] The merits of Panikkar's objection notwithstanding, we still need a working theory of religion. We need to define the ideas and prac-tices we consider religious. The field of religion is very broad. Religion is as ancient as humanity itself. From the very beginning of human existence human beings have been religious. Ancient civilizations like Egypt (c. 3100 BCE) Mesopotamia (c. 3000 BCE), and Babylon (c. 1792 BCE) were great not just because they had strong systems of government or because they engaged in commerce and trade with their neighbors, but also because they built their dynasties on strong religious (and ethical) systems. The legacy of their civilizations includes not only economics, but profound religious systems as well. They articulated in a unique way their "perception of that hidden power which hovers over the course of things and over the events of human history."[8] The Code of Hammurabi, named after King Hammu-rabi, who ruled from c. 1792 to 1750 BCE, is a well-ordered religious and a political text comprised of law codes put together for the good functioning of society. It stands in comparison to earlier law codes of ancient civiliza-tions, like the Code of Ur-Nammu (c. 2050 BCE) of King Ur, the Laws of Eshnunna (c. 1930 BCE), and later Hittite laws, Assyrian laws, and even the laws of Moses in the Hebrew Scriptures.

The word "religion" derives from the Latin *religio*, which was used to denote the act of performing a ritual with reverence or care. *Religio* itself may also have been derived either from the Latin *relegere*, which denotes people who were careful in their ritual actions, or *religare*, meaning "to bind." Early Latin Christian writers may have used the word *religio* to distinguish what they thought was true religion from false religion. For them *religio* would not extend to what we now know as "world religions" (like Hinduism, Bud-dhism, Islam, etc.). They applied the word only to what they thought was genuine and true worship, which for them was the Christian religion.[9] But a modern understanding of religion goes beyond the narrow definition of the ancient Christian writers and incorporates different historical traditions and practices—Islam, Hinduism, Buddhism, African Traditional Religions (ATRs), etc. Broadly defined, then, religion is "a system of symbols, myths, doctrines, ethics, and rituals for the expression of ultimate relevance."[10] The subject matter of religion is the human person, while God or deity may be considered the object or goal of religion. Viktor Frankl observed how those

---

7. See Schweitzer, *Contemporary Christologies*, 102.

8. See Nostra Aetate, no.2.

9. Kessler, *Eastern Ways of Being Religious*, 19.

10. Carmody and Brink, *Ways to the Center*, 1.

who died the quickest in the concentration camps were those who had lost self-determination and did not have anything to live for. He also observed that most of those who survived the horrors of the camps were those who had something to live for, such as their children or other loved ones, and who had attained self-actualization or self-transcendence—God. To better understand the meaning of religion we need to understand each of the five component parts in our definition.

A. **Symbol**: Why do Christians wear a cross around their necks? Why do Muslims who make the pilgrimage to Mecca wear white robes? Why do traditional Jewish men come to prayer with their *tallit* (prayer shawl)? A symbol is like a sign in the sense that it is used to represent something. A symbol is also like an icon because it presents something to the senses that ultimately needs to be interpreted. But more than a sign or icon, a symbol embodies that which it represents. A sign, for example, represents the object or idea to which it refers only in an arbitrary way. The relationship between the sign and the representation is determined merely by social convention. For example, we know by social convention that a red light means traffic must stop, but the red color of the light and the traffic's ability to stop are not inherently related in any way. It is just an arbitrary connection that can be changed whenever it is decided that there is a better way of signaling traffic to stop. But a symbol points to something beyond itself in a more evocative way. A symbol also has different levels of meaning. A symbol is better appreciated when it can be interpreted.

Christians wear a cross around their necks to symbolize who they are—followers of the man Jesus, who died on a cross and rose on the third day. Muslims on pilgrimage to Mecca wear simple white robes to symbolize the equality of all human beings and the purity that God expects of everyone. Jews come to prayer wearing the *tallit* to show that they remember the commandments given to them by Yahweh. Somebody on the outside may not be able to interpret or even appreciate a symbol the way a person on the inside does. This is because there is a difference between an insider's view and an outsider's view of religion.

Symbols are foundational to religion. Symbols, when used in religion, are meant to transport us out of our ordinary or mundane existence to the realm of the ultimate.[11] Religious symbols also inspire commitment on the part of those who belong to that religion. A cross

11. Ibid., 6.

is a Christian symbol that inspires commitment on the part of Christians. The crescent is a Muslim symbol that inspires a commitment on the part of Muslims. Symbols are not meant to be "believed," but revered.[12] Because they evoke reverence, symbols arouse passion. Religious people defend their religious symbols dutifully. What religious people do when they use a symbol is communicate something of deep significance that means the world to them.

B. **Myth**: Myth is usually confined to the realm of legends. We usually think of a myth as a story about a hero or an event that cannot be factually proven, or something that defies explanation. This common-sense definition assumes that a myth is not verifiable and not factual. But when used in religion, myth does not necessarily imply that we are dealing with an unverifiable fact. Rather than make factual claims, myths are to be understood as stories told and retold to express certain values. The question to be asked is not whether the truth claim of a myth can be verified, but whether the values it purports to convey can be vindicated.[13]

There is an episode in the life of Prophet Muhammad known as the *Miraj* (Ascension), which is referenced in Quran 17:1; 53:1–18. According to the way the story is told, the prophet was miraculously transported on a winged beast from Mecca to Jerusalem, where he ascended through the seven levels of heaven to the throne of God, and along the way met Moses, Jesus, and Abraham. The issue here is not whether we can factually determine that there are seven levels of heaven or whether a winged beast can transport a human person to heaven. Muslims who pray and venerate at the Dome of the Rock in Jerusalem (the site where Muhammad's heavenly journey began) are not concerned with such trivial matters. They are rather more concerned about preserving the sacred places of worship in Mecca and Jerusalem that the Quran prescribes.[14] The same thing can be said about the creation account in Genesis 1. The manner in which the story is told can be said to be a myth; it cannot be verified by the science of archeology. But the truth it expresses about the relationship between God and human beings and its basic assertion that God made man and woman in God's own image and likeness can be vindicated.

---

12. Ibid.

13. Ibid.

14. See Kaltner, *Introducing the Qur'an*, 52.

C. **Ritual**: "Rituals are prescribed, formalized actions that dramatize religious symbols."[15] Like myth and symbol, the primary purpose of ritual is "to connote some profound understanding or evoke some commitment within the person who hears the myth or participates in the ritual."[16] Because of the profound significance of the Quran in the daily life of Muslim believers, they engage the text of the Quran, both in their public and private recitation of it, in a variety of ways that might be considered ritualistic.[17] They engage in ritual behaviors like kissing the Quran, requesting a blessing from the Quran, weeping as the Quran is read, and placing the Quran in the home or somewhere outside the mosque as a sign of personal and communal devotion. These are prescribed obligatory rituals Muslims must perform.[18] In addition, Muslims also have a powerful ritual that is prescribed before prayer called *wudu* (ablution). Before prayer a person must clean with water his or her mouth, face, nostrils, forearms, elbows, feet, ears, and head. The only time one is exempted from this obligatory ritual is for women during menstruation. Christians likewise have prescribed obligatory rituals (like kneeling and standing at prescribed times during worship) they perform. In many cases, particular times for rituals are prescribed. For example, Catholic Christians are required to go to church on Ash Wednesday to receive ash on their forehead to mark the beginning of the Lenten season of fasting and abstinence, which lasts for forty days. The Jews eat the Sabbath meal at sundown on Friday, and what they eat and drink at this important meal are prescribed. Thus, often times "rituals are repeated in order to attain or sustain, the individual's contact with ultimate relevance and to consolidate the cohesion of the community."[19]

D. **Ethics**: People expect certain modes of behavior from religious persons. When a person who professes belief in deity acts in a way that is untoward or unbecoming, we usually express disappointment. This is because religions express values and have ethical prescriptions that hold their adherents to a very high standard. For example,

---

15. Carmody and Brink, *Ways to the Center*, 7.
16. Ibid., 8.
17. Kaltner, *Introduction to the Quran*, 32.
18. Ibid., 32–33.
19. Carmody and Brink, *Ways to the Center*, 7–8.

the Ten Commandments forbid lying, stealing, killing, bearing false witness, etc. These are ethical prescriptions for Jews and Christians, who accept these as divinely decreed by God. Buddhism prescribes the Middle Way (that one should avoid the extremes of sensual pleasure and the extremes of abstinence) and Eightfold Path: right speech, right understanding, right livelihood, right action, right effort, right mindfulness, right concentration, and right thought.

E. **Doctrine**: Religions have their own categorical statements about God, the origins of human life, sin, salvation, afterlife, etc. These are collectively called doctrine. In the Jewish prayer book (Siddur) there is a prayer (Shema Israel) there is a fundamental statement about God that takes center stage. It is a statement about the unity of God taken from Deuteronomy 6:4–9. A Jewish child learns the Shema and commits it to memory. An adult Jew is required to recite the Shema at least twice a day, once in the morning and once in the evening. Orthodox Jews cover their eyes with their right hand as a sign of reverence when it is recited in the synagogue. Buddhist doctrine is encapsulated in the Four Noble Truths: all life is suffering; the cause of suffering is desire; stopping desire will stop suffering; and the Eightfold Path is the best way to stop desire.

To be religious is therefore to be fully human. When we say this, however, as we pointed out earlier, we are by no means implying that people who do not consider themselves religious are less human. What we are saying unequivocally is that to be religious is to be human in a unique way. For religious people the knowledge of God, the supreme truth, brings radical change to a person's life in such a way that he or she lives no longer for him- or herself, but for others and God. "The human person cannot find fulfillment in himself that is apart from the fact that he exists 'with' others and 'for' others. This truth does not simply require that he live with others at various levels of social life, but that he seek unceasingly—in actual practice and not merely at the level of ideas—the good, that is the meaning of truth."[20]

---

20. Pontifical Council for Justice and Peace, *Compendium of the Social Doctrine of the Catholic Church*, 73.

IS RELIGION DIFFERENT FROM THEOLOGY?

Earlier we pointed out how Raimon Panikkar objected to the idea of having a universal theory of religion because of its implicit political overtones. He suggested that what is needed instead is a "theology for a post-colonial era."[21] Hints from Panikkar's suggestion already indicate that theology differs from religion. Religion seeks ultimate relevance. Theology attempts a reflection on religion and brings to light the significance and value of religion in a given culture.[22] The subject matter of theology (God) is also different from that of religion. Religion seeks to understand the human person as he or she expresses ultimate relevance. Theology attempts to understand God and God's response to human invocations. In the latter understanding, we can speak of a plurality of theologies—Christian theology, Islamic theology, Jewish theology, etc. Theology, like religion, has a history which has been understood differently, even by people of the same era. In Christian theology, for example, the early Christians had different understandings of Jesus. These different understandings led to divergent theologies of the person of Jesus Christ (Christology). Those who sought a political messiah who would deliver them from Roman oppression thought Jesus was a leader like Moses—a political liberator. Others who saw salvific value in their human suffering saw Jesus as one who would liberate them from sin and eternal punishment—a savior and religious leader.

The word "theology" is derived from the two Greek words, *theo* (God) and *logos* (discourse or study). From this etymological derivation theology can be conceived as the study of or reflection about God. Within a Christian context it denotes a person's reflections on the revelation given in and by Christ Jesus.[23] Christians, from the very beginning, have reflected on their understanding of God, i.e., how God has been revealed throughout human history, particularly in the Jewish and Christian scriptures. These reflections, as already indicated, have often led to different theologies. The reflections of the author of the Fourth Gospel (sometimes referred to as the Johannine community), for instance, have some marked differences with the reflections of the writer of Mark's Gospel (the Marcan community). The reflections of the writer of the Gospel of Luke (the Lukan community) are also different from the reflections or theology of the writer of the Gospel of Matthew (the Matthean community). Even between Peter and Paul, the two great leaders of the early Christian community, we see some differences in

---

21. Schweitzer, *Contemporary Christologies*, 102.

22. See Lonergan, *Philosophy of God and Theology*, 22.

23. Lonergan, *Method in Theology*, 296.

their theologies and understandings of Jesus. These marked differences may account for why Paul saw his own mission as that of an apostle to the Gentiles (Rom 11:13) and Peter as an apostle to the Jews (Gal 2:8). From these examples we see that even though theology attempts a reflection on God, "when we talk about God, we are also talking about ourselves in our contexts in nature, history, and culture."[24] We cannot talk about God without talking about ourselves, the human condition, and our search for meaning and ultimate relevance.

In the Catholic tradition the idea of theology has a complicated history. As reflection about God, theology was first carried out wherever there was a believing community. For some early Christians, like Clement of Alexandria (c. 150–220), theology was understood as "knowledge of divine things." The term "theology" could be used to describe the writings of ancient Greek writers like Homer, since the writings of these authors reflect their knowledge of divine realities, even if those divine realities are not Christian.[25] But more specifically, Christians of the third century used the word "theology" to mean only "talking about God in a Christian way," which means that they saw the study of theology as systematic thinking and articulation of the fundamental ideas of Christianity, i.e., the "intellectual reflection on the act, content, and implications of the Christian faith."[26] At this time theology was something that only monks and pastors engaged in. Theology did not develop into an academic discipline until the Middle Ages, the time of the scholastics, or "Schoolmen" as they were known (c. 800–1500). With these Schoolmen came the growth of universities and centers of learning, like those in Paris, Bologna, Oxford, Rome, and Naples. Theology then ceased to be the prerogative of bishops and pastors and developed into an academic discipline or science that was vigorously pursued by anyone interested in learning about divine realities, like the Schoolmen, monks, and abbots did. The Schoolmen were the first to reflect on the nature of theology as a science and address the question of its definition. They made the science of theology rigorous and methodical, researching, classifying, and interpreting commentaries on the books of the Old and New Testaments, as well as the works of eminent writers before them. One such example is the systematic compilation of Christian theology in the *Book of Sentences* (1150 CE) by Peter Lombard (1100–1160). For Schoolmen like Lombard, "theology became a way of knowing God's revelation more deeply, protecting it from erroneous understanding, and the advancement of some newer understanding of

24. Portier, *Tradition and Incarnation*, 148.
25. Cunningham, *The Catholic Heritage*, 107.
26. McGrath, *Theology*, vii.

that revelation by the application of human intelligence."[27] An examination of a few definitions of theology from the time of the Schoolmen to contemporary times will show us how the understanding of theology has evolved over time.

1. **Anselm of Canterbury** (1033–1109): A famous scholastic, monk, archbishop, and doctor of the church, St. Anselm of Canterbury, was one of the first to offer a systematic definition of theology. He is regarded as one of the fathers of scholastic theology. He became famous for introducing Aristotelian logic into medieval thought. Before he became the archbishop of Canterbury, Anselm served as the prior (religious superior) of the Abbey of Bec. He spent his time teaching and providing counsel to the monks under his care. The two major works for which he is known are the *Monologion*, which literally means "an address to God," and the *Proslogion*, another work in which he gave a systematic presentation of the existence of God known as the "ontological argument."

Anselm did not see much need for a rational proof of God's existence. In the medieval era in which he lived faith was taken for granted and philosophy was assumed to be a "handmaid" of theology. As a leader of a large community, Anselm wanted to reach out to those monks who were vigorously involved in pastoral and intellectual activities. Wanting to encourage them and give them reasons why they should not despair in the face of difficulties, he gave a detailed account in the *Proslogion* of how God exists both as a concept and in reality. Starting with the notion that God is "that than which nothing greater can be conceived," Anselm argued that what exists in reality must be greater than that which exists only in the mind, and since God is that than which nothing greater can be thought, God must exist in reality. Anselm understood his project to be *fides quaerens intellectum* ("faith seeking understanding"). In other words, rather than seeking rational proof for God's existence, he derived his understanding from a simple act of faith. Addressing God in the *Proslogion*, he exclaimed:

> Permit me, at least from afar or from the deep, to look upwards toward your light. Teach me to seek You, and reveal Yourself to me as I seek; for unless you instruct me I cannot seek You, and unless You reveal Yourself I cannot find You . . . For I do not seek to understand in order to believe but I believe in order to

27. Cunningham, *The Catholic Heritage*, 108.

understand. For I believe this: that I shall not understand unless
I believe.[28]

Fides quarens intellectum, which speaks to Anselm's search for
ultimate meaning, has been taken by many Catholic theologians to
be a classical definition of theology. Anselm's definition was influenced by the theological debate of the time concerning essence and
existence. The debate, dating back to the time of Aristotle, suggested
that everything comes into being by virtue of two principles: essence
and existence. The essence of a thing (what makes a thing what it is)
is different from its existence. There was also the debate as to whether
or not existence precedes essence. In his *fides quarens intellectum*, Anselm accepted the notion that in God essence and existence are one
and the same. For some of Anselm's peers who were trained in Aristotelian philosophy, the notion that God is that than which nothing
greater can be conceived was easily understandable, for such a notion
squares well with the Christian adaptation of the Aristotelian theory
of essence and existence. Regardless, some of Anselm's contemporaries
still questioned Anselm's definition on philosophical grounds.

2. **Thomas Aquinas (1224/5–1274)**: At the time of Aquinas what we call
"theology" was known as "natural theology." In book 6 of *Metaphysics* Aristotle, whom Thomas admired as an intellectual giant, treated
natural theology as part of philosophy. Not satisfied with this Aristotelian treatment, Thomas needed another term for natural theology. He
chose the term *sacra doctrina* ("sacred doctrine"), since it deals with
the wisdom of God that comes to us from revelation. In book 1, chapter 4 of *Contra Gentiles*, Aquinas gives three reasons why it is difficult
for some people to engage in diligent inquiry for truth: some are prevented because their physical disinclination makes them not disposed
to learning, others are prevented because of the pressures of family
life, and still others are prevented because of laziness. Aquinas suggests
that the reason why a person learns metaphysics (the study of divine
realities) is because the pursuit of truth requires such a considerable
effort, which unfortunately many are not willing to give. He argues
that there are two ways of knowing the truths about God. The first is
through natural reason, as in the case of those truths that have been
conclusively proved by philosophers. The other is through revelation,
by which we know those things that exceed the capacity of human reason, like the mystery of the Trinity (the fact that God is three persons
in one being).

28. St. Anselm of Canterbury, "Proslogion."

Aquinas defined theology as the "science of faith," and went to great lengths to discuss the nature of this science, contending that it is necessary for the salvation of the human person that there be a knowledge revealed by God that goes beyond philosophical science. Those truths that exceed human reason, according to Aquinas, are known by revelation, for without revelation "truth about God such as reason could discover would only be known by a few, and that after a long time, and with the admixture of many errors."

In the *Summa Theologiae* Aquinas devotes ten articles to investigating the nature and extent of *sacra doctrina*: (1) Whether it is necessary?; (2) Whether it is a science?; (3) Whether it is one or many?; (4) Whether it is speculative or practical?; (5) How it is compared with other sciences?; (6) Whether it is the same as wisdom?; (7) Whether God is its subject matter?; (8); Whether it is a matter of argument?; (9) Whether it rightly employs metaphors and similes?; (10)Whether the Sacred Scripture of this doctrine may be expounded in different senses? Here is an example of how he argued his position:

Article 1: Whether, besides philosophy, any further doctrine is required?
Objection 1: It seems that, besides philosophical science, we have no need of any further knowledge. For man should not seek to know what is above reason: "Seek not the things that are too high for thee" (Sirach 3:22). But whatever is not above reason is fully treated of in philosophical science. Therefore any other knowledge besides philosophical science is superfluous.
Objection 2: Further, knowledge can be concerned only with being, for nothing can be known, save what is true; and all that is, is true. But everything that is, is treated of in philosophical science—even God Himself; so that there is a part of philosophy called theology, or the divine science, as Aristotle has proved (Metaph. vi). Therefore, besides philosophical science, there is no need of any further knowledge.
On the contrary, It is written (2 Timothy 3:16): "All Scripture, inspired of God is profitable to teach, to reprove, to correct, to instruct in justice." Now Scripture, inspired of God, is no part of philosophical science, which has been built up by human reason. Therefore it is useful that besides philosophical science, there should be other knowledge, i.e. inspired of God.

I answer that, It was necessary for man's salvation that there should be a knowledge revealed by God besides philosophical science built up by human reason. Firstly, indeed, because man is directed to God, as to an end that surpasses the grasp of his reason: "The eye hath not seen, O God, besides Thee, what things Thou hast prepared for them that wait for Thee" (Isaiah 66:4). But the end must first be known by men who are to direct their thoughts and actions to the end. Hence it was necessary for the salvation of man that certain truths which exceed human reason should be made known to him by divine revelation. Even as regards those truths about God which human reason could have discovered, it was necessary that man should be taught by a divine revelation; because the truth about God such as reason could discover, would only be known by a few, and that after a long time, and with the admixture of many errors. Whereas man's whole salvation, which is in God, depends upon the knowledge of this truth. Therefore, in order that the salvation of men might be brought about more fitly and more surely, it was necessary that they should be taught divine truths by divine revelation. It was therefore necessary that besides philosophical science built up by reason, there should be a sacred science learned through revelation.

Reply to Objection 1: Although those things which are beyond man's knowledge may not be sought for by man through his reason, nevertheless, once they are revealed by God, they must be accepted by faith. Hence the sacred text continues, "For many things are shown to thee above the understanding of man" (Sirach 3:25). And in this, the sacred science consists.

Reply to Objection 2: Sciences are differentiated according to the various means through which knowledge is obtained. For the astronomer and the physicist both may prove the same conclusion: that the earth, for instance, is round: the astronomer by means of mathematics (i.e. abstracting from matter), but the physicist by means of matter itself. Hence there is no reason why those things which may be learned from philosophical science, so far as they can be known by natural reason, may not also be taught us by another science so far as they fall within revelation. Hence theology included in sacred doctrine differs in kind from that theology which is part of philosophy.

3. **Late scholastics and Reformation thinkers**: Aquinas' definition of theology as the "science of faith" was a ground-breaking definition at the time. It influenced other scholastics who saw the need to employ Aristotelian philosophy to improve on what Aquinas had begun. But with time abuses crept in and excessive use of Aristotelianism in theology, among other things, led to the demise of scholasticism. The sixteenth-century reformers presented a systematic argument against this dependence of theology on philosophy. One of Martin Luther's goals in the Reformation was to rid theology of philosophy. His program of *sola fide, sola scriptura* ("faith alone, Scripture alone") insisted on rejecting anything that was not scriptural, even if it meant renouncing all he had learned from the Church Fathers, including the learned Augustine, whom he revered. "At first, I devoured Augustine. But

when the door was opened for me in Paul, so that I understood what justification by faith is, it was all over with Augustine. The books of his *Confessions* teach nothing; they only incite the reader; they are made up merely of examples, but do not instruct."[29] The attitude Luther had toward Augustine was the same attitude he had toward the Church Fathers in general. He had no use for their understanding of theology: "Jerome can be read for the sake of history, for he has nothing at all to say about faith and the teaching of true religion. I have no use for Chrysostom either, for he is only a gossip. Basil doesn't amount to a thing; he was a monk after all, and I wouldn't give a penny for him. Philip [Melanchthon]'s *Apology* is superior to all the doctors of the Church, even to Augustine himself."[30]

Luther's criticism of the church's doctrine and practices culminated in the sixteenth-century Protestant Reformation. In spite of its public condemnation of Luther, the Catholic Church had to reexamine some of its doctrine and practices. This reassessment led to the establishment of seminaries and divinity schools after the Council of Trent (held between 1545 and 1563) for the formal training of priests and pastors. Theology would no longer be taught in the universities, but in seminaries established specifically for that purpose. To help those trained in the seminaries receive a solid theological education, theology was divided into four main areas:

a. **Biblical theology**: a branch of theology that deals with the study of Scripture. It concentrates on the Old Testament and the New Testament. It also pays attention to the study of the original languages, like Hebrew, Greek, Aramaic, Syriac, and Latin, in which the Bible was written.

b. **Historical theology**: a branch of theology that studies the history of Christian thought, ideas, and movements like the Reformation, Renaissance, and modernism, etc. It also pays special attention to patristic and historical figures like Augustine, Ambrose, Gregory the Great, and the Greek Church Fathers (Athanasius, Basil, Gregory of Nazianzus, and John Chrysostom).

c. **Systematic theology**: a branch of theology that studies Christian doctrine and dogma. It attempts a meaningful presentation of Christian beliefs, dealing also with the works and thought of systematic theologians like Bernard Lonergan, Karl Rahner,

29. Oakes, *Pattern of Redemption*, 107.
30. Ibid., 107–108.

Karl Barth, John Macquarie, Elizabeth Johnson, and Shawn Copeland.

d. Ethics, or moral theology: a branch of theology that deals with principles of Christian living and human conduct. It asks: How ought we to live as Christians?

4. **Modern era**: In the modern period theology has become specialized and has moved from the seminaries back to the universities, where it originally took shape as an academic discipline. Today theology is taught both in the seminaries and in universities that have departments of theology and/or religious studies. Modern theologians view theology somewhat differently from the way it was viewed in the past, as can be seen in the three modern definitions we shall examine: one by an Anglican theologian, another by a Catholic systematic theologian, and the other by an African-American womanist theologian.

a. **John Macquarrie (1919–2007)**: John Macquarrie was a Scottish-born Reformed (Protestant) systematic theologian and an ordained priest in the Anglican Church. He was raised in a Calvinist environment, near Glasgow, Scotland, where he was born. His father was an elder in the Presbyterian Church. His desire to explore the influence of Martin Heidegger's philosophy on Rudolph Bultmann's theology led to the publication of his now famous work *An Existentialist Theology* (1960). Macquarrie taught systematic theology from 1962 to 1970 at the University of Oxford, where he served as Lady Margret Professor of Divinity, a prestigious post he held until he retired in 1986. His works provide a broad methodology for investigating human nature. He analyzed human existence in light of Scripture, tradition, and reason, understanding that reason plays a special role in human life. In another important work, *Principles of Christian Theology* (1966), he defined theology as "the study, which, through participation in and reflection upon a religious faith, seeks to express the content of this faith in the clearest and most coherent language available."[31]

b. **Bernard Lonergan (1904–1984)**: Bernard Lonergan was a Canadian Jesuit philosopher, economist, and theologian. He was born in Buckingham, Quebec, on December 17, 1904. At the age of thirteen he left for the prestigious Loyola College, a Jesuit high school and junior college in Montreal, and at seventeen he

---

31. Macquarie, *Principles of Christian Theology*, 1.

entered the Jesuit novitiate at Guelph, Ontario. After his novitiate and juniorate, he left for Heythrop College at Oxford for studies in philosophy. He also pursued a degree at the University of London and was ordained a priest in 1936 after the completion of his studies.

As a student, Lonergan devoted his free time to reading St. Augustine and Plato's early dialogues. He also read the *Summa* of Thomas Aquinas and was impressed by it. While doing his doctoral work at the Gregorian in Rome in 1938, Lonergan wrote his doctoral dissertation, *A History of St. Thomas' Thought on Operative Grace: A Study of the Development of St. Thomas' Notions of Grace and Human Freedom*. After his dissertation he moved to Montreal and served as professor of theology from 1940 to 1946 at the Collège de L' Immaculée-Conception. Lonergan has written numerous works in philosophy and theology. Two of his famous books are *Insight: A Study of Human Understanding* (which he began writing in the early 1950s while teaching in Toronto) and *Method in Theology* (1971), where he developed what has been termed a "general empirical method." In *Method in Theology* Lonergan articulates his understanding of the general empirical method (also known as the "cognitional method") and shows its application to religion, faith (Christian faith especially), and human cultures. He distinguishes between religion and theology. For him, any attempt to identify theology with religion would be "to revert to the earliest period of Christianity." Yet, while religion and theology are be separate, they still remain interdependent and should be integrated.

Integrating religion and theology, Lonergan defines religion as a mediation between religion and culture and theology as that which "mediates between a cultural matrix and the significance and role of religion in that matrix."[32] From this descriptive definition, we see that Lonergan conceives of theology as a reflection on religion. This means that we cannot speak of one theology or of theology as exclusively Christian. Rather, there are as many theologies as there religions—Hindu theologies, Buddhist theologies, Islamic theologies, Christian theologies, etc. Also, within Christian theology itself we can speak of liberation theology, African-American theology, Black theology, Latino/Latina theology, feminist theology, womanist theology, etc.

---

32. Lonergan, *Method in Theology*, xi.

Theological reflection, for Lonergan, has two phases. In the first, the *mediating phase*, theological reflection ascertains the ideals, beliefs, and acts of the representatives of the religion under investigation. Here theological reflection encounters the past. In the second, the *mediated phase*, theological refection is not just content to narrate the belief system of others and what they propose; it also pronounces which doctrines are true, how they can be reconciled with one another or with the findings of science, and also how they can be communicated appropriately to people of every race and culture. In this sense then, theology confronts the future. To accomplish these responsibilities, Lonergan lists eight distinct tasks that a theologian performs: research, interpretation, history, dialectic, foundations, doctrines, systematics and communications. He calls these eight tasks the "functional specialties." The functional specialties are interrelated, with one leading and yielding to the other. It is like a wheel whose parts, when set in motion, work cooperatively to get to the intended destination. A good theologian, for example, is one who engages in research and gathers available data. The data gathered is scrutinized and interpreted so that only what is relevant to the investigation is advanced. The material gathered is situated in its historical context. The pros and cons of the material are weighed. The outcome is subjected to further discussion and dialogue. After dialogue, there emerges a set of beliefs. These set of beliefs are articulated and explained. Finally, what is articulated and explained is communicated in ways that are relevant to everyday living. This is how the functional specialties, i.e., operations performed by the theologian, work in concert.

c. **M. Shawn Copeland**: M. Shawn Copeland is Professor of systematic theology at Boston College. She is a former president of the Catholic Theological Society of America (CTSA). Her praxis-based theology engages the shifts in theological understanding of the human person, particularly as these play out in gender, class, race, and (female) body. Among her over 100 articles and books are *Enfleshing Freedom: Body, Race, and Being* (2010) and *The Subversive Power of Love* (2009). Copeland's political theology denounces "protracted intransigence toward Black and Womanist theologies" and what she deems the failure of mainstream theology to "interrogate the interaction of gender, race, and class." She suggests that European theological and philosophical sources are inadequate for dealing with "White America's intractable racism." She therefore calls for "a serious and exacting Black Catholic theology that goes well beyond historical retrieval." Copeland sees the need to uncover the particular, partial, and limited character of history. For her, theology should be used to contest and erase the distortions of Black men and women because, theology, strictly speaking, "clarifies how traditioning contributes to the constitution of cultural, social, and existential identity"[33] Copeland's understanding of theology follows that tradition (Black theology) that attempts to give hope to the suffering and oppressed of society by challenging societal structures and analyzing the meaning of hope in God. Thus, theology, for Copeland, must speak to the needs of the poor and oppressed.

STUDY GUIDE

Review

1. The relationship between religion and the search for personal identity and meaning.

2. What Viktor Frankl means by "spiritual unconsciousness" or "unconscious religiousness."

3. Difference between religion and theology.

4. Why there are different theologies.

5. Influence of scholasticism in the understanding of meaning of theology.

6. Anselm's argument in the *Proslogion*.

7. Meaning of "sacra doctrina"/Thomas' understanding of Theology.

8. Protestant Return to Scripture.

9. The four branches of theology

10. John Macquarrie's definition of theology.

11. Bernard Lonergan's definition of theology.

12. Shawn Copeland's definition of theology.

33. Copeland, "Guest Editorial," 604–05.

Discussion Questions

1. We have seen how, in non-Western cultural traditions, community practices were not separate from religious practices. Do you think these non-Western cultural traditions vindicate Viktor Frankl's argument that there is an "unconscious religiousness" within every human person? How can Frankl's idea of "unconscious religiousness" be of help to the modern person suffering from loss of identity and meaning?

2. Distinguish some key differences between religion and theology. Do you agree that there is a fundamental difference between religion and theology?

3. In what way is St. Anselm's definition of theology different from a modern definition, like that of John Macquarrie or Bernard Lonergan?

4. Do you think St. Anselm's definition would have been very appealing to his peers? To what extent was his use of Aristotelian philosophy helpful to his argument in the *Proslogion*?

5. Why did Aquinas not treat theology as part of philosophy, as Aristotle had done before him? Explain why you think Aquinas' idea of *sacra doctrina* was a more helpful term.

6. Critically evaluate Aquinas' argument in the *Summa* as to why the human person needs divine revelation.

7. Was Luther justified in his insistence on *sola fide, sola scriptura*? Explain your answer.

8. Which of the definitions of theology do you find appealing? Why?

2

Creation Accounts of the Abrahamic Religions

TODAY PHYSICISTS AND SCIENTISTS have a lot to say on the question of the origin of the universe. They suggest that an understanding of the physical laws that govern the universe and how these physical laws work hold the key to unlocking the mystery of the origin of the universe. Some physicists take a step further— that if we understand quantum mechanics (the branch of physics that studies atoms and tiny particles) and the theory of relativity (made famous by Albert Einstein) we will begin to understand how the universe came into existence. According to Quantum mechanics, there is no such thing as an empty space. What we assume to be a vacuum, according to Quantum mechanics, is not actually vacuous. Rather it contains tons of particles and antiparticles, which are capable of flaring into existence and fading back into nothingness. According to this theory (which seems unconvincing), the universe must have come into existence from these particles and antiparticles. Today some physicists are moving towards the idea that the universe may have begun with the Big Bang. The Big Bing theory is another cosmological attempt to explain the origin of the universe. There are different variations of the Big Bang theory. But the standard view is that the universe sprang into existence about 13.7 billion years ago. The theory suggests that the cosmic expansion of the universe led to the formation of subatomic particles that include protons, neutrons, and electrons, which after some cooling off stage, coalesced to form the stars and the galaxies as we know them today.

The question of the origin of the universe is a fundamental human question that religion also addresses. The three Abrahamic religions (Judaism, Christianity, and Islam) agree that the universe has a beginning. They differ with science on how the universe came into existence. For the three Abrahamic religions, the universe was created in time by God and this creation is not a natural event, but a supernatural act. We want to be clear that the Abrahamic religions were not the first to address the question of the origin of the universe in a religious way. From the beginning of human history the question of the origin of the universe, i.e., how the world as we know it came about, was a fundamental human question that ancient cultures addressed. It is part of the question of the meaning of life and ultimate significance that human beings, as religious persons, cannot escape. Every age and culture has its own constructed myths and stories aimed at answering this fundamental question. Many ancient cultures put the matter of the origin of the universe squarely in the hands of their gods. The great legacy of Mesopotamia, the site of several civilizations after 4000 B.C., was its creation myths.[1] Early civilizations that developed in Mesopotamia — the Sumerians, Akkadians, Chaldeans, Assyrians, and Babylonians — also used their creation myths to account for the plagues and natural disasters they experienced. These myths offered explanations for both the flood and drought that plagued the Tigris and Euphrates at various times. Ancient cultures, in general, cleverly devised myths as a way of explaining the flux and instability they experienced in their daily lives. What we find is a pattern in which civilizations that developed along rivers where the climate was unstable (like the Mesopotamians and Babylonians that developed along the Tigris and Euphrates) tend to have tons of creation myths, while those that developed along rivers where the climate was stable (like the Egyptian civilization along the Nile River) tend to have fewer creation myths. The myths serve both as an explanation to a problem and a possible solution.

JUDEO-CHRISTIAN ACCOUNTS

When we examine the canon of Hebrew Scriptures we see that as the canon of Hebrew Scriptures was taking shape Greek or Hellenistic culture was becoming dominant throughout the Eastern Mediterranean basin. As more and more Jews spoke Greek the demand for Greek translations of the Hebrew Bible increased. We also see that each of the books of the Hebrew Bible, particularly the first five that Jews call the Torah (Christians call the Pentateuch) have different authors and translators. Part of the reason for

1. Carmody and Brink, *Ways to the Center*, 62–63.

difference in translators is that they were not all translated at the same time. Although controversy persists about the circumstances that led to the translations of these books, there was no doubt regarding the importance of the exercise itself. The first book of the Hebrew Bible, Genesis, was translated into Greek about the 3rd century BCE in Alexandria, which was at the time a flourishing Greek-speaking Jewish community.[2]

The book of Genesis, like the various creation myths deriving from the civilizations that settled along rivers Tigris and Euphrates, attempts to tell its own creation story from an Israelite point of view, i.e., God's chosen people. The Hebrew title of the book, *Bereshit* (in the beginning) is the first phrase of the book. But in the Greek translation "Genesis" is a reference to the opening theme (i.e. creation) of the book.[3] The narrators creatively use the creation motifs of the Ancient Near East to express their own experience of Yahweh's creative work.[4] The book, which divides naturally into two parts: the story of creation and human origins (Gen. 1–11) and the story of the patriarchs, i.e., Abraham, Isaac, Jacob and Joseph, etc. (Gen. 12–50), in theory spans about 2307 years. This number was derived "by combining the ages of the fathers of humanity at the birth of their successors with the years that elapsed between the birth of Abraham and the death of Joseph."[5] Genesis 1–11 is called the primeval story because it tries to tell the story of the origin of the universe, from the time Yahweh Elohim created the world to the time the earth was populated by human beings, i.e., the beginning of civilization. The remainder of the book (Genesis 12–50) is an attempt by the narrators "to show that Yahweh had guided their ancestors in a way of promise up to the events of the exodus."[6]

It is helpful to keep in mind that the narrators of the Genesis story did not intend to give a scientific account of history as we know it today. Their story is rather a confessional statement about the origin of the universe, which they interpreted in light of Yahweh's mercy, kindness, and love. They narrated these stories with a good blend of myth and etiology (tales to explain a certain state of affairs). People sometimes tend to think of myth as contrary to facts. We pointed out in the last chapter that that is not necessarily true. Myth is a story about the past that is told and retold to express certain realities. Thus while myths do not pretend to have factual claims, they are told to express certain truths and values. Genesis 1–11 (primeval

---

2. Dines, "Imaging Creation," 439.

3. Cohn-Sherbok, *The Hebrew Bible*, 12–13.

4. Landry and Penchansky, "The Primeval Story," 20.

5. Sherbok, *The Hebrew Bible*, 13.

6. Boadt, *Reading the Old Testament*, 110.

history) then does not provide factual accounts of history in any scientific sense. In what way then are the stories historical?

> These stories are "historical" only in the sense that they plumb the depth of history's meaning and evince those fundamental experiences that have been common to human beings from the very dawn of history. The manner of presentation is poetic or pictorial, for the narrator is dealing with a subject that eludes the modern historian's investigation— namely, the ultimate source of the human drama in the initiative and purpose of God. Above all the narrative is written in the conviction that Israel's root experiences, Exodus and Sinai, provide the clue to the meaning of all human history, right back to the beginning.[7]

Two Creation Accounts

The primeval story begins with two accounts of creation. Apart from differences in style and vocabulary, the two stories differ significantly with respect to the order in which creation takes place, as well as in their portrayal of God. The traditions from which they drew their accounts probably had independent oral existences in the sense that people told the stories orally and passed them down to their descendants. In time they were written down and combined with other sources to assume the form in which they exist today.

Priestly "Elohim" Creation Story (Gen. 1: 1–2: 4a)	Yahwist "YHWH ELOHIM" Creation Story (Gen. 2: 4b–3:24)
1In the beginning when God created the heavens and the earth, 2the earth was a formless void and darkness covered the face of the deep, while a wind from God swept over the face of the waters.	4 These are the generations of the heavens and the earth when they were created.
3Then God said, "Let there be light"; and there was light. 4And God saw that the light was good; and God separated the light from the darkness.5God called the light Day, and the darkness he called Night. And there was evening and there was morning, the first day.	In the day that the Lord God made the earth and the heavens, 5when no plant of the field was yet in the earth and no herb of the field had yet sprung up—for the Lord God had not caused it to rain upon the earth, and there was no one to till the ground; 6but a stream would rise from the earth, and water the whole face of the ground— 7then the Lord God formed man from the dust of the ground,* and breathed into his nostrils the breath of life; and the man became a living being. 8And the Lord God planted a garden in Eden, in the east; and there he put the man whom he had formed. 9Out of the ground the Lord God made to grow every tree
6And God said, "Let there be a dome in the midst of the waters, and let it separate the waters from the waters." 7So God made the dome and separated the waters that were under the dome from the waters that were	

---

7. Anderson, *Understanding the Old Testament*, 160.

above the dome. And it was so. 8God called the dome Sky. And there was evening and there was morning, the second day.

9And God said, "Let the waters under the sky be gathered together into one place, and let the dry land appear." And it was so. 10God called the dry land Earth, and the waters that were gathered together he called Seas. And God saw that it was good. 11Then God said, "Let the earth put forth vegetation: plants yielding seed, and fruit trees of every kind on earth that bear fruit with the seed in it." And it was so. 12The earth brought forth vegetation: plants yielding seed of every kind, and trees of every kind bearing fruit with the seed in it. And God saw that it was good.13And there was evening and there was morning, the third day.

14And God said, "Let there be lights in the dome of the sky to separate the day from the night; and let them be for signs and for seasons and for days and years, 15and let them be lights in the dome of the sky to give light upon the earth." And it was so. 16God made the two great lights—the greater light to rule the day and the lesser light to rule the night—and the stars. 17God set them in the dome of the sky to give light upon the earth, 18to rule over the day and over the night, and to separate the light from the darkness. And God saw that it was good. 19And there was evening and there was morning, the fourth day.

20And God said, "Let the waters bring forth swarms of living creatures, and let birds fly above the earth across the dome of the sky." 21So God created the great sea monsters and every living creature that moves, of every kind, with which the waters swarm, and every winged bird of every kind. And God saw that it was good. 22God blessed them, saying, "Be fruitful and multiply and fill the waters in the seas, and let birds multiply on the earth." 23And there was evening and there was morning, the fifth day.

24And God said, "Let the earth bring forth living creatures of every kind: cattle and

that is pleasant to the sight and good for food, the tree of life also in the midst of the garden, and the tree of the knowledge of good and evil.

10 A river flows out of Eden to water the garden, and from there it divides and becomes four branches. 11The name of the first is Pishon; it is the one that flows around the whole land of Havilah, where there is gold;12 and the gold of that land is good; bdellium and onyx stone are there.13The name of the second river is Gihon; it is the one that flows around the whole land of Cush. 14The name of the third river is Tigris, which flows east of Assyria. And the fourth river is the Euphrates.

15 The Lord God took the man and put him in the garden of Eden to till it and keep it. 16And the Lord God commanded the man, 'You may freely eat of every tree of the garden; 17but of the tree of the knowledge of good and evil you shall not eat, for in the day that you eat of it you shall die.'

18 Then the Lord God said, 'It is not good that the man should be alone; I will make him a helper as his partner.' 19So out of the ground the Lord God formed every animal of the field and every bird of the air, and brought them to the man to see what he would call them; and whatever the man called each living creature, that was its name. 20The man gave names to all cattle, and to the birds of the air, and to every animal of the field; but for the man* there was not found a helper as his partner. 21So the Lord God caused a deep sleep to fall upon the man, and he slept; then he took one of his ribs and closed up its place with flesh. 22And the rib that the Lord God had taken from the man he made into a woman and brought her to the man. 23Then the man said,
'This at last is bone of my bones
    and flesh of my flesh;
this one shall be called Woman,
    for out of Man this one was taken.'
24Therefore a man leaves his father and his mother and clings to his wife, and they become one flesh. 25And the man and his wife were both naked, and were not ashamed.

3Now the serpent was more crafty than

creeping things and wild animals of the earth of every kind." And it was so. 25God made the wild animals of the earth of every kind, and the cattle of every kind, and everything that creeps upon the ground of every kind. And God saw that it was good.

26Then God said, "Let us make humankind in our image, according to our likeness; and let them have dominion over the fish of the sea, and over the birds of the air, and over the cattle, and over all the wild animals of the earth, and over every creeping thing that creeps upon the earth." 27So God created humankind in his image, in the image of God he created them; male and female he created them. 28God blessed them, and God said to them, "Be fruitful and multiply, and fill the earth and subdue it; and have dominion over the fish of the sea and over the birds of the air and over every living thing that moves upon the earth."

29God said, "See, I have given you every plant yielding seed that is upon the face of all the earth, and every tree with seed in its fruit; you shall have them for food. 30And to every beast of the earth, and to every bird of the air, and to everything that creeps on the earth, everything that has the breath of life, I have given every green plant for food." And it was so.

31God saw everything that he had made, and indeed, it was very good. And there was evening and there was morning, the sixth day.

2Thus the heavens and the earth were finished, and all their multitude. 2And on the seventh day God finished the work that he had done, and he rested on the seventh day from all the work that he had done. 3So God blessed the seventh day and hallowed it, because on it God rested from all the work that he had done in creation.

4These are the generations of the heavens and the earth when they were created. In the day that the Lord God made the earth and the heavens,

any other wild animal that the Lord God had made. He said to the woman, 'Did God say, "You shall not eat from any tree in the garden"?' 2The woman said to the serpent, 'We may eat of the fruit of the trees in the garden; 3but God said, "You shall not eat of the fruit of the tree that is in the middle of the garden, nor shall you touch it, or you shall die." ' 4But the serpent said to the woman, 'You will not die; 5for God knows that when you eat of it your eyes will be opened, and you will be like God,* knowing good and evil.' 6So when the woman saw that the tree was good for food, and that it was a delight to the eyes, and that the tree was to be desired to make one wise, she took of its fruit and ate; and she also gave some to her husband, who was with her, and he ate. 7Then the eyes of both were opened, and they knew that they were naked; and they sewed fig leaves together and made loincloths for themselves.

8 They heard the sound of the Lord God walking in the garden at the time of the evening breeze, and the man and his wife hid themselves from the presence of the Lord God among the trees of the garden. 9But the Lord God called to the man, and said to him, 'Where are you?' 10He said, 'I heard the sound of you in the garden, and I was afraid, because I was naked; and I hid myself.' 11He said, 'Who told you that you were naked? Have you eaten from the tree of which I commanded you not to eat?' 12The man said, 'The woman whom you gave to be with me, she gave me fruit from the tree, and I ate.' 13Then the Lord God said to the woman, 'What is this that you have done?' The woman said, 'The serpent tricked me, and I ate.' 14The Lord God said to the serpent,

'Because you have done this,
     cursed are you among all animals
     and among all wild creatures;
upon your belly you shall go,
     and dust you shall eat
     all the days of your life.
15 I will put enmity between you and the woman,
     and between your offspring and hers;

he will strike your head,
  and you will strike his heel.'
16To the woman he said,
'I will greatly increase your pangs in childbear-
ing;
  in pain you shall bring forth children,
yet your desire shall be for your husband,
  and he shall rule over you.'
17And to the man* he said,
'Because you have listened to the voice of your
wife,
  and have eaten of the tree
about which I commanded you,
  "You shall not eat of it,"
cursed is the ground because of you;
  in toil you shall eat of it all the days of your
life;
18 thorns and thistles it shall bring forth for
you;
  and you shall eat the plants of the field.

19 By the sweat of your face
  you shall eat bread
until you return to the ground,
  for out of it you were taken;
you are dust,
  and to dust you shall return.'

20 The man named his wife Eve,* because
she was the mother of all who live. 21And
the Lord God made garments of skins for the
man* and for his wife, and clothed them.

22 Then the Lord God said, 'See, the man has
become like one of us, knowing good and evil;
and now, he might reach out his hand and
take also from the tree of life, and eat, and
live forever'— 23therefore the Lord God sent
him forth from the garden of Eden, to till the
ground from which he was taken. 24He drove
out the man; and at the east of the garden of
Eden he placed the cherubim, and a sword
flaming and turning to guard the way to the
tree of life.

The first creation account, which was written at the time of the exile, comes from the Priestly writers who were in charge of cultic worship and whose duties as priests suggest that they were concerned with ritual matters. Their concern for rituals and worship was very evident in this creation account, which they framed in a seven-day structure, emphasizing how Yahweh imposed order on the watery chaos. In this (Priestly) account, which begins in Genesis 1:1–2: 3, Yahweh created the world out of nothing and completed His work in six days. "The distribution of the separate creative acts into six 24-hour days was a deliberate scheme utilized by the priestly writer. Organizing the activities in this way implies that God's design had rhythm and intentionality."[8] Human beings, made in the image of God, are the cream of Yahweh's creation. They are to assume leadership of created realities and take care of the earth. One of the goals of the Priestly account was to show creation as Yahweh's gift to humanity who in turn must worship Yahweh. The seventh day was given special status because it was the only day Yahweh blessed, a good reason to keep the Sabbath day holy.[9] The priestly writer deliberately emphasizes how the process of creation suggests that order and structure are pleasing to Yahweh, thereby suggesting that order and structure must also be present in the religious activities of Israel.[10]

The second creation account, which begins in Genesis 2:4b-3:24, comes from the Yahwist source. This account, which predates the Priestly account, describes creation as having taken place in different sequence and time frame. Unlike the remote and abstract God of the Priestly tradition, here God is portrayed as humanlike. God even comes down at certain time of the day to enjoy the garden He has made and to commune with humans.[11] The Yahwist writers were concerned with the problem of evil and proliferation of sin. These concerns make them to tell their story in a four-part story plot of sin, divine punishment, divine mercy, and further sin.[12] Their account details how Yahweh created human beings out of clay. The first human being to be created was Adam. After fashioning him from clay God breathed into him the breath of life. Adam seemed so lonely that God had to create for him a partner. God caused him to fall into a deep sleep and from his ribs created a woman whom the man, after seeing her, liked. He named her Eve (meaning mother of all the living). The two were placed in the Garden of Eden and were instructed to eat of all the trees in

---

8. Bandstra, *Reading the Old Testament*, 53.

9. Ibid., 60.

10. Landry and Penchansky, "The Primeval Story," 20.

11. Ibid., 21.

12. Boadt, *Reading the Old Testament*, 111.

the garden, except for the tree in the middle of the garden—the tree of good and knowledge. The serpent tempted them and they ate of the tree God had commanded them not to eat. As punishment for their disobedience God cursed them and expelled them from the garden.

What Questions does Genesis try to Answer?

At the time the Genesis account was written the ancient world was dominated militarily by the Babylonians and later by the Persians. The text addresses the questions: what divine force is in control of the world, given that it has been dominated militarily by the Babylonians? How does Israel forge its identity in a world that tries to deprive her of her identity?[13] Genesis 1–11 in particular is primarily a document of faith, i.e., a community's faith in a God who acts in human history.[14] The two creation accounts of Genesis are part of this confession of religious faith meant "to strengthen the community's faith in a God who acts in human history by grounding that activity in a story of God's acting in cosmic history."[15]

Genesis mounts a sustained attack on the polytheism of its neighbors. In contrast to the cosmic struggle of the Babylonian creation epic in which the national god, Marduk, subdues the primeval sea (Tiamat), Genesis reduces the "deep" sea to an impersonal matter, effortlessly shaped by a God who exists from the beginning. In contrast to the Sumerian epic in which the wind god, Enlil, brings order out of chaos, Genesis reduces the wind to an impersonal "thing" that does Yahweh's bidding.[16] "Light is created before the luminaries—before the sun god, in particular. Yahweh then separates light from darkness. They are not manifestations of the twin dualistic gods whom the Persians worshipped. The sun, the moon, and the stars also are objects created by Yahweh. They are not powerful gods, each with a sacred text, rituals, temple, and priesthood of its own, as in Mesopotamia and Canaan."[17] Some of Israel's neighbors were also attributing to certain animals divine power. Genesis shows that rather than bow down to the created order, humans are given dominion over these creatures.

The Priestly and Yahwist accounts of creation together "establish fundamental Hebrew truths about God in relation to the universe and humanity.

13. Bailey and Furnish, The *Pentateuch*, 127.

14. Tuohey, "The Gender Distinctions of Primeval History and a Christian Sexual Ethic," 175–76.

15. Ibid., 176.

16. Bailey and Furnish, The *Pentateuch*, 127–78.

17. Ibid.

God is sovereign and powerful, yet approachable and concerned."[18] The two stories complement each other. Both accounts tell us that the first human being, Adam, was made from the soil, *adama*, and that he became a living being only after Yahweh had breathed into him the breath of life. Both accounts also deal with "the deeper question of why man and woman, God's creatures, refuse to acknowledge the sovereignty of their Creator, with the result that history is a tragic story of banishment from the life for which they were intended."[19] The Garden of Eden story shows not only human rebellion against divine authority, but also human determination to assert independence by grasping for the fruit of the forbidden tree.[20]

CREATION ACCOUNTS IN THE QURAN

Like the Genesis creation story, the Quran speaks of God as creating the world in six days. "Indeed, your Lord is Allah, who created the heavens and earth in six days and then established Himself above the Throne. He covers the night with the day, [another night] chasing it rapidly; and [He created] the sun, the moon, and the stars, subjected by His command. Unquestionably, His is the creation and the command; blessed is Allah, Lord of the worlds" (Quran 7:54) The Quran is also clear that six day here should be understood only metaphorically because, for God, a day is like one thousand years and one thousand years is like one day (Quran 32:5). The word used to describe the world is *alamin*. God is the creator of everything (Quran 39: 62). But unlike Genesis where the creation accounts occupy the first two chapters of the book, creation accounts in the Quran are not located in one place. They are intentionally scattered throughout the book, for example Quran 7:54, 10:3, 11:7, 25:59, 32:4, 50:38, and 57:4.

The biblical account suggests that God created out of nothing. According to John Kaltner, there is little support in the Quran for *creation ex nihilo* (creation out of nothing), as we have in Christian teaching. In each of the passages (like Quran 40:68) that speak of creation, "there is already some 'thing' or matter to which God is speaking, and so it is better to think of this as transformation or reordering rather than calling something into being out of nothing."[21] Unlike the biblical account, the Quran also does not specify what was created in each of the six days that God created the world. It is only in Quran 41:9–12 that a distinction is made "between the first four

18. Bandstra, *Reading the Old Testament*, 69.

19. Anderson, *Understanding the Old Testament*, 161.

20. Ibid., 162.

21. Kaltner, *Introduction to the Qur'an*, 49.

days, when the earth was formed, and the next two days, during which the heavens were created."[22] The manner of creation in the Quran, however, is like that of Genesis where God spoke and what God commanded happened. In the Quran God had to speak in order to create something. God says "'Be' and it is" (Quran 40:68; 2:117).

The creation of Adam in the Quran is also similar to the biblical story. Adam was created out of clay (Quran 6:2; 15:26). Reference is also made to Eve in the Quran, but no allusion to the biblical account where Eve was said to have been created out of Adam's rib. But some Muslim interpreters have no problem accepting the biblical account that Eve was created from Adam's ribs because the story is found in the hadith (Prophetic traditions), though not in the Quran.[23] What Quran spells out is that Adam and Eve were instructed by God to reside in paradise and enjoy all the bounties God has placed in paradise for them, but with one exception, i.e., not to eat of the fruit of one of the trees. "Satan made them defy the divine commandment and they were ordered to descend to earth for a specified period of time (see Quran 2:35–36). Adam repented for his transgressions and was forgiven by the Lord (see Quran 2:37)."[24] The Quran is always quick to point out hat God is beneficent and merciful, always eager to forgive, if one repents of one's sins. That Adam repented and was forgiven by God is the Quran's way of showing Islam's disagreement with the Christian teaching of original sin (the sin of Adam and Eve, which in Christian teaching is inherited by everyone).

The Quran suggests that humanity is at the center of God's creation. God made them superior to other creatures. According to the Quran, the angels were with God when God created humans. The angels even protested when God wanted to create humans, telling God that human beings will bring nothing but trouble and mischief to God's creation. God ignored the angels' remonstration and created humans. After creating the first human being, Adam, God gives him a status higher than that of the angels by elevating him to the dignified position of *kalifa* or caliph (vicegerent or deputy of God). God teaches him the names of all the creatures but does not share the information with the angels, again showing God's predilection for humans.

> When your Lord said to the angels: 'I am placing a caliph on earth,' they replied: 'Will You put there one that will do evil and shed blood, when we have for so long sung Your praises and sanctified Your name?' He said: 'I know what you do not know.'

22. Kaltner, *Introducing the Qur'an*, 48.

23. Nawaz, *Islam*, 427.

24 Ibid., 426.

He taught Adam all the names and then set them before the
angels, saying: 'Tell me the names of these, if what you say be
true.' 'Glory be unto You,' they replied, 'we have no knowledge
except that which You have given us. You alone are wise and all-
knowing.' Then said He to Adam: 'Tell them their names.' And
when Adam had named them, He said: 'Did I not tell you that I
know the secrets of heaven and earth, and all that you hide and
all that you reveal? (Al-Baqarah 2:30–33)

When God asks the angels for the name of the creatures none of them was
able to name the creatures. Only Adam was able to name them. God then
asks the angels to bow down and do obeisance to Adam. All the angels did
except one, Iblis. God asks Iblis why he did not submit to Adam as he has
been commanded. Iblis answered: "I am better than he; Thou has created
me of fire, while him Thou didst create of dust" (Quran 7:12). God then
banished Iblis from the Garden for his arrogance. Iblis (sometimes understood as Satan) promised to get even by exposing to Adam and Eve their
nakedness. Iblis tricked them, telling them "Your Lord has forbidden you
this tree, lest you become angels or become of the immortals" (Quran 7:20).
After he lured them and they ate of the forbidden tree their nakedness became exposed to them and they began to put together leaves to cover their
nakedness. When they covered their nakedness God called out to them:
"Did I not warn you that Satan was your sworn enemy?" They replied, "Our
Lord, we have wronged our souls: if You do not forgive us and have mercy,
we shall be lost" (Quran 7: 23–24).

Unlike the Genesis creation story where God rested on the seventh day
(Sabbath), the Quran does not specify that God rested on the seventh day.
For the Quran, God "who created the heavens and the earth was not tired"
(Quran 46:33).

Creation of Heaven and Earth (Quran 14: 32–34	Creation in Six Days (Quran 7:54)	Human Beings Created from Dust (Quran 3:20)	God gives Authority to Humans (Quran 7:11)
It is Allah who created the heavens and the earth and sent down rain from the sky and produced thereby some fruits as provision for you and subjected for you the ships to sail through the sea by His command and subjected for you the rivers. And he subjected for you the sun, and the moon, continuous [in orbit], and subjected for you the night and the day. And he gave you from all you asked of Him. And if you should count the favor of Allah, you could not enumerate them. Indeed, mankind is [generally] most unjust and ungrateful.	Indeed your Lord is Allah who created the heavens and earth in six days and then established Himself above the Throne. He covers the night with the day [another night], chasing it rapidly; and [He created] the sun, the moon, and the stars, subjected by His command. Unquestionably, His is the creation and the command; blessed is Allah, Lord of the worlds.	And of His signs is that He created you from dust; then, suddenly you were human beings dispersing [throughout the earth].	And we have certainly created you [O Mankind], and given you [human] form. Then we said to the angels, "Prostrate to Adam;" so they prostrated, except for Iblis. He was not of those who prostrated.

PROLIFERATION OF SIN

According to the Genesis story, after Adam and Eve were expelled from the garden, they had conjugal relations, giving birth to their first son, Cain, and to another they named Abel. Cain was by profession a farmer. Abel was a shepherd. The two brothers offered sacrifice to God. God accepted Abel's offering but rejected that of Cain. Out of envy Cain slew his brother Abel, and by that singular act became the first murderer. The narrators of this story carefully show human belligerence and defiance even in the face of God's love and mercy. As punishment for his action, God cast a spell on Cain and he became a wanderer. After this incident Adam and Eve gave birth to their third son, Seth.

Human sinfulness and belligerence continue to get worse with successive generations. The sin of Cain continues in his lineage. Among his children were Enoch and Lamech. Genesis 4: 17 speaks of Cain as being "the founder of a city, which he named after his son, Enoch." This narrative tells us how human culture got off to a bad start, since, ironically the first city was built by Cain, a murderer.[25] Genesis 4: 17–24 also describes Lamech, Cain's other son, as a prototype of violent attackers. He even boasted to his wives about killing a man. Lamech also had three sons: Jabal, Jubal, and Tubal-Cain. Jabal was noted for domestication of animals, Jubal was famous for music, and Tubal-Cain famous for copper and iron industries. In spite of these achievements, sin continues to grow, as evident in Genesis 6: 1–4, an account of human intransigence, the intermarriage between the sons of God and the daughters of men. The narrators of these accounts try to tell us "cultural advance was accompanied by violence, lust, and unbridled passion—a chain reaction of evil that proceeded from bad to worse. The last straw that broke the camel's back, according to this epic scheme, was the violence perpetrated by heavenly beings ("the sons of God") who espied beautiful human maidens and had intercourse with them (6: 1–4)."[26] When God could not cope with human sinfulness God decided to destroy creation by sending the flood. But God spared Noah and his family whom God instructed to build an ark. The flood lasted forty days and forty nights. When the flood receded, God made a covenant with Noah and promised never again to destroy the earth with water. "Despite the blessing to Noah and the great increase of nations seen in Genesis 10, the people again rebel in pride to challenge God's rule by building a tower to heaven. God punishes them by confusing human languages, but again gives promise for the future in choosing Abraham."[27] The narrators tell us that even divine judgment could not check the evil impulses of human heart because human culture was already infected by evil.[28] Anderson gives a good concluding remark to the primeval history:

> Primeval history, then, had a sad outcome, for humanity failed to find true wholeness—life in communion with God and in community with fellow human beings. From Cain to the Tower of Babel the human tragedy increased, despite advances in the arts and the sciences. History was urged on by "evil impulse" that polluted God's creation, leaving human beings estranged

25. Anderson, *Understanding the Old Testament*, 163.

26. Ibid.

27. Boadt, *Reading the Old Testament*, 113.

28. Anderson, *Understanding the Old Testament*, 164.

from their Creator and at odds with one another. Taken by itself, the story would be extremely pessimistic. But the primeval history is now part of the larger Israelite epic. In this narrative context, it serves as a prologue to what follows: the call of Abraham and his venture of faith.[29]

Islam accounts for the proliferation of sin in ways that are somewhat similar and somewhat different from the Genesis story. One of the Quran's central message is that all created realities come from God, therefore everything in the heavens and the earth—sun, moon, stars, waters, and animals—are signs that point to God. "Time and again, the Quran repeats the theocentric message that everything was created by God and is controlled by God. Most of nature accepts that situation and does not try to rebel or deny God's authority. Only humanity attempts to wrestle control from God and assert its independence."[30]

The act of submission to God, which is a central tenet of Islam, is performed naturally by all of God's creation, except humanity. Recall that in the Quran Adam and Eve repented for their disobedience and transgression and were forgiven by God (Quran 2:37). The Quran would further describe subsequent human sinfulness as part and parcel of this human failure to submit to the will of God. The rivalry between Cain and Abel (Quran 5:27–31) is described in terms of human belligerence, which became more obtuse in the story of Sodom and Gomorra. "Prophet Lot, a nephew of the prophet Abraham, settled among the people of Sodom and Gomorra and preached the divine message to them. Those were the people given to the abomination of homosexuality and were destroyed with an intense shower of brimstone and baked clay (Quran 7:80–84; 11:77–83; 15: 58–77). The family of Lot was saved except his wife who betrayed her husband and denied the divine truth."[31]

Parallels in Ancient Near Eastern Texts

The two creation stories and the subsequent flood story in Genesis have parallels in the Ancient Near East. Both the cosmic order and language of the Genesis creation story are similar to the cosmic order and language of the Egyptian creation story and the Babylonian creation myth. In the *Memphite Theology*, for instance, Ptah, the sun god, creates by speaking.

29. Ibid., 166.

30. Kaltner, *Introducing the Quran*, 66.

31. Nawaz, *Islam*, 428.

By his spoken words the world comes to be and he declares it 'good;" and in the Babylonian *Enuma Elish* a firm dome separates the waters of chaos from the waters of creation and Marduk achieves his creation by imposing cosmic order on this chaotic preexistent cosmos.[32] There are also accounts of flood stories in the Ancient Near East, like the Deluge Tablet, where the hero, Ziusudra, survived the flood by building a boat. In the Gilgamesh epic of ancient Mesopotamia, the hero, Utnapishtim, survived the flood sent by the gods, and in the Atrahasis epic, Atrahasis survived the flood. See the table below for echoes of the ancient pagan accounts in the creation stories of Genesis.

32. Landry and Penchansky, "The Primeval Story," 20.

	Date	Location	Initial State	Creator	Method	Creation	Additional
Genesis 1	5BCE THE BEGINNING OF TIME	Israel	The earth was shapeless and void and darkness howered over the face of the deep	Yahweh	He created by his spoken words. He made the heavens and the earth in six days, fashioned Adam from clay, and from his ribs made Eve.	He created human beings, the heavens and the earth, and all the living creatures.	Yahweh rested on the seventh day, which he blessed and made holy.
Enuma Elish	1700 B.C.E.	Babylonia	Before earth was created there were two vast bodies of water. The male freshwater ocean was called Apsu and the female salt water ocean called Tiamat	Pantheon of gods came into being through the fusion of the male fresh water ocean Apsu and the female salt water ocean Tiamat	Younger gods came into being through sexual union	younger gods and human beings	Apsu wanted to dispose of the younger gods. Ea found out and instead killed Apsu. Tiamat, in seeking revenge for the death of her husband Apsu, disposed of the younger gods with the help of Kingu. Marduk decided to champion the cause of the younger gods. In the ensuing battle between Marduk and Tiamat, Marduk destroyed Tiamat and used her corpse to make the heavens. Marduk was enthroned as king of the gods by the lesser gods.
Atrahasis Epic	19th Century B.C.E.	Mesopotamia	Heaven is ruled by the god Anu, earth by the god Enlil, and ocean by the god Enki.	pantheon of deities	The goddess Mami by mixing clay and saliva and shaping them	Human beings and all living creatures	Atrahasis epic includes both a creation and flood account. In its flood story, as the human population grew, they began to disturb Enlil's sleep. Enlil, after sending several warnings and plagues decided to destroy the earth by sending the flood. But he spared Atrahasis by giving him advanced warning to build a boat, loaded with animals and creatures of his choice.
Creation From Egypt	3rd Millennium B.C.E.	Egypt	Cosmos was dark, formless, watery void, encased in darkness	Atum not only brought himself into being but also brought other creatures into being	Since he was male and had no mate he masturbated and brought lesser male and female deities into existence	"Lesser male" and female who populated the earth	Atum could also have created by naming his own body parts, from which came other separate beings.

CHRISTIAN APPLICATION OF CREATION STORY

Christian tradition uses the Genesis creation story to answer some basic human questions: Where do we come from? What is our origin? And what is the goal of human life? Christian doctrine teaches that creative act of God was creation *ex nihilo*, i.e. there was nothing in existence except the creator God who fashioned everything out of nothing. "In Christian doctrine, it is not even possible to talk of 'before' creation, except metaphorically, for there was no time before creation; nor is it possible to talk of creation as an event occurring in place, for there was no space in existence previous to creation for creation to happen 'in.'"[33]

The Christian doctrine of original sin has its scriptural basis in the Genesis account of disobedience of Adam and Eve who, against the directive of Yahweh, ate of the tree of the knowledge of good and evil. This loss of innocence or original sin is about a state that we (humans) exist in and cannot escape.[34] The story accounts for "a condition we find in ourselves and in the world. . . . It is precisely about something which has happened and cannot be undone."[35]

Human Dignity

In spite of the lost innocence of the Genesis creation account, Christian doctrine maintains that in human beings there is an imprint of the divine because man and woman are made in the image and likeness of God. In other words, there is some kind of resemblance between God and human beings that is not found between God and other animals.[36] In the narrative "humans are set off from all other creatures and are given power over them, immediately symbolized by Adam's naming of all the other creatures."[37]

The structure of the creation story suggests the special role assigned to humans in the whole narrative. Human beings were created last, meaning that they are the crown or apex of creation. Their being made in the image and likeness of God meant that Adam and Eve possessed some qualities that God possessed, qualities that distinguish human beings from other creatures. Medieval Christian theology used this to develop the idea that human beings have a *potentia obedientialis*—the human capacity to be open to God in a personal way, i.e. what in the Christian tradition is known as grace.

James Cone, the African-American liberation theologian, points out that the human person is not a collection of properties to be scientifically analyzed, but a being-in-the-world-of-human-oppression. For Cone, to be human is to be free. "But on the other hand, human existence also discloses

33. Smith, "Can Science Prove That God Exists?" 131.
34. Lowe, "Woman Oriented Hamarthologies," 128.
35. Ibid.
36. Landry and Penchansky, "The Primeval Story," 23.
37. Shannon, "Grounding Human Dignity," 114.

that the reality of evil is an ever-present possibility in our finite world, and to be (fully) human means to be identified with those who are enslaved as they fight against human evil. Being human means being against evil by joining sides with those who are the victims of evil."[38] Cone insists that the biblical notion of the human person as a being made in the image of God means that human beings are created in such a way that they cannot obey oppressive laws, for to be human is to be creative in ways that revolt against everything that is opposed to humanity.

STUDY GUIDE

Review . . .

1. Creation stories in Ancient Near East

2. The role of myth in creation stories of Mesopotamia

3. Meaning of Genesis and broad division of the Book of Genesis

4. How the Genesis creation stories differ from those of Israelite neighbors

5. Why and how Yahweh-Elohim created

6. Quran creation account

7. How the Quran's creation account differs from that of Genesis

8. Descendants of Adam and Eve

9. Christian view of creation

10. The human being as an image of God

Discussion Questions

1. What do you see to be the differences between the Priestly and Yahwist accounts of Creation? How can one account for these differences?

2. Explain the similarities and differences between the creation stories in Genesis and the Quran.

3. Situate the history of Israel in the context of Ancient Near East and show how the Genesis creation story is designed as a polemic against these neighbors.

38. James Cone, *A Black Theology of Liberation* Twentieth Anniversary Edition (Maryknoll, NY: Orbis Books, 2006), 87–88.

4. How does Genesis account for human belligerence in the face of all good and holy God? How did Cain and his descendants further deepen this divide between Yahweh and God's creation?

5. What does it mean to say man and woman are made in the "image of God?" Is Cone right to insist that to be human is to revolt against oppressive laws?

3

Judaism

JUDAISM IS THE PROPER name of the religious tradition of the people of Israel. Followers of this religious tradition began referring to themselves as Jews about the sixth century BCE, i.e., the same period the religion of Judaism gained currency. The term "Jew" serves as ethnic or national identity the same way a person might refer to one's self as an American, a German, Polish, Irish, an Indian or Togolese. One is considered a Jew if one is the son or daughter of a Jewish mother or a convert to Judaism.[1] The term "Jew" can be used in ways similar and yet different from 'Israel" and "Hebrew." Jewish people trace their origin to their patriarchs (fathers), one of whom was Jacob whose name Yahweh changed to Israel. Jacob himself was the son of Isaac who in turn was the son of Abraham. All three: Jacob, Isaac, and Abraham were Hebrews by tribe. As Hebrews they also spoke the Hebrew language (the language of the Hebrew Scriptures). To properly understand Judaism, the religion of the Hebrew or Jewish people, a background knowledge of the second book (Exodus) of the Hebrew Bible is important.

The second book of the Hebrew Bible, Exodus, is so called because the Greek word from which it derives its name means "departure." As the second book of the Hebrew Bible or Tanak, Exodus occupies an important place in the Torah and the Hebrew scripture as a whole. It is through the exodus event that the Hebrew people came to understand themselves as a nation. The book derives its name from an important event that happened in Israel's history: after four hundred years of slavery and oppression in the hands of the Egyptians, Yahweh, through the able leadership of Moses, miraculously

1. Carmody and Brink, *Ways to the Center*, 123.

46

delivered Israel, and led them through the Red Sea to Mount Sinai on their way to the Promised Land. At Mount Sinai the people of Israel entered into a special covenant with Yahweh. The book not only recounts how Yahweh delivered the Israelites from slavery, but also tells the Israelites how to live lives of gratitude for the freedom that land and children bring.[2] From the moment of their deliverance, the people of Israel will interpret reality from their perspective of a wandering people who were delivered from bondage by Yahweh.[3] Some think Exodus is "Israel's Magna Carta, Declaration of Independence, and national constitution rolled into one."[4]

SOJOURN IN EGYPT

How did the Israelites end up in Egypt? The Yahwist who contributed one of the creation stories in Genesis inherited patriarchal material about generations that carried on the story of Abraham, i.e., the story of Joseph, the son of Rachel and Jacob (the son of Isaac).[5] Their goal in using the Joseph story was to show how Yahweh's grace prevailed to save a good man in the face of human plot of wickedness. The Yahwists also show that through human history and the actions of bad and good people the purpose of Yahweh is worked out and Yahweh's promises kept.[6] In the narrative they recount how the sons of Jacob, out of envy, sold their brother Joseph into slavery. They lied to their father (Jacob) by telling him that Joseph had been devoured by a wild beast. The irony here is that Jacob, who as a young man, deceived his father, Isaac, and stole his brother's (Esau) blessing, was now being deceived by his own sons. "The Yahwist sees a line of guilt and suffering worked out in this family. And this inheritance of evil is used by God to bring about another phase in the history of the promise and its fulfillment."[7]

Meanwhile Joseph was brought to Egypt where he found himself in the house of Potiphar, an influential official of the court of Pharaoh. After some period of trials and tribulations, Joseph won the heart of Pharaoh and was entrusted with an important position in the royal court. As the story goes, after a series of events, Joseph soon reunited with his father Jacob (whose name had been changed to Israel) and his brothers, who came to Egypt to

2. Benjamin, *The Old Testament Story*, 73.

3. Tuohey, *The Gender Distinctions of Primeval History and a Christian Sexual Ethic,"* 175.

4. Bandstra, *Reading the Old Testament*, 131.

5. Swanston, *The Kings and the Covenant*, 80.

6. Ibid.

7. Ibid., 80–81.

join him. According to Ex.1: 1ff, about seventy direct descendants of Jacob went with him to Egypt. Jacob and his children, because of the influence of Joseph who had risen to a high position of authority, prospered in Egypt where they and their descendants lived for centuries. The descendants of Jacob were called the Israelites. "The Israelites were fruitful and prolific. They became so numerous and strong that the land was filled with them" (Ex.1: 7).

When Joseph died his descendants and the generation of Israelites were many. The prosperity of the Israelites soon landed them in trouble. "The Egyptians now regarded the Israelites as poor foreigners liable to be conscripted for the forced labor teams needed in the grandiose building schemes of Pharaohs. They had forgotten Joseph."[8] When a new king came to power, he decided to "deal shrewdly" with the Israelites "to stop their increase" (Ex.1: 10).

> Accordingly, taskmasters were set over the Israelites to oppress
> them with forced labor. Thus they had to build for Pharaoh the
> supply cities of Pithom and Ramses. Yet the more they were op-
> pressed, the more they multiplied and spread. The Egyptians,
> then, dreaded the Israelites and reduced them to cruel slavery,
> making life bitter for them with hard work in mortar and brick
> and all kinds of field work- the whole cruel fate of slaves (Ex.1:
> 11–14).

There has to be an explanation for the sudden reversal of the fortunes of Israelites in Egypt who went from being relatives of the chief minister to a slave population of a bitterly hostile country.[9] The narrators of this story used a technique called *chiasm* (derived from the Greek letter X, i.e. chi). Just as in chi (X) in which the top half of the letter is mirrored by the shape of its base, in *chiasm* the opening of a story is repeated at its closing. In the narrative of Exodus 1: 7–12 the authors, in their use of chiasm, were careful to begin with the words: "the Israelites were fruitful and prolific; they mul-tiplied and grew exceedingly" and end with similar words: "the more they were oppressed, the more they multiplied and spread."[10] Another possible explanation for this is that exodus as a whole was "not written to satisfy a de-mand for an historical narrative of Israel, at least not for that reason alone, but to show the men of the monarchy what Yahweh is like, how he always

8. Ibid., 83.

9. Ibid.

10. Benjamin, *The Old Testament Story*, 75.

acts, and how men should respond in loyalty to Yahweh's providence."[11] It was written down, probably, after King David's time.

Moses and the Burning Bush

The Yahwist shifts to the story of Moses' encounter with Yahweh at Mount Sinai. Some important events in Moses' life are carefully crafted to prefigure some major events in the life of the Israelites. "Moses goes into the Nile and is lifted up out of the Nile just as the Hebrews will go into the Red Sea and be lifted up out of it. He strikes down one Egyptian who was beating a Hebrew, just as Yahweh will strike down all the firstborn in Egypt. He goes into the desert and encounters Yahweh, just as the Hebrews will go into the desert and encounter Yahweh."[12] Exodus 2 narrates the story of the birth of Moses, in the face of Pharaoh's cruel decree to kill all male children of the Hebrews. To spare their son this cruel fate, Moses' mother put him in a basket and hides him on the bank of the Nile River. A puzzle is immediately introduced in the story: Pharaoh's daughter finds him and takes pity on him. She employs Moses' biological mother as his wet nurse and raises him in the courts of Pharaoh. "The birth of Moses shows that he was a miracle child destined by Yahweh from the very beginning of his life to fulfill a special role in Israel."[13]

Although Moses grew up in the court of Pharaoh, he never lost sight of his identity as a Hebrew. In fact, at one time he had to flee Egypt after killing an Egyptian taskmaster in defense of his Hebrew brother. Fearful for his life, he fled to the wilderness of Sinai. While there he married Zipporah. While tending the flock of his father in law, Jethro, Yahweh revealed Himself to Moses in a burning bush and told Moses that He has heard the afflictions of the Israelites in Egypt, and ordered Moses to go back to Egypt and negotiate their release. When Moses met Pharaoh, Pharaoh would not want the Israelites to be released. It was not until Yahweh afflicted the land of Egypt with series of plagues and natural disasters that Pharaoh acquiesced and allowed the Israelites to leave Egypt. The story of the plagues is found in Ex.7–12.

11. Swanston, *The Kings and the Covenant*, 84.

12. Benjamin, *The Old Testament Story*, 80.

13. Ibid., 81.

The Passover Meal

The last plague was the plague of death. In this plague Yahweh slew the first born of the Egyptians, humans and beasts alike. The book of Exodus ties this story to the Passover feast.

> The Lord said to Moses and Aaron in the land of Egypt, "This month shall stand at the head of your calendar. Tell the whole community of Israel: On the tenth of this month every one of your families must procure for itself a lamb, one apiece for each household. If a family is too small for a whole lamb, it shall join the nearest household in procuring one and shall share in the lamb in proportion to the number of persons who partake of it. The lamb must be a year-old male and without blemish. You may take it from either the sheep or the goats. You shall keep it until the fourteenth day of this month, and then, with the whole assembly of Israel present, it shall be slaughtered during the evening twilight. They shall take some of its blood and apply it to the two door-posts and the lintel of every house in which they partake of the lamb. That same night they shall eat its roasted flesh with unleavened bread and bitter herb. It shall not be eaten raw or boiled, but roasted whole, with its head and shanks and inner organs. None of it must be kept beyond the next morning; whatever is left over in the morning shall be burned up (Ex.12: 1–10).

At midnight, on the day of Passover, the Lord slew the first born of Pharaoh and every Egyptian. It was after the slaying that Pharaoh's heart softened and he gave the Israelites permission to leave the land. Even when he allowed the Israelites to leave Egypt, because of the hardness of his heart, Pharaoh and his army pursued the Israelites as they left the land of Egypt. With the Egyptian army in pursuit, Yahweh miraculously saved the Israelites as they crossed the Sea of Reeds (Red Sea). But he drowned Pharaoh and his army (Ex.14: 10–31). This miraculous departure from Egypt is known as the "exodus." The Jews, to this day, still celebrate the exodus event, which they call the **Passover** or **Pesach**, because it is a story of their liberation and coming to birth as God's people. Today Passover is celebrated as a spring festival to commemorate this defining moment in Israelite history. Jews also celebrate **Shavuot**, a wheat harvest festival that takes place seven weeks after

Passover. There is also another feast called the feast of **Booths** or **Sukkoth**, which is a fall harvest festival they celebrate by erecting straw booths or branch to commemorate the way God took care of them in the wilderness on their way to the Promised Land. Jews also have other feasts they celebrate throughout the year that is related to the Passover. One of these is **Yom Kippur** (Day of Atonement). This is somber and solemn ceremony in which Jews ask for forgiveness from their loved ones or anyone they have offended. There is also the feast of **Hanukkah** (festival of lights) in which Jews remember what God has done for them by liberating them through the hands of the Maccabees. The Maccabees led a successful revolt in 168 BCE against attempts to destroy traditional Judaism by Greek leaders who wanted to enthrone worship of Greek gods among the Jews.

THE COVENANT

Israel understands its existence as rooted in Yahweh's inescapable and unwavering commitment to its nationhood. In other words, Israel came to exist in the world of the Near East because of the decisive, sovereign, free, and initiatory action of Yahweh.[14] This inexplicable and irreversible commitment of Yahweh is rendered in the Sinai covenant narrative revolving around Moses, and also in the ancestor stories of Noah, Abraham, and the Patriarchs.[15] According to the terms of these covenants, Yahweh shows preferential treatment for the Israelites by promising to protect them, while the Israelites on their part would keep and observe Yahweh's laws. According to the story of the covenant in Exodus 24, after Moses entered the agreement with Yahweh, he related all the words and ordinances of Yahweh to the people who all answered in one voice, "we will do everything the Lord has told us" (Ex. 24: 3).

The word "covenant" (*berith* in Hebrew) is a biblical word for an agreement or treaty between Yahweh and Yahweh's people. The basis of the covenant, in Jewish understanding, is Yahweh's *hesed* (steadfast love). Aware of its divine predilection, Israel characteristically uses the verbs "love," "choose," and "set one's heart" to express its awareness that its existence is rooted only in Yahweh's commitment.[16] Yahweh is the one whose love for Israel causes Israel to be and in this act of love Yahweh assigns Israel a special role in the community of nations. "Yahweh's commitment to Israel is not simply a formal, political designation, but it is a personal commitment that

14. Bruggemann, *Theology of the Old Testament*, 414.
15. Ibid.
16. Ibid.

has a dimension of affection and in which Yahweh is emotionally extended for the sake of Israel."[17]

Covenant can also be conceived as a treaty, like that found in the ancient world between kings and their vassals. Extra-biblical materials support the idea that the making of treaties in the ancient world pre-dates Israel. The French archeologist, Jacques de Morgan (1857–1924) discovered the law stele of the Babylonian king Hammurabi (1901). The stele shows the king receiving laws couched in casuistic form from the god Shamash.[18] This is akin to Moses receiving the Laws from Yahweh. Since Morgan's discovery other ancient law codes have also been discovered. Reading the Israelite covenant law against "the background of this extensive corpus of cuneiform law reveals the extent to which early Israel appropriated an ancient and widespread legal tradition."[19]

The relationship between covenant and law in the ancient world was not always clear. While law was intended to be a social expression of the covenant bond, covenant was sometimes used for political treaty.[20] Scholars who, while studying the relationship between covenant and law and analyzing international treatises of the late second millennium B.C., have been able to distinguish two types of treaties or covenants in the ancient world: (a) Parity Treaty: treaty between equals and (b) Suzerain Treaty: treaty between a monarch and his vassals. "A parity covenant is reciprocal—- that is, both parties, being equal in rank, bind themselves to each other by bilateral obligations. The suzerain covenant, on the other hand, is more unilateral, for it is made between a suzerain, a great king, and his vassal, the head of a subordinate state."[21]

In the Suzerain treaty found in the ancient world, there are six legal steps or procedures to be followed:

- Preamble: the suzerain or king identifies himself or herself, e.g. thus speaks Marduk the great king of the Hittites.

- Historical Prologue or Antecedent History: reference is made to what happened in the past, e.g. things (acts of kindness) the king had done for his vassal, implying that the proper response of the vassal ought to be gratitude.

---

17. Ibid., 417.
18. Blenkinsopp, *The Pentateuch*, 201.
19. Ibid.
20. Anderson, *Understanding the Old Testament*, 98.
21. Ibid.

- Stipulations: the purpose of the treaty is stated, and stipulations are imposed on the vassal, i.e. loyalty and obedience, especially in time of war.

- Deposition: legal document is signed. Copies of the document are preserved in the temples of both countries and they are expected to be read once a year, as a reminder to both parties of the agreement they had entered.

- List of Witnesses: gods of both countries are invoked but precedent is given to the gods of the king.

- Curses/Blessings: violation attracts curse and faithfulness guarantees blessing.[22]

The covenant between Yahweh and Israel is patterned after the Suzerain treaty. Exodus 19:3ff, for instance, reflects a suzerain treaty. Here Yahweh is the Suzerain (King) whose all-seeing eyes and omnipotence are enough to protect Yahweh's client, Israel. Yahweh is portrayed as designating Israel as Yahweh's covenant partner and Israel is obligated to respond and meet Yahweh's expectations.[23] The relationship between the Israelites and Yahweh, and also the relationship between the Israelites, one to another, are governed by the terms of the covenant. The Decalogue or Ten Commandments become part of the terms of this agreement. This is why in the Ten Commandments found in Ex. 20 can be found prescriptions that guide the people's relationship to Yahweh (Thou shall have no other god before me) and also prescriptions that govern interpersonal relationships (Thou shall not covet thy neighbor's wife).

The Hebrew bible has several other instances of Yahweh's covenant with people Yahweh has chosen[24]:

1. Covenant with Noah: The first covenant Yahweh made is found in the primeval story of the flood. This is called the covenant of creation, the covenant Yahweh made with Noah in Gen.9: 1–17. This covenant prefigures the already effectuated covenant at Sinai as well as the covenant with David. In the flood story Noah was the hero whose life and that of his family was spared by Yahweh who later promised, after the flood, never again to destroy the earth with flood. The rainbow is traditionally assumed to be Yahweh's sign to Noah when Yahweh said to him, "I set my bow in the clouds to serve as a sign of the covenant between me and the earth" (Gen.9: 13). Subsequent covenants are going to be

---

22. Ibid., 100.

23. Bruggemann, *Theology of the Old Testament*, 416.

24. See Dempsey, "2 Samuel 7," 7–10

modeled after the covenant with Noah. In Genesis 15 and 17 (covenant with Abraham) and Exodus 19 (covenant with Moses) we are reminded of Yahweh's words to Noah before and after the flood, but here the words have new meanings.[25]

2. The second covenant is Yahweh's covenant with Abraham (Gen.12 & 15). This covenant with Abraham and the ancestors is one of divine initiative and may be considered unconditional.[26] When Abraham heeded Yahweh's call to leave his father's land and proceed to a foreign land, Yahweh assured Abraham of land and posterity (Gen.17: 1–21). According to the terms of this covenant, Yahweh promised to make Abraham "a great nation," and make the name of Abraham great. (Gen.12: 2–3). Yahweh changed his name from Abram to Abraham because he is to be the father of a host of nations. Yahweh continued this covenant with Abraham's son Isaac, and Isaac's son, Jacob, whose name Yahweh changed to Israel. "It is as "the God of Abraham, the God of Isaac, and the God of Jacob" that YHWH then appears to Moses (Ex. 3:6; cf. Ex. 3:15–16). YHWH had gotten attached to Israel's ancestors, had come to love them and had chosen them."[27] Yahweh's covenant with Abraham is very important in Christian scripture, the New Testament (covenant), and in Islam.

3. Then there is Yahweh's covenant with Moses at Mount Sinai (Ex.19–24). Yahweh's covenant with Moses is also a covenant between Yahweh and Israel. Here Moses acts as the representative of the people. "The Noah covenant neither required nor allowed for any human response. The Abram covenant required the mark of male circumcision and presupposed a broader commitment to a whole and open walk before God, but laid down no further specific expectations or requirements. The meeting at Sinai involves a renegotiating of these arrangements."[28]

The basis of the covenant is Yahweh Himself, although a responsive reciprocal commitment to Yahweh on Israel's part is an absolute necessity.[29] As part of the covenant relationship between Yahweh and Israel, Yahweh devised a set of moral principles that will govern and guide relationship between Yahweh and Israel on the one hand, and the Israelites with one another, on the other. These moral principles

25. Goldingay, *Old Testament Theology: Israel's Gospel*, 370.

26. Bruggemann, *Theology of the Old Testament*, 418.

27. Goldingay, *Old Testament Theology*, 302.

28. Ibid., 371.

29. Ibid., 372.

or guidelines are called the Ten Commandments. Yahweh gave these commandments to Moses at Mount Sinai. The Torah gives two different accounts of the Ten Commandments. The first account is found in Ex.20, while the second account is found in Deut.5. The latter account duplicates the former but with only minor variations. The Ten Commandments will form the backbone of Israel's law codes. Yahweh may punish the rebelliousness of Israel if they break the covenant, but that does not mean the covenant is annulled.[30]

4. At the time of the monarchy Yahweh also made a Covenant with David (Ps.89: 3–4, 19–37; Is.55: 3–5). A detailed account of Yahweh's covenant with David is found in 2 Samuel. David, after becoming king, wanted to build a house for the Lord, a place of worship where the twelve tribes of Israel would gather to worship Yahweh. But David is told through Prophet Nathan that he is not to build a house for the Lord but that the Lord will build a house for David. Yahweh promised David land and dynasty and assures him that his dynasty will last forever—that a descendant of David will always be on the throne. This is why the great Israelite kings always traced their lineage back to David. For Christians, the Lord's promise to David came to its full realization in Jesus Christ who was called "Son of David."

Law Codes in Ancient Near-East

Law is an important cultural convention that counters that which threatens the social order.[31] "Ancient Near Eastern cultures produced many kinds of legal genres, including loans, leases, contracts, pledges, marriage agreements, adoptions, real-estate transactions, lawsuits, royal edicts, and law codes, among others."[32] Israel's traditions do not stand in isolation from the traditions of the legally ordered societies of the ancient Middle East. The law codes of the nation of Israel have many points of contact with ancient extra-biblical law codes. "Archeology has uncovered no less than seven ancient codes of law from Israel's neighbors. They range from the Sumerian code of Ur Nammu in the twenty-second century B.C. down to the Babylonian codes of the sixth century B.C."[33] The seven famous law codes that have been found through the work of archaeologists are: the Sumerian

---

30. Ibid.

31. Sparks, *Ancient Texts for the Study of the Hebrew Bible*, 417.

32. Ibid.

33. Boadt, *Reading the Old Testament*, 186.

code of Ur-Nammu (c.22nd cent. B.C.E.), the code of Lipit-Ishtar, the code of Eshnunna, Middle Assyrian laws, Hittite laws, Neo-Babylonian laws and the code of Hammurabi.[34] Compare the following law of retribution or *lex talionis* taken from the Code of Hammurabi with that taken from the Book of the Covenant:

Code of Hammurabi	Law of Moses (Ex. 21: 23–25)
"If a man has destroyed the eye of another man, they shall destroy his eye. If he has broken another man's bone, they shall break his bone."	"If any injury occurs, you shall take life for life, eye for eye, tooth for tooth, hand for hand, foot for foot, burn for burn, wound for wound, beating for beating."

Apodictic or Case Law

The example (above) is called "case law." Case laws are different from "apodictic laws," e.g., the Commandments in Exodus 20. Apodictic laws are laws that are couched in absolute terms and do not admit of conditions. These absolute laws that are stated in sharp, terse language seem "to be more characteristically Israelite and expresses the unconditional demands of the covenant."[35] Apodictic laws are infrequent in Ancient Near East law codes, but appear frequently in the Hebrew Bible.[36] In ancient near East, the form of law was usually casuistic. A casuistic or case law specifies conditions and the consequences that will follow. A casuistic or case law is a "specific kind of legal article that states the facts of the case in the protasis ("when a person does X") and the legal consequences in the apodosis ("then Y follows")."[37] An example is found in Ex.21: 28–29: "If an ox gores a man or a woman to death, the ox must be stoned. . .but if the ox had the habit of goring in the past. . .then the owner must be put to death." This kind of law is also found in ancient law codes, especially the Code of Hammurabi.[38]

Jews are known for their adherence to the law. In fact, non-Jews tend to associate Jews with the Law or Torah. It is not only the Law that made Jews distinct and different from others. They also have dietary laws that are derived from their understanding of Torah. This dietary law or kosher has served as "a badge of Jewishness in many periods, serving to demarcate

34. Bandstra, *Reading the Old Testament*, 153–4.

35. Anderson, *Understanding the Old Testament*, 97.

36. Sparks, *Ancient Texts for the Study of the Hebrew Bible*, 417.

37. Blenkinsopp, *The Pentateuch*, 204.

38. Anderson, *Understanding the Old Testament*, 97.

Jews from Gentiles and helping preserve the purity of the chosen people."[39] Jewish dietary laws were constructed or framed on the model of God as One, Complete, and Whole. To be holy is to be whole because holiness is unity, integrity, and perfection.[40] The animals that the Jews considered unclean lacked completeness, unity, and perfection. In fact, they were not to be eaten because they were "imperfect members of their class."[41] These imperfect animals included "those that lived in the water but did not have fins and scales (eels, shellfish), birds of the air that at the same time lied in the water (gulls, pelicans). The pig was also unclean, for although it came within the category of cloven-hoofed animals, it did not chew grass like the edible goat and sheep."[42]

EXODUS A CREATION STORY?

The book of Exodus can be understood as a creation story or the continuation of the creation story already begun in Genesis. The God who delivers Israel from Egypt is the same Yahweh-Elohim who created the world. The conviction that Yahweh did deliver Yahweh's people was older than the conviction that Yahweh had created the world, the former being the origin of the latter.[43] Israel hardly thought about itself as a people brought into being by God without linking it with the way the world itself was brought into being by the same deliverer God.[44]

> Further, even if its story once began with the ancestors or the exodus, Israel did not rest content with that, but came to preface it with an account of creation. Exodus is not the first book in the Bible and the story of Israel's deliverance is not the beginning of its gospel. Its gospel has a plot, and to start reading its story by beginning with its deliverance from Egypt is like coming into the theater when the play has already reached scene 3. For individuals too, deliverance is not people's first experience, even in the case of newborn babies. Before they are delivered from oppression, they were born into the humanity created by God.[45]

39. Carmody and Brink, *Ways to the Center*, 135.

40. Douglas, *Purity and Danger*, 64.

41. Ibid., 55.

42. See Arbuckle, *Culture, Inculturation, and Theologians*, 42; referencing Douglas, *Leviticus as Literature*.

43. Goldingay, *Old Testament Theology*, 288.

44. Ibid., 289.

45. Ibid.

The language and structure of the deliverance story, especially of the death of the first born of the Egyptians in Exodus 1: 7–13:6 and the privileged position of the first born of Israel in 13:17ff are similar to the language of creation stories found in Ancient Near East.[46] These narratives, as creation stories, "follow the same basic pattern as the Enuma Elish Stories about Marduk who delivers Babylon from Tiamat and Kingu, and the Stories of Ea and Enki who deliver the household of Gilgamesh from Enlil, and the Stories of Ba'al and Anat who deliver Ugarit from Yam and Nahar."[47]

In the account of the firstborn of Egypt, Pharaoh is given a character similar to that of Enlil in the Atrahasis and Gilgamesh stories. Like Enlil, Pharaoh is perturbed by his slaves, and like Enlil tries a number of strategies to control his fears. Enlil resorts to plague, drought, and floods. Pharaoh tries slave labor and the killing of new male born. In the same manner, the character of Yahweh is patterned after that of Enki in the Atrahasis epic and that of Ea in the Gilgamesh epic. "Like Ea and Enki, Yahweh is a friend to humans. Like Ea and Enki, Yahweh prevents the divine assembly from completely destroying humans with a flood, and like Ea and Enki, Yahweh requires the people to leave the land of their divine enemy."[48] Israel's history is then the foreground against which the people understood the origin of the universe and the primeval history.[49] The primeval history is at the same time a narrative that grounds the Exodus event by rooting it within the cosmic history.[50] "The fact that the deliverer is the creator might merely have meant YHWH was sovereign over the whole world and therefore capable of acting on Israel's behalf against other peoples, in bringing Israel out of Egypt and taking it into Canaan."[51]

Jewish people have several rites with which they commemorate Yahweh's sovereignty over their life and the whole of creation. They do this in their various rites of passage: **Bris**—infant circumcision on the eighth day of a person's birth. Its significance is to show that the male child has entered the covenant community of Israel; **Bar Mitzvah**—celebrates the coming of age; and **Kaddish**—funeral prayer requiring ten Jewish males. These celebrations reinforce the idea that life is good and that one should be committed

---

46. Benjamin, *The Old Testament Story*, 74.

47. Ibid.

48. Ibid., 76.

49. Goldingay, *Old Testament Theology*, 290.

50. Tuohey, "The Gender Distinctions of Primeval History and a Christian Sexual Ethic," 175.

51. Goldingay, *Old Testament Theology*, 293.

to finding goodness in every stage of life, including death because death is not a final reality.[52]

PROPHECY AND THE PROPHETIC BOOKS

Charlotte Buhler's (1893–1974) psychoanalytic theory speaks of the human person as a being with intentionality, meaning that human beings live with a purpose. The purpose of human life, according to this German developmental psychologist, is to create values and give meaning to life. The search for meaning is not the same as the search for pleasure. Viktor Frankl (1905–1997) has also reminded us that the pleasure principle is self-defeating because the more one aims at pleasure the more one misses it. Pleasure-seeking, in Frankl's view, is responsible for the multi-layered sexual neurosis of our time. "Normally, pleasure is never the goal of human strivings but rather is, and must remain, an effect, more specifically, the side effect of attaining a goal. Attaining the goal constitutes a reason for being happy. In other words, if there is a reason for happiness, happiness ensures, automatically and spontaneously, as it were. And that is why one need not pursue happiness, one need not care for it once there is a reason for it."[53] In the ancient world of which Israel was a part, prophets were spiritually attuned people who, among other things, reminded their peers that the pursuit of happiness cannot be found in mundane or trivial pursuits.

Former Prophets and Latter Prophets

Ancient Israelite prophecy was a complex phenomenon that has been studied extensively by biblical scholars. Israelite prophets played a special role in the establishment of the Hebrew Covenant. The books of the prophets occupy an important place in the canon of Hebrew Scriptures. They are placed immediately after the Torah and before the Writings. The Prophetic books begin with six historical books (Joshua through Kings) that are sometimes called the Former Prophets. These historical books form a continuous history written according to the ideology of Deuteronomy, which scholars designate as Deuteronomist History.[54] "This history, which was composed toward the end of the monarchy, was probably revised and expanded upon during the exilic period, around the middle of the sixth century BCE.

52. Carmody and Brink, *Ways to the Center*, 138.
53. Frankl, *The Will to Meaning: Foundations and Applications of Logotherapy*, 34.
54. Blenkinsopp, *A History of Prophecy in Israel*, 11.

The book of Joshua recounts the story of Israel under the able leadership of Joshua. It tells the story of how Israel conquered the land of Canaan and defeated so many enemies with the help of Yahweh. The book of Judges tells the story of the rise of Judges who ruled Israel in the period before the monarchy. The books of Samuel and Kings narrate the rise of Monarchy in Israel, with Saul as the first king. They recount the rise of kingship, the development and growth of the Israelite kingdom and the division of Israel into two kingdoms, the Northern kingdom and the Southern kingdom. The story culminates in the eventual destruction of Judah by the Babylonians and their captivity and exile.

The Former Prophets give a detailed history of prophecy from Moses, who was considered the prophet par excellence, to Joshua, who received a share in his charisma, and those "servants of the Prophets" after Joshua who predicted the consequence of neglecting the Deuteronomic law.[55] Deuteronomy (18: 15–19) specifically interprets prophecy as a way of continuing the work of Moses throughout history and urges the observance and transmission of the same message to posterity.[56] The two books of Kings were the first to mention explicitly the existence of a large band of prophets that were active in the two kingdoms of Israel, but not the first to make allusions to the existence of prophetic activity in Israel.[57] Numbers 23–24 tells the story of Balaam, a non-Israelite prophet who, though was hired to curse Israel, chose instead to offer a blessing. Samuel, one of the great judges in the days Judges ruled Israel, was considered a prophet. Even at the time of the great king David, prophecy also played a special role, for David had two court prophets, Nathan and Gad, who offered divine guidance, especially in royal policies.[58]

The Latter Prophets were like the supervisors of the covenant who indicated the shape of Israel's prophetic ministry.[59] A good number of the Latter Prophets emerged after the kingdom of Israel had been divided into two. Some also emerged either during the exile, when the people of Israel were forlorn and in despair because they had been taken out of their homeland. Other Latter Prophets emerged after the exile, when the nation was struggling to rebuild. The collected oracles of these prophets have come down to us in books that bear individual names like Isaiah, Jeremiah, Ezekiel, Hosea,

---

55. Ibid., 12.

56. Ibid.

57. Boadt, *Reading the Old Testament: An Introduction*, 303.

58. Ibid.

59. Dumbrell, *The Faith of Israel*, 10.

and Amos.[60] The view of the Latter Prophets concerning Israel's inevitable dissolution did engender an eschatology, i.e., teaching about the final destination of God's people, to use Isaiah's vision (Is. 65–66) that looks toward a new beginning for a believing Israel and also toward a New Creation.[61] In order to understand the work of these prophets it is important that we first understand the meaning of biblical prophecy.

Former Prophets	Later Prophets	
Joshua	Isaiah	
Judges	Jeremiah	
1 Samuel	Ezekiel	
2 Samuel		
1 Kings	Minor Prophets:	
2 Kings		Hosea
		Joel
		Amos
		Obadiah
		Jonah
		Micah
		Nahum
		Habakkuk
		Zephaniah
		Haggai
		Zechariah
		Malachi

PROPHECY IN THE ANCIENT NEAR-EAST AND ISRAEL

The Hebrew Bible attests to the fact that prophecy was not confined to Israel.[62] To understand prophecy in Israel it is important to compare and contrast the nature of prophecy in Ancient Near East of which Israel was a part. The Ancient Near Eastern notion of prophecy is indispensable for the understanding of the prophetic phenomenon in general and also for the cultural and conceptual preconditions of prophecy in the Bible.[63] Although

60. Boadt, *Reading the Old Testament*, 303.

61. Dumbrell, *The Faith of Israel*, 10.

62. Blenkinsopp, *A History of Prophecy in Israel*, 41.

63. Nissinen, "What Is Prophecy? 28.

some contemporary scholars tend to reject the idea that Israelite prophecy was borrowed from one of the surrounding cultures,[64] Israelite prophecy was to a large degree dependent on the prophecies in Ancient Near East, especially, Mesopotamia, Egypt, Babylon, Assyria, and Canaanite societies. During the reign of Zedekiah, the last of the kings of independent Judah, the prophet Jeremiah (27: 1–15) was said to have urged rulers of the neighboring lands of Moab, Edom, and Phoenicia, not to give in to the demands of their prophets, divinizers, and the other intermediaries who were supporting a planned rebellion against Nebuchadnezzar. This has raised the question as to whether Israelite prophecy was one of several variations of a widespread cultural phenomenon. Were there special factors at work in Israel that dictated the direction in which prophecy developed?[65]

Archeological findings have also revealed that there existed in Ancient Near East a band of people called "seers" or "divinizers." In Babylonia, for instance, "divination was a highly technical job and the Babylonian priests have left many clay tablets of instructions on how to interpret such things as sheet livers. But beyond this type of seeking God's word, it was also recognized that God might speak directly to individuals in dreams or trances."[66] People went to these divinizers to discern either the mind of the gods or a particular life activity. They were like the astrologers or psychics of today. Even potentates and kings went to them for divination, either of a particular political or social affair, or to find out the will of the gods. In Babylonian society for instance, *baru* (priest or prophet) often used a divinization method to deliver the message of the gods to the people.[67] Ancient Near Eastern religions made no formal distinction between prophets and priests. In Phoenicia the existence of ecstatic prophecy was already well developed as far back at the 11th century B.C. The priest-prophet performed cultic duties and also had a lot of magical powers, which enabled them to serve also as physicians. They were believed to be inspired and specifically chosen to speak to the people that which they heard from the gods. They were also actively engaged in the political life of the state, especially foreign policy. "This is evident especially from the second-millennium Mesopotamia texts from Mari, where prophets advise kings in time of war and warn them of impending military disasters."[68]

---

64. Wilson, *Prophecy and Society in Ancient Israel*, 90.

65. Blenkinsopp, *A History of Prophecy in Israel*, 41.

66. Boadt, *Reading the Old Testament*, 304.

67. For more on this see Miller, Meet the Prophets.

68. Barton, *Isaiah 1–39*, 28.

Prophecy in Israel did not emerge *ex nihilo* but was a development of and a reaction to previous prophetic activity throughout the ancient world. To the extent that Israel was dependent on its neighbors in the areas of politics, arts, and culture, the Israelite religion, and prophecy in particular, were dependent on Ancient Near Eastern idea of prophecy. The idea of prophecy became ingrained in Jewish society. The Hebrew notion of the nature of God, however, was the unique basis of all prophetic activity in Israel. Since Yahweh is holy and righteous, Yahweh's people must also be holy and righteous. There is no area of life that the divine demands for righteousness and holiness do not penetrate.[69]

Prophets, who were known by various names, performed various functions. A prophet was a "Seer" who received the word of God (2 Sam.24: 11) and could divinize and tell the future (1 Sam.9: 6–11). They were sometimes hired to cast spells on the enemy as in the case of Balaam (Num.23–24). The prophetic insight of a Seer comes through some sort of "third eye" vision that is accompanied by words.[70] Some prophets were also isolated figures who lived alone (1 Sam 10), others lived with a band of prophets as in case of Elijah and Elisha (2Kgs 2). While some prophets divined Yahweh's word and received their message through dreams and oracles, others spoke with Yahweh "face to face" (Num. 12: 8).

The Prophets of Israel were people who knew their environment and spoke about events that related to their world. They were spiritually attuned individuals living within a given period of time, whether at the time of Davidic dynasty, destruction of the kingdom or at the time of Assyrian invasion, who tried to discern Yahweh's will. They spoke out against corruption and spiritual decline of their people and interpreted the events and catastrophes of their time in light of the people's rejection of the path of Yahweh. In some cases the prophets sought to give hope to a forlorn people.[71] If every social reformer has his or her utopia, then Hebrew prophets were not without their own idealized dreams of human society.[72]

In our day, owing to a misunderstanding of the Greek term *prophetes*, it is easy to assume that a prophet was one who told or predicted the future. But that is not the idea of biblical prophecy. The word "prophet" is derived from the Greek *prophetes* (a combination of the verb *phemi*, "to speak" and the prefix *pro*, "before" or "forth"), and it was usually given to a person connected with the oracles of Apollo and Zeus, and used to designate the one

69. Francisco, "The Moral Message of the Hebrew Prophets," 435.

70. Boadt, *Reading the Old Testament*, 305.

71. Brown, et.al., *The New Jerome Biblical Commentary*.

72. Francisco, "The Moral Message of the Hebrew Prophets," 441.

who "speaks forth" or "proclaims" the message of deity and interpret divine word for those seeking divine oracle.[73] But "because divine messages deal with future events, the *prophetes* later came to be seen as one who "speaks of the future," who "speaks before" events actually take place."[74] Predicting the future, however, is not the essential idea of biblical prophecy. For if the ability to predict the future was the main aim of a prophet then meteorologists, psychic hotline and horoscopes will qualify as prophets. "Predicting the future was not the major component of the prophetic task in the Israelite world. The most basic function of biblical prophecy was to analyze political and social policies in light of Yahweh's demands of justice, loyalty, and faith in him."[75] No one, however, denies that the prophets sometimes predicted the future. But that was not the purpose of the prophetic office:

> The purpose of God speaking through a prophet was not to communicate information about a timetable of events for the distant future. To be sure the prophets often made predictions, in the conviction that Yahweh was shaping the course of events leading from the present into the future. But these predictions, some of which came true and some of which did not, had reference to the immediate future, which impinged on the present. Just as a doctor's prediction that a patient has only a short time to live makes the patient's present moments more precious and serious, so the prophetic announcement of what God was about to do accented the urgency of the present. Their task was to communicate God's message for *now*, and to summon the people to respond *today*.[76]

The Hebrew word for prophet, *nabi*, derives from the Semitic verb "to call." A prophet then is either "one who is called" or "one who calls."[77] This indicates that the prophet does not speak his or her own words but the words of Yahweh who does the calling.[78] Amos was a herdsman and a dresser of sycamore trees whom the Lord called to prophesy to Israel (Amos 7: 14–15). Having received his divine mission, Amos called out (proclaimed) the word of God (Amos 8:4ff). A prophet then, was someone that was simply called by God, to deliver a message, and he or she was concerned about the moral and religious principles that govern the corporate and personal lives of the

73. Fenton, "Israelite Prophecy," 131.

74. Ibid., 22–23.

75. Bandstra, *Reading the Old Testament*, 210.

76. Anderson, *Understanding the Old Testament*, 249.

77. Bandstra, *Reading the Old Testament*, 210.

78. Boadt, *Reading the Old Testament*, 306.

people of God.[79] "This conviction that the words they spoke came directly from God was based on the prophetic experience of being summoned in some kind of a vision to hear God speak in the heavenly throne room."[80] Sometimes the message of the prophet was not palatable to the people who often sought to persecute them (Amos 7: 10ff). The prophets of Israel were not silent on the issues of just relationship between the people and the king. Wherever they found injustice they made their voices known.[81] But the prophets of Israel do not seek to overthrow the monarchy, but to restore justice, loyalty to the national deity and an informed and sensible handling of the dangerous forces at work on the international scene.[82]

Patterns of Prophetic Speech

Like the prophetical books of the Bible and the other documents from the Ancient Near East, the *ipsissima verba*, i.e. the actual spoken words of individual prophets, are difficult to find. "The development from oral performance to written record happened under material restrictions and linguistic constraints, and the path from the prophet to the recipient may have been a complicated one. Moreover, the Ancient Near Eastern sources include quotations that may be purely literary imitations of prophetic language rather than actually proclaimed prophecies."[83] This kind of enigma would also be found in the study of Israelite prophecy. Some have attempted a distinction between ancient Hebrew prophecy and biblical prophecy. According to this distinction, ancient Hebrew prophecy refers to "the concrete transmission of the divine word in the Hebrew language in ancient Palestine by persons that qualify as prophets, that is a phenomenon belonging to the context of Ancient Near Eastern prophecy," while biblical prophecy means "prophecy as interpreted by those who created the writings that gradually took the shape of what we call the Hebrew Bible."[84]

To the extent that Israel was a part of the Semitic world, its traditions, religious traditions especially, were indebted to the religious traditions of the Ancient Near East. "The prophetic literature has been thoroughly analyzed, and the literary history of the prophetic corpus has been traced. Scholars have succeeded in delineating the characteristic patterns of the

79. Bandstra, *Reading the Old Testament*, 210.

80. Boadt, *Reading the Old Testament*, 306.

81. Francisco, "The Moral Message of the Hebrew Prophets," 439.

82. Fenton, "Israelite Prophecy," 136.

83. Ibid.

84. Ibid., 31.

prophets' words and in some cases have been able to relate the various forms of prophetic speech to their original social settings."[85] In 1906, the biblical scholar, H. Gunkel, used the phrase *Sitz im Leben*, i.e. "setting in life," to develop the idea that all literary genres had a setting in the life of the people who used them. Since then "form critics have had a great deal to say about the literary genres of prophetic speech and about the original social matrix of the language of those genres."[86] Biblical scholars, using **Form Criticism,** have attempted to situate the language of the Hebrew Bible in its original real life situation. Form criticism or Form analysis, as a method used to examine the *Sitz im Leben* (original context) of biblical language, has been particularly productive especially in prophetic literature. Westermann has used such a method to demonstrate the origin of the phrase "thus says the Lord," which often prefaces the messages of Hebrew prophets. Westermann traced the phrase to the Ancient Near Eastern kings' method of sending messages to vassals or client states. The messenger carrying the message of the king committed the king's message to memory. On arriving at his destination, the messenger would recite the king's message as if he were the king himself, prefacing the message with "Thus says the King." Hebrew prophets took over such a procedure, prefacing their message with "Thus says the Lord" to establish their words as a message from God and anchor them in divine authority.

PROPHETIC BOOKS

Prophetic books, as we noted earlier, consist of the Former Prophets (Joshua—Kings) and the Latter Prophets comprising of the three Major Prophets (Isaiah, Jeremiah, and Ezekiel) and the twelve Minor Prophets. The latter prophets cover the period of Israelite history when the kingdom was divided into two: the north and the south, and continues into the exilic and post-exilic period. The influence of the prophets predominate the prophetic literature. We know a lot about some of the prophets and know little or nothing about others. In general, however, we know they knew their sense of mission and refused to compromise even in the face of persecution. Isaiah, for instance, described his divine commission: "In the year that King Uzziah died, I saw YHWH sitting on a throne, high and exalted. . . . Then I heard the voice of YHWH saying, 'Whom shall I send, and who will go for us?' And I said, 'Here I am, send me!'" (Is.6: 1–8). In spite of their wide

---

85. Wilson, *Prophecy and Society in Ancient Israel*, 1.

86. Ibid., 11. See also Gunkel, "Fundamental Problems of Hebrew Literary History," 61–62.

diversity, characteristics, and wide range of activities, the one feature common to all the prophets is their commission to speak in the name of Yahweh, for divine revelation is a sine qua non of prophecy.[87]

The prophets did not speak in a vacuum. They all had a social location from which they spoke. They also had different cultural backgrounds, some agricultural, others urban. They also came from different regions: Northern or Southern kingdom. While Isaiah, for instance, directed his oracles and pronouncements against the ruling elites in Jerusalem (Southern kingdom), Amos, a contemporary eighth century B.C. prophet, directed his pronouncements against the ruling class of Samaria (Northern kingdom). The prophets also lived at different times: pre-exilic, exilic or post-exilic. Some lived at the time before the Israelites were taken into captivity in Babylon. Others lived during the period of captivity. Still others lived and prophesied after the return to homeland. The concerns of the prophets also varied. While some were concerned with domestic issues or local politics, others were concerned with foreign affairs or international relations. There is also evidence that some of the prophets knew the prophetic oracles of either their contemporary prophets or the prophets before them. In some instances they even made use of the prophetic oracles of their predecessors. Isaiah, for instance, who lived in Jerusalem in the 8th century BCE (or at least those who compiled his sayings) knew of the prophetic oracles of Amos, Hosea, and Micah, and to some degree was influenced by them.[88] Thus, the prophets were dependent on the work of one another.

The final composition and editing of each of the prophetic books took a long period of time. It is essential to keep in mind, when reading a prophetic book that we are not dealing with a prophetic person, but prophetic personalities that may be behind the final editing and shaping of the book. Though a prophetic book may bear the name of a named prophet, it is by no means an autobiography of the prophet in question. We should by no means confuse the modern notion of authorship with the biblical notion. For the most part prophetic books may contain the ideas of a band of disciples who align themselves to the named prophet. These disciples take the message of the prophet, rework them, and apply them to their new circumstance. These disciples sometimes are behind the final shaping and editing of the prophetic books, a point Boadt explains very well:

> The titles of books under individual names such as Amos or Hosea do not imply that they contain just the words of Amos and Hosea, but also words *about*, and in the *tradition of*, the

87. Grabbe, *Priests, Prophets, Diviners, Sages*, 83.

88. Bandstra, *Reading the Old Testament*, 302.

prophet. Nor are the oracles sayings necessarily in the logical or chronological order that we would like. Ancient editors have collected and arranged words spoken by these prophets in an order that seemed important to them but often escapes us. Editors frequently added words taken from disciples of the prophet, or even unknown prophetic words that are similar in theme and which add to the thought of the prophet in whose book they are included. Even more dramatically, later generations who cherished the words of an Amos or Micah occasionally added new applications and comments from their own centuries to the collected words of the long-dead prophet.[89]

ISAIAH THE PROPHET

The story of Israel narrated in the book of Isaiah is, in a nutshell, a long account of Israel's life in the midst of a demanding sequence of imperial powers.[90] It was assumed until fairly recently that the story told in the book of Isaiah was the work of one single author, Isaiah of Jerusalem. This assumption was based on the fact that the book begins with the proclamation that it contains "the vision which Isaiah, son of Amoz, had concerning Judah and Jerusalem in the days of Uzziah, Jotham, Ahaz and Hezekiah, kings of Judah" (Is.1: 1). But far from being the work of a single author, scholars have discovered that the book contains prophetic materials and oracles that stretch over two centuries, "when Judah had fallen, when the people were in exile, and when Babylonia—then the superpower in the world—was about to fall before the rising empire of Persia."[91]

This discovery is largely due to the landmark work of Bernhard Duhm (1892) who, while building on the efforts of Doderlein (1775) and Eichhorn (1780–83), uncovered different thematic and historical interests.[92] The book of Isaiah is now believed to consist of three sub-collections, each sub-collection representing the oracle of a prophet who identified his/her name with Isaiah of Jerusalem. Only chapters 1–39 have been attributed to Isaiah of Jerusalem, the eighth century BCE prophet who lived at a time Israel was under the threat of the Assyrian empire. Due to differences in historical background, literary style, and theological emphasis, scholars believe that Chapters 40–66 could have come from anonymous disciples, probably at

---

89. Boadt, *Reading the Old Testament*, 313.

90. Brueggemann, *Isaiah 40–66*, 1.

91. Anderson, *Understanding the Old Testament*, 322.

92. Dumbrell, *The Faith of Israel*, 107.

the time of Cyrus of Persia (593 B.C.E), when the rising Persian empire displaced the brutal and hated domination of Babylon.[93] In fact, Chapters 40–55 have been attributed to a disciple of the prophet who lived during the time of the exile, suggesting that these chapters serve as prophetic interpretation and elaboration of the traditions of Isaiah 1–39.[94] Finally Chapters 56–66, assumed to have been written by a disciple of the disciple of the prophet who lived after the exile, elaborates and applies the message of Isaiah 40–55,[95] at a time "when Jews who had returned from exile went about the critical and difficult task of reshaping the community of faith after its long, exilic jeopardy."[96]

A Divided Kingdom

As we study Isaiah it is important to give a brief historical background of how the nation of Israel split into two kingdoms because such a background will help us better appreciate Isaiah when he makes references to places like Judah, Samaria, and even Israel as separate entities. For the prophetic activities of Isaiah Ben Amoz took place at a crucial time for both the northern kingdom (Israel) and the southern kingdom (Judah), i.e. it was a period of crises (national and international) and challenges in political as well as cultural life.[97]

Shortly after the death of Solomon, son of David, during the reign of his son and successor, Rehoboam, the nation of Israel split into two kingdoms: the Northern Kingdom and the Southern Kingdom. As told in 1Kgs 12, after the death of Solomon, representatives of people in the north came to Rehoboam and put before him the request that their burdens be lightened. Rehoboam's father, Solomon, had imposed forced labor on the people, including high taxes and levies. Rehoboam sought the advice of his counselors (called Elders) who advised him to heed the people's request. But he went against the advice of his wise counselors, and arrogantly declared: "My father put on you a heavy yoke, but I will make it heavier. My father beat you with whips, but I will beat you with scorpions" (1Kgs 12: 14). This angered the northerners who in mutiny exclaimed:

"What share have we in David?

93. Brueggemann, *Isaiah 40–66*, 3.
94. Dumbrell, *The Faith of Israel*, 108.
95. Ibid.
96. Brueggemann, *Isaiah 40–66*, 3.
97. Widyapranawa, *Isaiah 1–39*, xiv.

> We have no heritage in the son of Jesse
> To your tents, O Israel!
> Now look to your own house, David" (I Kgs 12: 16).

Ten of the twelve tribes that seceded became known as the Northern Kingdom, while the South was left with two tribes: Benjamin and Judah. Isaiah sometimes speaks of the Northern Kingdom as Israel and the Southern kingdom as Judah or Jerusalem. This is akin to what we see in modern day politics where political pundits sometimes refer to the former Soviet Union as Russia, the United Kingdom as London, and the People's Republic of China as Beijing. Some prophets of the South (e.g. Amos), who were Isaiah's contemporaries, prophesied at Bethel, the great center of worship in the North. They, like Isaiah, sometimes referred to the South as Jerusalem or Judah, and the North as Israel, Ephraim or Samaria.

First Isaiah (Chapters 1–39)

The material in this collection has been attributed to Isaiah Ben Amoz, sometimes referred to as Isaiah of Jerusalem (8th cent. BCE). First Isaiah contains pre-exilic materials, i.e. oracles or pronouncements that were delivered before the Israelites were taken into exile. Unlike some prophets of this period, we do know a little about the personal life of this prophet. From his own account we get to know that he was married to a woman whom he referred to as prophetess (Is.8: 3). He had two sons. One was called Shear-jashub, a name that means, "a remnant shall return" (Is.7: 3), and the other was called Maher-shalal-hash-baz, which means, "quick spoils, speedy plunder" (Is.8: 3).

Isaiah understands the symbolic meaning of his name and that of his two sons, which he applies to the nation of Israel: "Look at me and the sons the Lord has given me: we are signs and portents in Israel from the Lord of hosts who dwell on Mount Zion" Is.8: 18). Isaiah is also vast in the traditions of Jerusalem. He was from Judea and knows a lot about the Davidic dynasty, a dynasty he reveres greatly. He accepts the idea of the election of the Davidic line and expands this to include the concept of the Davidic Messiah (Is. 16: 5; 9: 6).[98] He is also well educated and probably was from the upper class family. "The prophet seems to have known and had access to members of the royal court (Is. 8:2; 22: 15–16), and he apparently had no difficulty gaining an unofficial audience with the king (Is. 7:3)."[99] He may also have

---

98. Wilson, *Prophecy and Society in Ancient Israel*, 270.

99. Ibid., 271

been educated in the royal court or in the temple, based on the "wisdom" language he sometimes uses.[100] In all likelihood, he is familiar with the prophetic oracles of the other eighth century prophets like Amos, Hosea, and Micah, and to some extent was influenced by them. While Amos and Hosea prophesied in the north, Isaiah was active in Judah.[101] Some scholars have established literary and theological similarities between Isaiah and Amos based on some of the words and phrases used by Isaiah in his prophetic oracles, which are typical of Judean prophets.[102]

Isaiah Ben Amoz lived and prophesied at a time Israel and Judah were under the threat of the Assyrians.[103] Isaiah receives his divine commission in the context of these turbulent times and sees his service to the king of Judah as a divine call, a divine commission he vividly describes in chapter 6. His call took place "in the year king Uzziah died," when Yahweh was "seated on a high and lofty throne."

> Notice the time and the place. It was a critical time, heavy with urgency and foreboding. That is the meaning of the reference to Uzziah's death. Uzziah had been a strong king, and even while his son Jotham was acting as regent Uzziah remained a pillar of strength for the people. . . . Hence Uzziah's death was an event that touched the life of the people, especially in view of the weakness of his son Jotham and the menacing shadow of Assyria.[104]

A lot of Isaiah's prophetic oracles relate to social justice. He cries out against the leaders and the people for social and cultic abuses, while still holding out the hope of salvation if they repent.[105] His cry for social justice is found in his famous Song of the Vineyard poem (Is. 5: 1–7), where the prophet, with good play of words, declared Yahweh's indignant disappointment:

> He looked for justice [*mishpat*]
> and behold bloodshed [*mispah*]
> for righteousness [*zedaqah*]
> but behold, distress [*ze'aqah*].[106]

100. Ibid.

101. Boadt, *Reading the Old Testament*, 324.

102. Wilson, *Prophecy and Society in Ancient Israel*, 270.

103. Bandstra, *Reading the Old Testament*, 303.

104. Anderson, *Understanding the Old Testament*, 324.

105. Wilson, Prophecy *and Society in Ancient Israel*, 272.

106. See Anderson, *Understanding the Old Testament*, 328.

Isaiah prophesied during the reigns of Ahaz (735–715 B.C) and his son successor, Hezekiah (715–687 B.C), especially during the Assyrian crisis (701 B.C). The prophet may have witnessed the invasion of Judah by Israel and Syria in their attempt to force Judah to join the anti-Assyrian coalition. Assyria conquered Israel and forced Syria and Judah to become their client state. Some of Isaiah's prophetic oracles were pronounced at this time. Isaiah was convinced of the majesty of God, "the Holy One of Israel" (Is.6: 1–13), who alone is King. The destiny of all nations, including the great ones, lies under the control of Yahweh. Isaiah made it clear that any kind of oppression against Yahweh's people offended Yahweh. Yahweh will redeem His own people at His own time. He then cautioned against the futility of Judah's attempt to control its own destiny by aligning with Assyria.

Immanuel Prophecy

First Isaiah has several themes: hope, restoration, and Davidic Promise. The Immanuel prophecy is one of the most important themes in this collection. Ahaz, the king of Judah, was faced with a serious political dilemma. Syria and Israel (sometimes referred to Ephraim in this book) were forming an anti-Assyrian coalition. Ahaz was not sure whether to join this anti-Assyrian coalition that the kings of Syria and Israel were pressuring him into. Isaiah felt compelled to tell Ahaz not to join the anti-Assyrian alliance and also to trust in Yahweh. But Ahaz, fearful of the consequences of not joining the alliance, was worried about Israel and Syria. Rather than join the coalition, he was inclined to seek the help of the Assyrians to ward off the threat from Israel and Syria. Isaiah advised Ahaz not to be afraid and guaranteed him of Yahweh's assistance in the present situation. To assure Ahaz of Yahweh's help, Isaiah asked Ahaz to ask for a sign from Yahweh. But Ahaz would not ask for a sign because he did not want to "tempt the Lord." Isaiah then gave him a sign: "Therefore the Lord himself will give you this sign: the virgin shall be with child, and bear a son, and shall name him Immanuel" (Is.7: 14). One assumption is that the young woman Isaiah was referring to was the queen, i.e. the wife of Ahaz. Since the name Immanuel means, "God is with us," Isaiah was assuring Ahaz that the son whom the queen will give birth to will continue the Davidic dynasty, a sign that the Lord is still with Judah. The wife of Ahaz, in fulfillment of Isaiah's prophecy, gave birth to a son who was named Hezekiah. Isaiah saw the birth of Hezekiah as a sign of good things to come:

> The people who walked in darkness have seen a great light;
> Upon those who dwelt in the land of gloom a light has shone.

You have brought them abundant joy and great rejoicing, as they rejoice before you as at the harvest, as men make merry when dividing spoils. For the yoke that burdened them, the pole on their shoulder, and the rod of their taskmaster .... For a child is born to us, a son is given us; upon his shoulder dominion rests. They name him Wonder-Counselor, God-hero, Father-Forever, Prince of Peace. His dominion is vast and forever peaceful, from David's throne, and over his kingdom, which he confirms and sustains (Is.9: 1–6).

Although Isaiah was not looking into the distant future, and although when Isaiah spoke of the "anointed one" he meant the reigning king, it is difficult to resist the conclusion that the child he meant, in this Immanuel prophecy, was to be a "messianic" figure, i.e. a deliverer.[107] But in spite of this Immanuel prophecy, Ahaz sought the help of Tiglath-Pileser III, the king of Assyria.[108] Tiglath-Pileser III helped Ahaz take care of the Syrian-Israelite threat. But the consequence of this was that Judah became an Assyrian client-state and remained so for about a century.[109] Upon the death of Ahaz, Hezekiah became the king of Judah. He began an expansionist policy that was to land him in trouble. He attacked some of his neighbors like Edom and Philistine, and revolted against Assyria by aligning with Egypt to form an anti-Assyrian coalition. Prophet Isaiah warned him, without success, not to join this coalition. The result was that he was swiftly attacked by king Sennacherib of Assyria (see Is.36–7). But Yahweh miraculously saved Judah from the invading Assyrians who had to retreat after suffering many casualties.[110]

Second Isaiah or Deutero-Isaiah (Chapters 40–55)

Israelite history is sometimes best told in the context of the fall and rise of foreign powers—Israelite neighbors. The Assyrian empire, which was a great threat to Israel in the eight century BCE at the time of First Isaiah, had disintegrated by the seventh century BCE and its capital city Nineveh left in ruins. In the vacuum left by the demise of Assyria Babylon, led by

---

107. Ibid., 334.

108. Assyria would be the modern day Iraq, Babylon the modern day Kuwait and Persia the modern day Iran.

109. Bandstra, *Reading the Old Testament*, 307.

110. Ibid., 308.

Nabopolassar (Nebuchadnezzar), became a formidable threat and "enacts the devastation of Jerusalem in 587."[111]

Second or Deutero-Isaiah is an exilic material composed by a prophet who lived in the Babylonian exile, about the middle of the 6th century B.C. "As Isaiah 1–39 had ended with the prospect of exile before Jerusalem, so Isaiah 40 commences the second half of the prophecy on the comfort to be extended to Jerusalem and the exiles in Babylon"[112] Although the Israelites were exiled in Babylon, at this time Persia, under Cyrus, was increasingly becoming a dominant power. Cyrus practiced a benevolent imperial policy, which permitted exiles to return to their homeland.[113] Second Isaiah saw Persia under Cyrus as an agent of Yahweh's restorative justice in the same way Jeremiah thought of Babylon under Nebuchadnezzar as an agent of Yahweh's judgment.[114] Second Isaiah tries to show that Yahweh, in the form of Persian army, will defeat Babylon and permit Judah to return in freedom to the beloved citadel of Zion.[115]

Unlike First Isaiah, we do not know the name of this prophet, since we have only scanty information about the prophet. "He has hidden his own identity behind that of the great prophet Isaiah so that those who hear or read his prophecies will see only the continuity of what God is doing from Isaiah's age to his own."[116] The anonymity of Second Isaiah may also be due to the common practice at the time of this prophet, i.e. the increase of prophetic anonymity resulting from concern over prophetic authority.[117]

> A number of the late prophetic writings are simply added on to earlier books, and in this way the anonymous author claims the authority of an earlier prophet who lived in a time when prophetic authority was still recognized. This device has been used by Second Isaiah, Third Isaiah, Second Zechariah, and Third Zechariah, among others. The tendency in this period to edit an existing prophetic book rather than create a new book may also reflect an attempt to gain support from the past.[118]

---

111. Brueggemann, *Isaiah 40–66*, 9.

112. Dumbrell, *The Faith of Israel*, 115.

113. Brueggemann, *Hopeful Imagination*, 91.

114. Ibid.

115. Brueggemann, *Isaiah 40–66*, 10–11.

116. Boadt, *Reading the Old Testament*, 417–8.

117. Wilson, *Prophecy and Society in Ancient Israel*, 291.

118. Ibid. Wilson notes some characteristics of late prophets: (i) the tendency to reuse earlier prophetic oracles to enhance their authority (ii) they did not draw their earlier material from only one prophetic tradition (iii) some of them used prophecy to advance their own views and oppose those of their opponents and (iv) the tendency to

In spite of the anonymity of Second Isaiah, this prophet has been described as "pensive" and "optimistic." In the prologue (chapter 40: 6–7), the prophet describes his divine commission, telling us how he heard a voice summoning him to preach. His faith in Yahweh seems unflinching. It would seem that the prophet "regarded himself as the lineal descendant of the pre-exilic prophets. This is shown, first, by the fact that in substantiation of his message he adduces a call, and, second, that like Isaiah and Jeremiah, his first reaction is to shrink from it."[119] When he demurs at the summons to preach, his initial refusal is not an expression of his own personal lament, but of solidarity with his fellow exiles who think that the collapse of their nation is an expression of divine judgment.[120] "The thoughts of his fellow-exiles were his thoughts, too, and he had been every bit as flagging and weary as they. It was a word from outside himself, a command that made him a prophet, as it had done his predecessors."[121] The prophet stresses the culmination of historical events in God's plan. Yahweh is the Lord of all creation and every human event works according to His grand design.[122]

We also see the prophet's disappointment with some of the captives in Babylon who, it would seem, had rejected the prophet. Some of these captives had thought that the destruction of Jerusalem and the Temple, and even their captivity, signaled the withdrawal of Yahweh and their abandonment. They thought Yahweh had perhaps withdrawn to the wilderness. The prophet denounced these people as being narrow minded and prophesied a new Exodus: Yahweh will reveal Himself and bring His people once again to the Promised Land. This time it would not be through the Reed Sea but through the pathways of the Arabian Desert. The prophet, more than other prophets, stresses the power of the word of God and encouraged the people to have faith in God.[123] He also stresses the centrality of Jerusalem and its Temple.

Second Isaiah is sometimes called the "Book of Comfort" or the "Book of Consolation" (Is. 40: 1–2, 6, 8) because "the prophet offers no judgment and condemnation of Israel, but only a message of trust and confident hope

---

overly use apocalyptic imagery, probably because they were becoming more and more isolated from the central social structure and so were beginning to formulate their own apocalyptic program.

119. Westermann, *Isaiah 40–66*, 7.

120. Ibid.

121. Ibid.

122. See Brown, et.al., *The New Jerome Biblical Commentary*.

123. Bandstra, *Reading the Old Testament*, 311.

that God is about to end the exile."[124] These other main features of Second Isaiah should also be noted:

- Encourages Israel to have faith in the new exodus (Is.43:16–19).

- Full of promises of hope and restoration. The prophet stresses that there will be a new creation because everything, including the wicked schemes of the nations, fall under the saving plan of God (Is. 40: 12–31, 48: 13–14).

- Second Isaiah has the Songs of the Servant passages: 42: 1–4; 49:1–6; 50: 4–11; 52:13- 53:12. In these passages Israel is described as the "servant of God" in whom God's predilection rests.

- Feminine imagery of God: compares God to a mother (Is. 42:14; 45:10; 49:10).

- While other prophets had implicitly allowed the idea of the existence of other gods, Deutero-Isaiah was the first to stress explicitly that there is no other God but Yahweh.[125]

Third or Trito-Isaiah (Chapters 56–66)

Third or Trito-Isaiah is a late 6th century post-exilic prophetic oracle about Judah. The viewpoint of the prophet is no longer that of someone in Babylon, but of one already back in the Promised Land.[126] In 538 Cyrus the king of Persia allowed the exiles to return home and issued an edict to rebuild the Jerusalem temple (see Ezra 6: 3ff). He also gave back the temple vessels that were carted off when Jerusalem was captured.[127] Situated within this context, Trito-Isaiah falls within the period between 537 and 455 BCE.[128]

Trito-Isaiah must have been an anonymous disciple of Second Isaiah. Where Second Isaiah mocks foreign idols and believes they have no power over Israel, Third Isaiah berates Israel for falling into idolatry (Is. 57: 1–13), and while Second Isaiah never accuses Israel of sin but assures them that their sins have been doubly forgiven, Third Isaiah is full of condemnation of Israel's sins (Is. 58: 1–9, 65: 1–7).[129] The prophet is confronted with a Jewish community in crisis and struggling to rebuild itself. There seemed

124. Boadt, *Reading the Old Testament*, 416.

125. See Laurance, ed. *Introduction to Theology*.

126. Boadt, *Reading the Old Testament*, 443.

127. Westermann, *Isaiah 40–66*, 295.

128. Ibid., 296.

129. Boadt, *Reading the Old Testament*, 443–4.

to have been conflicts between the returnees from exile and the remnants of Israel, i.e. those who never left the land. The problem could be both cultural and religious. The prophet continues the theme of Second Isaiah with prophetic messages meant to sustain the returnees from exile, and messages meant to reconcile the division in the community. The prophet feels he has been "anointed to bring good news to the afflicted. . .shore up the broken hearted, proclaim freedom to the captives and freedom to those in bondage" (Is.61:1–2). Third Isaiah has messages or themes of Hope, Consolation, and Restoration that were addressed to those who just returned from exile.

Christian Metaphors in Isaiah

The book of Isaiah has deep significance for New Testament writers. No prophetic book is quoted in the New Testament as often as the book of Isaiah. For the early Christians, Isaiah, together with Genesis and Psalms, form the core of the Old Testament.[130] In Christian New Testament Matthew 1:23 is seen as the fulfillment of the promise of Isaiah 7:14. Yahweh's promise to deliver Judah is seen as metaphor for the coming Messiah, Jesus Christ, whose virgin birth would be seen as a fulfillment of Yahweh's promise to deliver the whole world. Second Isaiah's image of highway for return of the exiles also becomes a powerful metaphor for Christians whose gospel accounts employ this image of Isaiah to show how the ministry of Jesus is good news for all down trodden people of the earth.[131]

STUDY GUIDE

Review . . .

1. Exodus as a book and an event in the life of the Israelites.

2. How the people of Israel ended up in Egypt.

3. Joseph's rise from slavery to a position of prominence in Egypt.

4. Pharaoh's decree to kill all male children of the Hebrew people and the birth of Moses.

5. Moses' encounter with Yahweh.

6. Meaning of biblical covenant.

130. Barton, *Isaiah 1–39*, 13.

131. Brueggemann, *Isaiah 40–66*, 19.

7. Differences between Apodictic law and Case or Casuistic law.

8. Covenant with the Patriarchs

9. Covenant as forms of treaty in Ancient Near East.

10. Exodus as part of creation story.

11. Prophecy in Israel and Ancient Near East

12. Prophetic Books and Isaiah

Discussion Questions

1. Recount the exodus event, beginning from the time Joseph was sold into slavery to the time Yahweh made a lasting and abiding covenant with Moses at Mount Sinai.

2. You will recall that the Yahwist writers inherited patriarchal material of the past they wanted to blend into general history. What is this patriarchal material? How did the Yahwist use this material to show that God's grace prevails even in the face of human plot and wickedness?

3. Explain the events that led to Moses' first encounter with Yahweh at Mount Sinai.

4. How are the plagues suffered by the Egyptians connected to the Jewish Passover?

5. In what way is the Hebrew covenant idea similar to treaties found in Ancient Near East?

6. In the Suzerain treaty of Ancient Near East there are six legal steps or procedures. Show how Exodus 19: 3ff is patterned after these legal procedures.

7. Identify similarities and differences between Yahweh's covenant with Moses and Yahweh's other covenants with the Patriarchs.

8. In what ways are the law codes of the Ancient Near East similar to the laws found in the Book of the Covenant.

9. To what extent can it argued that Exodus is a continuation of the primeval story already begun in Genesis?

10. Explain the role the prophets played in the establishment of the Hebrew covenant. Can their roles be accurately described as that of "watch dogs?"

11. What is the rationale for dividing the Prophetic books into Former and Latter Prophets? What books are considered Former prophets and what books are considered Latter Prophets? Do designations "Former Prophets" and "Latter Prophets" describe the chronological sequence of these books?

12. Explain the role of prophecy in the Ancient Near Eastern traditions. To what extent was Israelite prophecy dependent on this tradition? Does the dictionary definition accurately describe the meaning of biblical prophecy? If yes, why? And if no, why?

4

The Canon of the Hebrew Bible
and the Christian Old Testament

IN OUR DEFINITION OF theology in chapter one we saw how the sixteenth century Protestant reformation radically altered the way Christian theology was conceived. We also saw how the Catholic Church responded to Protestant criticism of some Church practices by establishing seminaries and divinity schools for the training of priests and pastors. It was after this shift that theology was divided into the four broad areas of Biblical, Historical, Systematic theology, and Ethics. A study of the Hebrew Bible (Christian Old Testament) need be studied in the context of the history of the peoples of ancient civilization of which the people of Israel were a part.

ANCIENT CIVILIZATION AND ISRAELITE HISTORY

In the past two centuries the science of archeology has revolutionized our understanding of human origins. We have learned a lot about the history of the human race, ancient civilizations, Israel's predecessors and neighbors, and the Bible.[1] One of the many things these archeological findings reveal is that the history of the people of Israel ought to be studied in relationship to that of their neighbors, whose history, compared to that of Israel, was politically, economically, and socially larger. This means that Israel's history is "a minor sideshow in the larger history of the Ancient Near East, and

1. Wright, Murphy, and Fitzmyer, "A History of Israel," 1220.

80

its culture is overshadowed by the more brilliant cultures of antiquity."[2] Among Israel's neighbors were the Sumerians, creators of civilization in Lower Mesopotamia in the Copper-Stone age (4500–3200 BCE) who introduced the pictographic (cuneiform) system of writing.[3] There were also the Mesopotamians who built strong civilization, and the Egyptians whose civilization was concentrated along the Nile River and who made great strides in the development of agriculture and irrigation and invented the hieroglyphic script. For more than two thousand years Egypt was a dominant power in the Middle East. But its rise to power and fame was checked in succession by the rise of the Persians, Assyrians, and Babylonians.

In trying to help us understand the different stages of human existence on earth, archeologists distinguish various stages according to the material commonly used as tools and weapons. There is the Old Stone Age or Paleolithic period, which was a period in time when people were hunters and gatherers and moved from cave to cave for food and shelter. This period was followed by the Middle Stone age or Mesolithic period (18,000–8000 BCE) when people made strides from hunter gatherers to domesticators of animals. Then there was the New Stone age or Neolithic period (8000–4500 BCE) when people lived more sedentary life and became food producers. In the Copper-Stone age or Chalcolithic period (4500–3200 BCE) that followed agriculture was vastly improved and expanded. The Bronze Ages are divided into the Early Bronze Age (3200–2000 BCE), Middle Bronze age (2000–1550 BCE), and Later Bronze Age. The Bronze Ages ended what is known as prehistory and ushered in a new era—history properly speaking.

The rise of the Israelite nation cannot be separated from the social upheavals of the Late Bronze age.[4] The Hebrew Bible did not set out to tell an all-out scientific story. It did not set out to tell a secular history of Israel either. The story the Hebrew Bible tries to tell is one of sacred history, namely that the God of Israel played a role in a very real human history.[5] The events covered by the Hebrew Bible, i.e., the time of Abraham and the patriarchs (the period from Abraham to Joseph) to the Maccabean revolt, span about two thousand years of history. Both Jews and Christians alike accept these narratives as sacred history—that in these historical experiences, as seen through the eyes of faith, the ultimate meaning of human life is disclosed.[6] As a story of Israel's testimony of faith- encounter with God,

2. Anderson, *Understanding the Old Testament*, 8.

3. Wright, Murphy, and Fitzmyer, "A History of Israel," 1221.

4. Lemche, "Hebrew," 95.

5. Lonergan, *Method in Theology*, 306.

6. Anderson, *Understanding the Old Testament*, 8.

both the Hebrew and Christian Bible have a lot in common. They share the conviction that God has revealed God's self to the people of Israel.[7] But there are also significant differences — the arrangement of the books, the terminologies used to describe them, and the fact that the Christian Bible has the New Testament. The Hebrew Bible does not have the New Testament because Jews do not share the Christian idea of Jesus Christ as the final and definitive revelation of God in human history.

NATURE OF THE BIBLE

The Bible is the word of God in human language. As the word of God, expressed in human language, the Bible has two authors: divine and human. The Church understands this to mean that God chose certain people and made use of their powers and abilities, so that with God acting in them and through them "they, as true authors, consigned to writing everything and only those things which [God] wanted" (Dei Verbum, 11). The divine author is technically then the Holy Spirit who reveals to the human author what God wants them to write. God's first act of self-disclosure is through creation. After creation God reveals God's self through events in human history. God always wants "to manifest and communicate both himself and the eternal decrees of his will concerning the salvation of humankind" (Dei Verbum 6). The Bible is understood to be the place where God definitively reveals God's self to humankind. This process of God's self-disclosure to the human person is called **Revelation**.

The human author writes under the promptings of the Holy Spirit. The Holy Spirit breathes on this person who has been specially chosen, telling him or her to write what God wants and only what God wants. This is called **Inspiration**. According to the Church's understanding therefore, "the books of both the Old and New Testaments in their entirety, with all their parts, are sacred and canonical because written under the inspiration of the Holy Spirit, they have God as their author and have been handed on as such to the Church herself (Dei Verbum, 11). Since the human author communicates only the truth of God and under the guidance of the Holy Spirit the Bible is said to be without error. This idea that Bible is free from error is called **Inerrancy** (see 2 Timothy 3: 16). "Therefore, since everything asserted by the inspired authors or sacred writers must be held to be asserted by the Holy Spirit, it follows that the books of Scripture must be acknowledged as teaching solidly, faithfully and without error that truth which God wanted put into sacred writings" (Dei Verbum, 11). If the Bible is inspired and is

---

7. Boadt, *Reading the Old Testament*, 14.

written by human authors under the guidance of the Holy Spirit, how do we determine which of the human authors wrote under the promptings of the Holy Spirit? Who adjudicates? The process of determining which books should be among the collections of the Bible and which should not is called **Canonicity** or **Canon**. "Canon" means "measurement," "rule," or "standard." We shall return to the question of canonicity later because of the difference between Catholic canon and Protestant canon.

The Hebrew Bible

The Hebrew Bible, sometimes referred to as **Tanak**, has three main divisions: the Law (Torah), Prophets (Nevi'im) and Writings (Ketuvim). The word Tanak is derived from the first consonants of these three parts of the Hebrew Bible: **T** from Torah, **N** from Nevi'im, and **K** from Ketuvim = TNK. The Jews added vowels to make for easy acronym Tanak. The Torah or Law, which Jewish tradition holds was written by Moses, is at the heart of the Tanak. It consists of the first five books in the Hebrew arrangement of the Bible: Genesis, Exodus, Leviticus, Numbers and Deuteronomy. The traditional division of the Hebrew Bible into Torah, Prophets, and Writings reflects the Jewish understanding that each division or block forms a unit. Observant Jews commit them to memory, especially the Torah, because of the belief that the Torah contains Yahweh's instruction for the people of Israel.

The second part of the Hebrew Bible, the Prophets or the Nevi'im, has three main subdivisions:

(a). The first block consists of the historical books of Joshua, Judges, 1 & 2 Samuel, and 1 & 2 Kings. These are sometimes referred to as the **Former Prophets**.

(b). The second block consists of the three Major Prophets of the Hebrews: Isaiah, Jeremiah, and Ezekiel.

(c). The third block consists of the Book of the Twelve, what in Hebrew tradition is known as the Minor Prophets: Hosea, Joel, Amos, Obadiah, Jonah, Micah, Nahum, Habakkuk, Zephaniah, Haggai, Zechariah and Malachi. The last two sub-divisions, i.e., the Major and Minor Prophets, are sometimes collectively referred to as the **Latter Prophets**. "The titles Former and Latter are unfortunate because they foster the perception that the Latter Prophets are later than the historical books."[8] The distinction that has been made between the Former

8. Bandstra, *Reading the Old Testament*, 204.

and the Latter Prophets does not refer to the chronology of the books but simply their placement in the Bible.[9] The prophetic books generally re-interpret some events in Israelite life and redact some of these events in light of the covenant—that faithfulness to the covenant leads to prosperity and violation of tenets of the covenant brings curses, like the removal of many leaders of the Israelite community and their deportation to Babylon in the sixth century B.C.E.[10]

The Writings or Ketuvim include books like Psalms, Job, Proverbs, Ruth, Song of Songs, Ecclesiastes, Lamentations, Esther, Daniel, Ezra, Nehemiah, 1 Chronicles, and 2 Chronicles. Though the Ketuvim have less status than the Torah or the Prophets, this collection includes later and disparate materials that have been considered authoritative interpretations of relevance to the existence of Israel.[11]

In light of these three broad divisions, the suggestion here is that the three divisions of the Hebrew Bible be understood as a scheme of three concentric circles. "The inner circle, the Torah, presents the basic story of the people and includes the laws which are to guide them in living. The next circle, the Prophets, is a critical commentary on the life of the people to whom the Torah is given. The outer circle, the Writings, a diverse and open-ended collection, broadens out from Israel's worship and festal celebration to wisdom reflections."[12] Not included in the official list of the Hebrew Bible are seven books that Catholics and Protestants "disputed" (Apocrypha books), but which made its way into the official collection of Catholic Bible (Tobit, Judith, I and II Maccabees, Wisdom, Ecclesiasticus, and Baruch). The Jews consider them sacred but do not include them in their official list or canon.

THE CHRISTIAN OLD TESTAMENT

The entire Hebrew Bible, the Tanak, is what Christians traditionally call the Old Testament. "Old" here implies a Christian reading of the Hebrew Bible. The use of the term "Old Testament" probably derives from a passage in Jeremiah that speaks of both the Old Covenant and a New Covenant to be established:

9. Ibid., 205.

10. Carmody and Brink, *Ways to the Center*, 124.

11. Ibid., 125–6.

12. Anderson, *Understanding the Old Testament*, 3. See also Brueggemann, *The Creative Word*, 170.

> The days are coming, says the Lord, when I will make a covenant with the house of Israel and the house of Judah. It will not be the covenant I made with their fathers the day I took them by the hand to lead them forth from the land of Egypt, for they broke my covenant and I had to show myself their master, says the Lord. But this is the covenant which I will make with the house of Israel after those days, says the Lord. I will place my law within them, and write it upon their hearts; I will be their God, and they shall be my people (Jer.31: 31–34).

To call the Tanak "Old Testament" can be a somewhat misleading if by "old" one understands something antiquated or something no longer relevant. In fact, Christianity rejected that idea when it was first expounded by Marcion in the second century CE. Marcion erroneously taught that the Old Testament has been rendered void because of the New Testament. Orthodox Christianity considers the Old Testament to be "an indispensable part of Sacred Scripture" because its books are divinely inspired.[13] In the eyes of the Christian church, even though the Old Testament may contain "matters imperfect and provisional" they were deliberately designed to "prepare for and declare in prophecy the coming of Christ." Since the Old Testament bears witness to the "whole pedagogy of God's saving love," in these same books the "mystery of our salvation is present in a hidden way."

The first five books of the Christian Old Testament are properly called the **Pentateuch**, a term derived from the Greek *pentateuchos*, meaning "five scrolls or containers." Origen Adamantius (182–254 CE), an early Christian theologian from Alexandria, was said to have been the first to refer to these books as Pentateuch. The early Christian Church was a Greek-speaking community and they read the scriptures in Greek, especially the more authoritative Septuagint (Greek translation of Hebrew Scriptures) that was begun in Alexandria, Egypt, in the third century B.C. E.[14] The second set of books is the Writings, which include the Psalms, Proverbs, Ecclesiasticus, etc. Here we see another difference between the Hebrew Bible and the Christian Old Testament. In the Tanak, for example, Daniel and Lamentations are grouped with the Ketuvim (Writings). But in the Christian Old Testament Daniel and Lamentations are considered prophetic books. The third part of the Christian Old Testament is the Prophets. The basic difference here between the Christian and the Hebrew arrangement of these Prophetic books pertains to Baruch, which is a canonical book in the Christian Old Testament but did not make it to the Hebrew canon. There is also

---

13. See *Catechism of the Catholic Church*, no. 121; hereafter referred to as CCC.

14. Anderson, *Understanding the Old Testament*, 125–6.

the case, as we pointed out earlier, with Daniel and Lamentations, which in the Christian Old Testament are prophetic books, but in the Hebrew Bible are grouped with the Writings. The Christian placement of the prophetic books as the last block of materials of the Old Testament is meant to convey the idea that the prophets of the Old Testament stand as a bridge between the Old Covenant and the New Testament, and that the events prophesied in the Old have found fulfillment in the New. In the standard version of the Bible, for instance, the book of prophet Malachi is the last book of the Old Testament. Malachi uses expressions like "my Messenger" and "sacrifice." The Catholic placement of this book as the last book of the Old Testament is to give the idea that John the Baptist, the last of the Old Testament prophets and the forerunner of Christ, is that "Messenger" Malachi spoke about and that the sacrifice of Jesus stands as the "sacrifice" foretold by the prophet. It is for this reason that the Christian reading of the Old Testament is often referred to as allegorical or typological readings, i.e., Christians read the Old Testament "in light of Christ crucified and risen," with the understanding that such typological reading "discloses the inexhaustible content of the Old Testament."[15]

CATHOLIC AND PROTESTANT CANONS

The Bible is not a single unified work, but a collection of books written by different authors spanning about seven century. Each author wrote for different audience, using different styles and modes of communication that appealed to their audience. Most of the books of the Old Testament were written in Hebrew, except for parts of the books of Daniel (2: 4–7:28), Ezra (4:6–6; 7: 12–26), and Jeremiah (10 and 11) that were written in Aramaic. The whole of the New Testament, on the other hand, was written in Greek. The process of gathering and putting together these various books into a single collection was a long and arduous process. During this long and difficult process some books were accepted and others were thrown out. Those books that were accepted as meeting all the criteria to be included in the official list of the Bible are said to have made the "canon." The word "canon" is from the Greek meaning "rule" or "measurement." The Jews made a decision about which books to be included in their canon at the end of first century C.E., at the Council of Jamnia (90 A.D), which officially accepted only 39 books (mentioned above). The Catholic decision about which books to be included in the canon did not come until the Council of Trent in the sixteenth century.

15. CCC. 129.

Catholic and Protestant Canons of the Old Testament

Christians, like the Jews, had a long deliberation about which books to be included in the canon of the Old Testament and the canon of the New Testament. They must have followed criteria such as (i) the content of the book (ii) the author of the book and (iii) how often was the book used in the Church's liturgy and teachings? At the end of the deliberations there was no unanimity between Protestants and Catholics regarding the canon of the Old Testament. Both Catholics and Protestants accept the division of the Bible into the Old and the New Testament, but differ on the issue of the number of books to be included in the Old Testament. The Catholic Church accepts 46 canonical books of the Old Testament while the Protestants, following strictly the Jewish canon, accepts only 39 books of the Old Testament. The canonical books of the Old Testament in the Catholic Bible are as follows: Genesis, Exodus, Leviticus, Numbers, Deuteronomy, Joshua, Judges, Ruth, 1 and 2 Samuel, 1 and 2 Kings, 1 and 2 Chronicles, Ezra and Nehemiah, Tobit, Judith, Esther, 1 and II Maccabees, Job, Psalms, Proverbs, Ecclesiastes, the Song of Songs, Wisdom, Sirach (Ecclesiasticus), Isaiah, Jeremiah, Lamentations, Baruch, Ezekiel, Daniel, Hosea, Joel, Amos, Obadiah, Jonah, Micah, Nahum, Habakkuk, Zephaniah, Haggai, Zechariah and Malachi. Most Protestant Churches accept these books as canonical except for the following seven: Wisdom, Ecclesiasticus, Baruch, Tobit, Judith, and I and II Maccabees. These seven disputed books are called the Apocrypha books.

Why the difference between Catholic and Protestant Bible? Early Christians "used an ancient Greek translation of the Old Testament (the Septuagint). This Greek version of the Bible had 46 books. Since most of the early Christians were Greek-speaking, the Septuagint was their preferred version. But when Judaism officially set out to determine its canon at the end of the first century, it drew up a shorter list of 39 books, mainly written in Hebrew. In the Reformation period, Protestants went back to this shorter Hebrew canon, considering it more authentic.[16] This difference aside, Protestants and Catholics accept twenty-seven books of the New Testament: the four Gospels — Matthew, Mark, Luke and John— the Acts of the Apostles, the Letters of St. Paul to the Romans, 1 and 2 Corinthians, Galatians, Ephesians, Philippians, Colossians, 1 and 2 Thessalonians, 1 and 2 Timothy, Titus, Philemon, the Letter to the Hebrews, the Letters of James, 1 and 2 Peter, 1, 2, and 3 John, Jude, and Revelation or the Apocalypse.

---

16. See General Introduction of *The Catholic Study Bible*, RG 3.

Deuteronomist History (DH)

What in the Hebrew Bible are referred to as the Torah and Former Prophets are sometimes collectively called **Primary History** because together these books give a complete account of the history of Israel, starting from the beginning of time in Genesis, when Yahweh-Elohim created the universe, to the time Israel's development as a nation ruled by Judges and Kings, and even up to the time they were taken into exile. In this narrative the book of Deuteronomy is pivotal. Deuteronomy also occupies a central position in the Tanak as a whole, especially for two reasons: First, Deuteronomy concludes the Torah, and second, it opens the door to the Former Prophets.

The Former Prophets are also called the **Deuteronomist History** (**DH**). This is because the historical and theological perspective of the Former Prophets was shaped, by and large, by the book of Deuteronomy.[17] DH should by no means be confused with Deuteronomic material. While Deuteronomic material refers to the materials found in the book of Deuteronomy (Deut. 5–28), DH refers to those writings that were "influenced by the Deuteronomic torah, that comprise the so-called Deuteronomist History that extends from Joshua through II Kings."[18]

There is a neat pattern in the history that Deuteronomist historian tells: that Israel's vitality and solidarity lay, not only in a united, exclusive loyalty to Yahweh, but also that obedience to Yahweh's torah leads to welfare and peace and disobedience results in hardship and defeat. The composition of DH is very complex, in particular because of its multiple themes. M. Noth (1943), who was the first scholar to develop a theory of DH, has argued that DH was composed to explain why Yahweh allowed the nation of Israel to be destroyed by the Babylonians in the sixth century B.C. DH was, for Noth, a book of judgment, for the reason that Yahweh allowed the nation of Israel to be destroyed because of their idolatry.[19] Building on the suggestions of Noth, G. von Rad (1962) suggested that in addition to the theme of judgment, DH was composed to show the Israelites that hope for the future was based on a total return to the covenant Yahweh made with the House of David.[20] Wolff (1982) who also developed a theory regarding the composition of DH added that DH was composed as a call to repentance, i.e., to show the

---

17. Bandstra, *Reading the Old Testament*, 205.

18. Anderson, *Understanding the Old Testament*, 183.

19. Bandstra, *Reading the Old Testament*, 206.

20. Ibid.

nation of Israel that if they repent and return to the covenant Yahweh would restore them to their pre-exilic state.[21]

In studying the Torah and the development of DH, the importance of Deuteronomy to the Torah and the Former Prophets cannot be disputed. But as more and more theories are developed, scholars seem to work with more or less than the Pentateuch.[22] For example, M. Noth have suggested that the first four books of the Tanak (Genesis, Exodus, Leviticus and Numbers) should be read as a unit. His suggestion yields what is known as **Tetrateuch**. Still others like G. von Rad suggest that the book of Joshua be added to the first five books of the Tanak, because Joshua continues the story already began in Deuteronomy. This suggestion that the Torah and Joshua be read as a unit yields a **Hexateuch**. These terms are significant because they "express a particular understanding of the formation and relationship of the books concerned."[23]

Themes in the Pentateuch

In the first five books of the Bible (the Pentateuch) can be found multiple themes: (i) Genesis 1–11 details primeval history. (ii) Genesis 12–50 recounts the story of Abraham and the ancestors and ancestress. (iii) Exodus 1–18 gives a detailed account of the exodus or the escape from Egypt. (iv) Exodus 19 through Leviticus and through Numbers 10 give an account of the Law and the Wilderness sojourn, and (v) Numbers 11ff gives a detailed account of the entrance into the Promised Land. Who put these stories together? In other words, who is the author of the Pentateuch?

PENTATEUCH AND HISTORICAL-CRITICAL METHOD

For a long time both Jewish and Christian traditions assumed that Moses was the author of the Pentateuch. As far back as the post-exilic period (after 539 B.C.), Moses was explicitly identified as the author of the Pentateuch.[24] Even renowned historians like Titus Flavius Josephus (37–100 CE), and the distinguished scholar and Jewish philosopher, Philo of Alexandria (25 BCE-50AD) took it for granted that Moses authored these books.[25] This assump-

21. Ibid.
22. Murphy, "Introduction to the Pentateuch," 3.
23. Ibid.
24. Boadt, *Reading the Old Testament*, 90.
25. Ibid., 92.

tion was based on the Jewish understanding of passages in the Hebrew Bible where references were made to Moses and the Law. The New Testament simply continues this Jewish view. In Mk 10:3ff and Matt. 19:7ff Jesus is said to have made reference to "the hardness of your hearts" which made Moses to permit, in the Law, "a bill of divorce." Acts 15:5 also makes reference to those Christians who wanted Gentile converts to be circumcised and be made to observe "the law of Moses." In the Tanak, we read that "Joshua inscribed upon the stones a copy of the law written by Moses" (Josh.9: 32). The argument for Mosaic authorship of the Pentateuch went unchallenged for centuries. It was not until the early middle ages that people began to examine more closely some passages in the Tanak that seem to cast doubt, not only on the Mosaic authorship, but also on the theory of one single author of the Pentateuch. One of such passages was Deut. 34: 5–6, which gives an account of the death and burial of Moses: "So there, in the land of Moab, Moses, the servant of the Lord, died as the Lord had said, and he was buried in the ravine opposite Beth-peor in the land of Moab, but to this day no one knows the place of his burial." How could Moses have written about his own death?

A thorough examination of passages that cast doubt on the Mosaic authorship, coupled with an examination of the language and style of the Pentateuch, led to the realization that the authorship of the Pentateuch was more complex than originally thought. The ground-breaking work of Richard Simon (1638–1712) and the milestone work of Jean Astruc (1684–1766) brought to an end the view that Moses was the single author of the Pentateuch. Simon and the Dutch philosopher Baruch Spinoza (1632–1677) found in the Pentateuch "repetitions and contradictions," which led them to conclude that these books "seemed to lack the style of a single author."[26] Simon developed a theory that the Pentateuch was derived from a compilation of a number of sources beginning from the time of Moses to the time of Ezra (5th century B.C. post-exilic material). Astruc discovered that the Pentateuch derives from a compilation of two major materials and several minor materials especially in the way the texts refer to God either as Elohim or Yahweh, but still thought that it was Moses who compiled these materials.[27]

The work of Simon and Astruc have led scholars, using **source analysis or literary analysis** to argue, not only for a multiple authorship of the Pentateuch, but also for a complex process of compiling and editing, of which Moses was not a part. Through the pioneering work of these men, scholars have come to understand that the purpose of Pentateuch was not

---

26. Ibid., 92.

27. Bandstra, *Reading the Old Testament*, 39–40.

necessarily to give a historical account of the people of Israel, but to express faith in Yahweh. In expressing this faith, the narrators told their stories in songs, epics, proverbs and various traditions available to them at the time. Through source analysis, scholars have also come to the conclusion that at least four different sources were used in the compilation of the Pentateuch: the Yahwist source (known as J), the Elohist source (known as E), the Priestly source (P), and the Deuteronomist source (D). This idea that the Pentateuch was a compilation of four main sources is called **Documentary Hypothesis**. Julius Wellhausen worked out this schema in its complete form and published it in his *Prolegomena to the History of Israel* (1878). According to Documentary hypothesis, the composition and final editing of the Pentateuch evolved over a long period of time.

Documentary Hypothesis

The Torah, as we have seen, is a very complex book. The complexity of these books calls for recognition of various strands and units. The pioneering effort of Simon and Astruc was synthesized by Julius Wellhausen (1844–1918), giving us what we now know as the Documentary hypothesis. Despite modifications that have been made since the synthesis of Wellhausen, biblical scholars still speak of these four documents: J (8th century BCE), E (8th century), D (7th century) and P (Post exilic, 6th century BCE). These four main, probably written sources, were eventually merged together in the postexilic period by the P tradition and another redactor. Five literary identifiers are used to distinguish the sources: (a) duplications and repetitions of material (b) different ways of referring to God (c) contrasting geographical and political perspectives (d) variation in vocabulary and literary style and (e) evidence of editorial activity.[28]

J/Yahwistic Source

- Dates back to the time of Davidic monarchy (1000 B.C.)
- Uses the name YHWH for God.
- Uses anthropomorphism (i.e. speaks of God as if God were a man).
- Vivid storytelling and theological vision.
- Recounts traditions of the Davidic monarchy.

---

28. Ibid., 40.

- Speaks of Jerusalem as the one center of worship.

- Tells the story of Israel as that of a people under the special guidance of Yahweh.

- This material was probably written or preserved in the Southern kingdom, Judah (c.8th century B.C.).

E/Elohistic Source

- Dates back to the Davidic monarchy.

- Uses the name Elohim for God.

- Emphasizes morality.

- Does not necessarily recount Davidic monarchy, but references tribal traditions of the conquest of the land.

- Recounts covenant traditions.

- Has flare for worship, but locates worship centers outside of Jerusalem. Probably originated in the northern kingdom (perhaps earlier than J) before the establishment of the monarchy (Like J, dated c.8th cent. B.C.).

D/Deuteronomist Source

- Recognized by style of the book of Deuteronomy— highlighting role of the Law of Moses.

- Exhortatory in style.

- It was understood to be instructional or preaching material that used language, concepts and theological perspectives similar to that found in the book of Deuteronomy.

- Stresses the faithfulness of God as found in covenant traditions.

- Stresses obedience as the proper response to God.

- Thought to have influenced some of the liturgical traditions of the books of Samuel and Kings as well as prophetical books.

- Scholars contend that there are two distinct phases in the editing or redaction of D materials. Some believe that an early form of D document existed during the reign of Josiah (c.621 BCE), which Josiah used as a basis for reform. After the exile, a later version of this material was re-edited to apply the theology of Moses to the crisis of exile.

P/Priestly Source

- Understood to be priestly material and focused on the concerns of priests serving in Jerusalem temple.

- Concerned with cult and rituals (book of Leviticus).

- Concerns itself with record keeping and legal traditions concerning the proper functioning of the temple.

- Concerns itself with ordering events into sequence, genealogies and keeping of religious laws.

- Concerned about atonement for sins.

- Like D, P contains traditions from all previous periods of Israel's history.

- Final shaping of P traditions is considered late in the development of the final form of the Pentateuch, since the priests emerged as leaders and wielders of power after the exile. Most P materials are post-exilic (5th cent. B.C. or later.)

STUDY GUIDE

Review . . .

1. The story of Israel in the context of the larger history of the Ancient Near east.

2. The meaning of Tanak.

3. Three concentric circles of the Hebrew Bible.

4. Meaning of the "Old Testament."

5. The canon of the Christian Old Testament.

6. The canon of the Christian New Testament.

7. Differences between Catholic and Protestant canons.

8. Deuteronomist History (DH).

9. Mosaic authorship of the Pentateuch.

10. Documentary Hypothesis.

Discussion Questions

1. Even though the Bible sets out to tell sacred history, in what way can the Bible be meaningful in the study of world history? To what extent should the historical accounts narrated in the Bible be used to augment ancient history? Do you think the Bible should be jettisoned wherever its historical narratives conflict with archeological evidence?

2. Give a detailed outline of the three parts of the Hebrew Bible.

3. Compare and contrast, the Hebrew Bible and the Christian Bible. Do you think it is appropriate to refer to the Hebrew Bible as the "Old Testament?" Can you come up with better terms Christians can use rather than "Old Testament?"

4. The Torah has ambiguous indications of authorship. Imagine yourself in an argument with someone who thinks Moses actually wrote the Torah. How would you go about convincing this person against the so called Mosaic authorship?

5. Whose pioneering efforts led to the identification of four literary sources in the Pentateuch? How did this lead to the theory of Documentary Hypothesis?

6. What is Deuteronomist History (DH)? How pivotal is the book of Deuteronomy to the overall narrative of DH?

7. What do you think of the different hypothesis regarding the Torah? Do they help reinforce your faith in the Bible or do they make you have doubts about the truth of the Bible?

8. Identify and explain the positions of three authors whose theories about DH have helped our understanding of DH.

9. Give the main characteristics of the four sources developed by Julius Wellhausen

5

The Christian New Testament

IN ITS EARLY BEGINNINGS Christianity was thought to have begun as a sect within Judaism by the ruling Roman authorities. What was thought to be a sect quickly gained ground and became, not only the official religion of the Holy Roman Empire, but also the most dominant religion in the whole of the western world. What was responsible for the growth of this religion? How did it start? And how did it spread and become dominant? New Testament scholars like to make a distinction between Jesus, the early church, and the author of the gospels (evangelist).[1] This distinction assumes that there is an interconnection between these terms and that the words and deeds of Jesus and the early Christian understandings of them were what was put into writing by the evangelists. The prevailing idea the gospel writers tried to communicate was that the God once understood in the Israelite tradition as an ethnic God (Yahweh) for a few "chosen people" has been revealed in the resurrection of Jesus of Nazareth as the God of all humanity and that everyone is now potentially a member of God's chosen people.[2]

THE GOSPELS

The Greek word for Gospel, *euangelion*, and its Latin form *evangelium*, literally means Good News. The term "gospel," as used in the New Testament, refers primarily to the oral proclamation of the Good News of salvation

1. Swartley, *Israel's Scripture Traditions and the Synoptic Gospels,* 9.
2. Malina and Rohrbaugh, *Social Science Commentary on the Synoptic Gospels,* 427.

95

whose core is usually the death and resurrection of Jesus Christ or the salvation message proclaimed by Him.[3] All four Gospel writers give an account of the Good News of Jesus Christ, even though only Mark begins his narrative with reference to the "gospel" of Jesus Christ. The different gospel accounts about Jesus were written by and for third generation followers of Jesus who wanted to know more about the first generation experience and about what Jesus said and did in ways that would be relevant to them, since second generation followers like Paul wrote almost nothing about what Jesus said and did.[4]

The Gospels were not the earliest Christian writings of the New Testament. But they occupy a central place in the New Testament and in the life of the Church. Some second generation writings, like the Pauline letters, which were thought to have been written c. 50–70 A.D. predate the Gospels, which were estimated to have been written between 65 A.D. and 100 A.D. During this time, i.e., the period between Jesus' death and the first canonical gospel, information about Jesus' life and death was transmitted orally.[5] It was not until much later that some of the circulating oral information was committed to writing in the canonical gospels. The first generation of Jesus' followers were dying and memories of life and teachings of Jesus were fast fading. Then there arose the need to record information about Jesus that had initially been transmitted orally.[6]

The order of arrangement of the Christian Gospels — Matthew, Mark, Luke, and John — is not necessarily the order of composition. Earliest Christian reflections on Jesus appealed to the Old Testament to interpret the meaning of faith in Jesus Christ,[7] for the early church understood the meaning of Jesus' life, death, and resurrection through the lens of the Old Testament.

Survey of the New Testament

The Christian church existed ever before there was such a thing as a New Testament writing. In the first and second century, there was no such thing as the New Testament, since none of the books we now call NT scriptures existed then. The Christian communities at the time only read the Hebrew

3. Duling and Perrin, *The New Testament*, 295.

4. Malina and Rohrbaugh, *Social Science Commentary on the Synoptic Gospels*, 16–17.

5. Freed, *The New Testament*, 38.

6. Ibid., 40.

7. Swartley, *Israel's Scripture Traditions and the Synoptic Gospels*, 9.

Scriptures. What is now today the New Testament were themselves crystallizations of the different documents and traditions of the early Christian communities who engaged the Hebrew Bible and interpreted the events of the Tanak in light of their understandings of God's new revelation in the man Jesus. What we now call the Gospels first circulated as stories that emerged from the preaching, worship, and teachings of the early Christian communities, while the Epistles "bear fragments of, and make allusions to, liturgical formulae, hymns, ritual practices, and prophecies."[8] The collection of books that came to be known as the NT developed gradually over the course of several centuries and attained the form in which we know them in the fourth century.[9] The earliest Christian writings of the New Testament were composed by credible leaders of these communities as exhortations, admonitions, and encouragement for suffering Christian communities. These letters were read publicly by the communities to whom they were addressed and these communities sometimes shared them with other Christian communities. For example, Paul's letters to the Christian communities he founded (the first Christian writings of the NT) were "used by churches other than the ones for whom they were originally written, and indeed were regarded as having a special authority."[10] The Church recognized these books as scriptures because they proved more helpful to the Christian communities than the available Jewish Scriptures.

The final and definitive canon of the New Testament was agreed upon after a lengthy and laborious process. Catholics and Protestants did not initially agree on the books of the New Testament mainly because of the event of the Reformation. Luther had insisted on scripture alone as the authoritative guiding principle of the Christian Church. But the Catholic Church, while not fundamentally disagreeing with Luther, insisted on Scripture and Tradition (Magisterium) as authoritative norms of the Christian life.

The Four Gospels and Criteria for Canonicity

The Christian Church, as we pointed out in our treatment of the Hebrew Bible, accepts 46 books of the Old Testament as divinely inspired. They saw these books as foreshadowing the new covenant to be inaugurated by the man Jesus Christ. It is still not clear why the early Christian Church accepted only four Gospels out of the many 'gospels' in circulation at the time, just as we are not sure when the events of the life of Jesus were committed

8. Johnson, *The Writings of the New Testament*, 596–67.

9. Gamble, *The New testament Canon*, 12.

10. Johnson, *The Writings of the New Testament*, 598.

to writing. For example, among the gospels that were known and used by the early Christian communities were the gospel of Thomas, the gospel of Peter, the Dialogue of the Savior, the gospel of the Hebrews, and the gospel of the Egyptians. The circulation of multiple gospels created some difficulties. "Just as each Gospel was composed in the first place with the aim of providing a sufficient and self-contained account, it was not easy for Christian communities to see why there should be more than one: a plurality of Gospels cast doubt on the adequacy of any."[11] With this came the need to re-assert the authority of the Gospels by authoritatively recognizing some as authentic accounts of the history of the life of Jesus. As early as 180 C.E., evidence from the writings of St. Irenaeus (130–202 CE), bishop of Lyon, suggested that the Christian Church had recognized only four Gospels out of the many in circulation. Another second/third century fragment, the Muratorian canon, also attested to the existence of four Gospels. What criteria were used in this selection? We shall return to this later. But one thing is clear, the four canonical Gospels were widely accepted and used by the early Christians. These Gospels, before their compilation, were written for individual Christian communities and for a specific purpose.

When the idea of devising a scripture emerged, five main criteria were used. (1) Apostolicity: Writings that had direct or indirect connection to the apostles were more likely to be recognized as authentic. (2) Catholicity: The ideal of catholicity means that a document has to have a wider appeal, i.e., it must be considered relevant to the whole Church, and not just a specific local community. (3) Orthodoxy: The document must be orthodox in the sense of being in agreement with the faith of the universal Church. (4) Usage in Christian Worship: A document must conform to the traditional practices of the Church to be considered authentic, i.e., it must have expressed the faith of the Church in a way that must have called for its use in Christian liturgy and worship. (5) Inspiration: since the Church is led by the Spirit, to the extent that a document conforms to the first four criteria and were so designated by the Church, the document was said to be inspired.

THE CENTRALITY OF MARK

A good number of New Testament scholars hold the view that the gospels were written by anonymous authors and that the present titles were probably a second-century addition. "Because the form of the title is the same for every gospel, a title was probably given to each only after the gospels had been collected as a group of four. Then the name of a well-known person

11. Gamble, *The New Testament Canon*, 30.

was included in the superscription of each gospel."[12] Second century Christians, "possessing anonymous manuscripts and eager to give names to them, fastened upon four historical figures—the Apostles Matthew and John, Luke the "beloved physician" of Paul (Col. 4: 14), and John Mark of Jerusalem, the 'son' of Peter (Acts 12: 12; I Peter 5: 13)"[13]

Viewed in this light, the issue of the authorship of the Gospel of Mark is still problematic. While some assume that an anonymous Hellenistic Christian who lived in Syria wrote the Gospel, tradition assigns it to John Mark whom Papias (135 A.D), bishop of Hierapolis in Phrygia, Asia Minor, describes as "an interpreter of Peter," and whom Peter described as "Mark, my son" (1 Peter 5:13). A tradition from Clement of Alexandria (c. 150–220) also associates Mark with Peter in Rome, which means that Peter was thought to be the authority behind Mark's gospel.[14] Thus, in the second century it was thought that the author of the Gospel of Mark was not an eyewitness of Jesus, but a personal associate of someone (Peter) who was.[15]

"Mark" probably was not his real name.[16] There are quite a few references to John Mark in the New Testament. Colossians 4: 10 identifies him as "the cousin of Barnabas," and Acts 12:25 identifies him as the one who accompanied Paul and Barnabas in one of their missionary journeys. 2 Timothy 4: 11 describes him as someone Paul wanted to meet because he was "helpful in the ministry." His mother's name was Mary, according to the account in Acts 12:12 and she was thought to be a devoted Christian because the Christian community sometimes gathered at her house for prayer. Eusebius of Caesarea (263–339 CE), the famous church historian of the fourth century A.D, in his *Ecclesiastical History*, credits Papias (c. 140 A.D) with the following, regarding Mark:

> Mark became Peter's interpreter and wrote accurately all that he remembered, not indeed, in order, of the things said or done by the Lord. For he had not heard the Lord, nor had he followed him, but later on, as I said, followed Peter, who used to give teaching as necessity demanded but not making, as it were, an arrangement of the Lord's oracles, so that Mark did nothing wrong in thus writing down single points as he remembered

---

12. Freed, *The New Testament*, 97.

13. Helms, *Who Wrote the Gospels?*, i.

14. Freed, *The New Testament*, 98.

15. Helms, *Who Wrote the Gospels?*, 2.

16. Anderson and Moore, "Introduction," 2.

them. For to one thing he gave attention, to leave out nothing of what he had heard and to make no false statements in them.[17]

Just as not much information was available regarding the author of the Gospel of Mark, not much information was available regarding its audience as well. "The Gospel was unsigned and undated and contains nothing that attests explicitly either to its geographical location or to the specific circumstances of its writings or even to the gender of its author."[18] But it is projected that the Gospel could have been written in Rome, sometime between 65 A.D. and 70 A.D. "The reason for the date A.D. 70 is that chapter 13 suggests Mark knew about the Jewish insurrection against Rome and the resulting destruction of the Temple in Jerusalem in A.D. 70."[19] Some place Mark's origin in Syria where Greek was the common language.[20] This is based on the argument that Mark wrote in koine Greek, a not very literate Greek, and he also knew Jesus' language of Aramaic and quotes several sayings of Jesus transliterated from Aramaic into Greek. With this kind of bilingualism some place the origin of the gospel in Syria, "where a substratum of Aramaic seems to have survived."[21]

There is a general agreement, however, that the Gospel was addressed to Gentile Christians who were facing rejection and persecution,[22] at a time the city of Jerusalem and the Jewish Temple were under siege. Perhaps "a Greek-speaking non-Jewish Christian wrote about Jesus for an audience like himself of non-Jewish Christians who mistakenly expected that the destruction of Jerusalem was the beginning of the end of the age."[23] The persecution of these Christians came from both Judean and Roman authorities.[24] These Gentile Christians did not know a lot about Jewish laws and customs. The period was particularly a difficult time for Christians because the Romans regarded them as Jews while the Jews regarded them as outcasts. Moreover, their apocalyptic and eschatological expectations were intensified and Christians living in Rome, Syria, and Galilee would have been greatly affected by the tumultuous times.[25] The author of this gospel tries to explain some Jewish customs, emphasizes Christ's passion, and en-

17. Ibid., 3.

18. Rhoads, Dewey, and Michie, *Mark As Story*, 1.

19. Davis, *The New Testament*, 90.

20. Helms, *Who Wrote the Gospels?*, 9.

21. Ibid.

22. Roads, Dewey, and Michie, *Mark As a Story*, 2.

23. Helms, *Who Wrote the Gospels?*, 9.

24. Roads, Dewey, and Michie, *Mark As a Story*, 2.

25. Freed, *The New Testament*, 98.

courages the community to stand steadfast in the midst of persecution. The author seems to tell the Gentile Christians that membership in the family of Jesus is not so much by blood as it is by faith. Only those who acknowledge him, as did the Gentile Centurion who acclaimed him as the "Son of God" (Mark 15:39) can lay claim to the family of Jesus.

The Gospel of Mark is "a collection of what had previously been unconnected fragments about Jesus, units of oral tradition, and brief written stories and sayings that reveal a long history of transmission before they reached Mark; the collection looks nothing like the 'reminiscences' of Peter, though its lack of a clear chronology accounts for Papias' sense that it is 'not in order.'"[26] Mark is the shortest of the four Gospels. St. Augustine thought Mark copied and summarized Matthew "like a slave,"[27] an idea that has since been discarded, since it is now generally believed that Matthew expanded upon Mark. This gospel has a literary device called the "Messianic Secret," according to which the identity of Jesus is not known by his family and friends who thought he was either "possessed by Beelzebul," (Mark 3:22) or he was "out of his mind" (Mark 3: 21). Even though his family and friends do not know him, the demons knew who he was and called him "Jesus of Nazareth, the Holy One of God" (Mark 1:24).

The discovery of the "Messianic Secret" in the Gospel of Mark was largely due to the efforts of William Wrede whose publication of The Messianic Secret (1901) noted a pattern in Mark, especially in Mark 9:9 where Jesus specifically directs his disciples not to tell anyone what they have seen until He rises from the dead. On many occasions Jesus tries to keep his identity secret. In Mark 1: 34 he refuses to let the demons speak "because they knew him." In Mark 1: 43 he heals a leper and commands him to "say nothing to anyone." In Mark 5: 43 he raises a young girl from the dead and strictly orders that "no one know about this." Even in discussing with his disciples in Mark 8 he refuses to speak openly about his identity and commands silence when someone recognizes that he is the messiah (i.e. the "anointed one" like Israel's Kings).[28] Mark wanted the truth about Jesus to be proclaimed at the moment of his death, even if all the disciples had fled.[29] Wrede notes that the "messianic secret is not a historical fact so much as a theological idea, the idea that Jesus became Messiah through his resurrection."[30]

26. Helms, Who Wrote the Gospels?, 3.

27. Anderson and Moore, "Introduction," 3.

28. Ehrman, The New Testament, 75.

29. Davis, "Mark's Christological Paradox," 177.

30. Anderson and Moore, "Introduction," 3. See also Wrede, The Messianic Secret, 129.

The "Messianic Secret" is Mark's invention, and not part of the stories of the Christian tradition Mark inherited.[31] It is the "central theological idea pervading the entire Gospel and which concretely determines its structure."[32] By using this device Mark wants to show that "contrary to the popular understanding, the job of the Messiah is not to rule at first, but first to suffer and die before returning to rule."[33] Mark depicts the content of Jesus' preaching as proclaiming that the kingdom of God is at hand and that there is need for repentance and faith in God. The gospel begins with the story of John the Baptist, the precursor and baptizer, who baptized Jesus and preached this need for repentance. The death of John the Baptist is going to prefigure the death of Jesus. Jesus taught his disciples by parables. He also performed miracles. The greatest of all miracles was his death and resurrection. In Mark (16:8) even the resurrection is part of the Messianic Secret, for only the three women at the tomb are told about it and, because they were afraid, they said nothing to anybody.[34]

Mark emphasizes the passion of Jesus, stressing the necessity of His suffering and death. The German philosopher-theologian, M. Kahler (1835–1912) observed in this gospel the pattern of "the passion narratives with extended introductions."[35] Mark's interest in the passion of Jesus is both to convey the significance of the person and work of Jesus and also to stress the meaning of true discipleship. The structure of Jesus' prediction of His passion is always the same: Jesus' prediction, the disciples' misunderstanding, and Jesus' sayings about what is required of those who follow him.[36]

The Synoptic Problem

The gospel of Mark has a lot in common with the gospels of Matthew and Luke. These three gospels have so much in common that they are significantly different from John. In the eighteenth century the first three Gospels came to be called the Synoptic Gospels. The German biblical scholar, J.J. Griesbach, was the first to label these gospels Synoptic Gospels.[37] When

---

31. Helms, *Who Wrote the Gospels?*, 12.

32. Ibid., 13; quoting Conzelmann and Lindemann, *Interpreting the New Testament*, 219.

33. Ibid., 12.

34. Ibid., 13.

35. Freed, *The New Testament*, 101.

36. Ibid., 101–02.

37. Carson, et. al., *An Introduction to the New Testament*, 19.

placed side by side (synoptically) these three Gospels have a lot in common. Griesbach's choice of the word was influenced by the high degree of similarity he found in these gospels presentations of the ministry of Jesus, particularly similarities in structure, content, and tone.[38] It is enlightening to view them (-optic) with (syn-) one another, alongside one another.

Example 1.

Matt: 8: 16–17	Mark 1: 32–34	Luke 4: 40–41
When it was evening, they brought him many who were possessed by demons, and he drove out the spirits by a word and cured all the sick, to fulfill what had been said by Isaiah the prophet: "He took away our infirmities and bore our diseases."	When it was evening, after sunset, they brought to him all who were ill or possessed by demons. The whole town was gathered at the door. He cured many who were sick with various diseases, and he drove out many demons, not permitting them to speak because they knew him.	At sunset, all who had people sick with various diseases brought them to him. He laid his hands on each of them and cured them. And demons also came out from many, shouting, "You are the Son of God." But he rebuked them and did not allow them to speak because they knew that he was the Messiah.

Matthew, Mark, and Luke, in ways significantly different from John, structure the ministry of Jesus according to a general geographic sequence, i.e. Jesus' Galilean ministry, ministry in Judea, and final ministry in Jerusalem. In content, in ways significantly different from John, they relate many of the same events, i.e. Jesus' teaching and healing ministry. In tone, contrary to the more mellow and meditative tone of John, Matthew, Mark, and Luke convey a tone of intense, rapid-fire action by juxtaposing Jesus constant movement and teaching with miracles.[39]

38. Ibid.
39. Ibid.

Example 2: Triple Tradition.

Mark 2: 10–11	Luke 5: 25	Matthew 9:6
But that you may know that the Son of Man has authority to forgive sins on earth"— he said to the paralytic, "I say to you, rise, pick up your mat, and go home"	But that you may know that the Son of Man has authority on earth to forgive sins"—he said to the man who was paralyzed, "I say to you, rise, pick up your stretcher, and go home"	But that you may know that the Son of Man has authority on earth to forgive sins" —he then said to the paralytic, "Rise, pick up your stretcher, and go home." He rose and went home

According to The New Jerome Biblical Commentary, Mark has 661 verses, Matthew has 1068 verses and Luke has 1149 verses. About 80 percent of Mark is found in Matthew, and about 65 percent of Mark is found in Luke. (Material found in Mark that are in Matthew and Luke is known as the **Triple Tradition**). But in spite of these similarities we still see some significant differences between these gospels (materials that Matthew and Luke have in common, about 220 verses, that are not found in Mark is known as the **Double Tradition**). How could one account for the similarities and differences without recourse to the Holy Spirit?[40] The problem of determining the similarities and differences between these three Gospels is what is known as the synoptic problem.[41] In other words, synoptic problem is the study of the similarities and differences of the first three Gospels in an attempt to explain their literary relationship.[42]

How then do we solve the synoptic problem, since we are dealing with three known documents (Matthew, Mark, and Luke) plus unknown hidden factors, such as the possibility of written fragments and oral traditions?[43] There seems to be an agreement in language and order of narratives among these gospels. Is it possible that any of the evangelists had access to one or more gospel accounts? J.A. Fitzmyer has observed that the history of the synoptic research has shown that the synoptic problem is practically insoluble.[44] What Fitzmyer means is that the argument that Matthew and

40. Anderson and Moore, "Introduction," 5.

41. See Brown, et.al. *The New Jerome Biblical Commentary*. .

42. Goodacre, *The Synoptic Problem*, 16.

43. Fee, "A Text-Critical Look at the Synoptic Problem," 164.

44. Ibid., 163.

Luke used a second source in addition to Mark is no longer guaranteed, nor can the priority of Matthew or proto-Luke hypothesis resolve the synoptic problem.[45] But given that there seems to be direct literary dependence among the gospels, "that Gospel is to be preferred as having priority which best explains how the others came into existence."[46] In other words, what hypothesis best accounts for the combination of exact agreement and the divergence that characterizes Matthew, Mark, and Luke?[47]

Solution to the Synoptic Problem?

Different theories have been offered as solution to the synoptic problem:

1. In 1771 the German literary critic, G. E. Lessing, propounded the idea of an "Ur Gospel," an original gospel written in Hebrew or Aramaic that the synoptics relied on. In Lessing's view, this common dependence on one original gospel accounts for the relationship among the synoptics.[48] Some scholars, like Eichhorn, have adopted and modified this theory, postulating the existence of several lost gospels as the sources of Synoptic Gospels.[49]

2. Some who disagreed with Lessing, like the German J. G. Herder, suggested that the interdependence among the synoptics can be accounted for by their dependence on some common oral sources.[50]

3. The German theologian, Fredrich Schleiermacher, came up with a theory of common dependence on gradually developing written fragments, suggesting that "several fragments of the gospel tradition exited in the early church and that these gradually grew until they became incorporated into the Synoptic Gospels."[51]

4. Finally, there is the theory of interdependence; that two of the evangelists have used one or more of other gospels.[52] There are several variants of this theory as we shall explain below.

---

45. Luhrmann, "Q: Sayings of Jesus or Logia," 97.

46. Fee, "A Text-Critical Look at the Synoptic Problem," 164.

47. Carson, et. al., *An Introduction to the New Testament*, 27.

48. Ibid.

49. Ibid.

50. Ibid., 28.

51. Ibid., 29.

52. Ibid.

Two-Source Theory or Two Document Hypothesis

There are two facets of the Two-Source Theory: the Priority of Mark and the Q hypothesis.[53] This hypothesis which was postulated in the eighteenth century and developed in the nineteenth century states that Mark was the first written gospel and that Matthew and Luke depended on Mark. This hypothesis explains the pattern of divergence by proposing that although Matthew and Luke used Mark as a common source, they diverge from Mark at certain points because they wrote their accounts independently.[54] Investigation of parallel units of these three Gospels "reveals that where Matthew deviates from Mark, Luke usually doesn't, and that where Luke deviates from Mark, Matthew usually doesn't."[55] How then does one account for the Double tradition, i.e. the non-Marcan materials that are in Matthew and Luke? One posits the existence of a lost writing, the "Q" source. The "Q," which derives from the German word Quelle (source) was understood to be a written work that contained "Sayings" of Jesus from which Matthew and Luke each drew. Thus the Q hypothesis holds that both Matthew and Luke, independently of each other, besides Mark, used a second source.[56] In the earliest phase of this hypothesis it was generally assumed that Q was a written document.[57] But in the light of the understanding that in "the early years of Christian history, there seems to have been a great deal of freedom to move back and forth between written and oral tradition,"[58] scholars are willing to allow "some influence of the oral tradition between the time of its crystallization and its use by the two Synoptists."[59] Although the original language of written Q was thought to be Aramaic, it is safe to assume "that Q was a Greek document with only pre-literary connexion [sic] with Aramaic."[60] Thus, at the time the Q document was used by Matthew and Luke, Q was in a fixed written form, although "some sayings might have undergone slight alterations due to the influence of the oral traditions."[61]

The priority of Mark does not sufficiently resolve the synoptic problem. What about the materials unique to Mathew that are not found in Luke

53. Goodacre, *The Synoptic Problem*, 20.

54. Masson, *The Charmed Circle*, 118.

55. Ibid.

56. Vassiliadis, "The Nature and Extent of the Q-Document," 138.

57. Ibid., 139.

58. See Beardslee, *Literary Criticism of the New Testament*, 73; cited in Vassiliadis, "The Nature and Extent of the Q Document," 143.

59. Vassiliadis, "The Nature and Extent of the Q Document," 143.

60. Ibid., 146.

61. Ibid., 160.

and materials unique to Luke that are not found in Matthew? How do we resolve these? Scholars acknowledge the existence of a hypothetical "M" for materials found only in Matthew but not found in Mark or Luke and hypothetical "L" for materials found in Luke but not in Matthew or Mark.[62] It is not clear whether M or L is only one source or group of sources, or whether it was written or oral. What it suggests is only that it represents a single or multiple documents available to the author of Matthew or Luke and most likely stories that had been transmitted orally.[63]

A. M. Honore of Oxford, in his statistical study of the synoptic problem, arrived at the following conclusion:

- Mark is the main link between Matthew and Luke.
- Matthew and Luke used Mark.
- Matthew did not use Luke.
- Luke did not use Matthew.
- Matthew and Luke used sources other than Mark (i.e. Q).
- Q is not a single document.[64]

Those who reject the Two-Source theory posit the **Priority of Matthew**, also known as the **Griesbach Hypothesis**. This hypothesis, which goes back to the time of Augustine (4th cent) and reformulated by J.J. Griesbach (1789), states that Mathew was the first written Gospel, and that Luke depended on Matthew and Mark then abbreviated Matthew and Luke. This theory was revived in 1964 by William Farmer[65] who dispenses with the two facets of the Two-Source Theory, assigning the order of composition as Matthew, Luke, and Mark.[66]

CRITICAL RECONSTRUCTION OF THE LIFE OF JESUS

The Christian religion is anchored on the events surrounding the life of Jesus of Nazareth. As a historical person who lived and walked among us, Jesus had a history, a history that changed the course of world events. Some have sought to understand this history beyond the events narrated in the

62. See Brown, An *Introduction To The New Testament*. See also Johnson, *The Writings of the New Testament*.

63. Ehrman, *The New Testament*, 89.

64. Honore, "A Statistical Study of the Synoptic Problem," 110.

65. See Farmer, *The Synoptic Problem*.

66. Goodacre, *The Synoptic Problem*, 22.

canonical Gospels. But research into Jesus himself has long been controversial.[67] Many wonder if there is still something new to be said about Jesus and if the attempt to say something new is not a denial of Christian tradition and the sufficiency of Scripture.[68] Those who want to reconstruct the life of Jesus argue that "even in a human relationship of knowledge and love there can be misunderstandings, false impressions, wrong assumptions, which need to be teased out and dealt with, how much more when the one to whom we are relating is Jesus himself."[69] To reach Jesus himself, the argument continues, there is the need to go beyond the four canonical Gospels, the New Testament information about Jesus, and even the Greco-Roman Christian sources. This critical probing or attempt to reconstruct the life of Jesus is known as the Quest for the Historical Jesus.

The Quest for the Historical Jesus

The Gospels are confessional statements about Jesus, the Christ. Unlike other New Testament writings, the Gospels make their confession by going back to tell the story of Jesus' earthly life and ministry. With their backward glance the Gospels present us with a challenge of faith in Jesus and with a problem about Jesus.[70] In addition, when read with the intent of finding information about the life of Jesus, the Gospels pose a particular historical problem, stemming from their conspicuously different images of Jesus presented by the Synoptic Gospels on the one hand and John on the other. Moreover, these sources, i.e. the Synoptics and John, "exhibit, each within itself, a striking contradiction. They assert that Jesus felt himself to be the Messiah; and yet from their presentation of his life it does not appear that he ever publicly claimed to be so. They attribute to him, that is, an attitude which has absolutely no connection with the consciousness which they assume that he possessed."[71] Related to this is the lack of connecting thread in the materials they offer. While the Synoptics seem to be mere collections of anecdotes, John seems selective in his account of events and discourses.[72] "Not only do the events lack historical connection; we have no indication of a connecting thread in the actions and discourses of Jesus, because the sources give no hint of the character of his self-consciousness. . . . All that we

67. Wright, *The Challenge of Jesus*, 13.

68. Ibid.

69. Ibid., 14.

70. Tatum, *In Quest of Jesus*, 87.

71. Schweitzer, *The Quest of the Historical Jesus*, 9.

72. Ibid., 8.

know of the development of Jesus and of his messianic self-consciousness has been arrived at by a series of working hypothesis."[73]

These and similar difficulties have led to the question as to whether the Jesus portrayed in the Gospels is the same Jesus that lived and walked in Galilee. In other words, is Jesus of faith the same as Jesus of history? The critical investigation of the life of Jesus is one of the greatest achievements of German theology,[74] an investigation carried out in opposition to the "tyranny of dogma."[75] The issue, as Schweitzer posed it a century ago, is this:

> Is it possible to explain the contradiction between the messianic consciousness of Jesus and his non-messianic discourses and actions by means of a conception of his messianic consciousness which will make it appear that he could not have acted otherwise than as the evangelist describe; or must we endeavor to explain the contradiction by taking the non-messianic discourses and actions as our fixed point, denying the reality of Jesus' messianic self-consciousness and regarding it as a later interpolation of the beliefs of the Christian community into his life?[76]

Since Albert Schweitzer's ground breaking work, *The Quest for the Historical Jesus* (1906), it has become customary to attribute the origin of the "Quest for Historical Jesus" to Hermann Samuel Reimarus (1694–1768) in the eighteenth century.[77] Reimarus who's *Fragments* were posthumously published in 1778 by G.E. Lessing, was out to prove that the traditional European idea of Jesus was based on historical distortion or fantasy.[78] When the *Fragments* made their appearance in Germany they created an intellectual excitement.[79] Influenced by deism and the liberal enlightenment views, Reimarus argued that Jesus was no more than a Jewish revolutionary.[80] He saw the Gospels' story of Jesus' death and resurrection as "a creation of the disciples of Jesus after their disappointment over Jesus' crucifixion."[81]

Reimarus' view of the Christian religion was conditioned by the prevailing liberal enlightenment environment that saw history and faith

73. Ibid.

74. Ibid., 3.

75. Ibid., 5.

76. Ibid., 11.

77. Wright, *The Contemporary Quest for Jesus*, 1.

78. Ibid., 6.

79. Talbert, ed., *Reimarus*, 1.

80. Wright, *The Contemporary Quest for Jesus*, 7.

81. McKnight, *Jesus Christ in History and Scripture*, 8.

as antithetical,[82] splitting history and faith, facts and values, religion and politics, and nature and super nature.[83] The liberal view of early Christianity rested on four assumptions:[84]

1. The life of Jesus can be neatly divided into two periods: an earlier, successful period of ministry and a later journey to Jerusalem characterized by hostility and eventual death.

2. The passion narratives have been influenced by the Pauline notion of atonement.

3. The kingdom of God, a theme that dominates the passion narrative, is conceived as an ethical society of service to humanity and

4. The success of the passion depended on the disciples' understanding of the kingdom.[85]

David Friedrich Strauss (1808–1874) in *Life of Jesus Critically Examined* presented a different reconstruction of the life of Jesus.[86] Although Strauss did not share Reimarus' desire to discredit Christianity, he found in Reimarus "a valuable ally in his fight for a mythical view of the miracle tradition in the Gospels."[87] Strauss first portrayed Jesus as a disciple of John the Baptist who regarded himself as the messiah and had premonitions about his own death; and later under the influence of Hegelian philosophy "omitted the apocalyptic aspects of his earlier portrait of Jesus and presented him as a man with an intense consciousness of the sacred."[88] Strauss' goal was in part to show that while Christianity may not have resulted from a fraud as Reimarus thought, neither was it supernatural as his nineteenth century contemporaries thought.[89]

The last truly significant effort along these lines was Schweitzer's 1906 study.[90] "His survey of prior attempts to retrieve the "real" Jesus illustrated the obvious difficulty. Each interpreter found a different Jesus. Moreover, each found his own ideals embodied in Jesus."[91] Schweitzer objected to some liberal views by pointing out that while Reimarus was right to see

82. Wright, *The Challenge of Jesus*, 15.

83. Ibid., 21.

84. Weaver, *The Historical Jesus in the Twentieth Century 1900–1950*, 28.

85. Ibid.

86. McKnight, *Jesus Christ in History and Scripture*, 8.

87. Talbert, *Reimarus*, 36.

88. McKnight, *Jesus Christ in History and Scripture*, 8.

89. Talbert, *Reimarus*, 36.

90. Masson, *The Charmed Circle*, 116.

91. Ibid.

Jesus in the context of first century Judaism, he was wrong to see him as a revolutionary.[92] "Jesus shared the first century apocalyptic expectation of the end of all things, and though he died without it having come about, he started the eschatological movement that became Christianity."[93] For Schweitzer, "there never was a Jesus who cavorted around Galilee happily winning converts with his message about an ethical kingdom of human service; the service of which he spoke was the necessary repentance providing moral renewal as preparation for the supernatural kingdom."[94] For him, the Christian faith stands by the question of Jesus' messianic consciousness, for if Jesus did not know himself as the messiah then the judgment of the early church is not binding on us.[95]

Although the quest for the historical Jesus continues to this day, thanks to Ernst Kaseman's 1953 lecture, "The Problem of the Historical Jesus," which revived the quest in the modern time, the historical investigation of the real Jesus beyond the confines of dogma continues to prove difficult. In fact, some have tagged the attempt a complete failure. "The quest for the historical Jesus did not fail because the gospels are unreliable sources. The quest failed because interpreters like Reimarus misunderstood what kind of sources the gospels were and so asked the wrong sorts of questions."[96]

Non-Scriptural Sources of the Life of Jesus

Although the canonical Gospels of Matthew, Mark, Luke, and John remain "the most complete sources for a study of Jesus," they are not the only sources.[97] Some New Testament writings give information about Jesus and even some early Christian writers whose work did not make the canon of the New Testament give some information about Jesus, just as there were some writers in the first century CE who, in interpreting Jewish traditions and recording Roman history, make references to Jesus:[98]

1. Talmud: Jesus is sometimes mentioned in Jewish literature, especially "in the Jewish materials that came into fixed form in the Talmud, the repository of Jewish interpretation of the Law from the time of Ezra

---

92. Wright, *The Contemporary Quest for Jesus*, 10.

93. Wright, *The Challenge of Jesus*, 28.

94. Weaver, *The Historical Jesus in the Twentieth Century* 1900–1950, 29.

95. Ibid., 30.

96. Masson, *The Charmed Circle*, 117–8.

97. McKnight, *Jesus Christ in History and Scripture*, 28.

98. Ibid.

to the middle of the sixth century CE."[99] Some Talmudic references to Jesus contradict the Christian account. One possible explanation might be because some Talmudic traditions "attempt to destroy the validity of Christian truth by altering and interpreting the Christian tradition."[100] But even in doing so they do not destroy the basis of Christian truth.

2. Flavius Josephus: Some information about Jesus is found in the work of the Jewish historian Josephus. His work, Antiquities, references James as "the brother of Jesus, who was called the Christ."

3. Pliny: In a second century CE correspondence between Pliny the Younger, the governor of Bithynia, and Trajan, the Roman emperor, there were specific references to Christians and what they believe and references were made to Christ in the context of the existing hot political climate. In a letter to the emperor, Pliny notes how Christians "were in the habit of meeting before dawn on fixed days and singing hymns to Christ as to a god."[101]

4. Tacitus: The Roman historian, Tacitus, in two celebrated works, Histories and Annals gave information about the Christian religion and the man called Christ, who was crucified under Pontius Pilate.

5. Suetonius: Suetonius, a fried of Pliny's, while acting as secretary to Emperor Hadrian, published The Lives of the Twelve Caesars, mentions the persecution of Christians and the expulsion of those Jews from Rome who made disturbances at the instigation of "Chrestus."[102]

6. Agrapha: There are documents, Agrapha (meaning "unwritten things") that contain words ascribed to Jesus. They probably were words of Jesus that were first circulated orally by his followers before they were eventually written down. "Some of these sayings of Jesus are found in New Testament writings outside the Gospels. First Corinthians 11: 23–25 and Acts 20: 35 contain sayings that are clearly attributed to Jesus."[103]

7. Apocryphal Gospels: Some information about Jesus is found in the non-canonical or apocryphal gospels.

---

99. Ibid., 28–29.

100. Ibid., 29.

101. Amiot, "Jesus, an Historical Person," 8.

102. McKnight, *Jesus Christ in History and Scripture*, 33–34.

103. Ibid., 34.

THE STAGES IN-SETTING OF THE GOSPELS

On October 30, 1902, Leo XIII established the Pontifical Biblical Commission (PBC) because he was worried that Catholics were giving in to the opinions of "heterodox writers," and seeking understanding of Sacred Scripture in the "researches, which the erudition of unbelievers has arrived at."[104] The pope charged the PBC to give a "thorough interpretation" of the text of Sacred Scripture and shield it "from every breath of error . . . [and] temerarious opinion."[105] In 1979, however, the PBC ceased from being an official organ of the Catholic Church, in matters of scriptural interpretation. It is now a consultative body of scholars whose conclusions are revered and esteemed in the Church.

The PBC has issued some helpful documents regarding the methods of interpretation of Scripture. One of such documents was the 1964 document, *On the Historical Truth of the Gospels,*[106] in which the PBC sets some guidelines for Catholic exegetes. The Catholic exegete, the PBC admonishes, must make use of all the resources for the interpretation of the sacred text, which the Church has provided, such as the writings of the Fathers and Doctors of the Church.

> In order to bring out with fullest clarity the enduring truth and authority of the Gospels he must, while carefully observing the rules of rational and of Catholic hermeneutics, make skillful use of the new aids to exegesis, especially those which the historical method, taken it its widest sense, has provided; that method, namely, which minutely investigates sources, determining their nature and bearing, and availing itself of the findings of textual criticism, literary criticism, and linguistic studies. The interpreter must be alert to the reminder given him by Pope Pius XII of happy memory when he charged him "to make judicious inquiry as to how far the form of expression or the type of literature adopted by the sacred writer may help towards the true and genuine interpretation, and to remain convinced that this part of his task cannot be neglected without great detriment to Catholic exegesis."[107]

While encouraging the use of historical method, the PBC also urges caution because "the method in question is often found alloyed with

104. See Enchiridion Biblicum, 141.

105. Ibid., 139.

106. Pontifical Biblical Commission, "Instruction on the Historical Truth of the Gospels," 299–312.

107. Ibid., 306.

principles of a philosophical or theological nature which are quite inadmissible, and which not infrequently vitiate both the method itself and the conclusions arrived at regarding literary questions."[108] The PBC hinges its caution on the following areas of concern: (a) Some who have used the method have not only been led astray by "rationalistic prejudices," which made them not only to deny the existence of the supernatural order, but also to deny the reality of prophecies and miracles. (b) Some with erroneous view of faith advance the view that "faith is indifferent to historical truth, and is indeed incompatible with it." (c) Some deny the historical value and character of the documents of revelation and finally (d) some underestimate the authority of the apostles as eyewitnesses of Christ and their influence in early Christian community.[109]

In order to guard against these errors, the PBC endorsed the following three stages of the development of the Gospel tradition and asked the interpreter to take careful note of these "stages of tradition by which the teaching and life of Jesus have come down to us."

(a). First Stage, **the Public Ministry**: Jesus chose disciples who worked with him and were first hand eyewitnesses of His life and teaching. Jesus proclaimed His message orally and accommodated His teaching to the mentality of his audience and disciples. The disciples correctly understood the teachings, miracles, and other events in the life of Jesus. The disciples "grasped correctly the idea that the miracles and other events of the life of Jesus were things purposely performed or arranged by Him in such a way that men would thereby be led to believe in Christ and to accept by faith the doctrine of salvation."[110] Raymond Brown, commenting on this, asserts, "It is important for modern readers to keep reminding themselves that these were memories of what was said and done by a Jew who lived in Galilee and Jerusalem in the 20s. Jesus' manner of speaking, the problems he faced, his vocabulary and outlook were those of that specific time and place."[111]

(b). Second Stage, **the Apostles**: The apostles were witnesses to Jesus. His resurrection was the key turning point. They proclaimed His death and resurrection, and preached the events of His life, taking into account the circumstances of their hearers. Jesus was a Galilean, who spoke Aramaic. His message was proclaimed in Greek, a language he never or rarely spoke. Raymond Brown comments that this "change

108. Ibid.

109. Ibid., 306–7.

110. Ibid., 307.

111. Brown, An *Introduction to the New Testament*, 107.

of language involved translation in the broadest sense of that term, i.e. rephrasing in vocabulary and patterns that would make the message intelligible and alive for new audiences."[112] The PBC continues that after Jesus "had risen from the dead, and when His divinity was clearly perceived, the faith of the disciples, far from blotting out the remembrance of the events that had happened, rather consolidated it, since their faith was based on what Jesus had done and taught."[113] The disciples did not turn Jesus into a "mythical" personage, nor did they distort His teaching. Rather they handed on faithfully their understanding of the words and deeds of Jesus and interpreted them according to the "mentality of their hearers." The disciples illumined their own faith by their post-resurrection kerygma. They understood their mission as people sent forth to bring others to faith by proclaiming the risen Lord.[114]

(c). Third Stage, **the Sacred Writers**: The sacred authors, for the benefit of the Church, took what was first handed orally, and later written, and drew up a narrative that resulted in the four Gospels. "They selected certain things out of the many which had been handed on; some they synthesized, some they explained with an eye to the situation of the churches, painstakingly using every means of bringing home to the readers the solid truth of the things in which they had been instructed."[115] The PBC continues:

> For, out of the material which they had received, the sacred authors selected especially those items which were adapted to the varied circumstances of the faithful as well as to the end which they themselves wished to attain; these they recounted in a manner consonant with those circumstances and with that end. And since the meaning of a statement depends, amongst other things, on the place which it has in a given sequence, the Evangelists, in handing on the words or the deeds of our Savior, explained them, one Evangelist in one context, another in another. For this reason, the exegete must ask himself what the Evangelist intended by recounting a saying or a fact in a certain way, or by placing it in a certain context. For the truth of the narrative is not affected in the slightest by the fact that the Evangelists report the sayings or the doings of our Lord in a different

112. Ibid., 108.

113. PBC, *Instruction on the Historical Truth of the Gospels*, 307.

114. Ibid.

115. Ibid., 308.

order, and that they use different words to express what He said, not keeping to the very letter, but nevertheless preserving the sense.[116]

The exegete must consider these factors, which have a bearing on the origin and composition of the Gospels, if the exegete is to ascertain the true intentions of the sacred writers. The teachings and life of Jesus, according to the PBC, were not recounted just to be kept in remembrance, but were "preached" to furnish "the Church with the foundation on which to build up faith and morals."[117] The PBC then called on the exegete to "cherish a spirit of ready obedience to the Church's teaching authority,"[118] bearing in mind that the Apostles who proclaimed the Good News were filled with the Holy Spirit who preserved them from error when they committed the Good News to writing.

The three stages noted by the PBC are commonly referred to as three "settings-in-life". . . (1) in the life of Jesus before his resurrection, (2) in the life of the Church, i.e. of early Christians before the Gospels were written, and (3) the setting in the context of the Gospel writers and their shaping of the written Gospels, i.e. Jewish setting, Jewish-Hellenistic setting, and the purpose of the evangelists.

THE FOUR SENSES OF SCRIPTURE

The Christian Church venerates the scriptures as the word of God in human language. Earlier we saw that there are two authors of the sacred text, human and divine—that God is the author of Sacred Scripture in the sense that God revealed God's divine word to human beings who committed them to writing under the inspiration of the Holy Spirit. God chose certain men, whom he inspired, made full use of their own faculties and powers and guided them through the power of the Holy Spirit to write down only whatever God wanted. We also saw that sacred Scripture is inerrant (without error)—that God inspired the human authors of sacred scripture and they committed to writing only what God intended. The sacred scriptures firmly, faithfully and without error teach the truth God wanted to convey to human beings for our salvation.

116. Ibid., 309.

117. Ibid.

118. Ibid., 309–310.

There are two senses of scripture, according to ancient tradition: the literal sense and spiritual sense. The spiritual sense has three subdivisions: allegorical, moral and anagogical senses.

a. The Literal sense: This is the meaning conveyed by the human author. All other senses of scripture are based on the literal sense.

b. Allegorical sense: This is the profound understanding of the text by recognizing its significance in Christ. When the Hebrews crossed the Sea of Reeds for instance, the crossing of this sea is a type of baptism in Christ.

c. Moral sense: This is the ethical interpretation of the text of sacred scripture such that it helps us lead a good/moral Christian life.

d. Anagogical sense: Viewing the text of the sacred scripture in terms of their eternal significance, such that it leads us to our eternal home, heaven.

HERMENEUTICS AND THE NEW TESTAMENT

The English word hermeneutics is derived from the Greek verb *hermeneuin*, which means "to make known" or "to translate." Greek mythology depicts "Hermes" as the god whose duty it is to communicate to human beings the message of the gods. Later Hermes came to be known as the patron of communication and understanding. Hermeneutics, deriving from this mythic god-messenger, Hermes, means the art or science of interpretation. As Hermes bridged the gap between two realms: the divine and human realm, hermeneutics examines the relationship between two realms: the realm of the text and the realm of those who wish to understand the text.[119] In classical Greek literature, especially that beginning from Plato, hermeneutics "referred to the interpretation of divine signs and oracles as they related to the fate and destiny of people or individuals."[120] Properly speaking, hermeneutics is a branch of philosophy that is concerned with human understanding and interpretation of a written text. It examines the way one understands a text or a work of art.[121] Hermeneutics seeks to answer the question: how can a text that originates in a particular historical context be unfolded in a different (later) cultural setting? In their study and analysis of literature, the ancient Greeks looked for coherence and consistency in grammar, style,

119. Jeanrond, *Theological Hermeneutics*, 1.

120. Houtepen, "Hermeneutics and Ecumenism, "1.

121. Henn, "Hermeneutics and Ecumenical Dialogue," 47.

and logic. Later Hebrew also responded to the need to interpret Hebrew Scripture.

Need for Hermeneutics

Christians venerate the Bible as the revealed Word of God and are challenged to be obedient to God's Word. But "it can be daunting to face a voluminous Bible full of alien genealogies, barbaric practices, strange prophecies, and eccentric epistles."[122] There is also the fact of linguistic, historical, social, and cultural gaps between the ancient world of the scriptural writer and the modern world that needs to be bridged.[123] This then calls for a proper method of interpretation, hermeneutics. To properly understand the revealed word of God "we need an approach and methods that are appropriate to the task. Hermeneutics provides the means for acquiring an understanding of the Scriptures" in ways that avoid arbitrary and erroneous interpretation that suits our whims.[124]

A written or oral communication involves three layers of meaning: what the speaker or writer intends to convey, what the listener or recipient actually understands, and what meaning is actually encoded in the text or utterance itself.[125] "Authors may occasionally unconsciously convey more than they intended, but the point is that they normally determine what they will say, how they will encode their message, and what results they hope to achieve."[126] Since the biblical author is not available to make these known to us, it is only by means of biblical texts that we can reconstruct what the authors intend to convey and what their audiences understood.[127]

The Jews recognized the importance of scriptural interpretation very early in their history. Scholars allude to II Chronicles 35: 13, which attempts to reconcile the paschal prescriptions of Exodus 12:9 and Deuteronomy 16:7, as proof that what was later called rabbinic exegesis had long existed in the Jewish reading of Scripture.[128] In the late sixth century BCE, when the Jews started returning home from exile, the Levites were said to have helped Ezra the scribe interpret the Mosaic Law. The Jews who returned from exile did not speak Hebrew. They spoke Babylonian version of Aramaic. Accord-

---

122. Klein, et. al., *Introduction to Biblical Interpretation*, xxv.

123. Ibid., 5–6.

124. Ibid., 5.

125. Ibid., 8; paraphrasing Caird, *The Language and Imagery of the Bible*, 32–61.

126. Ibid.

127. Ibid., 9.

128. Halivni, "Aspects of Classical Jewish Hermeneutics," 77.

ing to the story attested in Nehemiah (8: 7–8), whenever Ezra proclaimed the Mosaic law during solemn assembly, it was the Levites who, in addition to explaining to the people what Ezra was reading, translated and interpreted the text. This practice led to what was later known as the *Targum*, the translation and interpretation of biblical texts in the period known as the intertestamental period. They interpreted the text in ways that explain obscure words and reconciles conflicting passages, and also found ways to apply the text to the daily life of the people.[129]

There was also the widespread use of the Midrashim in Hellenistic Judaism, when Greek culture and influence predominated in the period that followed the inauguration of world-wide transnational culture due to the conquest of the civilized world by Alexander the Great in about 333 BCE. Midrash is a Hebrew word that denotes "a method of reading details" into the biblical text. It is essentially a way of searching for the meaning of a biblical text. In the Hellenistic period, especially in the cultural center, Alexandria, hermeneutics assumed a more scientific style. Hellenistic scholars sought the origin and meaning of a given work by attending carefully to the logic, style, and grammar of the text. The method proved so useful that the Church Fathers applied it to the study of the New Testament. They favored allegorical reading of scriptural text over its literal meaning and found, in reading the Old Testament, a "hidden" meaning. They saw the Old Testament as pre-figuration of the New Testament.

The teaching office of the Catholic Church, the Magisterium, favors proper interpretation of the biblical text and sees this as essential to its duties of preserving the Christian faith and tradition. In its concern for correct scriptural interpretation, the Magisterium sometimes intervenes in cases where they believe individuals or schools of thought are misrepresenting a scriptural text. The Magisterium's intervention in scriptural matters has been well documented, especially since the last century, beginning with Leo XIII, who in 1902 established the Pontifical Biblical Commission to oversee issues of scriptural interpretation. Pius X, following Leo's lead, founded the Biblical Institute in 1909. In 1920 Benedict XV issued an encyclical on the interpretation of the Bible to celebrate the 1500th anniversary of the death of St. Jerome, the patron of Catholic biblical scholarship, and in 1965, the Second Vatican's Council's document, Dei Verbum, gave another boost to Catholic biblical studies. The involvement of the Catholic Church in Biblical studies, however, has been defined mainly by two encyclicals, Leo XIII's Providentissimus Deus (November 18, 1893) and Pius XII's *Divino Afflante Spiritu*.

---

129. Klein et.al., *Introduction to Biblical Interpretation*, 24.

On April 23, 1993, the centenary anniversary of Providentissimus Deus, the Catholic Church released another landmark document for Biblical studies that was prepared by the Pontifical Biblical Commission (PBC) titled, "The Interpretation of the Bible in the Church." The PBC "is not an organ of the teaching office, but rather a commission of scholars who, in their scientific and ecclesial responsibility as believing exegetes, take positions on important problems of Scriptural Interpretation and know that for this task they enjoy the confidence of the teaching office."[130] This PBC document examines modern approaches to biblical interpretation, its advantages and disadvantages, and outlines ways of knowing (interpreting) the meaning of a text. In this document, PBC notes that its intention is "to indicate the paths most appropriate for arriving at an interpretation of the Bible as faithful as possible to its character both human and divine."[131] In laying this path for correct interpretation of biblical texts, the document begins with a cautionary note, denouncing the hermeneutics of some rationalist philosophers.

Does Philosophical Hermeneutics have a Place in Biblical Interpretation?

Hermeneutics or the theory of interpretation of texts has "provided occasion for the elaboration of the impressive epistemological and metaphysical constructions associated with names such as Schleiermacher, Dilthey, Heidegger, Gadamer, Habermas and Ricoeur."[132] It was against their involvement in matters of hermeneutics that the Pontifical Biblical Commission (PBC) directed its cautionary note because they "stressed the involvement of the knowing subject in human understanding, especially as regards historical knowledge."[133] In the assessment of PBC, however, if this involvement of the knowing subject is seen in terms of rationalistic philosophical thought, especially that of the 18th century German philosopher, Immanuel Kant (1784–1804), it undercuts true interpretation. Kant had denied metaphysical knowledge since, for him, we cannot know the metaphysical world, the world of "noumena," as he calls it. In their concern, the PBC notes:

---

130. The Pontifical Biblical Commission, *The Interpretation of the Bible in the Church*, 28.

131. Ibid., 34.

132. Henn, "Hermeneutics and Ecumenical Dialogue," 47–48.

133. *The Interpretation of Bible in the Church*, 76.

In its recent course exegesis has been challenged to some re-thinking in the light of contemporary philosophical herme-neutics, which has stressed the involvement of the knowing subject in human understanding, especially as regards historical knowledge. Hermeneutical reflection took new life with the publication of the works of Friedrich Schleiermacher, Wilhelm Dilthey and, above all, Martin Heidegger. In the footsteps of these philosophers, but also to some extent moving away from them, various authors have more deeply developed contem-porary hermeneutical theory and its applications to Scripture. Among them we will mention especially Rudolph Bultmann, Hans Georg Gadamer and Paul Ricoeur. It is not possible to give a complete summary of their thought here. It will be enough to indicate certain central ideas of their philosophies which have had their impact on the interpretation of biblical texts.[134]

1. Friedrich Daniel Ernst Schleiermacher (1768–1834): a German phi-losopher/theologian who became deeply involved in the Romantic Movement in Berlin. Romanticists believed in individualism and ex-pression of individual freedom. Schleiermacher was sympathetic to the French Revolution.

2. Hans Georg Gadamer (1900–2002): a German philosopher/theolo-gian, and a student of Heidegger. His most famous work was *Wah-rheit und Methode* (Truth and Method) in which he argues that the element of effective history is operative in all understanding of tradi-tion. Gadamer stressed the historical distance between the text and its interpreter. "That the text is the object of interpretation means that it presents a question to the interpreter. To understand the text is to un-derstand the question of the text. Whoever wishes to understand the text must see it as the answer to the question. But the interpreter does not come as an empty vessel; the interpreter comes with a horizon of meaning that is broadened so as to become fused with that of the text."[135]

3. Paul Ricoeur (1913–2005) a French philosopher who was influenced by the work of Gabriel Marcel. Ricoeur was preoccupied with what has been known as the hermeneutic of the self, i.e. need to make one's life intelligible to oneself. He refers to a principle approach in his her-meneutic method as **hermeneutic of suspicion**, because every dis-course both reveals and conceals something about the nature of being.

134. Ibid.
135. McKnight, *Jesus Christ in History and Scripture*, 150.

Hermeneutic of Suspicion has been appropriated by Liberation theologians, especially Latin American liberation theology, Feminism, and Black theology. Feminist theologians and Black theologians alike look at such texts as these with suspicion:

- "Wives should be subordinate to their husbands as to the Lord. For the husband is the head of his wife just as Christ is the head of the Church" (Eph.5: 22–24).

- "Slaves be obedient to your human masters with fear and trembling, in sincerity of heart, as to Christ. . ." (Eph. 6: 5–6).

Historical-Critical Method and Biblical Analysis

The PBC considers the historical-critical method an "indispensable method for the scientific study of the meaning of ancient texts,"[136] in as much as the sacred scripture is the word of God in human language. The historical-critical method makes it possible to understand more accurately the intention of the authors and editors of the bible. The origin of the method goes back to antiquity, to Greek commentators of classical literature, and to the Patristic period (Origen, Jerome, Augustine, etc.). At this time the method was still in its infancy and less developed.

The PBC traces the modern form of the method to the refinements of the humanists of the Renaissance who called for *recursus ad fontes* (return to the sources). The work of Richard Simon (17th cent), who drew attention to the doublets, discrepancies in content and style of the Pentateuch ushered in the beginning of Literary Criticism. His discoveries disproved the notion of Moses as the single author of the Pentateuch. Literary criticism was further developed and in the 19th century there developed from it the **Documentary hypothesis,** which posits that four documents have been woven together to produce the Pentateuch. These four documents, as we have seen, are the Yahwist (J), the Elohist (E) the Deuteronomist (D) and the Priestly (P). Literary criticism has also been applied to the Gospels, yielding, for instance, the **Two Source Theory or Two Source Hypothesis**, which states that the synoptics, Matthew and Luke, in composing their gospels, relied on Mark and a collection of the Sayings of Jesus called Q.

The PBC, however, maintains that this kind of literary criticism, in its desire to establish chronology of the biblical text, restricts "itself to the task of dissecting and dismantling the text in order to identify the various

136. Pontifical Biblical Commission, *The Interpretation of the Bible in the Church,* 35.

sources,"[137] and as such does not pay sufficient attention to the final form of the biblical text, i.e. the work of the final editor. The PBC also notes the insufficiency of textual criticism and the Form criticism, which Martin Dibelius and Rudolph Bultmann applied to the synoptic gospels, and also the insufficiency of Redaction criticism. What this means, according to the PBC is that the historical-critical method sometimes dissolves and destroys the text. But it still "opens up to the modern reader a path to the meaning of the biblical text."[138]

The Pontifical Biblical Commission, far from endorsing any particular method of biblical analysis, states that no method of biblical analysis, no matter how scientific, is adequate enough to comprehend the richness of the biblical text. In this respect then, the historical-critical method is necessary but not altogether sufficient for grasping the richness of the biblical text. The PBC also examined other methods of literary analysis, like Rhetorical Analysis, Narrative analysis, and Semiotic Analysis, pointing out their usefulness as well as limitations.

Rhetorical Analysis is a systematic way of studying the biblical text by analyzing its rhetoric or pattern of speech. Rhetoric is the art of persuasion. Classical rhetoric distinguished between three modes of discourse or three different modes of public speaking:

1. Deliberative rhetoric that was used in political assembly

2. Judicial rhetoric that was used in the court of law and

3. Demonstrative rhetoric that was used in festivities or occasions that called for celebration.

In classical Greco-Roman literature, in every discourse (whether deliberative, judicial or demonstrative discourse) were present three basic elements: the speaker, the discourse or speech, and the audience. The quality of the speech is determined by three factors: (i) ethos, i.e. the authority of the speaker, (ii) logos, i.e. the force of the argument, and (iii) pathos, i.e. the feelings or emotions aroused in the audience.

Biblical scholars, recognizing the influence of rhetoric in Hellenistic culture, now pay attention to the rhetorical features of scripture. The PBC acknowledges that the Bible is not simply a statement of truths and that its message carries within it a function of communication within a particular context. In so far as rhetorical analysis recognizes the power of argument and rhetorical structure of the bible, the PBC says of rhetorical analysis, "Because of the enrichment it brings to the critical study of the text, such

137. Ibid., 36.
138. Ibid., 42.

rhetorical analysis is worthy of high regard. . . . It makes up for negligence of long standing and can lead to the rediscovery or clarification of original perspectives that had been lost or obscured."[139] PBC also points out the limitations of rhetorical analysis: (i) rhetorical analysis sometimes remains on level of description and therefore concern itself only with style (ii) Rhetorical analysis cannot claim to be an independent method which would be sufficient in itself. Thus its application to the biblical text raises several questions, which cast doubts on the use of the method.

Narrative Analysis attempts to understand the biblical message in form of story and personal testimony. The Hebrew Scriptures, for instance, according to this analysis, presents the story of salvation which finds expression in the profession of faith and liturgy of the Hebrew people, and the Christian New Testament presents a sequence of telling the story of the life, death, and resurrection of Jesus Christ. Narrative analysis often makes distinction between "real author" (the person who actually composed the story) and "implied author" (image of the person or author the text progressively creates) and "real reader" (the one who has access to the text from those who first read it) and "implied reader" (the reader the text progressively creates). The PBC says of Narrative analysis that it is well suited to the narrative character, which so many biblical texts display. But its distinction between "real author" and "implied author" makes the problems of interpretation more complex.

Semiotic Analysis used to be called Structural analysis or Structuralism, and traceable to the work of Swiss linguist, Ferdinand de Saussure, whose theory claimed that language is a system of relationships that obey fixed laws. One of the prominent biblical scholars who have refined the method and applied it to the bible was Algirdas Grimas. In the way Grimas used it, semiotic analysis is based on three principles or presuppositions: (a) the principle of immanence, in which a text forms a unit of meaning complete in itself (b) the principle of the structure of meaning, in which the analysis of the text consists in establishing network of relationships between the various elements of the text and (c) the principle of the grammar of the text, in which every text follows a 'grammar' or certain number of rules or structures.

According to the PBC, "by directing greater attention to the fact that each biblical text is a coherent whole, obedient to a precise linguistic mechanic of operation, semiotics contributes to our understanding of the Bible as the Word of God expressed in human language."[140] But the PBC also

139. Ibid., 45.
140. Ibid., 51.

cautions that the semiotic approach must be open to history, i.e. history of those who play a part in the texts, history of the authors and readers. "The great risk run by those who employ semiotic analysis is that of remaining at the level of a formal study of the content of texts, failing to draw out the message."[141]

CHARACTERISTICS OF CATHOLIC EXEGESIS

The first interpreters of scripture in the Christian church were the Church Fathers. The Fathers made sure that their exegesis was relevant to the needs of the Christians of their day. According to the PBC, what the bible and the history of its interpretation show is that there is a need for a hermeneutics, an interpretation that addresses the peculiar needs of our time. But the fundamental question remains: which hermeneutical theory or combination of methods best leads to the profound reality of which scripture speaks and its meaningful expression for people today? In light of this question, the PBC states that one must admit that some hermeneutical theories are inadequate for scripture. The PBC lists Bultmann's existentialist interpretation and its excessive "demythologization" of scripture, as an instance of an inadequate hermeneutic.

The Pontifical Biblical Commission lists the following as the characteristics of Catholic exegesis:

- Catholic exegesis is not tied to any particular scientific method but recognizes that the biblical text is the word of God expressed in human language by the human author who expressed this message in the social context of his time.

- Catholic exegesis makes use of scientific methods and approaches that allow for a better grasp of the meaning of the text in its linguistic, literary, socio-cultural, religious and historical contexts.

- Catholic exegesis is situated within the living tradition of the Church and concerns itself with fidelity to the revelation attested by the Bible.

141. Ibid.

STUDY GUIDE

Review . . .

1. Why the evangelists set out to write an account of the life and teachings of Jesus.

2. The central position of the Gospel of Mark.

3. Author, audience, and purpose of the Mark.

4. Messianic Secret.

5. Synoptic Problem.

6. Triple Tradition and Double Tradition.

7. Two-Source Hypothesis and Griesbach Hypothesis.

8. Solution to the Synoptic Problem.

9. Q Source.

10. Hermeneutics and the New Testament

Discussion Questions

1. Why is it that the second generation followers of Jesus did not write a Gospel account of the life and ministry of Jesus? To what extent should the four canonical Gospels be considered a reliable source for understanding the events in the life of Jesus?

2. Why is the issue of authorship of the Gospel of Mark difficult to ascertain? How do we go about figuring the author of this Gospel? What features does this Gospel share with the other two synoptics? What are the distinctive features of this Gospel?

3. What is the Synoptic Problem? Why does Joseph Fitzmyer argue that the issue of the synoptic problem is practically insoluble?

4. Use passages from the synoptic Gospels to account for the central position of the Gospel of Mark in relation to the Synoptic Problem.

5. How does the author of the Gospel of Mark use "Messianic Secret" to show that the passion and death of Jesus is the central event in the life of the Messiah?

6. What is meant by Triple Tradition and Double Tradition? Explain the roles of J.J. Griesbach and F. Schleiermacher in relation to the Synoptic Problem.

7. Attempt a solution of the Synoptic Problem. Do you think your solution can stand the test of time?

6

Two Great Influences

CHRISTIANITY — THE SECT within Judaism in the mind of the Roman authorities — had become well established in the Empire by the end of the fourth century CE. The growth continued at a very fast pace that by the Middle Ages Christianity had become entrenched and synonymous with Western civilization. Among the many factors responsible for this were the influences of two great theologians: Augustine of Hippo in the fourth century and Thomas Aquinas in the thirteenth century. Their writings, which were formative and influential for the Church, will ironically become the key reference points for the 16th century reformers. Luther and some of the Churches of the reformation that severed relations with Rome will appeal to Augustine's doctrine of grace to validate one of their key positions, i.e., human depravity and inability of human free-will to bring about salvation. The Roman Catholic Church will counter by appealing to Thomism (theology of Thomas Aquinas) and seeking a synthesis of faith and reason.

Fourth century CE Christian communities were organized along the Mediterranean coastlands, from modern Egypt and Libya through Tunisia, Algebra, Morocco, and Mauritania. But the fourth century was also a time of crisis for the Church because of Diocletian (284–305 CE) persecution. Nero (Roman Emperor from 54–68 CE) began the era of formal persecution of Christians and Diocletian brought it to an art form. Making matters worse for the Christian communities scattered all over the Mediterranean coastlands, the proconsul of Africa, Anullinus, "exceeded the requirements of the Diocletian edicts and directed the persecution not only at the hierarchy, in order to discredit it, but also at the laity."[1] The persecution made the Christian communities in North Africa (or North African Church) the hot bed of martyrdom. North African church produced many martyrs, like Perpetua (a twenty-two year old woman from a noble family in Carthage) and her slave girl Felicitas. The two women and their companions were thrown to the lions. There were also other witnesses like Cyprian, the Bishop of Carthage (c.200–258CE).

AURELIUS AUGUSTINE (354–430)

It was into this Church community of martyrs that Augustine of Hippo, the most well-known Christian theologian of antiquity, was born. Rome had destroyed Carthage and annexed it about 500 years before. Ancient Carthaginians spoke Latin (the language of Rome) as well as their own Berber and Punic languages. We know a lot about Augustine's early life from his own detailed account in the *Confessions*, which he wrote when he was about 43 years old. Augustine was almost certainly a Berber (a tribe in present day Libya). He was born in Thagaste, an insignificant town in Numidia, a center of Berber culture. His name Augustine is "a typical version of a Berber honorific name."[2] His other name, Aurelius, suggests that his family was among those who made Roman citizens, thanks to the edict of Caracalla. Roman citizenship was a prized possession that granted privileges to anyone that had it. The edict of Caracalla (212 CE), promulgated by Emperor Caracalla, granted Roman citizenship to all free-born inhabitants of the empire. It conferred the same privileges enjoyed by male Roman citizens to any free-born male in the empire and conferred the same privileges enjoyed by female Roman citizens as well to all females in the empire. Before the edict Roman privileges was enjoyed only by those living in Italy. It was not extended to anyone in the provinces controlled by Rome.

Augustine was born of a pagan father, Patricius, a name that indicates that he must have been wealthy and well to do, and a Christian mother, Monica, a name that derives from the Berber deity Mon. Augustine was attached to his mother, but alienated from his father. He moved to Carthage in search of education. In Carthage he lived a licentious life and had a mistress who bore him a son, Adeodatus (God-given). Augustine does not mention the mother of his mistress who bore him Adeodatus in the *Confession*.

Augustine was interested in learning. He was also drawn to literature, rhetoric, and philosophy, particularly the philosophy of Plato. This desire

---

1. See Fitzgerald, ed., "North African Church," 185.

2. Thompson and Ferguson, *Africa in Antiquity*, 184.

for learning led him to Manicheanism, a religious sect in North Africa. He spent nine years as a member of this sect. Manicheanism was dualistic. It taught that matter or flesh was bad and sprit was good. Manicheanism condemned all sexual unions. The Manicheans considered it a crime to give birth to children because matter was thought to be evil. Giving birth to children would be to needlessly imprison their soul in the body. The Manicheans proposed a mythical explanation for the problem of evil (theodicy) and suggested that there was a perpetual struggle between co-eternal principles of light and darkness. Manicheanism also denied liberty. It offered a scientific explanation of nature that contradicted sacred Scripture. Augustine was fascinated by the teaching of the problem of conflict between two forces, matter and spirit.

The sect was hierarchically structured. According to their degrees of membership, priest or "elect" was the highest and "auditor" was the lowest. Members of this sect go through initiation rite to be considered an "elect." The "elect" performed rigorous ascetical practices. But auditors were permitted to engage in sexual relations, though they were forbidden to reproduce. Augustine never attained the degree of "priest" or "elect" and probably never went beyond an "auditor." In the end Manicheanism did not satisfy his quest for knowledge and he left the sect after nine years. Later as a Christian Augustine would counter the Manichean idea that sexual union and procreation are bad. Augustine the Christian would see marriage as ordained by God and sexual union as having its place only in marriage.

Augustine's spiritual yearning led him to Neo-Platonism, a teaching that derived from Plotinus (207–270 CE). Augustine learned Neo-Platonism through the Latin translations of Victorinus. Plotinus himself was an Egyptian by birth. He taught that humans participate in divine activity through the mind and that a person should reject material things as a way of purifying the soul and unifying oneself with what he called the One. Augustine was fascinated by the Neo-Platonic teaching that evil was a privation of the good. But again in the end Neo-Platonism did not completely satisfy Augustine's spiritual quest. In fact, his confidence in Neo-Platonism "was shaken by the discovery that the Neo-Platonist Victorinus had joined the Church and made a public confession."[3] Later as a Christian Augustine would see aspects of Neo-Platonism to be in harmony with Christian teaching. In fact, when he became a Christian Augustine and some other early Christian thinkers used the neo-Platonic theme of emanation (the doctrine that the Mind or "Nous" and the Soul or "Psyche" derive from the One) to explain the Christian teaching of *exitus et reditus* (that God is the be-

3. Bainton, *Christianity*, 118.

ginning and final end of human life). Augustine would also realize much later, as a Christian, that evil is not merely an absence of the good as the Neo-Platonists suggested, but a rebellion against God. Augustine turned to the New Testament upon the urging of his mother.

Augustine went to Rome in 383 CE and accepted a teaching position in Milan in 384 CE. Milan at the time was an important cultural and intellectual center in all of the Roman Empire. The see of Milan was overseen by an influential bishop, St. Ambrose of Milan (339–97 CE). Ambrose was a scholar, a powerful orator, and preacher. His preaching made great impressions on Augustine who became a catechumen. After eight months of studying and reflecting in solitude at Cassiciacum, near Milan, Augustine was baptized in 387 CE on Easter eve. Augustine tells us in his *Confession* that apart from the preaching of Ambrose two other factors were responsible for his about face: his mother Monica who prayed for 30 years for his conversion and his reading of *The Life of St. Anthony of Egypt* by St. Athanasius. Augustine was impressed by the way the holy monks were able to control their passions. When he became a Christian and accepted baptism Augustine was baptized alongside his son, Adeodatus, and his friend Alypus.

Augustine returned to Africa immediately after his baptism and was hit by tragedy soon after. His mother died on the way to Africa, in Ostia in 387 CE. His son Adeodatus also died in 390 CE upon arrival. Augustine never again left the African soil. His reputation as a Christian grew and he was consulted by many on various topics and subjects. At this time "the power of Rome was then rapidly declining and Christianity was still a minority religion, with many of the wealthiest citizens and officials still attached to the old religions or to a degenerate Neo-Platonic philosophy with its hedonistic culture."[4] Severed from all family ties, Augustine established a semi-monastic community in Thagaste to help him and other Christians live ascetic life. He studied for the priesthood and was ordained in 391 CE. When Valerius, the bishop of Hippo, died in 396 CE Augustine was appointed to succeed him. He became the bishop of Hippo at the age of 42 and held the position for thirty-four years.

The Donatist Controversy

As bishop Augustine was beset by many problems. One of these was the Donatist controversy. Diocletian persecution forcefully removed Christians from their place of worship. Christians were also made to renounce their faith and hand over sacred Scripture and holy Church artifacts to the Roman

4. Sanneh, *West African Christianity*, 12.

authorities. Those who refused to comply suffered martyrdom while those who did were spared. In the eyes of the Church those who recanted were apostates, guilty of sin of apostasy (denial of faith). Those who surrendered church property for destruction were called the *dies traditores*. Their crime was considered by some Christians to be more heinous than those of the apostates because they handed Church property to the Romans.

As persecutions wane, questions arose regarding what the Church should do with the traditores. Some Christian in North Africa came up with the idea that neither the traditores nor anyone associated with them can get to heaven. They also adopted a policy to exclude the traditores and everyone associated with them from the Church. These Christians who wanted the traditores excluded from the Church adopted a strict and austere lifestyle. It became a standard insult to associate a Christian or Catholic bishop with traditores.[5] Even when martyrdom ceased and Christianity became a legal and accepted religion in Roman Empire these people still continued their austere lifestyle by seeking other forms of martyrdom, like mortification (denial of self from pleasure).

In 321 CE a Christian man named Caecilian was consecrated bishop of Carthage. One of those who consecrated him bishop, Felix of Aptuca, had been a traditores. The bishops from all areas of Numidia protested and re-fused to recognize the consecration of Caecilian as valid. They chose instead Donatus. When Donatus was appointed bishop of Carthage he identified Carthage as the "church of the martyrs" and soon after Carthage became the center of activity of those Christians who wanted a strict and austere church. "Donatus gave his name to the church community that was galva-nized by his presence, and then by his memory for more than a century."[6] This singular act distinguished the Donatist from orthodox Christianity.

There were also socio-economic differences between the Donatists and the rest of the Church. Many of the Donatists were pagan converts and a whole lot came from the Berber people of North Africa who were usu-ally poor and rural. Donatism became for these Berbers a vehicle of Ber-ber patriotism and socio-economic protest "against a Church increasingly closely identified with the landowning classes and imperial authority."[7] But this is not to suggest that Donatism was limited only to the rural areas or that Donatism was just an African phenomenon. Donatism was as much an urban phenomena as it was rural. The phenomenon extended from North Africa to Spain and Gaul (France). In the main, what distinguished

---

5. See Fitzgerald, "Church of North Africa," 185.

6. Ibid.

7. Isichei, *A History of Christianity in Africa*, 37.

the Donatists was their ideology—their concept of the Church as a small body of the chosen.[8] They wanted the Church to remain holy and demanded the highest moral standard. As far as they were concerned, the validity of the sacraments depended on the worthiness of the priest or minister. The Donatists thought they were the true Church and demanded a rebaptism of lapsed Christians and clergy. The Donatists also had their own peculiar way of interpreting the Scripture. Given their African root, "they cherished texts that could be construed to mean God's special predilection for Africa, such as a version of the Song of Solomon 1:6 ('my beloved is from the South')."[9]

Augustine defended the Catholic Church against what he saw as the Donatists' attack. To Augustine who was more interested in the unity of the Church, it was bizarre to suggest, as the Donatists did, that God's Church was primarily located in Africa.[10] Augustine compared the Donatists to "frogs in a pond, who thought that they were the universal Church."[11] Augustine also stressed that Church contains both good and bad because the Church is at one and the same time holy and sinful. He also argued that the validity of the sacraments does not depend on the worthiness of the minister (*ex opere operantis*), as the Donatists suggested, but on the fact that the sacraments have their own validity (*ex opere operato*) on the correct celebration by the Church.[12]

The Pelagian Controversy

After the Donatist controversy Augustine was embroiled in another huge argument—the Pelagian controversy. A British monk by the name Pelagius propounded a teaching that denied original sin. The human person, according to Pelagius, is born without the stain of sin. Adam's sin, therefore, was a personal sin which does not extend to his offspring. A person, according to Pelagius, can also attain salvation unaided by God's grace. A person can choose good over evil without divine help. Augustine denounced the Pelagian teaching and reiterated the Church's teaching that everyone inherits the guilt of original sin (see Rom.5:12), meaning that everyone is deserving of hell. But baptism cleanses original sin. Augustine also taught that human nature is seriously flawed because it has been corrupted by original sin. Because of our fallen nature the human person needs God's grace to

8. Ibid., 38.

9. Isichei, *A History of Christianity in Africa*, 38.

10. Ibid.

11. Ibid.

12. Holmes and Bickers, *A Short History of the Catholic Church*, 41.

attain salvation. Even though the human person is free, God predestines us to salvation. Grace is irresistible for those whom God has predestined. This teaching, sometimes called Predestination, will be at the center of controversy much later in the 16th century Church. Towards the end of Augustine's life, a moderate teaching of Pelagian teaching (known as Semi-Pelagianism) resurfaced again. It was propagated by those who misunderstood the role of human cooperation in the process of human salvation.[13] Augustine responded "that even the initial desire to change one's life or to accept the Christian faith was the work of God's transforming power of love and grace."[14]

Augustine's Writings

Augustine was a true pastor and theologian who had genuine concern for the salvation of his flock.[15] He composed a vast body of literature, totally over twelve hundred, on a variety of subjects as a response to the many theological questions and socio-political problems facing the Church.[16] Augustine started writing the *Confession* shortly after becoming a Christian. The *Confession* is not an autobiography, but Augustine's own illustration of a human person's capacity for corruption, imperfection, and redemption.[17] It is divided into 13 Books. Each book is in turn divided into chapters. Augustine's other well-known works are *The City of God* and the *Enchiridion* (handbook on the Grace of God).

CONCLUSION

Augustine spent his whole life trying to answer the questions: Who am I? How does one find true happiness? What is salvation? And what is the role of one's neighbor or community in the search for true happiness and salvation?[18]Augustine gathered together strands from Christina thought, as well as strands from classical philosophy, and creatively wove them into a

---

13. McGonigle and Quigley, *A History of Christian Tradition*, 114.

14. Ibid.

15. Ibid., 112.

16. Ibid.

17. Bainton, *Christianity*, 116.

18. McGonigle and Quigley, *A History of Christian Tradition*, 111.

new fabric that would profoundly influence Christian thought until it would be surpassed in the Middle Ages by the genius of Thomas Aquinas.[19]

Augustine was a controversialist. Many of his works were written in the heat of debate with his opponents. Because of this his writings are sometimes difficult to follow as he moves from one subject to another. "In the midst of controversy an author often overstates his case and emphasizes certain factors that would be more carefully balanced in a less intense situation."[20] Augustine has also been criticized for some of his theological views. Some have wondered how much of his theological views (e.g., transmission of original sin and his views on marriage) were influenced by Manichean piety. When he was preparing for baptism in Cassisiacum as a catechumen Augustine wrote some works like "Dialogues," "Contra Academicos," "Providential Order of the World and the Problem of Evil," and "God and the Soul." Some have questioned whether he wrote these works as a Christian or as a non-Christian. The importance of Augustine, however, cannot be diminished, His life "coincides with the end of classical era and the beginning of the Middle Ages. He was a man who looked back to the past as well as one who predicted the future, and his life would become a paradigm for subsequent Christian understanding of the individual's journey to salvation."[21]

THE MIDDLE AGES AND CHRISTIANITY

Some Christian theologians see the historical study of the Middle Ages as a gift to our century.[22] It was in the Middle Ages that people discovered that the study of theology was useful for the understanding of God, the human person, and the world at large. Christian faith flourished in the Middle Ages, particularly the thirteenth century that has been considered the golden age of Church intellectual history. What might be called Catholic conservatives or traditionalists in the likes of Hilaire Belloc (1870–1953) and G.K. Chesterton (1874–1936) look to the thirteenth century as the "greatest of centuries" and point to it as the high point from which all later history has been mostly a dismal decline.[23] But some more contemporary theologians, like the Swiss Hans Urs von Balthasar (1905–1988), thought the decline of

---

19. Bainton, *Christianity*, 115.

20. McGonigle and Quigley, *A History of the Christian Tradition*, 113.

21. Ibid., 111.

22. O'Meara, *Thomas Aquinas Theologian*, xii.

23. Oakes, *Pattern of Redemption*, 160–4.

modern theology began in the thirteenth century because of scholasticism, a system of philosophy we shall explain later.

What is it that makes the Middle Ages significant and contentious at the same time? Three important developments took place in the 13th century. First, there was the founding and flourishing of universities and centers of learning — Bologna, Paris, and Oxford. These centers became places where the study of theology and rigorous intellectual activities took place. Second, there was the establishment of mendicant orders — Dominic de Guzman (1170–1221) and Francis of Assisi (d.1226), for example. The mendicant orders brought to a Church in need of reform a new spirit of evangelical poverty that appealed to laity that was sick and tired of corruption and abuses by clergy. Dominic founded the Order of Friars Preachers (Dominicans) in 1216, stressing apostolic preaching and assiduous study. Francis founded the Franciscans in 1210, stressing evangelical poverty and the imitation of Christ. Both Dominic and Francis are now canonized saints. The third great development of the 13th century was the discovery in the Latin West translations of Aristotle's works, a discovery made possible by Jewish and Arabic philosophers, like Moses Maimonides (1138–1204), Ib'n Cina or Avicenna (980–1037), Avicebron (1021–1058), and Averroes (1126–1198). The discovery of Aristotle supplanted the influence of Plato's philosophy hitherto employed by neo-Platonic Christians

When the Latin West first discovered Aristotle it was not without skepticism and suspicion, mainly because the works in question were mediated by Arabs and Jewish scholars who translated and commented on them. These two groups were at the time considered arch enemies of Christians. There was also the problematic of Aristotle's own teaching on the eternity of the universe. Aristotle taught that the universe was eternal and uncreated. This teaching and his other thoughts on the immortality of the soul seemed to contradict Christian teaching of creation of the universe. These difficulties led to three major reactions or responses to Aristotle. One group, known as the Augustinian group, refused to accept anything that contradicted the teachings of St. Augustine. They were led by the Franciscans, particularly Bonaventure (1221–1274). Bonaventure himself "was skeptical of the ability of the human mind, unaided by God, to reach the truth. He maintained that any philosophical propositions which were contrary to faith must be dismissed, and he reminded people that, in his opinion, philosophy was very much at the service of theology."[24] The second group, the Averroists, championed by Siger of Brabant (1240–1280), accepted Aristotle's teachings, but tried to find a middle ground whenever Aristotle contradicted

24. Holmes and Bickers, *A Short History of the Catholic Church*, 94.

Christian teaching. "When Aristotle contradicted Christian teaching the Averroists tried to overcome the difficulty by what was called the 'theory of double truth.' According to this, as philosophers they accepted the teaching of Aristotle and as Christians the teaching of the Church. In other words, they claimed that the conclusions of theology and philosophy could contradict each other while both remained valid."[25] The third and final group attempted a synthesis or harmony of Aristotelianism with Christian teaching. They tried to show that Augustine and Aristotle were not in any way opposed to each other, that what was needed was a correct interpretation of Aristotle. To this group belonged Thomas Aquinas, a key figure we shall examine later.

The Middle Ages was also the age of Dante Alighieri (1265–1321) and Albert the Great (1193–1280), among many others. It was, among other things, the age of the Schoolmen, affectionately called scholastics. The Schoolmen were idealized by Pope Leo XIII as the "Doctors of the Middle Ages" who set out to do a work of very great magnitude by diligently gathering for their use and convenience of those who came after them the "rich and fruitful crops of doctrine scattered everywhere in the mighty volumes of the Holy Fathers."[26] The Schoolmen or scholastics were "teachers" of the "new period' after the barbarian invasions of Rome. The ideal they embodied found expressions in the works of two great saints of the period: the Dominican Thomas Aquinas and the Franciscan Bonaventure. Both men saw ancient wisdom in the teaching of the Church Fathers and found ways to make them relevant to their time by employing Aristotelian and Platonic philosophies. Leo XIII spoke lovingly of "the angelic St. Thomas, and the seraphic St. Bonaventure" as "two glorious Doctors" who brilliantly unfolded the scholastic method.

The Catholic Church relies greatly on their method, particularly St. Thomas, for correct interpretation and understanding of Scripture, for reading and expounding the Fathers with clarity, and for answering different errors and heresies. Although Aquinas to this day "still fashions ways in which Roman Catholics think,"[27] not everyone agrees with St. Thomas and his ways of thinking. It was precisely his style of thinking and the undue influence of scholasticism on Christian theology that Protestant theology opposed during the Reformation. Thomas and scholasticism were, for some of the reformers, the epitome of the stagnancy of the medieval church. Prot-

25. Ibid.

26. Leo XIII, Aeterni *Patris* [On the Restoration of Christian Philosophy According to the Mind of St. Thomas Aquinas, the Angelic Doctor], xiv.

27. O'Meara, *Thomas Aquinas Theologian*, xiv.

estant theology viewed "Thomas and his times as just what they were trying to escape" and the Middle Ages as "a great backwater into which the river of history poured for centuries before finally, in the sixteenth century, making a new start."[28]

THOMAS AQUINAS (1224/5–1274)

Thomas was born to a noble family in Roccasecca, near Aquino, north of Naples, in Southern Italy. His father, Landulph, was the Count of Aquino, and his mother, Theodora, the Countess of Teano.[29] The exact date of his birth is still disputed. Catholic hagiographers approximate the date of his birth on the basis of the date of his death. The consensus is that he died in 1274, on his way to the Council of Lyons, although some still contend that he died in 1276 or 1277. What is more probable in all these conjectures is that Thomas "had completed forty-nine years and begun his fiftieth year" before he died. On the basis of this calculation, 1224/25 has been suggested as the probable year of his birth. His father had at least nine children (four boys and five girls). As the youngest of the sons, Thomas was destined, according to the custom of the time, for an ecclesiastical position. His father offered him as an oblate to the Benedictine monastery of Monte Cassino, hoping that someday he would become an abbot.

At age five Thomas was enrolled in the school run by the Benedictine monks of Monte Cassino where he had his elementary education and was exposed to the Benedictine religious life of prayer, scriptural reading, and manual labor. Even at this tender age he was said to have shown signs of a future scholar. One of the monks of Monte Cassino who noticed his talent and passion for learning advised Landulph (Thomas' father) to send him to Naples to study at the prestigious University of Naples. The University of Naples was founded by the emperor of the Holy Roman Empire, Frederick II, for the education of his court functionaries. At the time Naples was the only university to be teaching Aristotelian logic that was then beginning to infiltrate the borders of Christendom by way of Islamic scholars in Spain.[30] Thomas proceeded to this university in 1236, at the age of fourteen, and received training in the liberal arts.

At Naples Thomas was fascinated by the life style of a new religious Order of Preachers that was founded a decade earlier. This newly formed mendicant Order that went by the name Dominicans was quite popular in

---

28. McDermott, ed., *St. Thomas Aquinas Summa Theologiae*, xvii.

29. Torell, *St. Thomas Aquinas*, 1–9.

30. McDermott, *St. Thomas Aquinas*, xviii-xix.

the city because of their commitment to the evangelical vows of chastity, poverty and obedience and also because of their dedication to the preaching apostolate. They based their life on the Gospel mandate (Luke 9: 1–6) to go out and preach, two by two, taking nothing for the journey. "If Aristotle represented a new current in secular thinking, the friars were the most radical representatives of the new spirit of reform within the church." Their life of preaching and austere poverty made a great impression on the young Thomas who decided to join their ranks.

In 1244, against the wish of his family, Thomas made the official move to join the Dominicans. The Dominicans at this time were beginning to devote their attention to preaching in the universities and committed to exploring the newly translated works of Aristotle that were seen by some to be a threat to the Catholic faith. Theodora, his mother, was particularly distressed by her son's decision to join this brand of preachers. Thomas joining the Order of Preachers would jeopardize her grand plan for him to become the abbot of the Benedictine monastery of Monte Cassino and so she did all she could to stop him. At her instigation Thomas was kidnapped by two of his brothers who kept him in solitary confinement for two years, hoping to dissuade him from joining the Friars. But rather than be discouraged, Thomas' time in captivity reinforced his decision to fully commit himself to the order who's preaching apostolate he has come to love so much.

After Thomas was released by his family in the summer of 1245, the Dominicans in Naples, fearing another kidnap plan, thought it unsafe to keep him around. They sent him to Rome from where he would proceed to Paris to begin studies at the University of Paris, under the famous German Dominican friar, Albert the Great. Albert, at this time, was just beginning his encyclopedic commentaries on Aristotle. Three years after this turn of events, Albert was sent to Cologne on a mission to begin a Dominican study house. Thomas went with him to Cologne and taught as a Bachelor under Albert the Great.[31] For some reason his peers there nicknamed him the "dumb ox." Albert was so impressed with the talent of Thomas that he remarked that one day this "dumb ox" would make a great impression on the world.

Under the tutelage of Albert, Thomas was excited when he discovered the works of Aristotle whom he called "the Philosopher." Thomas's friend and confrere, William of Moerbeke, helped him translate the works of Aristotle from Greek into Latin. While many at that time saw Aristotle's work as "pagan" and incompatible with the Christian message, Thomas saw in the

31. Bachelors are like today's Teaching Assistants. They assisted the Masters or Scholastics who taught in the universities.

works of this great philosopher a gold mine and found ways to harmonize them with Christian doctrine. It was not only the work of Aristotle that Thomas examined, he also studied the works of some prominent Greek, Latin, and Arab philosophers of the time (chief among whom were Averroes and Avicenna) and acknowledged coming to know more about Aristotle through them.

Thomas was sent to Paris in 1252, at the recommendation of Albert the Great, to fill a vacant position of Bachelor at the Dominican center for studies. This event proved to be the turning point of Thomas' illustrious career. While in Paris, he lectured and commented on the Sentences of Peter Lombard (1100–1160), the most referenced theology textbook of the time. Upon completion of his formal studies he received his master's degree and at the age of thirty-two occupied the chair of theology Albert once held. After three years in Paris as professor of sacred theology he was sent to Italy where he spent six years at the papal court in Orvieto. He also spent another two years at the Dominican study center in Rome and one year at another papal court in Viterbo before returning to Paris 1269. After three years in Paris he finally returned to Naples in late 1273. Thomas had a mystical experience in Naples on December 6, 1273, an experience that made him abandon all teaching and writing. The force of his mystical experience was so great that Thomas had to declare that all he wrote was "mere straw" compared to the divine revelation that was revealed to him. He died shortly after this revelation.

Authority of Thomas Aquinas

Thomas Aquinas was the most influential Christian philosopher of the Middle Ages. He ranks as one of the outstanding Christian thinkers in the history of Western civilization. His work was seminal in the formulation of Catholic teaching and doctrine. His authority is so revered in Catholic circles that the Code of Canon Law legislates that the clergy receive their philosophical and theological formation according to the methods, doctrine, and principles of the Angelic Doctor. Pope Leo XIII glowingly paid tribute to the authority of Thomas in his 1879 encyclical *Aeterni Patris* in which he called for the revival of Thomism. As the Pope recalled it, "in the midst of the Council of Trent, the assembled Fathers so willing it, the Summa of Thomas Aquinas lay open on the altar, with the Holy Scriptures and the decrees of the Supreme Pontiffs, that from it might be sought counsel and reasons and answers."[32]

32. Leo XIII, "On the Restoration of Christian Philosophy According to the Mind

Thomas was canonized on July 18, 1323, by Pope John XXII who extolled Thomas' devotion to study and prayer and pronounced him a model of fidelity to the Roman Church. His canonization paved way for other titles his disciples and admirers had adjudged for him. Even as far back as 1317, he was already called *doctor communis* by the faithful at the University of Paris. The title *doctor Angelicus* was attributed to him in the second half of the fifteenth century, and a hundred years later, on April 15, 1567, Pope Pius V, a Dominican pope, proclaimed him *doctor ecclesiae* (Teacher of the Church). On August 4, 1880, Pope Leo XIII declared him patron of all Catholic schools and institutions.

Although the title doctor ecclesiae was not exclusively applied to St. Thomas, it was still a significant achievement when he received this encomium, especially when one considers the fact that there were only four Doctors of the Church when he was given the title (St. Ambrose, St. Jerome, St. Augustine, and St. Gregory the Great). Doctor ecclesiae is a special title the Church reserves for distinguished saints whose writings and teachings have been adjudged useful in the formulation of Christian doctrine. In addition, the universal church is invited to honor them and celebrate their feasts in the Church's liturgy. When Pius V accorded the honor to St. Thomas, he also announced four other great Doctors of the Eastern Church: St. Athanasius (c. 293–373), St. Basil the Great (c.329–79), St. Gregory of Nazianzus (c. 325–89), and St. John Chrysostom (c. 347–407).

The Works of Thomas Aquinas

Thomas wrote for various occasions and lectured on different subjects. Some of these have been collected and edited by his disciples. There is, for example, edited commentary on the *Sentences* of his Parisian days. There are also collections of his lectures on Matthew's Gospel, Isaiah's Prophecies, the books of Job, Jeremiah, and the epistles of Paul. Some of his debates on theological questions of his own choosing have also been collected in the *Quaestiones Disputatae de Veritate*, his Rome public debates in *de Potentia, de Malo,* and *de Spiritualibus Creaturis* and questions thrown at him by his audience have been collected in *Quaestiones Quodilibetales.*[33]

Thomas began writing a comprehensive theology manual in 1266 and left it unfinished before his death. Some of his writings give us his insight into some contemporary controversies. He wrote volumes on the theology of angels. No wonder he was called "Doctor Angelicus." He also

---

of St. Thomas Aquinas, the Angelic Doctor," xvi.

33. McDermott, *St. Thomas Aquinas*, xx.

has commentaries on well-known traditional texts, which speaks to why he was called "Doctor Communis," i.e. common teacher of all Christians. His four major works in theology are: *A Commentary on the Sentences of Peter Lombard* (1256), *A Compendium Theologiae* (an incomplete work that has not been satisfactorily dated), the *Summa Theologiae* and the *Summa Contra Gentiles* (1264). Of the four, the last two are well known and widely used. The *Summa Theologiae* (Summary of Theology) is regarded as the most comprehensive treatment of the relation of philosophy and theology. Thomas was dissatisfied with the then existing manual of instruction and intended this work to be a systematic introduction to theology for Dominican novices. The *Summa Contra Gentiles* (Summary against the Gentiles) was also designed to be an apologetic work. Thomas again intended it as an aid to his brother Dominican missionaries in their efforts to convert Muslims in Spain and North Africa. He probably composed the *Summa Contra Gentiles* at the request of his religious superior, Raymond of Penafort, who would have asked Thomas to equip the Dominican missionaries working in the Muslim world, particularly Spain, with the necessary intellectual tools. But the *Contra Gentiles* today is more than a missionary manual.

In these works Thomas shows inclination towards apophatic theology, that there is nothing to know about God except to know that which God is not. Apophatic theology attempts to distinguish God from all that is not God, moving from negation to negation to arrive at the knowledge that God is distinct from everything. In addition to apophatic theology, Thomas also shows in these works how Christian theology is the sum and summit of all sciences. He establishes revelation as a source of knowledge because (i) it aids us in comprehending truths already known by reason and (ii) it is the absolute source of knowledge of Christian mysteries. Consistent with his apophatic approach, Aquinas built his system around two sources of knowledge: revelation and human reason. Revelation is not scripture alone but scripture and tradition. Reason is not just individual human reason, but collective reason, the foundation of natural truth (philosophy), as in the philosophies of Aristotle and Plato. For Aquinas, reason alone is not a sufficient guide for human actions. Reason has to be aided by revelation, for faith and reason are not opposed to each other.

The Plan of the Summa

The *Summa Theologiae* is today the most widely used work of Aquinas and without doubt the central source for a discussion of his theology and the climax of his life work and synthetic masterpiece.[34] But it was not widely received in Aquinas' lifetime. His ideas frightened authorities during and immediately after his lifetime that his work faced ecclesiastical censorship. He was even denounced as a heretic because of the Aristotelian influences in his work. Aristotelian philosophy was then considered a "pagan" philosophy. In 1276, for instance, Albert the Great, Thomas' mentor, reported knowing certain bishops who lumped together all who used Aristotle in theology, calling them "Averroists," which means that they were more Muslim than Christian. Thomas was among those branded "Averroists." The Bishop of Paris, at the decree of Pope John XXI, ordered an investigation of theologians who employed Aristotelianism. On March 7, 1277, the third anniversary of the death of Aquinas, as many as 200 propositions, some of which were found in the work of Aquinas, were condemned and those who taught them excommunicated. It was only through the insistence of his Order and Dominican confreres who vigorously defended him and promoted his course that the ecclesiastical censorship against his work was lifted and it was gradually brought back into the mainstream of Catholic theology.

Between 1286 and 1405, after Aquinas's work had been rehabilitated, although the Sentences of Peter Lombard and Sacred Scripture were the normal text of the universities, the leadership of the Dominican Order insisted that Aquinas' writings be part of their school curriculum. With much insistence and maneuvering the Summa in time became the accepted textbook of Catholic theology, supplanting even the Sentences of Peter Lombard as a symbol of Catholic orthodoxy. Many find the originality and style of the summa appealing. "The greatness and originality of a philosophical or theological work," remarked M.D. Chenu of the Summa, "are not measured primarily by the amplitude of its conclusions, but by the order of its construction in the light of principles which determine logically and spiritually the conception and the arrangement of its parts."[35]

St. Thomas' unique style sometimes makes him difficult to read, especially for beginners not familiar with the scholastic method. If great minds are difficult because they write in a kind of code, the "code" in which Aquinas wrote his Summa is decipherable in the context of medieval debate, an expression of the thought-form of his culture. Here is a description of the format of medieval debate:

34. O'Meara, *Thomas Aquinas Theologian*, xv.

35. M.D. Chenu, "The Plan of St. Thomas' Summa Theologiae," *Cross Currents* 9 (1959): 67.

> At the beginning of the disputation the master would announce the [36] "Article" or subject to be debated, which was itself a subdivision of a broader "Question" being discussed. This was followed by a number of objections which were put forward by the audience, to which preliminary responses were made by "bachelors" (in present-day terms, teaching assistants) who were working with the master (professor), possibly also referring to authorities who held views contrary to the objections. The next day the master would give his response ("I answer that") to the basic issue or issues posed and would follow this with formal replies to each of the initial objections. The disputation was sometimes taken down by a secretary and later edited by the master for publication. The oral disputation thus gave rise to the formal structure used by the scholastics to analyze philosophical and theological problems- a statement of an issue, alternative opinions or objections, contrary quotations from recognized authorities, the author's response to the problem, followed by answers to each of the initial objections.

Following this conventional method of debate, a medieval text, when printed, is divided into hundreds of topics called questions. Each topic consists of a sequence of dilemmas called articles. In a dilemma are three short arguments, i.e. objections, against some traditional position called the *sed contra*. They are resolved by an argued point of view called *responsio* which are applied to each objection in answers to the objections.

The *Summa Theologiae* is patterned after this medieval method of debate. The Summa is composed of series of questions or discussion topics, each question further divided into articles. Since the intent is to dialogue with an imaginary dialogue partner, Aquinas always gives an alternative view after stating the question. He will give a *Sed Contra* (on the Contrary), which would contradict the alternative view he has stated, and often close to Aquinas' own view. Then at the end he gives a *Responsio* (response or formal replies), where he offers reasons for rejecting the alternative views and even gives reason why reasons given for the rejection of the alternate views may not be adequate.

Traditionally the Summa Theologiae is divided into three parts.

(I.) The First Part: The first part is called the *Prima Pars* (**Ia** pars). Here Aquinas takes up the Neo-platonic theme of emanation and shows how God is the First Principle of human life. He also discusses the

---

36. See Sigmund, ed., *St. Thomas Aquinas on Politics and Ethics*, xvii.

basis of theology and issues like Sacred Doctrine, God, Trinity, Providence, Predestination, creation, angels and human beings.

(II.) The Second Part: Theology for Aquinas and the scholastics is the science of God. Here Aquinas discusses all things in their relation to God, *exitus reditus*, i.e., either God as their origin or final end, which was Aquinas' intelligible way of explaining everything and human action in light of God. Due to the wide range of topics treated here, the second part of the Summa is divided into two parts. The first part is called *Prima Secundae* (**Ia IIae** pars), i.e. First part of the Second part. It deals with the goal of human existence, human acts, passions, character development, virtues, vices, sin, law and divine grace. The second part is called *Secunda Secundae* (**IIa IIae** pars), i.e. second part of the Second part. It deals with the theological virtues, the cardinal virtues and the vices opposed to these virtues.

(III.) The Third Part: The third part is called the *Tertia Pars* (**IIIa** pars) and is also divided into two parts, though not by design. Aquinas died before he could complete the *tertia pars* and so his disciples added this sequel, known under the name of Supplement. The first part of the tertia pars contains some of the original thought of Aquinas. Since the *exitus et reditus* (the going forth from and the return to God), according to Aquinas, is accomplished in Christ, here Aquinas discusses the Life of Christ, Sacraments (Baptism and Eucharist), and the Christian conditions for that return. The second part of the tertia pars is called *Supplementum Tertia Pars*. It deals with Penance, Extreme Unction (now called Anointing of the Sick), Holy Orders, Matrimony, Resurrection, and Appendices.

Content of the Summa

In spite of its abrupt ending, i.e., because of the mystical experience and untimely death of the angelic doctor, it was the intention of St. Thomas to divide the Summa into three parts. He begins the Summa with this prologue, which gives the intent and context of his work:

> Because the Master of Catholic Truth ought not only to teach the proficient, but also to instruct beginners, we purpose this book to treat of whatever belongs to the Christian Religion, in such a way as may tend to the instruction of beginners. We have considered that students in this Science have not seldom been hampered by what they have found written by other authors,

partly on account of the multiplication of useless questions, articles, and arguments; partly also because those things that are needed for them to know are not taught according to the order of the subject matter, but according to the plan of the book might require, or the occasion of the argument offer; partly too, because frequent repetition brought weariness and confusion to the minds of the readers. Endeavoring to avoid these and other like faults, we shall try, by God's help, to set forth whatever is included in this sacred science as briefly and clearly as the matter itself may allow.[37]

Thomas begins by speaking about God in the Prima Pars, the movement of rational creature toward God in the Secunda Pars, and finally in the Tertia Pars about Christ who, according to his humanity is, for us, the way that leads towards God.[38]

1. Prima Pars: Q.1 treats the nature and extent of sacred Doctrine. QQ.2–26 treat those things that belong to the divine essence and QQ. 27–43 those that belong to the distinction of persons. Since God is the beginning and the end of all things, QQ 44–46 treats creation in general, QQ.48–49 the distinction and cause of evil, QQ.50–64 regarding angels, QQ.65–74 regarding the six day creation story, QQ.75–102 treats the human person as a creature made in the image of God, and QQ.103–19 treats of the way God governs creation through the mediation of secondary causes.[39]

2. Secunda Pars: The second part has two subdivisions. Aquinas devotes these to the orientation or movement or return of rational creature to God who is the goal or end of human life. He begins the prologue of the treatise on the last end with the statement: "Now that we have treated of the exemplar, i.e., God, and of those things which came forth from the power of God in accordance with His will; it remains for us to treat of His image, i.e., man, inasmuch as he too is the principle of his actions, as having free-will and control of his actions."[40] QQ.1–5 treats this end of human life as consisting in beatitude. QQ 6–48 begin Aquinas treatment of means of arriving at this end, beginning with voluntary and free acts of the will and the passions of the soul. QQ. 48–49 deal with virtues and vices, QQ. 90–108 with law as exterior

---

37. St. Thomas Aquinas, *Summa Theologica*, vol.1, xix.

38. Torrell, *Saint Thomas Aquinas*, 148.

39. Ibid., 149.

40. Thomas Aquinas, *Summa Theologica* vol2, 583.

principles influencing human activity, and QQ.109–114 concludes the Prima Secundae with Aquinas' treatment of grace.[41]

Secunda Secundae continues Aquinas' theme of the return of rational creature to God. QQ.1–46 probes how this return can be achieved by dedication to the theological virtues of faith, hope, and charity. QQ. 47–170 analyzes the cardinal virtues of prudence, justice, temperance, and fortitude, specifying both their proper acts and contrary sins. QQ. 171–89 concludes the Secunda Secundae with a treatment of charism and ecclesial diversity that ends with the contemplative life.[42]

> 3. Tertia Pars: Aquinas begins his treatment of Jesus Christ as the savior who brings salvation to human race. In the prologue he states: "It is necessary in order to complete the work of theology that after considering the last end of human life, and the virtues and vices, there should follow the consideration of the savior of all, and of the benefits bestowed by Him on the human race."[43] QQ.1–26 treats the mystery of the incarnation and QQ.27–59 examines the mystery of the suffering of Christ and the salvation he brings to the human family. The second section of the Tertia Pars, beginning with QQ.60–90, examines the sacraments of the church as means of arriving at this salvation. The third part, which Thomas was not able to write, was to "consist of a detailed reflection on the end to which we are called, eternal life, into which we enter by being raised through Christ."[44]

REVIVAL OF THEOMISM

Although the philosophy of St. Thomas was not properly received in the 14th and 15th centuries, the significance of the Summa Theologiae as a symbol of Catholic orthodoxy has not been disputed since his philosophy (Thomism) became the official Catholic philosophy. At the Council of Trent, the Summa, in a symbolic gesture, was laid on the altar alongside the Scriptures and decrees of the popes. While for Catholics that may have been a symbol of Catholic orthodoxy, for Protestants it was a metaphor for adulteration of the pure word of God. The limitations of Thomism were of course the reasons for its decline and rejection, not only among Protestants but in Catholic circles as well. For example, "one can notice in lines of Aquinas some naïve

---

41. Torrell, *Saint Thomas Aquinas*, 149.

42. Ibid., 149–50.

43. Thomas Aquinas, *Summa Theologica* vol.4, 2019.

44. Torrell, *Saint Thomas Aquinas*, 150.

exegesis, some limits of past science, and a sparse view of history. Some moderns have been distracted by the un-modern pattern of centering all on God or by the teleological dynamic."[45] Another reason for the collapse of Thomism stemmed from its identification as perennial philosophy. "This encomium, hastily imposed by anxious theologians and church authorities, presumed that time and culture had little impact on human consciousness, and implied that one philosophical theology could serve all people. By claiming too much it rendered Thomism bland and arrogant."[46]

Learned Catholics have on several occasions attempted a revival of Thomism as a good representation of official Catholic teaching. The most recent and authoritative attempt was Leo XIII's 1879 encyclical, Aeterni Patris, which called for the revival of scholasticism and gave official support for the study of Thomism as the best means of realizing scholastic thought. Leo extolled the virtues of St. Thomas:

> There is no part of philosophy which he did not handle with acuteness and solidity. He wrote about the laws of reasoning; about God and incorporeal substances; about man and other things of sense; and about human acts and their principles. What is more, he wrote on these subjects in such a way that in him not one of the following perfections is wanting: a full selection of subjects; the best method of treating them; certainty of principles; strength of argument; perspicuity and propriety in language; and the power of explaining deep mysteries.[47]

Leo concluded with the exhortation that Thomism be considered a perennial philosophy and itemized four reasons why modern youths should engage in the study of the Angelic Doctor. First, young men and women are faced with a world besieged by "the wiles and craft of a certain deceitful kind of wisdom." Therefore those growing up "ought to be fed with healthful and strong food of doctrine."[48] Second, there are those who, "with minds alienated from the Faith," hold that reason alone is their teacher and guide. "To heal these men of their unbelief and to bring them to grace and the Catholic Faith, We think that nothing, after the supernatural help of God, can be more useful in these days than the solid doctrine of the Fathers and the Scholastics." Third, family life and civil society are greatly threatened by "pestilence of perverse opinions." A doctrine more in unison with the

45. O'Meara, *Thomas Aquinas Theologian*, xiv.

46. Ibid., 156.

47. Leo XIII, "On the Restoration of Christian Philosophy According to the Mind of St. Thomas Aquinas, the Angelic Doctor," xv.

48. Ibid., xvii.

perpetual teaching office (Magisterium) of the Church, as found in the works of Thomas Aquinas would be more suitable for the universities and schools. Lastly, the pope reasoned that it is a proven fact that the liberal arts have been most flourishing when the honor of philosophy has stood inviolate and neglected and almost obliterated when declining philosophy has been enveloped in errors and absurdities. Hence the pope called for the restoration of philosophy according to the ancient wisdom of "Thomas, and Blessed Albert the Great, and other princes of the Scholastics [who] did not so give themselves up to the study of philosophy, as to have little care for the knowledge of natural things," as part of the process of rehabilitating and restoring the dignity of the liberal arts.

CRITIQUE OF THOMAS AQUINAS

In spite of his creative genius, the work of St. Thomas contains "some naïve exegesis, some limits of past science, and a sparse view of history."[49] The contemporary person who takes seriously the issues of race, gender, and class will find some of Aquinas' work a little troubling. Liberation theologians are quick to remind us that the problem of human suffering is inextricably tied to race, class, and gender, issues that St. Thomas did not give considerable attention. Thomas accepted the world order of his time, which makes his views on women and slaves completely unacceptable to the modern person.

On the issue of women, Thomas followed Aristotle who described the female as a male manqué, meaning that females are conceived from a "weak seed." Thomas used this to support his argument on "the natural inequality and subordination of women to men, who are by nature more reasonable and discerning." In *Summa Theologiae* (Q.91. Art.1, Pt.1) Thomas reiterates his argument that the production of woman comes from "defect in the active force or from some material indisposition," that nature's intention for the woman is only for "generation," and that the woman was not made to be man's helpmate but man's "helper." Thomas held a view of women as "an occasion of sin to man" and follows Paul's literary injunction that women not be allowed to teach in public.

Black people also find St. Thomas' view on slavery a little disturbing because some of his views have been used historically to justify the subordination of people of color. Thomas did not challenge prevailing views on slavery. Although slavery at the time of Thomas was not the same as the trans-Atlantic slave trade that dehumanized Africans that were brought

49. O'Meara, *Thomas Aquinas Theologian*, xiv.

to the Americas, Thomas accepted slavery as a human institution or contrivances designed for the good of society. He took for granted that some people are meant to be subordinate to others. Such subordination, in his view, "would have existed in the state of innocence, since man is by nature a social animal, and people living a social life need some single authority to look to their common good. If some men are more knowledgeable and just than others the right thing is to use that to the others' benefit."[50]

STUDY GUIDE

Review. . .

1. Life of Augustine and his influence in Early Christianity.

2. Donatism and Pelagianism.

3. How Augustine was able to overcome difficult theological problems of North African Church.

4. Reasons why the Middle Ages symbolize different things for Catholics and Protestants, and mean one thing for conservative Catholics and another for liberal Catholics.

5. The influence of Aquinas' family in his education and vocation.

6. Why the authority of Aquinas surpassed that of other scholastics.

7. The structure of the Summa.

8. Parts of the Summa.

9. The role of the Dominican Order in rehabilitating the work of Aquinas.

10. Themes treated in each part of the Summa.

11. Limitations of Thomism.

12. Reasons for the revival of Thomism.

13. The role of Pope Leo XIII in the revival of Thomism.

14. Weaknesses of Aquinas' theology.

Discussion Questions

1. Who was Augustine of Hippo? Describe his role and influence in establishment of Christian doctrine.

50. McDermott, *St. Thomas Aquinas*, 147.

2. We have seen how the parents of St. Thomas Aquinas attempted to frustrate his efforts to join the Dominican Order, even though according to the customs of the time, Thomas was destined for the Church. What do you think was the motive of his parents? Why did they eventually release him from his house arrest knowing fully well that Thomas was still going to go ahead with his plans to join the mendicants? Was there a way they could have prevented the turn of events?

3. Explain what you understand by scholasticism. What is scholastic method? To what extent was Thomas Aquinas original in his style and to what extent was he culturally conditioned? Do you think scholastic method makes texts easy to understand? Compare the scholastic method with the modern way of writing.

4. Give an account of the themes treated by Thomas Aquinas in the *Summa Theologiae* and show how they fit into his grand scheme of theology.

5. We have seen that Aquinas intended to divide the Summa into three parts but died before he could finish his work. What do you think about the plan of the Summa and the arrangement of the materials discussed by Aquinas? Do you think Aquinas was right to have stopped writing before he died because of his mystical vision? Do you think if he had put the revelations of his vision into writing the Summa would have been significantly different and better? Do you think St. Thomas actually had a mystical experience or that he could have suffered a terrible illness?

6. What is Thomism? What are some of the limitations of Thomism? Do you think it was right for the Church to attempt a revival of Thomism, given the negative realities that led to its demise and the cultural differences between the world in which Thomas wrote and modern culture?

7. Explain reasons Pope Leo XIII gave for the revival of Thomism. To what extent can the pope's reasons be vindicated in light of the contemporary problems in human society?

8. Compare and contrast the influence of Augustine of Hippo and Thomas Aquinas in the development of Christian doctrine.

7

The Church, Christology, and Salvation

THE PSYCHOTHERAPIST VIKTOR FRANKL always began his therapy sessions by asking his patients why they have not committed suicide. He discovered astonishingly that for every patient there was a different answer to the question, why have you not attempted suicide? People's motivations and will to meaning in life differ. For one it may be the love of children, for another it may be the love for a talent yet to be used, still for another it may be a lingering memory worth preserving. The human will to survive in the face of inexplicable odds is what Frankl captures in his book about his prison camp experience. He relates how his parents, brother, and wife were gassed to death in Nazi gas chamber. As Gordon Allport sums it up in the preface to Frankl's book: "To live is to suffer, to survive is to find meaning in the suffering. If there is a purpose in life at all, there must be a purpose in suffering and dying. But no man can tell another what this purpose is. Each must find out for himself, and must accept the responsibility that his answer prescribes."[1]

THE PROBLEM OF EVIL

As human beings we are always confronted with the reality of evil. We experience natural disasters, like hurricanes, tornados, and earthquakes. We are aware of moral evils, like the holocaust, slavery, and the extermination of Native Americans. We also know of structural evils, like abuse of women and the oppression of the poor and minorities. We experience evil as a fact

1. Frankl, *Man's Search for Meaning*, 11.

and a reality. In June 2001, America woke up to one of such realities that shocked the moral fibers of our nation. A woman in Houston, Texas, Andrea Yates, confessed to drowning her five children in the bathtub. As details of the tragedy emerged, we came to discover that Andrea Yates had been suffering from postpartum psychosis. Although the jury later convicted Yates for killing her five children, many believed that she was a victim of forces beyond her control. Andrea Yates was not evil. But in her actions many experienced the troublesome problem of evil. To cite one more example, in the last couple of years the world's attention has turned to the rising incidents of anti-semitism in Europe. In March 2012 a gun man went to a Jewish school in Toulouse, France, and killed a rabbi and three Jewish children. In 2014 French authorities reported that a 19 year old girl that was raped in Paris was targeted and raped because she was Jewish. These are just a tip of the iceberg of the rising wave of anti-semitism in Europe (and France especially) that has led to about about 7000 French Jews emigrating to the state of Israel in 2014 alone.

This brings us to the complex problem of suffering and the age-old question: what is evil? What forces, if any, are responsible for evil? Where is God in relation to this pervasive problem? Jews who have been victims of anti-Semitism have a cultural connection to Judaism. Their cultural connection to the sufferings of their fellow Jews during the holocaust and sufferings of Jewish people throughout history may help them pull through. Believing in a hopeful future promised by God in the Torah, some Jews use the tragedy of the past as lessons towards realizing the promise. In theological terms, the attempt to articulate the problem of evil is known as **theodicy**. Christianity, like Judaism and Islam, recons with the fact of evil. These religious traditions take a hopeful view that a person can transcend his or her predicament and that in the face of suffering one can discover meaning in life. Viktor Frankl tells of a promise he made to himself the first day he arrived in concentration camp in Auschwitz. The camp in Auschwitz was surrounded by electric wires to prevent prisoners from escaping. If prisoners touched the electric wires they were electrocuted instantly. Prisoners who could not tolerate the horrors of prison camp took to suicide as an escape. One popular method of suicide was to run into the wire and touch the electrically charged fence. The phrase "run into the wire" became a common phrase among prisoners. Frankl made himself a promise not to "run into the wire."[2] In his work on Logotherapy, Frankl distinguishes between different forms of neurosis "and traces some of them (the noogenic neuroses)

---

2. Frankl, *Man's Search for Meaning*, 37.

to the failure of the sufferer to find meaning and a sense of responsibility in his existence."[3]

The practical problem is not whether evil exists, but what can be done about it? Life holds a potential meaning under any circumstances, especially the most miserable ones.[4] Since God is the ground of all human endeavors, the question is also about what God is and what God has been doing about the fact of evil. The question of what God is doing about the fact of evil is what is known as **special transcendent knowledge—that God must be doing something about evil, if God truly loves humanity**.[5] For Christians, God explicitly addressed the problem of evil by sending Jesus to die on the cross. We shall examine the meaning of the church in the next section, but not before examining the causes of evil.

Causes of Evil

When we speak of human evil we are talking of the human person who in freedom chooses to do this as opposed to that or refrains from doing this as opposed to that. Human existence comes with freedom and responsibility. In freedom we give determinate validity to our life. Given this human ability to choose and make determinations for one's life, there is an extent to which human beings are responsible for the evil in the world. Some evil are brought about by our excessive desires and lusts for power, which sometimes lead to war. Some evils are as a result of the pollution of the environment and lack of adequate care of our natural resources. Ignorance, i.e., wrong or erroneous belief, is also to some degree responsible for evil. An example of this may be the issue of global warming. For a long time it was erroneously thought that we humans had nothing to do with the changing climate. But scientists are now discovering that we can do a lot to help reduce global warming. Among the many evils that afflict the human person and the human community at large there is none worse than the erroneous beliefs that distort a person's mind and make systematic aberrations of their conduct.[6] The September 11 terrorist attack in New York is a good example. The terrorists who hijacked planes and crashed them into the Pentagon and the World Trade Center, we are told, were convinced of their cause, "martyrdom," but their belief was erroneous. Something can be also be said of athletes who knowingly take drugs and unintentionally cause bodily harm to themselves because of

3. Ibid., 10.
4. Ibid., 16.
5. Lonergan, *Insight*, 709.
6. Ibid., 709.

the erroneous belief that taking drugs can make them better athletes. The course of action that people choose reflect either their ignorance or their bad will or even their ineffectual self-control. This is called sin in Christian theology.[7]

The reality of sin is at times evident in the way societies are configured. Some societies have structures that are in themselves unjust and sinful. In many countries, especially developing countries of Africa and Latin America, the structures of society are such that the rich get richer and the poor get poorer. Nowhere is this more evident than in Latin America where Liberation theologians have spent a great deal of time challenging structural injustice. One of the prominent voices in this regard is the Peruvian born theologian Gustavo Gutierrez who insists that the situation of the poor in Latin America calls for a revolutionary transformation of the very basis of society. Gutierrez calls for a theology that addresses this need (Liberation Theology), insisting that true liberation has three main dimensions: (1). It involves political and social liberation that eliminates the immediate causes of poverty and injustice. (2) It involves the emancipation of the poor and marginalized from those things that inhibit their capacity to develop themselves freely and with dignity. (3) And finally, true liberation involves liberation from selfishness and sin and a reestablishment of right relationship between God and God's creatures. Liberation theology has been continued in Latin America by theologians like the Brazilians Clodovis and Leonardo Boff, Juan Luis Segundo of Uruguay, Ignacio Ellacuria of El Salvador, Dom Helder Camara, the Catholic Archbishop of Olinda and Recife (Brazil), and the Brazilian educator Paulo Freire.

Are We Responsible for Evil?

We know that greed, avarice, and insatiable human appetite are at the root of human pain. Buddhism suggests the doctrine of the Four Noble Truths as panacea for human suffering. The Four Noble Truths teach that (i) All life is suffering (ii) The cause of suffering is desire (iii) Stopping desire will stop suffering (iv) the eight fold path (i.e., right views, right intention, right speech, right action, right livelihood, right effort, right mindfulness, and right concentration) is the best way to stop desire.[8] Some Christian theologians are beginning to adopt positions similar to the Buddhist notion that ignorance or erroneous beliefs are responsible for some of our bad actions. According to Bernard Lonergan, as a person advances in truth he or she

7. Ibid., 711.

8. See Carmody and Brink, *Ways to the Center*, 224–25.

begins to acquire the capacity to correct his or her errors. "Our advance in understanding is also the elimination of oversights and misunderstandings."[9] If ignorance is in part responsible for erroneous belief, which in turn leads to concrete act of evil, it is necessary to take steps to free oneself from false beliefs. If there are erroneous beliefs that make evil possible, it also means that there must be opposite intelligible good choices that lead to good acts. To make good choices is to be attentive, intelligent, reasonable, and responsible. While rational and responsible decision-making processes do not completely eliminate evil, they significantly reduce them. People who are attentive, intelligent, reasonable, and responsible may still have to suffer from the evil of those who are not as intelligent and reasonable. This is one of the reasons why Viktor Frankl speaks of suffering as what one may sometimes be required to accept, i.e., an act of fate or even a cross to be borne. "When a man finds that its his destiny to suffer, he will have to accept his suffering as his task; his single and unique task. He will have to acknowledge the fact that even in suffering he is unique and alone in the universe. No one can relieve him of his suffering or suffer in his place. His unique opportunity lies in the way in which he bears his burden."[10] But why do the just have to suffer?

The problem of evil raises for us the question of God whose all-knowing and all mighty power can remedy all evils. Since God is good and wills the goodness of all of God's creatures, it is meaningless to speak of a problem of which there is no solution.[11] The fact of evil means that God is doing something about it. The reality of God must have meaning and value for us. The Bible is very clear about God's participation in human events, a reason for which God intervened in human affairs by sending Jesus as the savior who would deliver God's children from sin and evil. The promise of a savior was realized in the man Jesus Christ who was miraculously born of the Virgin Mary. The story of Jesus is preserved by the Church. What is the Church? Who was Jesus Christ? In what way was he a savior? If he was a savior, was he a savior for a select few or savior of the whole world?

THE CHURCH

The Church is identified with the person and work of Jesus. While on earth Jesus knew himself to be the "absolute mediator of salvation."[12] The Bible

9. Lonergan, *Method in Theology*, 110.

10. Frankl, *Man's Search for Meaning*, 99.

11. Lonergan *Insight*, 716.

12. Rahner, *Foundations of Christian Faith*, 322.

describes him as "the Lamb of God who takes away the sin of the world" (John 1:29). In carrying out his mission on earth, Jesus did not found an institution or a large cathedral church, like the ones we see in major metropolis. Rather, he went about preaching the good news, healing the sick, and forgiving sins. "He did take a stand and gathered people around himself as disciples and called them to stand with him. He defined this stance in terms of symbols like the Kingdom of God and the 'twelve' (representative of the tribes of Israel) and in terms of a call for a qualitatively radical conversion."[13] Jesus shared his healing powers with the disciples who took a stand with him. On the eve of his death he shared a special meal with his disciples (the Last Supper) and commanded them to do this often "in memory of me" (I Corinthians 11:24). The followers of Jesus, after his death, called themselves *ekklesia*, the Greek term for "assembly" or "gathering" of a people set apart. They considered themselves to be an assembly or community that was different from the existing Jewish community and the rest of society. At Pentecost the followers of Jesus received the power of the Holy Spirit (Acts of the Apostles 1:18) and were emboldened to proclaim the coming of the kingdom of God. The power they received on Pentecost empowered them to scatter all over Palestine where they founded more communities. The different Christian communities founded by the apostles met regularly to celebrate the Eucharist as Jesus had directed them. They also had a governmental structure—bishops, presbyters, and deacons. Thus, it is this line of continuation of Christ through the believing community who profess faith in him and knew him to be the savior of the world that we call "church."[14]

Because of the 16th century reformation that led to division in Christian unity today we have different ecclesial communities that call themselves "church." This sometimes lead people to wonder which one of these different ecclesial communities is the true church of Christ. According to Karl Rahner, "the question of the church which was really intended and founded by Christ" is one of the most difficult questions in Church history.[15] What we mean by "church," therefore, is best spoken in terms of models. Speaking of the church in terms of models leaves space for different ecclesial communities to identify with any of the models. People throughout Christian history have come up with different models. The American Jesuit, Avery Dulles (1918–2008), has offered six good models that can help our discussion.[16] .

---

13. Masson, *The Charmed Circle*, 221.

14. Rahner, *Foundations of Christian Faith*, 322.

15. Ibid., 324.

16. See Dulles, S.J., *Models of the Church*.

1. Church as institution. Today the word "structure" carries negative con-
    notation because of the awareness of the dangers structures can pose
    and how structures of society can be institutionalized to legitimize op-
    pression. Often when we speak of institution we think of unjust struc-
    tures, like those that marginalize women and ethnic minorities. Ap-
    plying the metaphor to the church may seem problematic. But when
    we speak of the church as an institution it is intended to mean that the
    Church teaches and rules with the authority of Christ (Mathew 16:18).
    It also intended to highlight the fact that the church has a govern-
    mental structure (Pope, Bishops, Priests, and Deacons) responsible for
    administering the sacraments and clarifying doctrines.

2. Church as Community: the church is the Body of Christ or a fellow-
    ship of love where members reflect in their relationship to one another
    the love between God the Father, the Son, and Holy Spirit (Romans
    12; I Corinthians 12). The Catholic Church emphasizes two aspects of
    the community that are related to each other: the local church and the
    universal church. The local church is where the believing Christians in
    a given locale gather for worship. A local church is related to all other
    sister churches. The church then is a place where everyone is truly wel-
    comed and becomes part of a community. "One of the great human
    paradoxes" of the church community as Dennis Doyle observed, "is
    how we can all be so different and yet so similar."[17]

3. Church as Sacrament: the Church is a visible manifestation of God's
    grace in human community. The Church manifests grace in the way it
    witnesses and in the way it worships (I Peter 2:9; Ephesians 5:32).The
    Belgian Catholic theologian, Edward Schillebeecks (1914–2009) was
    one of the chief proponents of the typology of Church as Sacrament.
    Traditionally, a sacrament is "an outward sign instituted by Christ to
    confer grace." The Catholic Church teaches that there are seven sac-
    raments and that they all confer grace. Schillebeecks was concerned
    about some misunderstandings in the way grace is conferred. He
    thought that some Catholics were beginning to treat the sacraments of
    the church like magical rituals and therefore saw the need to reshape
    the Church's teaching on the sacrament. In his book, *Christ the Sacra-
    ment of the Encounter with God* (1963), Schillebeecks pointed out that
    Jesus Christ is the proto-sacrament in whom God's love for humanity
    became visible and irrevocable. He also pointed out that in so far as
    the mission of the Church is to make visible the love God has shown
    us in Jesus Christ that the Church is equally a sacrament. Before his

17. Doyle, *Communion Ecclesiology*, 7.

death in 2009, Schillebeecks took his typology of church as sacrament a step further, emphasizing how our encounter with the poor and the marginalized provide us an opportunity to encounter God.

4. Church as Herald: the Church is God's faithful people who hear God's word and keep it alive (Mathew 28; Acts 2). This model places emphasis on the mission of the Church to proclaim the Good News of the coming of God's kingdom.

5. Church as Servant: the Church is an instrument by which God brings justice and peace on earth (John 13:34). This model emphasizes the mission of the Church to reach out to the poor and marginalized people of the earth.

6. Church as Discipleship: the Church is a group of people who follow Christ and learn from him. According to this model, the Church, as followers of Christ, learn from Christ and try to live out the life of Christ in the world.

CHRISTOLOGY

Christology is an attempt to understand Jesus Christ. Was Jesus human or divine? Or was he human and divine? If he was human, we have a fairly accurate knowledge of the point in time in which he became man, since we know of his virgin birth. But if he was divine, when did he become divine? Was he always divine? As a man did he know he was divine? If he was aware of his divine nature at what point did he know it? Was he fully conscious of his mission as divine redeemer? If he was, why did he not explicitly say so?

The Gospel of John answers some of these questions. The author of this gospel, sometimes referred to as the Fourth Gospel, begins the prologue by asserting the divinity of Jesus: "In the beginning was the Word, and the Word was with God, and the Word was God" (John 1:1). The author immediately tells us that it was because of God's kindness to give to the human race "grace upon grace," that made Jesus become one like us: When he "became flesh and made his dwelling among us" (John 1:14), Jesus, as it were, identified with our frail human nature. He did not identify with us just to sympathize with us. Rather, he identified with us so he could do something about it, something he accomplished through suffering, death, and resurrection.

The resurrection of Christ is for the New Testament writers the cornerstone of the Christian faith. It is a testimony that God, at a particular moment in history, decided to do something about human sinfulness. Faith in God's decision to act was based on faith in the Lord Jesus. The apostle Paul states that if Christ had not risen from the dead we (Christians) are the most pitiable of people. The word "Christ" is a Greek translation of the Hebrew word Messiah, meaning an "anointed one." For Christians, Jesus' death and resurrection prove that He was the "anointed" One chosen by God to redeem God's people from the evil of sin and death. Jesus was the messiah prophesied in Old Testament scriptures. In him the messianic hope long awaited by the people of Israel was fulfilled.

Early Christological Controversies

Faith in the Lord Jesus was not always a given. The contemporaries of Jesus did not all accept him as the promised messiah. Worse still, the early Christian Church did not always understand his divinity. The Church was for a long time embroiled in controversies regarding the person of Jesus and his mission. These led to heated debates—the Christological controversies. The first seven ecumenical councils of the Church dealt with these controversies. The first problem had to do with the human and divine natures of Christ. Subsequent Christological controversies dealt with the question of how Jesus Christ can at one and the same time be human and divine.

In the early Church there were three patriarchates (theological centers): the two rival schools of Alexandria and Antioch, and Rome, which enjoyed the special privilege as "overseer" of the Church. The theological center of Alexandria boasted of eminent theologians like Clement of Alexandria (150–215 CE) and Origen (182–254 CE) and was noted for its allegorical interpretation of scripture. Allegorical interpretation is a method of interpretation that assigns contemporary meanings to Old Testament passages and words. The Alexandrian emphasis was on the unity of the human and divine natures of Christ. The rival school of Antioch, on the other hand, preferred literal interpretation of scripture. Their emphasis was on the humanity of Christ. The Christological controversies unfolded in this arena, i.e., the two contrasting styles or starting points of theology. The first council of Nicaea (325 CE) was convened in response to the Arian problem. Arius (256–336 CE), a priest from Alexandria had claimed that Jesus was a creature and not God as God the Father is God. After much deliberation and heated arguments, Nicaea affirmed that Jesus was one in "being (essence) with the Father," "begotten not made," and "homoousios (consubstantial) with the Father." Constantinople (381 CE) affirmed the decisions of Nicaea and added that the Holy Spirit is "the Lord the Giver of Life who proceeds from the Father [and] together with the Father and the Son is to be adored and glorified." A more refined definition of the relationship of the human and divine natures of Christ was given at Chalcedon (451 CE). According to the decree of the Council, the two natures of Christ were "unmixed and unchanged, undivided and unseparated," and the qualities of each nature were by no means destroyed in this union, but preserved and united in one person (*prosopon*) and one *hypostasis*. The word "hypostasis" signifies that there is a real distinction between the Father, the Son, and the Holy Spirit, all of them being unto themselves supreme reality in divine substance, essence, and nature.

Church as Sign of God's Desire to Save Humanity

God's universal salvific will is continued in the Church, an institution, if you like, established by Jesus. In so far as the Church is a continuation of the work of Christ, the Church is a sign of salvation or what Karl Rahner calls "the basic sacrament of salvation." As sacrament of salvation, the Church is not only for those who profess to be Christians, but for all of God's people. God's desire to save humanity (salvation history) "has entered into its final, eschatological and irreversible phase."[18] The Church is not the salvation, but a sign of that salvation that comes from Christ. Christ established within the church means of attaining salvation—sacraments. The Catholic Church speaks of seven of these sacraments. The origin or institution of these sacraments "can be understood in a way which is analogous to the institution of the church itself by Jesus."[19] The seven sacraments are baptism, eucharist, confirmation, anointing of the sick, holy order, penance, and matrimony.

Baptism, Confirmation, and Eucharist are called sacraments of Christian initiation. Baptism is the sacrament that washes away original sin and makes a person a member of the Church. "Membership in the church and belonging to the church is the first and most immediate effect of this sacrament of initiation which every Christian receives, and which for every Christian is the foundation of his Christian existence."[20] Confirmation is the sacrament that perfects the grace of baptism in that one receives the Holy Spirit and becomes an adult member of the church. It is the sacrament that strengthens a person's faith "against the powers and forces of this world, the powers of untruth and of disbelief, and of the demonic hybris to want to redeem oneself."[21] The Eucharist is at the center of the Church's liturgi-

18. Rahner, *Foundations of Christian Faith*, 412.

19. Ibid., 413.

20. Ibid., 415.

21. Ibid., 417.

cal life. It is a memorial sacrifice that is offered for the nourishment of the Christian and reparation of sin. Rahner calls the Eucharist the sacrament of the church in "a very radical sense" because of this sacrament's "decisive importance for the founding of the church and for the self-understanding of Jesus as the mediator of salvation."[22]

The sacraments of penance and anointing of the sick are called the sacraments of healing because they take away sins that are committed after baptism and reconcile the sinner to God. The last two sacraments: Holy orders and matrimony are called the sacraments of Christian vocation because they are geared towards the service of others. Matrimony is a sacrament of marriage while Holy orders is the sacrament of consecration of priests by which the apostolic mission of the church is continued.

CATHOLIC AND CATHOLICISM

We need to distinguish between two words that are related but nonetheless not synonymous: "catholic" and "Catholicism." The word "catholic" is from the Greek kat'holou, meaning "to be whole" or "to be complete." The word "catholic" is usually used in contrast to sects or schismatic groups, like the Donatists or the Arians that were sectarian or provincial, as we saw earlier. "Catholic" is usually used as an adjective or a noun to denote universal. St. Augustine used the term "catholic" exactly this way in his dealings with the Donatists. He spoke of the Church of Christ as "catholic," meaning universal, as against the Donatist who were sectarian (incomplete) and parochial (limited). The Donatist wrongly taught that the church was the church of the few, not for everyone. In the way Augustine used the term, the word "catholic" denotes something that is complete or a faith that is unified and orthodox. The Council of Nicaea (325 CE) and Council of Constantinople (381 CE) also used the word "catholic" as a rallying point for unity of faith. In fact, the first person to use the word "catholic" was St. Ignatius of Antioch (50–117 CE) who stated: "Wherever the bishop is to be seen, there let all his people be, just as wherever Jesus Christ is present, we have the Catholic Church." The bishop, represents for Ignatius and the Fathers of the Church, a symbol of orthodoxy.

The word "catholic" became problematic and took a new twist in the eleventh century when the Eastern Church (Orthodox Christianity), for political and theological reasons, separated and severed ties with Rome (Western Church). The Western Church held on to the title Catholic Church, while the Eastern Church became the Orthodox or Byzantine Church. It

22. Ibid., 425.

was called Byzantine because it had its capital in Byzantium. The meaning of the word "catholic" got even more complicated in the sixteenth century when those Western Christians who severed relations with Rome during the Protestant Reformation took the name Protestants. Those who retained ties with Rome were called Catholics, as a way of distinguishing them from the Protestants. Thus, as a result of the eleventh century split between the East and West and the subsequent sixteenth century Protestant Reformation, the meaning and understanding of the word "catholic" became severely distorted from its original meaning. Today it is not only the Roman Catholic Church that calls itself "catholic." There are several other ecclesial communions, like the Armenian, Byzantine, Coptic, Ethiopian, East Syrian, and Maronites that call themselves "catholic."[23] Therefore, we may say that to be Catholic "is to be a kind of human being, a kind of religious person, and a kind of Christian belonging to a specific Eucharistic faith-community within the worldwide, or ecumenical, Body of Christ."[24]

We see from our analysis of the word "catholic" that the Church is composed of many churches, which means the noun "church" can refer to the Catholic Church, the Orthodox Church, the Baptist Church, the Lutheran Church, and the Presbyterian Church, etc.[25] If as we said in our earlier chapter that to be religious is to be human in a unique way, we might also say that to be Catholic is an instance of this unique or specific way of being human. Catholicism (as used to mean the Roman Catholic Church) is a particular understanding, affirmation, and expression of this unique affirmation of human existence.[26] Catholicism in this sense is also a religious perspective that offers an understanding of God, an understanding that is "the foundation and context for tis understanding of creation, redemption, incarnation, grace, the Church, moral responsibility, eternal life, and each of the other great mysteries and doctrines of Christian faith."[27]

Characteristics of Catholicism

Christians generally affirm the uniqueness of Jesus and how God, in Jesus, actualized God's desire to save humanity. Be that as it may, many Christians also admit that there is no one way of talking about how Jesus affects our lives and for this reason think that we should be open to developing new

23. See McBrien, *Catholicism*, 5.

24. Ibid., 6.

25. Ibid., 7.

26. Ibid., 6.

27. Ibid., 7.

images that can help us understand how his mission of salvation affects our lives.[28] The Catholic approach to Christian life is different from non-Catholic, particularly the Protestant approaches to Christian life, in many ways. These differences are what characterize Catholicism.

1. Sacramentality: Catholicism has a practical commitment to the principle of sacramentality. Catholicism sees all reality as sacred. It does not make sharp distinction between nature and grace (divine presence). It sees human nature as already from the beginning graced; that the world is good, even though sin is in the world. This Catholic approach of nature-grace harmony differs from the approaches of the ecclesial communions deriving from the Reformation. Take the example of Jehovah's Witnesses who generally believe that a blood transfusion from one person to another violates God's law against ingesting blood. Jehovah's Witnesses believe that person who accepts blood transfusion from another human being risks losing eternal salvation because the act violates biblical prohibition against ingesting blood. For this reason parents who are Jehovah's Witnesses do everything in their power to prevent their children from receiving blood transfusions. They would not want to preserve human life of their children at the expense of their eternal life. But the Catholic sacramental principle accepts genuine advancement in human medicine as an instance of graced nature. The spiritual is in the material because God plays an active part in human history and God has a hand in modern medicine. Thus, the Catholic sacramental principle affirms that God is already present in human life and history. This sacramental vision sees God in all things, in the whole cosmos, and in all human events.[29] "The great sacrament of our encounter with God, and of God's encounter with us, is Jesus Christ. The Church, in turn, is the fundamental sacrament of our encounter with Christ, and of Christ with us."[30] Catholicism, in a nutshell, does not follow a grace or nature, but a graced-nature approach.

2. Mediation: Catholicism holds that the human encounter with God is mediated through persons or created realities. "Catholicism's commitment to the principle of mediation is evident especially in the importance it has placed on the ordained ministry of the priest. . . . The function of the priest as mediator is not to limit the encounter between God and the human person, but to focus it more clearly for the sake

28. See Knitter, "Five Theses on the Uniqueness of Jesus," 4.

29. McBrien, *Catholicism*, 10.

30. Ibid.

of the person and ultimately for the sake of the community of faith."[31] Catholicism's principle of mediation is seen in the emphasis it places on the role of Mary, the mother of Jesus, in salvation history, as well as emphasis it places on intercession of the saints. Catholicism "engages in the veneration (not worship) of Mary and asks her to intercede for us, not because Catholicism perceives Mary as some kind of goddess or super creature or rival of the Lord himself, but because she is a symbol, image, and instrument of God."[32] Mary and the saints, like sacraments do, signify and cause grace.[33] But the churches deriving from the Reformation differ from Catholicism in this regard and deemphasize any mediatory or intercessory roles for Mary or the saints for that matter. Their emphasis is only on Jesus, the one mediator.

3. Communion: In some cultures, particularly "the dominant European culture of the United States, ultimate significance is often placed on the individual, on personal rights and freedoms, sometimes even to the extent that the relationship of the individual with the social groups to which he or she belongs gets overlooked."[34] But Catholicism affirms that our way to God is not only mediated but is also communal because God's encounter with individuals is always mediated through the community of faith. This means that for Catholicism "there is no relationship with God, however profound or intense, that dispenses entirely with the communal context of every relationship with God."[35] Catholicism, for this reason, speaks of the communion of saints and the Church as a community where the human person encounters God through the sacraments and the various ministries and gifts God has endowed the Church. Take the example of what happened in 1992 in New York City when the Ancient Order of Hibernians organized St. Patrick's Day Parade but refused to allow gays and lesbians of Irish descent to join the parade. The exclusion of gays and lesbians from the march, as would be expected, was controversial. The city of New York took a legal action, accusing the Hibernians of violating the city's law against discrimination. In their defense, the Hibernians argued that they belonged to the Roman Catholic communion and that they were following their charter, which following Roman Catholic teachings considers homosexuality objectionable. The following year, 1993,

31. Ibid., 12.

32. Ibid.

33. Ibid.

34. Huff and Wetherilt, *Religion*, 11.

35. McBrien, *Catholicism*, 13.

the city of New York denied the Hibernians permit to hold their annual parade in so far as they cannot hold a more inclusive parade. The Hibernians sued the city for denying them permit, an act they thought violated their own First Amendment rights. The Hibernians won the case on the argument that their parade was designed "to honor the patron saint of Ireland and to proclaim their allegiance to the Roman Catholic Church and its teachings."[36] Although the surface issue in this case is discrimination, the underlying issue was religious autonomy.[37] The Hibernians demonstrated that they belonged to a religious community and that though they respect the laws of the state, their primary allegiance was to a community of faith to which they belong. This Catholic idea of communion is also found in the ecclesial communions that separated themselves from Rome, but in a different way.

4. Sacred Tradition: Catholicism places great emphasis, not only on Scripture, but also on sacred tradition. Catholicism sees "a close connection and communication between sacred tradition and Sacred Scripture. For both of them, flowing from the same divine wellspring, in a certain way merge into a unity and tend toward the same end" (Dei Verbum, 9). Catholicism recognizes that even the Bible itself is a product of many traditions that have come down to us through the Church. It therefore sees the history of the Church as part and parcel of divine revelation.[38] Unlike many of the ecclesial communions deriving from the Reformation that adopt a Scripture alone approach, Catholicism adopts Scripture nourished by tradition approach. For "Sacred Scripture is the word of God inasmuch as it is consigned to writing under the inspiration of the divine Spirit, while sacred tradition takes the word of God entrusted by Christ the Lord and the Holy Spirit to the Apostles, and hands it on to their successors in its full purity" (Dei Verbum, 9). Thus, the Catholicism teaches that since it is not from Scripture alone that the Church draws its certainty, but Scripture nourished by sacred tradition, "both sacred tradition and Sacred Scripture are to be accepted and venerated with the same sense of loyalty and reverence" (Dei Verbum, 9).

5. Reason: Because Catholicism recognizes that all created reality is a graced reality, it places emphasis on the use of reason in the understanding of faith. Fideism (naïve faith) cannot grasp the mysteries of

---

36. See Carter, *The Culture of Disbelief,* 34.

37. Ibid.

38. McBrien, *Catholicism,* 14.

God. Faith needs reason.[39] Back to our earlier example of Jehovah's Witnesses who refuse blood transfusion on the argument that it violates Sacred Scriptures prohibition against ingestion of blood, the US courts have on many cases forcibly ordered blood transfusions to save the lives of Jehovah's Witnesses. Even some hospitals require doctors to refer protesting Jehovah's Witnesses to psychiatrists because they suspect "the patient was not acting rationally in rejecting medical advice for religious reasons."[40] Catholicism does not follow an either faith or reason or law or Gospel approach, but reason illumined by faith and law inspired by the Gospel approach.

6. Analogy: Catholicism affirms that we come to our knowledge of God through our knowledge of created realities and therefore that God can be known analogically. In other words, we come to a knowledge of God through our own human experience. The Catholic analogical thinking is a way of thinking about God and understanding our encounter with God by seeking "'similarity in difference,' in contrast to a more typically Protestant way of thinking that is dialectical—emphasizing always what is unique in God and, therefore, the radical dissimilarities that exist between the divine and the human."[41]

7. Universality: Catholicism prides itself in being at one and the same time a Church universal and local. Catholicism is not a Church that is tied to one culture. It can find expression in any culture that accepts the Gospel. Catholicism reflects on questions like: How do we reevaluate the Christian message in a world of cultural pluralism in such a way that it does not become disruptive to other people's cultural identities? How is an African or Asian, for example, to live and express his or her faith in such a way "that the Christian faith does not become an alienating reflection of a foreign world behaving aggressively towards indigenous African customs and beliefs?"[42] The Catholic universal principle makes it to be radically open to anything that has truth and value.[43] Catholicism is not about unity or diversity but unity in diversity.

39. See Orji, *The Catholic University and the Search for Truth*, particularly chapter 7.

40. Carter, *The Culture of Disbelief*, 14.

41. McBrien, *Catholicism*, 15.

42. Orji, *A Semiotic Approach to the Theology of Inculturation*, 31.

43. McBrien, *Catholicism*, 15.

STUDY GUIDE

Review . . .

1. Viktor Frankl and the problem of evil.

2. Causes of evil.

3. What God is doing about evil.

4. The saving significance of Christ.

5. Christological Controversies.

6. The Church as Sacraments.

7. The Seven Sacraments of the Church.

Discussion Questions

1. Compare the experience of Viktor Frankl in prison camp with the story of Andrea Yates and explain how human beings are responsible for the problem of evil.

2. Can you make an argument for the position that "erroneous belief" is responsible for the problem of evil?

3. How did God intervene in human affairs? Did Christ, by his death and resurrection, bring to an end to the problem of evil?

4. How are the sacraments of the Church a continuation of the saving work of Christ?

5. How would you characterize "Christological controversies?" How were some of these controversies resolved by the early Christian church?

6. How would you describe the Church? Explain the different models of the Church and identify any two models that appeal to you most.

7. What is Catholicism? What are some of the characteristics of Catholicism.

8

Development of Christian Doctrine and Spritiuality

CHRISTIAN DOCTRINES DEVELOPED, NOT in abstract, but in historical contexts. In some cases these doctrines developed simultaneously with the Church's attempt to define itself and shape its identity in a culture that already had its own religion and socio-political structures. To understand Christian doctrine, therefore, is to understand how the Church evolved over time, beginning from its Jewish roots to its foray in a Hellenized Roman world. "All History, that of the Church included," writes Glenn Olsen, "has taken place under the sign of contradiction and has been full of irony, tragedy, success that breeds failure, failure unexpectedly successful, roads not taken, and roads taken that should not have been taken."[1]

It is easy to assume today that Christianity was from the very beginning different from Judaism. But the difference between the two religions was not always clear, at least in the eyes of the Roman government. One of the first steps taken by the early Christians was to assert their autonomy from Judaism. When the distinction between Christianity and Judaism did become clearer to the Roman government, it was not without some bloodshed. The birth of Jesus in Bethlehem and his upbringing in Nazareth essentially made him a Jew in the true sense of the term. According to the gospel account of Luke 2, Jesus was born during the reign of Augustus Caesar, at the time Herod the Great was king of Judea, and Quirinius the governor of Syria. As a devout Jew, Jesus read and knew the Hebrew Scriptures. He also received

1. Olsen, *Beginning At Jerusalem*, 13.

rabbinical education. Called like a prophet to communicate God's message to his fellow Jews, Jesus began his public ministry at the age of 30. He went to the Temple and synagogues where he taught his followers and gathered disciples. His main message was that "the kingdom of God has come near! Repent and believe in the good news" (Mk.1:15). After his death and resurrection, his disciples continued to worship in the Temple and synagogues, proclaiming Jesus Lord and the promised Messiah.

The Roman conflict with the people of North Africa, the Carthaginians, with whom the Romans fought three Punic wars, began as far back as the middle of the third century BCE and came to an end when Rome became the undisputed power of the western world. Roman control of North Africa and the Mediterranean world meant that such a huge empire would be ethnically and religiously diverse. The policy of religious freedom or toleration, which the Roman rulers introduced for practical reasons, had some political risks because the policy also threatened the unity of the empire. The Roman authorities decided, in the interest of the unity of the empire, to have a uniform religion and mandated one public religion for everyone, i.e., the worship of Roman gods (which later evolved into worship of Roman emperors). "This was not so much a religious obligation as a political one. The acceptance of the Roman gods was an acceptance of Roman governmental authority."[2] But the Jews on their part were not going to compromise the worship of the one true God. Through some political negotiations they were able to gain some religious concession from the emperor. Respect for the antiquity of their monotheistic tradition was a rationale for this exception, at least in the Roman view. Even those Jews who had settled in other cities (Jews of the Diaspora) benefited from this concession, "which safeguarded their freedom of worship, gave them exemption from the Cult of the Emperor and allowed them to be judged by their own civil law, a law which assumed enormous importance in their lives."[3] Christians enjoyed these same benefits as long as they were thought to be members of the Jewish people. But when it was clear that Christians were different from Jews and that Christianity was different from Judaism this Christian self-assertion led to conflicts with the Roman authorities, conflicts that produced both martyrs (people who shed their blood for the Christian faith) and apologists (people who vigorously defended the Christian faith by their writings).

2. Hogan, *Dissent from the Creed*, 17–18.

3. Holmes and Bickers, *A Short History of the Catholic Church*, 11.

CHRISTIAN COMMUNITIES IN ASIA MINOR

Acts of the Apostles, the New Testament book that takes up the story where the Gospel of Luke left off, gives a detailed account of the development of the Church from its humble beginnings in Jerusalem to its growth in parts of the Mediterranean basin. The story in Acts is a story of how Christianity defined and distinguished itself from Judaism and Jewish traditions. The first Christian community, according to the story in Acts, was in Jerusalem where the disciples, together with some women and Mary the mother of Jesus, devoted themselves to prayer and fasting. These disciples, under the leadership of Peter, saw the need to choose a replacement for Judas who had committed suicide after betraying Jesus. They cast lots to choose a successor. The lot fell on Matthias, who then became one of the Twelve (Acts 1: 15–26).

The city of Jerusalem was important for early Christians. Jesus had commanded them not to leave the city until they had received "power from on high." Acts 2 tells the story of how the disciples received the gift of the Holy Spirit on Pentecost, which in effect signaled the beginning of the Christian church, as we know it today. The Pentecost experience emboldened the disciples who began to preach and witness to Jesus, even in the face of persecution. This preaching and the persecution that followed it took them to cities other than Jerusalem where Jews had taken up residences. From there they founded Christian communities all over Asia Minor.

One of the early Christian converts was Saul of Tarsus, a zealous Pharisee, who was christened Paul after his conversion, and who proclaimed himself an apostle to the Gentiles. "Paul was certain that he too was an apostle, although he went up to Jerusalem to meet with Peter three years after his conversion (Gal.1:18)."[4] His new-found vocation impelled him to embark on three great missionary journeys between 46–58 CE. He founded Christian communities in many of the cities he preached. Some of his communities included Corinth, Philippi, Galatia, Thessalonica, Ephesus, and Rome. He was also associated with the community at Antioch, where Gentiles were first admitted to the Christian faith.[5] Acts tells us that it was at Antioch that the Disciples of Christ were for the first time called Christians (Acts 11: 26). Paul himself preached first to Jews wherever he went, then to "God-fearing" gentiles, admirers of Jewish monotheism.

There were also other Christian communities founded by disciples other than Paul. Philip, for example, founded the community at Samaria. Christian tradition also links Mark the Evangelist to Alexandria, the

---

4. McEnhill and Newlands, *Fifty Key Christian Thinkers*, 215.

5. Ibid., 216.

commercial capital of Egypt and one of the early centers of Christianity. Christian tradition also links Andrew, the brother of Simon Peter, to the community in Constantinople, and Peter with Rome, not as its founder, but as its leader.[6] These Christian communities had one thing in common: they had to deal with two tough issues: the Roman authorities that barely tolerated them, and Jewish authorities whose hostility towards Christians was clearly obvious.[7]

THE FIRST MINISTERIAL POSITION: THE DIACONATE

While the early Christian community was dealing with the external threats of Roman authorities and Jewish hostilities on the one hand, it was also barraged with hosts of internal conflicts on the other hand. The internal conflict, which had ethnic and cultural undertones, had to do with the Hellenists (Greek-speaking Jews) question. The first recorded account of this problem is found in Acts 6: 1–7. The Hellenists had complained against the Hebrews that their widows were being neglected in the daily distribution of food. The issue was brought to the attention of the apostles who wisely discerned that it was not right for them as apostles to neglect the word of God for the distribution of food. They asked the community to choose from among them "reputable men, filled with the Holy Spirit and wisdom," to help in this task. After some prayer and discernment, the community chose seven men, all with Greek names: Stephen, Philip, Prochorus, Nicanor, Timon, Parmenas, and Nicholaus of Antioch. The Greek name of these diaspora-born Jews was a testimony of the attraction of the Gospel to people other than Jews. They became the first seven deacons of the Christian Church. According to the story in Acts, the Jewish authorities stoned to death Stephen, the best known of the seven deacons. Following Stephen's death, more persecutions followed under Herod Agrippa (c.42 CE), who made a calculated risk that by harassing followers of Jesus he would win the support of the Jewish authorities.

The Council of Jerusalem

The election of the seven deacons did not put an end to rift in the Christian community. Soon after they settled the Hellenist problem, the community at Antioch was faced with another problem: the question of whether it was

---

6. Holmes and Bickers, *A Short History of the Catholic Church*, 13.

7. Ibid.

proper for Gentile Christians to undergo circumcision. Unable to resolve this, the community sent Paul to Jerusalem to consult with Peter, James, and the other Apostles. Paul met with the Apostles in Jerusalem (c.50 CE), at a meeting popularly referred to as the **Council of Jerusalem**. The Council resolved the Gentile question by insisting that Gentile Christians not be forced to go through the Jewish rite of circumcision. While that momentous decision may have temporarily resolved the tension between Jewish Christians and non-Jewish Christians, it did nothing to alleviate the wider problem between Judaism and Christianity. The hostility between the two religious groups reached its climax sometime between 66–70 CE, when a Jewish political group, the Zealots, orchestrated a revolt against the Roman authorities.[8] The Romans, led by a commander, Vespasian, who later became emperor, attacked Judea in 67 CE and conquered Jerusalem in 70 CE, destroying the Temple, except the Western or the Wailing Wall.[9] In the period following this revolt, Jewish Christians emigrated to Pella, an act which was regarded as treachery by those Orthodox Jews who remained to fight, in spite of the destruction of the city.[10] The destruction of the Temple around this period played a significant role in the growing distinction between Christianity and Judaism.

Era of Formal Persecution of Christians

Attempts by the Roman authorities to unify the empire, as we pointed out earlier, led to the imposition of one state-sanctioned religion, the Cult of the Emperor. Refusal to partake in this cult (except for the Jews who gained religious exemption) was considered treasonous, a crime punishable by death. The era of formal persecution began with Nero who ruled from 54 to 68 CE. The apostles Peter and Paul died under Nero. Some accounts of this persecution come from the Roman historian, Tacitus (c. 55- 120 A.D), who recorded in his *Annals* that Christians were made a scapegoat for everything that went wrong. According to the report of Tacitus, who was himself a non-Christian, when fire gutted the city of Rome in 64 A.D Nero accused Christians of setting the fire. Tacitus also reports that Christians were charged with crimes of atheism, immorality, and cannibalism.[11] The Christian writer, Tertullian (c. 160–225), in corroborating Tacitus' account of how Christians were made scapegoats for everything that went wrong,

8. Ibid., 12–13.

9. Hogan, *Dissent from the Creed*, 18–19.

10. Holmes and Bickers, *A Short History of the Catholic Church*, 13.

11. Ibid., 15.

reported "that if the Tiber flooded its banks or the Nile failed to flood, or if the stars stood still or the earth trembled, the cry in the streets was always the same: 'Christians to the lions!'"[12] Christians were made to suffer the humiliation of social and legal legislation: they were forbidden access to public places; those who did not recant their faith were tortured and put in prison. Those who survived the prison experience were sent to the amphitheater as baits for the wild animals.[13]

In the second century other prominent Christian, like Ignatius of Antioch (d.107 CE), Justin Martyr (100–165 CE), and Polycarp of Smyrna (69–155 CE), died in the draconian policy of Emperor Trajan (98–117 CE). The general policy and severity of persecution at times depended on local circumstances and individual emperors. During the reign of Decius (249–251 A.D), for instance, the Roman Empire was under severe threats from its neighbors. It was threatened by the Visigoths who attacked from the western Mediterranean and by the other Barbarian tribes who attacked from the Roman borders of Gaul, Spain, and Asia Minor. Decius ordered every citizen to offer sacrifices to the Roman gods, as a symbol of solidarity and as an invocation of help from the Roman gods.[14] According to the terms of this edict, all the inhabitants of the empire who offer public sacrifice to the Roman gods were be supervised by an elected official who in turn will issue a *libellus* (certificate) stating that one had offered the desired sacrifice. Some Christians refused to partake in this sacrifice and their refusal made the Roman authorities to view Christianity as a dangerous sect and a threat to the security of the state. Christianity, for them, violated the Roman pietas, i.e. the virtue by which citizens showed their love and respect for the state. This virtue of Roman pietas was outwardly expressed through the rites and usages by which the gods of Rome were honored such that refusal to participate in this common expression of pietas was considered criminal, blasphemous, and treasonous.[15]

In all, apart from the persecution initiated by Nero, there were at least nine other recorded formal persecutions of Christians in the Roman Empire: Domitian (c. 80 CE), Trajan (c.108 CE), Marcus Aurelius (c. 161 CE), Severus Septimus (c. 192 CE), Maximus (c. 235 CE), Decius (c. 249 CE), Valerian (c. 257 CE), followed by the Aurelian persecution (c. 274 CE) and Diocletian persecution (c. 303 CE). The Diocletian persecution, sometimes called "the Great Persecution," lasted from 303–312 CE and was the last of

12. Cunningham, *The Catholic Heritage*, 11.

13. Ibid., 11–12.

14. Ibid., 12–13.

15. Ibid., 10–11.

the formal persecutions in the Roman Empire.[16] All the emperors adopted a policy that made Christians who refused to sacrifice to idols to be treated like criminals.

The persecution of Christians, which increased significantly during the reign of Marcus Aurelius (c.161- 180 A.D.), went hand in hand with literary polemics against the Church. One of those who attacked Christians with his writings was Celsus, whose book, *True Discourse*, painted a grim picture of Christians and attacked them on the level of both doctrine and practice.[17] These literary attacks gave a false picture of the Church and left Christians more vulnerable in a society that was ever ready to increase its hostility towards those who would not abide by the Roman pietas. As persecution against Christians persists, increase in literary attack against the Church put Christians in a position where they had to defend themselves against such attacks. There emerged, about the second century CE, a group of Church leaders called the **Apologists** who devoted time and energy defending the Church against offensive literary attacks. Christians were accused of acts of immorality and spreading teachings that made no sense. The Apologists "wrote a series of works with the double purpose of denying the false rumors regarding Christian practice and of showing that Christianity was more than mere nonsense."[18] Thus, in providing the intellectual basis of Christian doctrine, the Apologists wrote literary works, "Apologies," i.e., legal briefs, in defense of the Church's doctrine and practice. The most famous of the apologists and one who gave the strongest argument in defense of the Christian faith was Justin Martyr (100–165 CE). Justin suffered martyrdom during the reign of Marcus Aurelius. Justin was born of pagan parents. After his baptism he moved to Rome where he opened a philosophical/theological school. His best known work was the *Dialogue with Trypho the Jew*. Among Justin's teachings was that in Jesus Christ the prophecies of the Old Testament had been fulfilled and that life in Christ is initiated by baptism and sustained in the Eucharist. He also argued that Jesus was the "Logos" or Word of God. Justin suggested that since Jesus is the "Logos" of God, the "Logos" or Word of God illumines everything that came before and after the incarnation. On the basis of this argument Justin accepted anything of value in pagan philosophy.[19] His teaching that anything of value in pagan philosophy can illuminate the Christian faith will later have significant impact on Christian theology. Other notable apologists were Melito

---

16. Ibid., 13.

17. Holmes and Bickers, *A Short History of the Christian Church*, 19.

18. Gonzalez, *Church History*, 27.

19. Ibid.

of Sardis (d.180 CE), Quadratus (d. 129 CE) and Aristides both of Athens (d. 133 or 134 CE), Athenagoras of Athens (133–190 CE) and Theophilus of Antioch (d.181 CE), and Tatian (120–180 CE). Tatian was later forced out of the Church because he wrote a controversial work *Diatesseron*, "a highly influential harmony of all four Gospels"[20] that tried to create a single gospel narrative out of the many existing ones. After the apologists there followed a list of great teachers of the faith, among whom were Tertullian, Clement of Alexandria, Origen, and Cyprian of Carthage. We shall discuss their impact and contribution to development of Church doctrine in the next section. But enough to say that the conversion of Constantine brought Christians a much-needed reprieve. In 313 A.D. Constantine promulgated the edict of religious toleration, **Edict of Milan**, which gave Christians right to freedom of worship. With the Edict, Christianity was at first tolerated and later flourished under Constantine (c. 380 CE) to become the official state religion. "In consequence, the church, which until then was composed mostly of people from the lower echelons of society, made headway among the aristocracy."[21]

CHURCH LEADERSHIP AND ORGANIZATION

Conversion of Constantine to Christianity radically changed things for Christians. Transitioning from outlawed religion to one officially recognized as the state religion was not easy for some Christians who were used to persecution. Their response to the new situation varied significantly, depending on the social location. "Some were so grateful for the new situation that it was difficult for them to take a critical stance before the government and society. Others fled to the desert or to remote places and took up the monastic life. Still others simply broke away from the majority church, insisting that they were the true church."[22] This means that the Church could only survive the new situation with true leadership and guidance. Thankfully the Church was blessed with a new crop of Church leaders in the second century CE. These new leaders came after the apologists and wrote works of great significance. They thought of themselves as following apostolic succession—in the footsteps of church leadership of which Peter the apostle was the first in line.

From the time Jesus called Simon and changed his name to Peter, meaning rock (Luke 5: 1–11), it was clear that Peter was the uncontested

20. Anderson and Moore, "The Lives of Mark," 1–2.

21. Gonzalez, *Church History*, 12.

22. Ibid., 12–13.

head of the apostles and he assumed this leadership role until his death. After Peter's death, and death of the other apostles, the leadership of the church fell on a group of people who were themselves disciples of the apostles. These were known as the **Apostolic Fathers**. Prominent among them were Clement of Rome (d. 99CE), Ignatius of Antioch (d.107 CE), Polycarp of Smyrna (69–155 CE), and the Shepherd of Hermas (2nd century CE valuable Christian work). The Apostolic Fathers provided the church with much-needed leadership at a time the church was struggling for survival in the Roman Empire. There was also the leadership provided by late second century CE Christians, like Quintus Tertullian (160–220 CE), Irenaeus (130–202 CE), Clement of Alexandria (150–215 CE), Cyprian of Carthage (d. 258 CE), and Origen (182–254 CE). Apostolic succession and leadership became a fortress that held the church together.

Tertullian was from Carthage in North Africa. "He wrote in defense of the faith against pagans, and also against several heresies. He was the first to use the formula 'one substance, three persons' to refer to the Trinity, and also the first to speak in terms of 'one person, two substances' in Jesus Christ."[23] Irenaeus was from Smyrna, a town in Asia Minor, but spent most of his adult life in Lyon (modern day France). He devoted a great deal of time defending and strengthening the faith of Christians under his care against the threat of heresy. Clement of Alexandria preoccupied himself with the issue of how to adapt Greek philosophy and make it relevant to the Christian faith. Cyprian was a church leader and bishop of Carthage who died in 258 CE during the persecution of Christians. Origen was also "a prolific writer, much inclined to philosophical speculation. Although after his death many of his more extreme doctrines were rejected and condemned by the church, for a long time the vast majority of Greek-speaking theologians were his followers in one way or another."[24] In all, these late second century CE group of church leaders wrote great theological works and treatises that answered questions on various subjects. The theological works they produced before Christianity became official state religion to a great extent helped Christians struggling to adapt to their new situation as members of the only recognized state religion until the sacking of Rome in 410 CE by the Visigoths and the Germanic peoples, a sacking that finally led to the last of the Western Emperor, Romulus Augustus, being deposed in 476 CE.[25]

23. Ibid., 30.

24. Ibid.

25. Gonzalez, *Church History*, 13.

Internal Problems: Heresies

Although the sacking of Romulus Augustus by the Visigoths in 476 CE, as well as the Barbarian invasion of Rome, greatly devastated the power and influence of Rome, it did not decimate the rising influence of Christianity. Before the invasion of Rome, for administrative reasons the Roman Empire was divided into two parts: the Western half, which spoke Latin, with its capital in Rome and the Eastern half, which spoke Greek, with its capital in Byzantium. The invasion of Rome by the Visigoths and Barbarians "had a much deeper impact on the Latin-speaking Western church than on the Eastern and Greek-speaking branch of Christianity."[26] Church doctrines that developed around this time developed mostly as a response to heresies (false teachings) that the Church had to correct. It is difficult to put a timeline on some of these heresies because some predate the sacking of Rome. The expansion and growth of the Church brought to it "people of various religious backgrounds, and this in turn gave rise to diverse interpretations of Christianity."[27] Some of these interpretations, which bothered on what the Church would later consider heresies (false teachings) represent internal threats to the Church. There were for example, Gnosticism, Marcionism, and Montanism, etc. All threatened to tear Christians apart even before Christianity became official state religion of Rome. These heresies merit some attention because of their significance in the development of church doctrine.

(a) Gnosticism: There are different variations of Gnosticism. But in general terms, Gnosticism is derived from the Greek *gnosis* (knowledge) and *gnostikos* (good at knowing). The Gnostics were an elitist group that taught that one could be redeemed only through knowledge (cosmic redemption through knowledge). As an elitist group, they separated themselves from other people, i.e. people who in their interpretation lacked knowledge. The Gnostics had a dualistic view of reality: spirit and matter. Spirit was good and matter evil. Matter was considered evil because it is a deterioration of spirit. Gnostics denied creation, holding that the created world was the work of a lesser god, demiurge. Human beings, according to their teaching, are prisoners in this world of matter. The ultimate goal of human existence is union with the Supreme God, not the lesser god. This, according to them, can be achieved only through *gnosis*, knowledge, which only a few people possess. The considered the vast majority of human beings to be doomed.

26. Ibid.

27. Ibid., 28.

The Gnostic doctrine was essentially in conflict with the Christian doctrine. One implication of their teaching was that Christ could not have been human, since anything human or material was evil. They, in fact, taught that Christ came to bring gnosis to effect a union with Supreme God. Though no one can tell precisely the origin of Gnosticism, its origin is generally held to have pre-dated Christianity. Its rise was mainly due to the influence of Greek philosophy.

(b) Marcionism: Marcion of Sinope (85–160 A.D.), an influential early Christian writer, was a native of Asia Minor who was influenced by the gnostic doctrine. Like gnostics, Marcion denied that the material world was the work of the good God. Denying the goodness of creation, Marcion took the gnostic position further, formulating a doctrine that made a sharp distinction between the God of the New Testament and the God of the Old Testament. For Marcion, the God of the Old Testament was a God of Law and the God of the New Testament the God of Love. Marcion considered the God of the Old Testament to be inferior to the God of the New Testament. He also rejected the Old Testament and drew his own canon of scripture. His canon consisted mainly of selected letters of St. Paul's writings and selected parts of the Gospel of Luke. Like the Gnostics, Marcion promoted austere lifestyle.

(c) Montanism: Montanus (c. 2nd -3rd cent. A.D.), the founder of this sect, claimed to be a prophet called to speak on behalf of the Holy Spirit. He taught the need for austere lifestyle and perpetual fasting. His followers were called Montanists. They promoted a doctrine of the imminence of the Second Coming of Christ. They also taught their followers not to avoid martyrdom, but to seek it and embrace it.

The Church responded in various ways to threats posed by heresies. Against the gnostic distinction between supreme (good) God and evil god (demiurge), the Christian church insisted that there is only one good God. It also rejected the gnostic dualism of spirit (good) and material (evil) universe, insisting on the goodness of the whole created universe. Against Marcionism, the church formulated its own canon of scripture (i.e., books officially recognized as part of Christian Scripture). Individual church leaders like Justin, Tertullian and Irenaeus also refuted Marcion's teaching by insisting on a Church with a more organization and well defined doctrines and practices. We shall discuss other heresies, particularly Arianism and other Christological controversies, in the context of the ecumenical councils since it was these councils that clarified the Christological problems and authoritatively defined the Church's creed. But key to the unity of the Christian churches scattered throughout the Roman Empire was the institution of Roman primacy whose origin goes back to the primacy conferred on Peter by Jesus. We already saw how the city of Antioch was very important for early Christians, since it was there that the disciples of Jesus were for the first time called Christians. Two other cities, in addition to Antioch, emerged as an important center of Christian activity: Rome and Constantinople. Each of these cities or centers of Christian activity had its own leader to whom the local Christian faithful looked up for leadership. But the bishop of Rome enjoyed enormous power and influence over the whole Church. "The primacy conferred by Christ on Peter was in no way a temporary, circumstantial affair, fated to disappear when Peter died. It was a permanent institution, an earnest of the permanence of the Church, something that would be valid for all times."[28] There were also other reasons for the esteemed position of the bishop of Rome. First, Rome was the capital of the Roman Empire before Constantine moved it to Byzantium in 324 CE. Second, the apostolic witness of Peter (the first bishop of Rome) and Paul, who were both martyred in Rome under Nero, helped raise the status of Rome. Third, the relocation of the capital of the empire to Constantinople helped consolidate Rome's position for this reason: in the separation of East and West that followed, the emperor became the major power in the East, while the bishop of Rome emerged as the major rival power in the West. Speaking of the esteemed position the bishop of Rome enjoyed over the whole Church, Ignatius of Antioch spoke of Rome as the "bond of love" uniting the whole church. Damasus, who was the Bishop of Rome from 366–84 CE not only referred to Rome as the "Apostolic See," but also referred to other bishops as "sons." He claimed that the primal place of Rome was due to divine will. Siricius, who became the bishop of Rome from 384–399 A.D. was believed to be the first to use the title "pope" (father). He was also the one that began a tradition later popes would follow, i.e., meddling and giving decisions in cases of dispute, something referred to as the decretals.[29] The eminent position of the bishop of Rome assumed great importance during the pontificate of Leo the Great (440–461) who championed the theory that the Bishop of Rome was the successor of the apostle Peter.

28. Orlandis, *A Short History of the Catholic Church*, 20.

29. Holmes and Bickers, *A Short History of the Catholic Church*, 39.

ORIGIN AND RISE OF MONASTICISM

Constantine's conversion to Christianity left a remarkable imprint on Christianity. By the time he died Christianity was not yet the official state religion of Rome. But "his policies and those of his successors left their mark in the religious life of the Roman Empire"[30] that by the time Christianity became the official state religion in the late fourth century "the church, which until then was composed mostly of people from the lower echelons of society, made headway among the aristocracy."[31] Constantine, before his death, supported the Christian faith with the power of the state, building churches in Byzantium (which he changed to Constantinopolis, meaning the City of Constantine).[32] Some of the net result of Constantine's conversion was codification of Christian worship. "Christian worship became ever more formal, in part imitating the usage of the court. There also began to develop a typically Christian architecture, whose most common expression was the type of church known as 'basilica.'"[33]

The support the Church got from the state as the official state religion was a mixed bag. "The change was not easy, and Christians responded in many different ways. Some were so grateful for the new situation that it was difficult for them to take a critical stance before the government and society."[34] Some who were fed up with the level of corruption or the level of "worldliness" Christianity had degenerated in the empire began to flee to the desert, particularly the desert of Egypt, to practice what in Greek was known as *askesis* (athletic training), i.e. asceticism. These people lived a life of total self-denial, which they saw as a new form of martyrdom. They were described as "athletes for Christ."[35] Their goal, which was to attain *apatheia* (a state of inner peace), was achieved in a two-step process: *apotasis*, i.e. total renunciation of the world, and *enkrateia*, subduing one's passions by living a life of poverty, chastity, and obedience.[36] This became the origin of monasticism. Athanasius, the bishop of Alexandria (c. 297–373), writes in his biography, *The Life of Anthony* that the first person to practice this kind of life was Anthony of Egypt. Anthony withdrew to the deserts of Egypt in 271 CE to live a life of hermit (solitary life). He sought perfection in prayer,

30. Gonzalez, *Church History*, 33.

31. Ibid.

32. Ibid.

33. Ibid., 34.

34. Ibid.

35. Cunningham, *The Catholic Heritage*, 28.

36. Ibid., 29.

fasting, and penance. He began a lifestyle known as the eremitical tradition of asceticism. Eremitical tradition of asceticism is a solitary lifestyle in which a hermit seeks perfection by waging spiritual war against his own demons. A second form of asceticism was begun by Pachomius (290–346 CE) who practiced cenobitical lifestyle (life in common or community). This was communal-based— a group of like-minded people lived together in search of perfection. This kind of monastic life is known as cenobitical tradition of asceticism. Like hermits, cenobites (monks who live in common) pursued a life of prayer, fasting and self-denial. The cenobitical lifestyle soon became popular throughout the Christian world, thanks to the efforts of men like Basil the Great (c. 329–379). Basil wrote a Rule to guide the day-to-day life of the monk. He also put great effort into organizing cenobitical style of monasticism. There was also Benedict of Nursia (c. 480–547 A.D.), whose monastic Rule was adopted in the West. Another great advocate of monasticism was Augustine, one of the most important figures of Western (Latin) Christianity whose life journeys and encounter with Christianity we discussed at length in chapter six.

EARLY ECUMENICAL COUNCILS

We have seen some of the internal threats that plagued the Christian church in the early years of its existence. We also saw how the Church dealt with these threats that came in the form of heresies (false teachings), particularly Gnosticism, Montanism, and Marcionism. But as debilitating as these threats were, they pale in comparison to the controversy surrounding Arianism, a theological problem that began in Alexandria and would later spread to the whole of the Christian world. The controversy led to the first ecumenical Council that authoritatively defined the Christian creed (statement of faith about God, church, and human salvation).

The Council of Nicaea (325 CE)

The conversion of Constantine that helped the Church politically did not put an end to the Church's internal conflicts. A priest in Alexandria, Arius, became the focus of a theological dispute that threatened to split the church. By the fourth century, as we pointed out earlier, there had developed in the early Church two important theological centers that rivaled each other and tried to outdo the other. One was the theological school of Antioch in Syria and the other was the theological school of Alexandria in Egypt. Arius, who

grew up in Libya, was a product of the school of Antioch.[37] In his interpretation of the Logos in John 1:1 and the relationship of this Logos to the
Father, Arius argued that the Logos was God's first creature, but a created
being nevertheless. This teaching, which subordinates the Son to the Father
and which gained popular appeal among the followers of Arius, is sometimes known as subordinationism. Arianism or subordinationism led to a
big theological controversy that forced Constantine to convoke a council
to settle the dispute. This council, which was attended by as many as three
hundred bishops from Asia Minor, opened in Nicaea on May 20, 325 A.D.

Constantine convoked the Council by virtue of his position both as
the emperor and the pontifex maximus (chief priest or "bridge builder"), a
title he assumed after his victorious battle over his rival Maxentius, which
made him to think he was put on the throne by God to be the chief defender
of the Christian faith.[38] Although Nicaea was the first official ecumenical
gathering of the Church, there is no official record of the proceedings of the
Council.[39] But we do know that those in attendance were unanimous in
their condemnation of Arius. They affirmed the divinity of the Son, Jesus,
and produced a creedal formula, the **Nicene Creed**, which proclaimed the
Son as being *homoousios* (consubstantial) with the Father. But this non-
scriptural Greek word, *homoousios*, which some of the bishops felt had its
origin in gnostic literature, would later become another contentious issue
for the Church to deal with.

The Council of Constantinople (381 CE)

The condemnation of Arius by the Council of Nicaea did not fully resolve
the Arian controversy, especially for three reasons. First, there was the
contentious issue of *homoousios*. Second, Arianism resurfaced in different
forms, taking different variations: the *Anomeans* who stressed the difference
between the Father and the Son, the Semi-Arians who stressed the likeness
between the Father and the Son, and the *Homeans* thought there was (only)
a similarity between the Father and the Son. Third, the death of Constantine in 337 A.D. At Constantine's death the empire was divided between
his three sons, each one favoring a different theological position, further
fueling the theological divide in the empire. There were, however, those like
Athanasius who continued to champion the Nicene orthodoxy. When Athanasius died in 373 A.D. the Cappadocian Fathers (Gregory Nizianzus, Basil

37. Hogan, *Dissent from the Creed*, 79.

38. Ibid., 82.

39. Jones, *Constantine and the Conversion of Europe*, 129.

of Caesarea and his brother Gregory of Nyssa) emerged as the leaders of the Nicene orthodoxy and laid the groundwork for the impending Council of Constantinople.

The Cappadocian Fathers, realizing that the Western part of the empire and the Eastern half of the empire were drifting more and more apart because of cultural, linguistic, and theological differences, saw "no solution to the continuing theological difficulties unless the West and East could talk with each other and understand what the other was trying to say. Further, they understood that some solution to the question of the Holy Spirit had to be found."[40] They sought imperial cooperation which they thought was needed to settle the divisive question of the relationship of the Holy Spirit to the Father and the Son.

In May 381 emperor Theodosius saw the need for a council of the Church in Constantinople. Appolinarius (c.310–395 A.D.) taught that Christ was not fully human, that in Christ the human spirit was replaced by the divine logos. Apollinarius went on to affirm the divinity of Christ while denying his humanity. The council of Constantinople that met in 381 A.D. condemned Apollinarius, reaffirmed the decisions of Nicaea and added a statement about the Holy Spirit to the creed. This statement states that the Holy Spirit "proceeds from the Father," and is not, therefore, created, but strictly speaking divine like the Son. Thus the additions of the council of Constantinople to the Nicene Creed gave birth to the Nicaea-Constantinople creed. Although the council of Constantinople was the second ecumenical council of the Church, it was not until the fourth ecumenical council at Chalcedon in 451 (70 years later) that the 381 council of Constantinople was officially recognized as the ecumenical council of the whole Church.[41] We should point out that in 9th century CE the West added the phrase "and the Son" to Constantinople's statement about the procession of the Holy Spirit. This changed the text to read, at least in the West, that the Holy Spirit "proceeds from the Father and the Son." This addition, which in Latin was known as the *filioque*, had no Greek equivalent. It became a source of more argument and misunderstanding and (unwarranted) mutual condemnations between the East and the West.

The Council of Ephesus (431 CE)

The Christological controversies soon took a new twist. The Church had struggled with how best to respond to people who denied the divinity of

40. Hogan, *Dissent from the Creed*, 97.
41. Ibid., 98.

Christ (Arianists) and those who denied the humanity of Christ (Apollinarians). Since there was no precise terminology to express the union of these two natures in Christ, it seemed to some that there were two persons in Christ.[42] Related to this was the popular piety that emerged very early in the Church's liturgical life in which Mary, the mother of Jesus, was venerated and honored as "Theotokos," i.e. God bearer. The origin of this title goes back to the struggle against Apollinarius who had been condemned for propounding a doctrine that questioned the humanity of Christ. The opponents of Apollinarius countered by affirming the divinity of Jesus. If Jesus is God and Mary is the mother of Jesus then Mary must be the mother of God, they reasoned. But such honorific title did not go down well with Emperor Theodosius II and the bishop of Constantinople, Nestorius (c. 428 A.D), who decided to clamp down on those promoting the Marian title because of its negative link with the heretic, Apollinarius. But what the emperor and the bishop did not realize was that in spite of its connection with Apollinarius, the Marian title, *theotokos*, had assumed a position of orthodoxy and was now championed by such eminent personality as Cyril of Alexandria who had earlier been involved in other controversies with Nestorius. The conflict between Cyril and Nestorius "was partly a clash of strong personalities. In addition to the personality clash, there was also the rivalry between Antioch, represented by Nestorius, and Alexandria, represented by Cyril. . . Alexandria emphasized the divinity of Christ, while Antioch was more concerned (but not exclusively so) with Christ's humanity."[43]

The Christological issue now turned into a conflict between Cyril of Alexandria and Nestorius who saw an opportunity to charge Cyril with heresy. For Nestorius, Mary could not be properly called the "Mother of God" but the "Mother of the Christ." Nestorius offered two good reasons for his argument. First, if Mary is the mother of God it would imply that the divine nature was born, suffered, and died. Second, since God is unchangeable one can never impute to God the changing process of birth, suffering, and death.[44] Cyril denounced Nestorius' view, charging that Nestorius denied the divinity of Christ and offended the dignity of Mary by refusing to apply to Mary the title "Theotokos." A general council was convened in Ephesus in 431 CE to settle this Christological question. Nestorius refused to attend and was charged with heresy by the council which deposed him and sided with Cyril. They affirmed the Nicene and Constantinople creed and declared "Theotokos" orthodox Christian doctrine.

42. Ibid., 123.

43. Ibid., 127.

44. Ibid., 124.

The Council of Chalcedon (451 CE)

Another controversy broke out in 446 CE, this time regarding a leader of a large monastery in Constantinople, Eutyches, who denied the two natures of Christ. This heresy known as monophysitism emphasized the divinity of Christ while denying his humanity. It was popular among local Christians in Egypt. The council of Chalcedon met in 451 CE, condemned monophysitism, and declared: "We believe and we teach one and the same Christ in two natures, unmixed and unchanged, undivided and unseparated." The union of the two natures of Christ, according to the Council, is preserved in one hypostasis (person). Some Christians, especially Egyptian Christians, refused to accept the declaration of Chalcedon and held on to Monophysite doctrine and later formed their own Coptic church.

CHRISTIANITY IN AFRICA

Africa is the ancient home of the Christian religion. It is common today to hear some Christian antagonists call Christianity a "white man's religion." In our chapter on Islam we shall discuss Islam as a religion, beginning from its early beginnings in Arabian Peninsula to its development in non-Middle Eastern cultures, like the United States. We shall see how Black Muslims in the US, i.e., Muslims who belong to the Nation of Islam, refer to Christianity as a "white man's religion," as part of their effort to show Black Americans why they should discard Christianity and embrace Islam. But Jesus was, from the very beginning, connected to Africa. The Gospel narratives relate how Jesus was born in Bethlehem at a time the whole civilized world was under the rule of Roman Empire. The greatness of Rome, apart from its military might, was evidenced in how it united and brought distant provinces under its control by a unified administration with an efficient communication and transport system. Jesus' parents, according to the Gospel narratives, out of concern for the safety of the infant Jesus, had to flee Bethlehem in a hurry for Egypt because of threat from Herod, the district governor of the Romans. The flight to Egypt was in effect the first tradition connecting the Christian story to the African continent.[45]

Apart from refuting the mistaken notion that Christianity is a "white man's religion," the history of Christianity cannot be complete without situating it in its African context. From the very beginning "Africans played a prominent role in the life and expansion of the early Church."[46] Some of the

45. Sanneh, *West African Christianity*, 1.
46. Ibid.

best and prominent theologians of the early Church came from Africa. A famous early center of Christian activity was the ancient city of Alexandria, Egypt, the other two being Rome and Antioch. As part of the Roman Empire, Alexandria also had some sizeable Jewish population. Jews had been attracted to Egypt when Egypt became part of the Roman Empire in 30 BCE. Many of them took part in the research and scholarship that was going on in Alexandria and some were converted to Christianity. One of such men was Philo of Alexandria who attempted a synthesis of the Christian faith using Greek philosophy. As far back as 280 BCE what is known as the Septuagint, the Greek translation of the Old Testament was carried out in Alexandria—"the first translation of any part of the Bible into a foreign language. It was later used by Christians who, in response to Jewish taunts that they had no access to the Hebrew original, developed a myth that the Septuagint was divinely inspired, the work of seventy translators in seventy days, working independently and producing miraculously identical texts."[47]

The Catechetical school of Alexandria, which was famous for its great learning and allegorical interpretation of scripture, was led by Clement of Alexandria. Although Clement was not a native of Alexandria (he was born in Greece and migrated to Alexandria in 180 CE), Alexandria produced some famous second century figures like Origen and Athanasius, and the fourth century dominant figure, Cyril of Alexandria. By the 7th century BCE Greeks had populated the ancient city of Alexandria that was in 331 BCE named after one of the foremost rulers in Greek history, Alexandria the Great.

There were several prominent Church theologians of African origin in North Africa, like Tertullian of Carthage who in the third century became the first Christian theologian to use Latin in his writings instead of the customary Greek, and the great Augustine of Hippo of the fourth and early fifth centuries.[48] Tertullian brought vitality and vigor to early Christianity. "He is regarded as the father of Latin Christianity in the sense of having created a Latin vocabulary for Christian theology. He was the first to formulate and coin the term 'Trinity,' marshalling reasons as to its central place in the Church's teachings.[49] Pope John Paul II did not mince words in recalling the glorious splendor of Africa's Christian past: "We think of the Christian Churches of Africa whose origins go back to the times of the Apostles and are traditionally associated with the name and teaching of Mark the Evangelist. We think of their countless Saints, Martyrs, Confessors, and Virgins,

---

47. Isichei, *A History of Christianity in Africa*, 16.

48. Schwarz, *Theology in a Global Context*, 501.

49. Sanneh, *West African Christianity*, 8.

and recall the fact that from the second to the fourth centuries. Christian life in the North of Africa was most vigorous and had a leading place in theological study and literary production."[50]

Asceticism and the African Origins of Monasticism

Christian monasticism began in Africa. Its origin is traceable to Anthony of Egypt (251–356 CE) who fled to the desert of Egypt to seek communion with God. Anthony began the eremitical tradition of monasticism, living alone as a hermit. There was also Pachomius (290–345 CE), the man from Upper Egypt who was born of pagan parents. He converted to Christianity and began the cenobitical tradition of monasticism. The cenobitical tradition stressed communal life and ascetical practices under the leadership of an elected leader called the abbot. Anthony and Pachomius were the first founders of the monastic life that later spread and further developed in the East and West. According to John Paul II, it was because of the examples of these saintly men that Africa produced some saintly (African) Popes in the likes of Victor I, Melchiades, and Gelasius I whose noble examples enrich the common heritage of the Christian Church. There were also, in the first century Church of Africa, saintly African Christian women like Saints Perpetua and Felicitas, Saint Monica, and Saint Thelca.[51] Perpetua was an African woman mystic. She was married with a son. She and her slave Felicity and their other companions were martyred in Carthage in 203 CE. Their martyrdom and sacrifice was symbolic of the sacrifices of early African Christians who gave their lives for the faith at the time of great persecution.

Arab Conquest of North Africa

Islam came to Africa in the 7th century when an Arab force invaded Egypt seven years after the death of the Holy prophet Muhammad. The invading Muslims surrounded Egypt and the whole of North Africa, renaming it the "Maghrib," an Arabic word for "West." Before the Arab conquest Christianity had concentrated mainly in North Africa. "The Sahara and the difficult terrain of the mountain Berbers sealed off the church from active contact with sub-Saharan peoples, whom Christianity was to reach mainly by way of the sea."[52] The Arab conquest further prevented the spread of Christianity to

---

50. John Paul II, *Ecclesia in Africa* 31; quoting Pope Paul VI.

51. John Paul II, *Ecclesia in Africa*, 31.

52. Sanneh, *West African Christianity*, 13.

the southern interior. Even North Africa that had been Christianized before the conquest, Christianity completely disappeared in several places with the exception of Egypt where the Orthodox Coptic Church remained powerful. The people known as the Copts were ancient Egyptians who lived mostly in the rural areas and practiced the old religions of the Pharaohs before the advent of Christianity. In the middle of the third century many Coptic villages and towns along the Nile embraced Christianity.[53] The Copts were noted for their rich liturgical and sacramental practices. Even when Islam took over North Africa the Copts still kept their Christian traditions. The Muslim conquerors must have been lenient with Copts who paid their poll tax in return for religious toleration. The Arabs appreciated the Copts as taxpayers and even sometimes intermarried with them and allowed them to keep their language and traditions. By the end of the tenth century most Egyptian Christians spoke Coptic. But by the end of the twelfth century most spoke Arabic and thereafter Christian literature was translated into Arabic.[54]

By the beginning of the eleventh century there was hardly any trace of Christianity in that region of Africa known as the Maghrib. Islam had predominated and Christian churches and cathedrals had been converted into mosques. The Portuguese who explored the coast of Africa in the fifteenth and sixteenth century attempted a re-evangelization of the African continent, setting up posts in the present day Benin, Sao-Tome, Angola, Mozambique, and Madagascar. The Portuguese did not only come for evangelization, they also came for commerce, dealing with the export of slaves from Africa to Europe and the New World which they monopolized between 1440 and 1640.

In 1491 Christian missionaries from Europe sailed into Pinda, the mouth of the Zaire River and with the help of the great king of Congo, Nzinga-a-Nkuwu, set up Christian missions and erected Episcopal Sees. The result of this mission was the consecration in 1518 by Pope Leo X of Don Henrique, the son of Don Alfonso I, King of Congo, as Titular Bishop of Utica. Don Henrique went on to become the first native bishop of Black Africa.[55]

The second phase of the evangelization of Africa came to an abrupt end in the eighteenth century, making way for the third phase, which began in the nineteenth century with the European exploration of the African interior. European powers established colonies throughout Africa, ushering

53. Ibid., 8.

54. Isichei, *A History of Christianity in Africa*, 43.

55. John Paul II, *Ecclesia in Africa*, 32.

in the era of colonialism. It is in this colonial context that Christianity was re-introduced to Africa. This is why we have "predominantly Roman Catholic-Christianity in the former Belgian Congo region, British (Anglican) Christianity in Kenya, and a strong Lutheran church in Namibia. South Africa was settled in the seventeenth century by Dutch immigrants and later conquered by the British, so Anglican and Dutch Reformed churches prevail there."[56]

In the Roman Catholic context, the list of saints that Africa gives to the Church continues to grow: Blessed Clementine Anwarite, a virgin and martyr of Zaire was beatified in 1985 by Pope John Paul II; Blessed Victoria Rasoamanarivo of Madagascar and Blessed Josephine Bakhita of Sudan were also beatified by John Paul II, Blessed Isidore Bakanja, martyr of Zaire, there were also the Martyrs of Uganda and Blessed Cyprian Tansi of Nigeria, to mention a few.

56. Schwarz, *Theology in a Global Context*, 501.

9

Schism and Reformation

C.S. LEWIS FAMOUSLY DESCRIBED the history of the Church as similar to that of an onion, each period becoming a new layer. Using this metaphor, Glenn Olson notes: "If, under the assumption that the best was at the beginning, one attempts to peel through the accrued layers in search of the purported pure and perfect beginnings beyond which all development was distortion or decline, one ends up destroying the onion."[1] The history of the Reformation has been written from different viewpoints. But like an onion, some of its layers are pleasant and joyful, others not so pleasant. And far from being completely peeled off and consigned to the annals of the past, the effects of the unpleasant (layer) division of the body of Christ linger to this day. "Our pasts have made us whatever we are and on that capital we have to live or else we must begin afresh."[2] To retrieve the past, consider:

> Suppose a man suffers total amnesia. He no longer knows who he is, fails to recognize relatives and friends, does not recall his commitments or his lawful expectations, does not know where he works or how he makes his living, and has lost even the information needed to perform his once customary tasks. Obviously, if he is to live, either the amnesia has to be cured, or else he must start all over.[3]

It is erroneous to think that the Reformation was caused by a single act. The events that led to the Reformation were an accumulation of many factors:

1. Olsen, *Beginning At Jerusalem*, 39.
2. Lonergan, *Method in Theology*, 181.
3. Ibid.

economic, social, political, and religious, some of which the participants at the time were oblivious.

THE GREAT SCHISM AND CONCILIAR MOVEMENT

A movement known as **Conciliarism** emerged in the Middle Ages. Conciliarism taught the doctrine of supremacy of general councils over the pope, not only in matters pertaining to the well-being of the whole Church, but also in matters of faith. The conciliar movement gained momentum because of the failure of the popes to provide leadership to a fragmented Church in need of reform. It was also impelled by the Great Western Schism. Both, particularly the Great-Schism that ranks as one of the most difficult problems of late Medieval Church history,[4] combined to create a degenerate condition that later 16th century reformers would capitalize on,

The Great-Schism produced two popes, Urban VI (1378–89) in Rome and Clement VII in Avignon (1378–94), each one claiming to be the legitimate pope and denouncing the other as schismatic heretic. This rivalry led to a divided loyalty, not only among the hierarchy but especially among the faithful. Italy, England, Hungary, most of the German empires, and the Nordic countries, for example, recognized Urban as the true pope, while France, Naples, Savoy, Scotland, Aragon, and Castile pledged allegiance to Clement.[5] The situation got messy when Urban was succeeded by Boniface IX (1389–1404) and Clement was succeeded by Benedict XIII (1394–1423). Boniface died in Rome and was himself succeeded by Innocent VII. Innocent died within two years and was succeeded by Gregory XII (1406–15).

The rival claimants to the papacy before it was finally resolved were Pope Gregory in Rome and Pope Benedict in Avignon. When the schism finally ended, thanks to the Council at Pisa (March 1409-August 7 1409), which declared (June 5, 1409) the Roman see vacant and the two rival popes "notorious schismatics and obdurate heretics," the schism had lasted for more than thirty years.[6] In the interest of peace the cardinals of the two rival camps united and elected a neutral pope, the archbishop of Milan, who took the name Pope Alexander V (1409–10). Although the election of Alexander V brought temporary relief, the damage had been done. The schism severely impaired the Church and the "division of allegiance to the 'heads'

---

4. Fink, *History of the Church*, 402. See also La Due, *The Chair of Saint Peter*, 157.

5. La Due, *The Chair of St. Peter*, 157.

6. Ibid., 157–58.

of Christianity greatly accelerated the break-up of Western Christendom in the sixteenth century."[7]

The relief brought by the election of Alexander V did not last long. "Benedict XIII (Avignon) and Gregory XII (Rome) still had their faithful followers, so the crisis in many ways became more pressing than ever. Now the Christian people had to deal with three papal claimants."[8] Since the schismatic popes did not provide the kind of leadership the church needed, some learned men (conciliar theorists) suggested that only a general council of the church could carry out the much-needed sweeping reforms. Also men like Pierre d'Ailly (1351–1420) and Jean Gerson (1363–1429) of France, and Nicholas of Cusa (1401–1464) of Germany advanced the argument that "only a general council represented the will of the entire Church and could end the schism, reform the church, and put an end to heresy."[9] There were also some teachers of cannon law who suggested that the cardinals have a right to call a council and that when such councils convene the popes should be bound by the decisions of the council. These canonists or decretists (commentators on the Decretum of Gratian, 1140) as they were called, argued that although the Church itself could not err in declaring the faith, the pope alone did not enjoy that prerogative since previous pontiffs had fallen into error.[10]

> Accordingly a number of cardinals from each papal obedience, or rule, agreed to call a meeting of a council at Pisa in 1409. Although this body acted too rapidly and made matters worse by creating a third pope without compelling the other two to resign, the principle of a limited papacy had gained wide acceptance. The Council of Constance (1414–18), called at the insistence of Emperor Sigismund, proceeded more cautiously and finally succeeded in ending the papal schism. Although it failed to solve the problem of heresy by having Hus, Jerome of Prague, and the bones of Wycliffe burned, and made little progress with reforms, it enunciated two revolutionary decrees. The one, called, *Sacro sancta* (1415), stated that the general council had its authority directly from Christ and that therefore the entire church was bound by its decisions. The second, called *Frequens* (1417), provided for regular meetings of the general council.[11] .

7. Ullmann, *The Origins of the Great Schism*, 96. See also La Due, *The Chair of Saint Peter*, 157.

8. Ibid., 158.

9. Grimm, *The Reformation Era: 1500–1650*, 45.

10. La Due, *The Chair of Saint Peter*, 158.

11. Grimm, *The Reformation Era*, 46–47.

The Council of Constance (1414–1418) may have ended the Great Western Schism, at least temporarily. But the problem persisted when the Fathers of the Council elected Martin V pope, and the long awaited reform failed to materialize.[12] The French clergy, dissatisfied about the inability of the church to carry out reforms, took advantage of the weakness of the hierarchy during this Great Schism and appealed to Charles VII to convene an assembly of his clergy at Bourges for the purpose of carrying out reforms in the French church. At Bourges (1438) the French church not only reaffirmed the conciliar theory of the supremacy of the council over the pope, but also laid down some basic liberties ("Gallican liberties"):

1. The right of the French church to elect its own clergy without papal interference

2. The prohibition of the payment of *annates* (taxes on inferior benefices and tithes) to the papacy and

3. The limitation of the number of appeals from the French courts to the Roman Curia.[13] .

Tensions between the papacy and the conciliarists continued even after the "Gallican liberties." The Council of Basel (1431–49) attempted to resolve this problem, as well as the issue of reform and heresy. The conciliarists continued to stress the supremacy of the council over the papacy and the role of the council as the supreme authority in the Church. Though at the close of the Council of Basel in 1449 there emerged the recognition of papal power as the supreme authority, the tension between papalism and conciliarism was to be one of the battleground issues of the reformation. Sadly, some of the popes preoccupied themselves with temporal (secular) matters, concerning themselves less with religious affairs. Much of their time and energy were devoted to politics, a trend that was resented by many.[14]

Growth of Humanism

Although humanism was by no means identical with the Reformation, it did much to prepare the way.[15] The beginning of the humanist movement is traceable to one of the famous poets of the 14th century, Francesco Petrarch (1307–74) who, drawing his inspiration from ancient writings, particularly

---

12. Kapr, *Johann Gutenberg,* 59.

13. Grimm, *The Reformation Era,* 46.

14. Holmes & Bickers, *A Short History of the Catholic Church,* 118.

15. Grimm, *The Reformation Era,* 85.

Greek and Roman literature, emphasized the importance of education.[16] Petrarch's love for ancient wisdom inspired him to learn Greek. He was struck by the works of Homer, which he translated into Latin for the benefit of his contemporaries who could not read Greek. Petrarch was able to express in his poetry the beauty of nature and the uniqueness of each individual human person.[17]

The work of Petrarch sparked interest in education and the study of languages. Other humanists soon emerged and began to concentrate their energy on literature, biblical exegesis, and general education, their priority being to reform the church. They saw education as the only effective means of achieving this goal. Like Petrarch, the humanists saw good in the human person. The human person, for them, is not just a rational being, but a sentient rational being who can appreciate music, literature, and the arts. The impact of the humanist ideals was felt in Rome. Though some popes seemed hostile to the humanist ideals, others embraced their devotion to music and the arts. During the reign of Sixtus IV (1471–84), for instance, a lot of renovations were carried out in the Palace Chapel of the Vatican.[18] The famous Sistine Chapel was built at this time. Julius II (1503–13) commissioned the building of St. Peter's basilica and the re-painting of the Sistine Chapel by Michelangelo. All these were largely due to the influence of the humanists whose love for music and the arts was unparalleled.[19]

The humanist movement paved way for what would become the Renaissance (15th /16th cent). Renaissance is from the Italian *rinascuta*, meaning "rebirth." It was used in reference to the rebirth of the styles of ancient Rome and Greece in the spheres of literature and art.[20] Towards the end of the Middle Ages, some Italian cities, Venice and Florence especially, spurred by economic prosperity, on the one hand, and the desire to free themselves from excessive Church control (papal domination), on the other, strove for independence from the Holy Roman Empire.[21] They saw no reason why the church should interfere in the secular affairs of the city-states. The humanists turned to the work Cicero to propound their theory of city-state. "Just as Thomas Aquinas previously had turned to Aristotelian theory to develop the concept of the state, the early civic humanists turned

16. Holmes & Bickers, *A Short History of the Catholic Church*, 119.

17. Ibid.

18. Ibid., 121.

19. Ibid.

20. Ibid., 119.

21. Feldman, *Please Don't Wish Me A Merry Christmas*, 50.

to Cicero."[22] They emphasized the Ciceronian concept of virtues (that virtue which unites wisdom with eloquence) and sharply contrasted it with the Thomistic-Augustinian Christian view of human nature.[23] "Whereas Augustinians saw only human depravity and sin, the humanists believed people, as citizens, could achieve excellence in political and civil society."[24] It was in this new context that the notion of "the Middle Ages' arose. The period between classical culture and the Renaissance now was seen as a sort of cultural depression between two creative periods.

The humanist ideals were expressed in the Renaissance and led to the theory of separation of church and state, separation of temporal and spiritual powers. The most renowned humanist whose work embodied the call for separation between the two powers was the sixteenth century political writer, Niccolo Machiavelli (1469–1527) who believed that the preservation and liberty of the republic are the highest values (common good) that every citizen should do whatever it takes to preserve. He argued that Christianity undermines the citizen's devotion to liberty because it renders people humble and feeble, making them too willing to submit to tyranny. He saw Christianity as something inimical to the preservation of the republic.[25] Machiavelli further opened the conceptual gap between church and state, arguing in *The Prince* (1513)[26] that the state would do better without religion because Christianity corrupted political affairs.[27]

Johann Gutenberg & William Caxton

The birth of Johann Gutenberg (1396–1468) was to be an added impetus to the cause of the humanist movement in the 15th century. Gutenberg was born in Mainz (anywhere between 1394 and 1404) where he also went to school and developed his bent for research and discovery.[28] Gutenberg discovered the first printing press when in 1450 he invented a typecasting machine and in 1455 printed the "Gutenberg Bible," also known as the "42 line bible" because it had forty-two lines to each column.[29] The cause of the

---

22. Ibid.
23. Ibid.
24. Ibid.
25. Ibid., 52.
26. See Machiavelli, *The Prince*.
27. Feldman, *Please Don't Wish Me A Merry Christmas*, 52
28. Kapr, *Johann Gutenberg*, 25.
29. Holmes & Bickers, *A Short History of the Catholic Church*, 122.

humanists, in general, was helped by the discovery of printing, a discovery that was to play a pivotal role during the reformation.

The Englishman William Caxton (1422–91) was another key figure in the printing field. Caxton did not invent printing; he merely introduced it to England.[30] In 1474 he printed, in Cologne, the first book in English, The Histories of Troy. He also established in Westminster a printing press, the place that printed in 1476 The Indulgence of Sixtus IV, the first book printed in England, and in 1484 printed Chaucer's *Canterbury Tales*.

Erasmus & Thomas More

Most of the 15th century humanists were what was considered then as ordinary non-ordained people. Since they were not ordained members of the Church they were virtually free from any kind of censorship that could come from the church. They devoted their time to scholarship and were, for the most part, critical of the church, bringing to light the weaknesses and abuses in the church. They were irked by what was perceived as the igno-rance of the clergy and their lack of education. They also spoke out against over clericalization of the church and some of the popular piety of the time, which in their view, bordered on superstition. Two of the famous humanists of this period were Erasmus, who incidentally was an ordained clergyman, and Thomas More, a lawyer and statesman. These two spoke out against the abuses in the church, called for reform, but refused to be part of the reform movement that severed ties with Rome. One of More's main works was *Utopia* (1516), a work in which he satirically presented the dilemma of the Christian religion in a world subject to fools as leaders and followers.

Erasmus (1466–1536) was concerned with Christian history. His con-ception of history was Christocentric. For him, all history was, in a sense, Christian history. He saw Christian history as proceeding in the wrong di-rection. "In the Middle Ages, especially in the last few centuries, faith had grown cold, and humanity had become distracted by care for mere outward things. Erasmus saw it as his task, at least in his mature years, to direct the process and to lay the foundations for liberation of the soul."[31] In his view, sacred and cultural history were inextricably intertwined and he saw in the study of ancient literature, i.e. Greek and Latin classics and the Bible, the restoration of cultural, intellectual, moral, and spiritual standards of the society that had hitherto been in decline because of the neglect of these

---

30. Blake, *Caxton and His World*, 13.

31. Bejczy, *Erasmus and the Middle Ages*, xiii.

studies.[32] Erasmus blamed the intellectual decline of the high Middle Ages on the moral degeneration of the Christian world of the time and criticized the clergy and religious for what he perceived as their ignorance, pride, idleness, luxury, and superstition.[33]

The Rise of Mysticism

The medieval Church, especially the 14th / 15th century Church, witnessed a spiritual revival that blossomed into a mystical piety. Not all popular piety which the humanists criticized for their superstition boarded on superstition in the true sense of the word. There were some real genuine piety that led to the rise of mysticism. Mysticism was a natural product of the flourishing monastic life of the period. "The two usual preconditions for mysticism, an ascetic life that allows one to overcome the pull of the body's delight in things physical and a life devoted to prayer, meditation and contemplation that open one to the 'still, small voice,' are more easily attained by nuns, monks, anchoresses and hermits than by lay people whose lives are dominated by the affairs of daily life and the needs of the body—food, drink, shelter, children."[34] Though most of the well-known mystics lived in the 14th century, their influence was all the more felt in the 15th century and greatly impacted the Reformation.

> Usually, this mysticism did not attack the church openly, nor was it characterized by the intense emotional exaltation that is usually called mysticism. On the contrary, most of these mystics of the late Middle Ages were quiet and scholarly persons, who devoted themselves to study, meditation, and contemplation, but who did not set out to convert the entire church to their understanding of the Christian life. Nevertheless, their mere existence and their exemplary lives, coupled with the fact that many of them made little of the ecclesiastical hierarchy, made many wonder whether this was not an alternative way of being Christian.[35]

(a) Brethren of the Common Life

The origin of this group goes back to Gerard Groote (1340–84 A.D) who devoted himself to a life of simplicity. Groote studied in Paris

32. Ibid., xiv.

33. Ibid., 96–97.

34. Fanning, *Mystics of the Christian Tradition*, 75.

35. Gonzalez, *A History of Christian Thought*, 19.

and taught briefly in Cologne before he turned to asceticism. His preaching won him a band of followers who adopted a semi-monastic lifestyle known as the Brethren of Common Life.[36] Groote's preaching brought him in conflict with the diocesan clergy and the Mendicants who were bitter about his criticism of their way of life. He was accused of heresy and banned from preaching. His movement however continued. His followers spent time in prayer, devotion, and manual labor. They contributed to the mass production of manuscripts and the creation of schools where the best available education of the time was made available to the youth.[37]

The most famous student of the Brethren of the Common life was **Thomas a Kempis** (1380–1471), who was a student in Deventer, in the Netherlands. Though Thomas did not remain a member of the Brethren, he was partly responsible for one of the most famous spiritual classics of the time, *The Imitation of Christ*, a book that invites the reader to seek perfection through an assiduous following of Christ.[38] The book has four main divisions or sections: The first section stresses the need for self-control and aims to help the reader gain inner peace of mind by helping the reader to become humble. The second section deals with the need to persevere through suffering. The third section stresses God's power in aiding us through God's gift of grace. The fourth section deals with the sacrament of Holy Communion and gives the reader three practical exercises to help the reader appreciate the power of God's love.[39]

(b) German Mysticism

The origin of German mysticism goes back to **Meister Eckhart** (1260–1327/8). Eckhart was born Johannes Eckhart in Tubingen, Germany. He joined the Dominican Order at the age of fifteen and took up studies in Cologne, Germany, where he also taught and was given the title "Meister." Eckhart was a powerful preacher and spiritual director and wrote his works in German and Latin.[40] He later became the Dominican provincial of Saxony and was active in the administration of the Order. His mystical writings emphasized union with God through a mystical union of the soul. His mystical ideas were thought to have had much in common with Eastern thoughts, especially Ve-

---

36. Holmes & Bickers, *A Short History of the Catholic Church*, 124.

37. Gonzalez, *A History of Christian Thought*, 19.

38. Holmes & Bickers, *A Short History of the Catholic* Church, 125.

39. Ibid.

40. Fanning, *Mystics of the Christian Tradition*, 103.

dantic Hinduism and Zen Buddhism.[41] The Archbishop of Cologne later accused him of heresy and Pope John XXII condemned several propositions found in his works. This condemnation prevented many from embracing his teaching. His disciples, however, felt that he was not treated fairly and some took up his cause.

One of Eckhart's most famous disciple was **John Tauler** (1300–61). Tauler did not know Eckhart personally. He only came to know him through his writings. Tauler was born into a wealthy family in Strasbourg, at the time a German city and part of the Roman Empire. He joined the Dominican Order in 1314 and became famous for his preaching and spiritual directions.[42] Tauler, like Eckhart, stressed union with God through mystical union of the soul. He ensured the survival of the core of Meister Eckhart's apophatic mystical theology, admonishing that Christians shun vices, cultivate the virtues, and detach themselves from anything that is not God.[43] For Tauler, union with God is achieved through practical Christian charity.

Another disciple of Eckhart's and contemporary of Tauler's was the highly influential **Henry Suso** (1295–1366) who was born to a noble family in Constance, Switzerland. His real name was Henry von Berg, but he adopted the family name Sus (Latinized into Suso) to honor his mother.[44] Suso joined the Dominican Order in Constance at the tender age of thirteen. He went to Cologne for studies and there encountered Eckhart. He fell in love with the Meister's teaching and soon became a loyal disciple. Suso greatly defended the teachings of Eckhart, a defense that brought him in conflict with his Dominican superiors. He wrote a practical book of meditation called *The Little Book of Eternal Wisdom*.[45]

(C) English mystics

One of the famous English mystics was **Richard Rolle** (1300–49), a hermit from Yorkshire, who wrote most of his works in English and Latin. He went to school in Oxford but had to drop out because of what he perceived as the "aridity of the curriculum."[46] He considered what was taught at the universities "an arid and barren tower of truth" and turned to true prayer, which he claimed could never be found

41. Ibid; see also Eckhart, *Selected Writings*.

42. Fanning, *Mystics of the Christian Tradition.*, 104.

43. Ibid., 104–5.

44. Ibid., 105.

45. Holmes and Bickers, *A Short History of the Christian Church*, 123–4.

46. Ward, "The English Mystics," 50.

in another false tower, i.e. the monastery.[47] He became a hermit in Yorkshire where he sought mystical experience with God. He expressed his experience with God with three words: "heat," "sweetness," and "song" (*calor, dulcor, canor*). Rolle was also a prolific writer. Some of his works include, *The Fire of Love* and *The Emending of Life*. He also wrote several mystical works and scriptural commentaries.[48] He served as spiritual advisor and counselor to many Christians at the time. He extolled the solitary life as the surest way of experiencing God. He died in 1349, during the Black Death.[49]

There was a popular book at the time that was very much in the tradition of Richard Rolle, but not written by him, *The Cloud of Unknowing*. Though the author of the book is still unknown, it stresses the need to know God, not by reason, but by God's self-revelation, stressing also the need for contemplation and prayer.[50] The author of this work must have known the mystical theology of Pseudo-Dionysius because he or she refers to Dionysius by name. The author must have also been familiar with the apophatic approach of Pseudo-Dionysius who denied that God could be found through intellect and reason. Rather, "the Cloud of unknowing," that surrounds God, the author insists, can be penetrated only by love.[51] The author insists that true prayer means an increase in love, a love that goes beyond knowledge, leading to a new way of understanding or responding to God's call of love.[52]

Another influential English mystic was the lady **Julian of Norwich** (1342–1413). Her actual name is unknown. She is referred to as Julian only because of her association with the church of St. Julian in Norwich.[53] She told the story of how she became ill at the age of thirty and during her illness fell into a trance lasting about five hours during which she received fifteen revelations. She received another vision the following day and after years of reflecting on her visions wrote *The Revelation of Divine Love*. Her book stresses belief in the passion and cross of Christ and the eventual triumph of love as seen in the final expulsion of evil.[54] Julian may have had a single, near-death

---

47. Ibid., 51. See Rolle, *The Fire of Love* and Rolle, "The Form of Living."
48. Holmes & Bickers, *A Short History of the Catholic Church*, 125–6.
49. Fanning, *Mystics of the Christian Tradition*, 119.
50. Holmes & Bickers, *A Short History of the Christian Church*, 126.
51. Fanning, Mystics *of the Christian Tradition*, 124.
52. Ward, "The English Mystics," 55. See also Walsh, ed., *Cloud of Unknowing*.
53. Fanning, *Mystics of the Christian Tradition*, 124.
54. Holmes and Bickers, *A Short History of the Catholic Church*, 126.

mystical experience, an experience that completely changed her life, making her to become an anchoress in a single-room cell attached to the church of St. Julian.[55] Julian was noted for having popularized the feminine imagery of God. She constantly referred to God as mother, a maternal imagery that goes back to Paul and the Hebrew Scriptures. But Julian emphasized it more frequently that she became associated with it.

Popular Piety

Due in part to the influence of the mystics and the spiritual classics that were circulating in the 15th century, two major themes dominated the preaching manuals of the time: Death and Judgment. The preachers of the gospel were primarily concerned with preparing people for death. They encouraged the dying person not to despair at the moment of death, but to look at the crucifix and remind themselves of the death of Christ. They also reminded people the judgment that follows death and stressed in graphic pictures the fate of those who go to heaven and the fate of those who go to hell.[56] In emphasizing the passion and death of Christ they hardly mentioned the resurrection, thereby portraying God, not as a loving Father, but a judge. Even the story of the prodigal son and the good shepherd, which portray God as a loving Father, was hardly ever mentioned. Instead the people got a good dose of the parable of the last judgment, i.e. the separation of the sheep and goats. This kind of preaching gave the people an image of a distant God, even Christ, the sole mediator between God and his people seemed distant.[57]

Such a terrifying image of God led to a popular piety in which people approached God through the help of mediators. Mary was seen as a person who could help in averting the anger and judgment of this distant and angry God. The Dominicans and Franciscans championed this cause of seeking intercessions through Mary. They stressed the recitation of the rosary. From this Marian devotion also emerged the cult of the saints. "In the Middle Ages its growth was luxuriant, and few valleys, territories, diseases, or professions lacked their specific saint, at once a protector and refuge in difficult times and an embodiment of some aspect of God's truth to be emulated."[58] The saints were seen as friends the people could turn to for help, so much so that with time some saints began to be associated with some specific skills.

55. Fanning, *Mystics of the Christian Tradition*, 125.

56. Holmes and Bickers, *A Short History of the Catholic Church*, 127.

57. Ibid.

58. Olsen, *Beginning At Jerusalem*, 49.

The early venerated saints were largely martyrs, except for Saint Martin of Tours who was born about four years after the conversion of Constantine and who died in 397 CE.[59] People turned to these saints for different favors. For instance, people turned to St. Dennis when they had headache because he was known for averting headaches, St. Vitus was for people suffering from epilepsy, St. Barbara for people afraid of lightning, St. Christopher for those in need of safe journey, and St. Margaret for people suffering from insanity.[60] Superstition aside, there were those who genuinely saw the saints as God's continuing revelation, each saint's life revealing something universal in something particular.[61]

Although the material remains of martyrs (relics) were accorded great respect in the early Church by Christians who celebrated the Eucharist over the tombs of the martyrs, devotion to the saints in the medieval church increased the importance attached to relics. There was increase in the demand for relics and in some cases some dismembered the saints' bodies and transferred them from place to place just to meet the demand for relics. People who went to Rome for pilgrimage often came back with bones and other objects of the saints. It was often not easy to verify such claims. Some saints were associated with particular shrines to which people made pilgrimages. Relics and pilgrimages were connected with indulgences. People believed they could be released from their temporary punishment from sin if they had particular relics or made particular pilgrimages. The reformers were quick to point out the abuses of such practice.[62]

In the early Church the Eucharist was the center of the Church's liturgical life. It was primarily community worship, the whole community gathered around the local bishop as a sign of this unity. The 15th century church seemed to depart from this practice. There was a fundamental change in the way the Eucharist was celebrated and also notable abuses. One of the abuses was the rise of "Private Mass," where the priest alone celebrated the mass in private. There was also the barrier that came from the use of Latin as the sole language of the liturgy. The bread used for mass was replaced with a thin wafer. The priest stopped offering the chalice to the laity. The laity was discouraged from receiving communion on a regular basis lest they receive it unworthily. There was also the fact of language. Given that the language of worship was Latin, people no longer understood what was going on at mass and depended on the priest for their understanding.

59. Ibid., 50–51.

60. Holmes and Bickers, *A Short History of the Catholic Church*, 127–8.

61. Olsen, *Beginning At Jerusalem*, 51.

62. Holmes and Bickers, *A Short History of the Christian Church.*, 128.

There were also some architectural changes: the priest now said mass with his back towards the people because altars were placed against the East Wall, side altars were built to facilitate private masses, communion rails were introduced, which mandated that the people kneel to receive communion in their tongue, "rood screens" were erected, which heightened the sense of awe, but also further increased the distance between the people and the priest. Emphasis was shifted from receiving communion to "seeing" the host. In an attempt to accommodate this, elevations of the consecrated host now lasted longer and bells were rung to remind people that elevation was going on. When bells rang, people rushed to catch a glimpse of the host in the belief that their fortunes would change for the better. In spite of the good intentions of these practices, a great deal of superstition crept into the Mass.[63] There was, to say the least, a great deal of change in the liturgy in the 14th/15th century. Some were positive changes, but a great deal bordered on superstition and abuses. The humanists and the reformers were quick to highlight these deficiencies but their call for change was stymied by the papacy.

SOCIAL CHANGES IN EUROPE

Remarkable change took place in the social structure of Europe at the end of the 15th century. The population of Western Europe that was hitherto 53 million in 1350 had risen to about 70 million in the 1500s. There was an uneven distribution of wealth. Most wealth was concentrated in the hands of a few. For the poor and underprivileged, the standard of living took a turn for the worse. This led to a lot of disaffection among the poor and underprivileged.[64] Much of the dissatisfaction among Europeans at the end of the 15th century and the beginning of the 16th century centered on economic changes. The economic prosperity that was achieved in the 13th century was giving way to a prolonged period of economic depression, caused largely by plagues and farming, and even wars, which greatly decreased the population and hampered trade.[65] While the majority of the people were suffering from deprivation, the rich landowners and traders were amassing more and more wealth. This further enlarged the gulf between the rich and the poor, the lower class and the aristocracy. "The peasants, who had retrogressed rather than advanced in status since the thirteenth century, joined

---

63. Ibid., 128–9.

64. Ibid., 130.

65. Grimm, *The Reformation Era*, 6.

the malcontented groups whenever the opportunity to register protests presented itself."[66]

On the positive side, important discoveries took place at this time as well. These were phenomenal discoveries of new lands led and championed by Spain and Portugal. The discoveries led to a Commercial Revolution—rapid increase in commercial activities in Europe and the new found lands.[67] Portugal established trading posts in Africa, thanks to people like Bartolomeu Dias (1450–1500) who sailed around the coast of Africa and established the Cape of Good Hope in 1487. In 1488 Vasco Da Gama (d. 1524) discovered India by sailing off the eastern coast of Africa, and Pedro Cabral (1467–1520) discovered the coast of Brazil and South America in 1500. The Italian explorers and navigators Christopher Columbus (1451–1506) and John Cabot (d. 1498) circumnavigated the world. Columbus made four voyages from 1492–1502 and sailed to places like West Indies, Panama, Trinidad, and northern coast of South America. The discoveries of Columbus were to be followed by the discoveries of other Spanish explorers to such places as Yucatan, Mexico, Florida, and the lands along the Rio Grande and Colorado rivers of North America, as well as to some South American countries.[68] These voyages gave Spain much control of the New World.[69] Although the English did not follow the discoveries of Cabot with territorial claims in the New World or the Far East until the middle of the sixteenth century, the discoveries and expansions themselves increased trade and commerce, leading to the emergence of a strong middle class. A strong middle class deeply altered the existing social order.

In 1493 Pope Alexander VI divided the discovered lands between Spain and Portugal.[70] National consciousness or the spirit of nationalism now reigned supreme. In Spain the marriage between Ferdinand of Aragon and Isabella of Castile not only united the two most powerful families in Spain, but also heightened national pride, especially when Spain controlled almost the whole of the Iberian Peninsula.[71] This enabled Spain to follow the lead of Portugal in establishing colonial empire in places like Africa. England at this time was still reeling from Henry Tudor's success in the 1485 War of the Roses. The twenty-four year rule of Henry Tudor gave England a new spirit of national consciousness. The landscape of Europe was chang-

66. Ibid.
67. Ibid.
68. Ibid., 8.
69. Ibid.
70. Holmes and Bickers, *A Short History of the Catholic Church*, 131.
71. Ibid.

ing and the world was changing socially, economically and politically.[72] All these changes also paved way for a church in need of change.

The social position of the clergy also added impetus to the reform movement. There was in the sixteenth century a big gulf between the clergy and the laity. "By means of a number of election decrees, the laity had been excluded from the administrative affairs of the church, which consequently became in personnel, cult, and culture intrinsically a church of priests."[73] Lay people were further and further distanced from the mass, their role became more of onlookers than that of worthy participants. A good number of the clergy had enriched themselves and their attention focused more on secular matters. "It is no wonder that many townsmen looked upon the clergy as hoarders of wealth who drained their cities and lands of gold and silver. The poorer classes also often resented the wealth, as well as the tremendous power which the clergy exercised over them 'from the cradle to the grave.'"[74] The situation with the hierarch was far worse, a situation into which Martin Luther was born:

> The pope, as the absolute ruler over the clergy and all the church lands, ranked among the highest monarchs of Christendom, while his magnificent court in Rome became the envy of the most powerful kings. The cardinals, the high officials in the papal Curia, the archbishops, bishops, and abbots, and all the higher clergy throughout Europe lived on a relatively high social plane. Usually men of noble birth who had obtained their positions through political influence or by the expenditure of large sums of money, they lived on a par with kings and princes. This was particularly true in western Germany, where, for example, the archbishops of Mainz, Trier, and Cologne were also electors in the Holy Roman Empire and ruled their territories like kings.[75]

Martin Luther (1483–1546)

Martin Luther was born in the town of Mansfeld in Saxony, Germany, on Nov. 10, 1483, at a time the wind of change was blowing. It was a time when national consciousness was gaining ground and central authority of

72. Ibid.

73. Grimm, *The Reformation Era*, 17.

74. Ibid., 18.

75. Ibid.

Christendom with its concentration of power on the pope was seriously challenged.[76] Luther was baptized a day after his birth and named after St. Martin of Tours. His parents gave him a very strict, conservative, and puritanical religious upbringing. As a child, Luther feared God whom he saw as a judge. His family moved to Mansfeld where he went to school. At the age of fourteen Luther moved to Magdeburg to continue his education and attended a school run by the Brethren of the Common Life. He went to the University of Erfurt where he came under the influence of Ockhamism. There he got his bachelors and masters degrees. Luther entered the Reformed Monastery of the Augustinians at Erfurt, in spite of his father's objections.[77] His father wanted him to pursue a career in law but Luther instead chose to become a monk after a frightening experience during a thunderstorm in which he feared he would die without receiving the sacraments.[78] Erfurt was at the time a leading center of monastic ideal among Augustinians, an institution that stresses the fact of human sinfulness and the need of salvation effected only by the intervention of grace in Christ Jesus.[79] Luther made his religious profession in 1506 and in 1507 was ordained a priest. He was haunted by his fears and scruples and was convinced of his own unworthiness.

> As a pious and faithful monk Luther followed the penitential process but felt that his sins were still with him. It did not seem to matter how rigorous he was in observing the rule of his order, he could not find a gracious God, nor achieve any certainty with respect to salvation. He was always aware that he was not contrite enough, that he had omitted something from his act of confession. In short he seems to have suffered from a particularly acute religious conscience and could not understand how he, a sinner, could make an act of sufficient contrition or penance that would satisfy a righteous and just God. The righteousness of God was a fearsome concept that hung over Luther like a cloud, for he believed that he could do nothing that could please such a God. If God was truly righteous and just and judged everyone impartially then surely God could only condemn the sinner that Luther knew himself to be.[80] .

Luther acknowledged the enormous influence Johann Staupitz, the Vicar-General of the Augustinians and professor of Scripture at Wittenberg

---

76. Holmes and Bickers, *A Short History of the Catholic Church*, 132.

77. Ibid., 132–3.

78. McEnhill and Newlands, *Fifty Key Christian Thinkers*, 180.

79. Ibid.

80. Ibid., 181.

University, had on him during his formative years. Staupitz tried to help Luther overcome his fears. In 1508 Luther became professor of moral theology at Wittenberg. In 1510 he was sent to Rome to represent Erfurt at a conference of Augustinians. Luther recounts how in Rome he was shocked by the "abomination" of the papacy, which he saw first-hand. Luther received his doctorate in theology in 1512 and succeeded Staupitz as professor of Scripture at Wittenberg University. Luther became more convinced that faith alone justified a person and nothing could alter that fact. He stressed the primacy of the Word of God over anything else.

Luther had a revelation experience, the famous "Tower Experience," while studying in the tower of the monastery in Wittenberg. His experience taught him that it is God who justifies one by God's gift of faith. This changed, in his mind, the picture of God whom he had feared as a judge from his youth. Now salvation, he realized, was a free gift of God; faith alone, not a person's works, brought justification before God. This realization gave him the courage to speak out against the so called "Indulgence Preachers." In 1505 Pope Julius II (1503–13) in rebuilding St. Peter's Basilica in Rome announced the issuance of indulgence (granting of 'spiritual' benefits) to help finance the cost. In 1514 Albert of Magdeburg paid a huge amount of money to the curia to become the archbishop of Mainz. Part of his deal with the curia was to allow preachers to come to his diocese and preach indulgences. Tetzel, the Dominican priest, preached indulgences to help build the Basilica of St. Peter, and many flocked to hear him. Luther took exception to the indulgences. He wrote the Archbishop of Mainz criticizing the way indulgences were being preached. He also sent to the Archbishop a copy of the 95 Theses, which he wrote to clarify the teaching on indulgences. The Archbishop failed to act and Tetzel dismissed Luther's objection as heretical. Legend has it that Luther nailed his famous 95 Theses to the door of the church in Wittenberg with the hope that it would encourage academic and scholarly discussion, especially regarding the sale of indulgences.[81]

Luther was ordered to Rome on August 7, 1518 after attempts to silence him failed. He openly challenged the authority of the Pope and some church practices. These forced him into a series of debates with prominent church members— the Heidelberg Disputation of 1518, the Leipzig Disputation of 1519 in which he debated John Eck, and the debate with Erasmus on the Freedom of the Will, which led to the publication in 1524 of *De Servo Arbitrio*.[82] Pope Leo X sent Cardinal Cajetan to Germany to try Luther in Germany. Luther and Cajetan met in Augsburg and the meeting ended

---

81. Ibid., 184.
82. Ibid.

inconclusively. "The meeting in Augsburg was a disappointment, because Cajetan did not allow Luther to debate the issues, but only gave him an opportunity to recant. When the interview was finished rumor reached Luther that the Cardinal was empowered to arrest him, so by night Luther escaped from Augsburg."[83] Cajetan asked the secular ruler of Saxony, Frederick the Wise, to extradite Luther to Rome. Frederick the Wise rejected the appeal of Cardinal Cajetan to either extradite Luther or banish him from his territory. Frederick the Wise held Luther in protective custody. "The Roman curia now tried diplomatic means to settle the affair. A series of negotiations and debates followed, culminating in Luther's hearing before the German Diet (or Parliament) in the town of Worms in 1521."[84] But Rome had already pre-judged the issue without waiting for the hearing, and in 1520 sent a papal bull to Luther declaring that he was a heretic and was excommunicated from the church.[85] In the same year (1520) Luther wrote "An Open Letter to German Nobility" in which he claimed that the Roman church had erected three 'walls,' which had effectively blocked all attempts to reform. These three 'walls' were (i) the claim that spiritual jurisdiction was superior to the secular (ii) that the pope was the sole interpreter of scripture and (iii) that the pope alone could summon a general council. In October of the same year Luther published *The Babylonian Captivity of the Church* where he denied the seven sacraments and charged that the Roman church had "shackled" the Eucharist by refusing the chalice to the laity, maintaining the doctrine of transubstantiation, and reducing the Mass to a "good work."[86]

The June 1520 bull *Exsurge Domine*, which Leo X issued, condemned forty-one of Luther's theses as heretical. Luther responded by making a last attempt to come to peace with Rome and wrote "The Freedom of a Christian," a kind of diplomatic letter that summarizes his theology. In it he stressed his three major doctrines: primacy of scripture, justification by faith alone, and priesthood of all believers. On January 3, 1521, Luther was formally excommunicated and he severed himself from the church in 1524 when he married ex-Cistercian nun, Katherine von Bora. Luther assumed leadership of the Reformation in Wittenberg and the whole of Germany.[87] His books were burnt in some cities in Germany, while he remained under the protective custody of Frederick the Wise in Saxony. His excommunication was to be "the beginning of the division in the church which was to

83. Groohans, *Luther*, 6.

84. Ibid., 7.

85. Ibid.

86. Holmes and Bickers, *A Short History of the Catholic Church*, 136–7.

87. Ibid., 148.

lead to the formation of the new Protestant Churches, and was to influence dramatically the political history of Europe and beyond."[88]

Ulrich Zwingli (1484–1531)

Ulrich Zwingli was born in 1484 in Wildhaus, a village high in the Alps of the Toggenburg, a duchy allied with the Swiss Confederacy.[89] He was educated at the universities of Basle and Vienna where he was introduced to the scholastic style education and the newly emerging humanist approach to faith and learning.[90] He was ordained to the priesthood in 1506 and served as chaplain to the Swiss mercenary forces that fought at the battles of Novaro (1513) and Marignano (1515).[91] The carnage that he witnessed as chaplain made him to be critical of the Swiss practice of using mercenary soldiers to fight foreign wars, even in the name of the Pope.[92] In 1515 he met Erasmus, the emerging scholar and leading figure of humanism in Europe, and both discussed the many abuses in the church and the overtly military nature of Pope Julius' reign.[93]

Zwingli went to Zurich in 1519 where he preached against the abuses in the church. In the same year he came in contact with Luther's work. Though he claimed to have been independent of Luther, contact with Luther's works no doubt intensified many of the issues he was addressing. Unlike Luther, he did not have trouble with conscience. In fact, he was said to have had sexual lapses even as a young priest. An accusation was brought against him in 1518 when he was called to be the preacher at the Great Minster in Zurich. In his defense, Zwingli regretted his failure to fulfill his vow of celibacy and argued that although he was guilty of sexual immorality, he had never defiled a virgin, a nun or a married woman.[94] He demanded primacy of the Word, rejected the authority of the pope, clerical celibacy, invocation of the saints, fasting, the doctrine of purgatory and monasticism, and the sacrifice of the Mass. Zwingli became the leader of the Swiss reform. In 1525 the Roman Mass was abolished and replaced with Zwingli's communion

---

88. Grosshans, *Luther*, 7.
89. Lindberg, *The European Reformations*, 170.
90. McEnhill & Newlands, *Fifty Key Christian Thinkers*, 269.
91. Ibid., 270.
92. Ibid.
93. Ibid.
94. Ibid., 271.

service. Zwingli rejected the idea of real presence and accepted "symbolic" presence.[95] Zwingli is noted for the so-called "Affair of Sausages."

> During Lent of 1522, Zwingli was at the house of Christoph Froschauer, a printer who was laboring over the preparation of a new edition of the epistles of Paul. In order to refresh his dozen tired workers, Froschauer served sausages. Was it just coincidence that the number of participants and the manner of distribution recalled the Lord's Supper? This public breaking of the Lenten fast flouted both medieval piety and ecclesiastical and public authority. The Zurich town council arrested Froschauer, but not Zwingli, who himself had not eaten the meat. Zwingli, who held the eminent post of people's priest at the Great Minster church in Zurich, could have smoothed everything out. Instead, he made a public issue out of the incident by preaching a sermon, "On the Choice and Freedom of Foods" (23 March 1522) that was soon enlarged into a printed pamphlet (16 April 1522). Almost certainly influenced by Luther's earlier (1520) treatise on Christian freedom, Zwingli argued that Christians are free to fast or not to fast because the Bible does not prohibit the eating of meat during Lent. "In a word, if you will fast, do so; if you do not wish to eat meat, eat it not; but leave Christians a free choice in the matter."[96] .

John Calvin

John Calvin was born in the Cathedral city of Noyon (north-east of Paris) in 1509. His father was the notary and solicitor to the Bishop and Cathedral chapter at Noyon and he used his influence with the bishop to secure chaplaincies and benefices for Calvin and his other two brothers.[97] Calvin's father was excommunicated in 1528 because of suspicion of financial and other irregularities.[98] At the time of Calvin's birth in 1509, Henry VIII was king of England, Louis XII king of France, Ferdinand king of Spain, Julius II was pope, and the young Luther was 26 years old.[99] Calvin went to Paris in 1523 to continue his education. He enrolled in the Sorbonne in 1528. Soon

---

95. Holmes and Bickers, *A Short History of the Christian Church*, 139.

96. Lindberg, *The European Reformations*, 169.

97. McEnhill and Newlands, *Fifty Key Christian Thinkers*, 91.

98. Holmes and Bickers, *A Short History of the Catholic Church*, 141.

99. Ibid.

after he left for Orleans to study law and completed this study in 1532.[100] Calvin soon came in contact with humanist philosophy and made friends like Pierre Robert and Melchior Wolmar who had identified themselves with the Reformation and were sympathetic to the ideals of reform in the church.[101]

After his studies, Calvin encountered a little problem with the local authorities, a problem that forced him to leave France entirely. But after his father's death in 1531 he returned to Paris to continue his literary studies and in 1532 published his first work, *De Clementia*, a work that betrayed his indebtedness to the humanist ideals.[102] "It is not clear, however, precisely when Calvin moved from being a humanistically inclined Catholic, with moderate intentions to reform the Church, to being someone who was wholeheartedly identified with the Protestant cause."[103] The only clue we have was his statement in the preface to the *Commentary on the Psalms* (1537) where he referred to himself as "someone obstinate in their attachment to the Church of Rome until God made his heart teachable."[104]

In 1534 Calvin fled France for Switzerland when the French authorities initiated a fresh persecution against the reformers and their allies. Calvin at first settled in the Swiss city of Basle where he published *The Institutes of Christian Religion* (1536), a systematic presentation of his reformed theology. In 1537 he went to Geneva and submitted to the city authorities his Articles on Ecclesiastical Organization.[105] The city authorities were not receptive to his confessional statement and he was forbidden to preach and banished from Geneva in 1538. Martin Bucer, one of the leading figures of the Reformation, invited him to Strasbourg. His association with Bucer put him in contact with the Lutheran scholar, Melanchthon, another leader of the reform movement. In 1541 he was invited back to Geneva by the city authorities to reform that city according to the principles of Holy Scripture.[106] In 1559 Calvin became a citizen of Geneva and became the head of the reform movement in the city. He was noted for his doctrine of predestination, his work on the Trinity, the Person and Work of Christ, the Word and Sacraments and the Church. He died in 1564, but not until he had transformed Geneva as the capital of Swiss reform.

---

100. Ibid.

101. McEnhill and Newlands, *Fifty Key Christian Thinkers*, 91.

102. Ibid., 92.

103. Ibid.

104. Ibid.

105. Ibid.

106. Ibid., 93.

John Knox (1513–1572)

John Knox was born in 1513 in Scotland. He was educated in Glasgow where he came under the influence of the reformers. Knox fled England during the reign of Queen Mary Tudor. While in exile he met Calvin. He returned to England in 1559 after the death of Mary and continued his reformed policies. He persuaded the Scottish parliament to abolish the mass, reject papal authority and accept his Confession of Faith.

The English Reformation

The reformation going on in England was by and large different from that going on in the continent in that the reformation in England was an act of the state, under the leadership of the king, who was supported by the parliament.[107] Most historians agree that the English Reformation began more as a political rather than a religious dispute.[108] The Reformation began with Henry VIII, King of England (1509–1547) who was far from being a religious revolutionary.[109] Though the Reformation began as an act of the state the point also has to be made that neither England nor Scotland was isolated from the reformations taking place in the European continent, and as such the initiation and advance of reformation ideas and convictions did not begin with nor completely dependent on royal actions alone.[110]

The 15th century church in England experienced the same abuses and problems (absenteeism, low moral standards, lack of education for the clergy, ignorance and superstition, etc.) as the rest of Europe.[111] At the center of the English Reformation was King Henry VIII who needed papal dispensation to have his marriage to Catherine of Aragon annulled so he could marry his new love, Anne Boleyn.

> Henry was theologically trained and even published in 1521 an Assertion of the Seven Sacraments, which defended the seven Roman Catholic sacraments against Luther's attacks. Pope Leo X then declared Henry to be the "Defender of the Faith." In any event, Henry had long been married to Catherine of Aragon. Because Catherine had been the widow of Henry's older brother, a papal dispensation had to be granted to authorize Henry

107. Holmes and Bickers, *A Short History of the Catholic Church*, 148.

108. Feldman, *Please Don't Wish Me A Merry Christmas*, 81.

109. Ibid.

110. Lindberg, *The European Reformations*, 309.

111. Holmes and Bickers, *A Short History of the Catholic Church*, 148.

and Catherine's marriage in the first place. In 1527, though, two factors prompted Henry to seek an end to his marriage with Catherine. First, he had fallen in love with Anne Boleyn; second, he wished to have a male heir. Catherine was unlikely to have any more children, and to that point she had borne Henry only one surviving daughter, Mary. Since divorce as we currently know it did not exist then, Henry claimed that from a religious standpoint, the marriage had been invalid at the outset and that the pope should therefore officially annul it.[112]

When the pope, for political (the Emperor of the Roman Empire, Charles V, was Catherine's nephew, and the pope was not inclined to offend Charles V) and religious reasons, refused to grant this dispensation, Henry VIII, with the help of his Lord Chancellor Thomas Cromwell (1485–1540), transferred ecclesiastical jurisdiction from the hand of the pope to the crown and declared himself the supreme head of the Church of England. In August 1532, Henry divorced Catherine, married Anne Boleyn in a secret marriage supervised by Thomas Cranmer, the Archbishop of Canterbury. Henry had a daughter by Anne Boleyn, Elizabeth (who later became Queen Elizabeth). Pope Clement VII condemned Cranmer's action, denounced Henry's second marriage, and excommunicated him. Henry enacted series of legislations that led to the final separation with Rome.[113] He solidified England's break from Rome by procuring several key parliamentary enactments, the most important of which was the 1534 Act of Supremacy, which declared that "the king's majesty justly and rightfully is and ought to be the supreme head of the Church of England."[114]

John Wycliffe (1329–84)

Though the reformation in England was an act of the state, there were some notable individuals who worked relentlessly to bring about reform. One of such men was the Oxford reformer John Wycliffe. Wycliffe was critical of the abuses in the church and did not hide his disdain for papal authority. He believed that everyone had the right to study the bible, insisting that the Bible was the sole authority in a Christian's life. The medieval church used the Latin version of the Bible, the Vulgate. The Vulgate was prepared by St. Jerome, at the request of Pope Damasus (c.382 A.D). Jerome translated the

---

112. Feldman, *Please Don't Wish Me A Merry Christmas*, 80.

113. Holmes and Bickers, *A Short History of the Catholic Church*, 148.

114. Feldman, *Please Don't Wish Me A Merry Christmas*, 80.

New Testament from the Greek, and in 405 produced Latin Old Testament translated from the Hebrew.[115]

Wycliffe made attempts to translate the bible into English. "He and his followers, the Lollards, emphasized in their preaching the supreme authority of the Scriptures. But to 'search the scriptures' men needed a Bible in their own tongue."[116] Wycliffe and his followers made two translations of the Vulgate available in English. The first translation (1381–1383) was a word for word rendering of the Vulgate, and the second translation (1395) was "less literal and less Latinate."[117] In 1408 the Synod of Oxford forbade translation of the Bible into English, failure to comply earned one the ignoble charge of heresy.[118]

William Tyndale (1493–1536)[119]

The first real English translation of the bible was undertaken by William Tyndale and through the efforts of Miles Coverdale the first printed English bible appeared in England in 1535.[120] William Tyndale was a student at Oxford where he earned his B.A. in 1512 and M.A. in 1515. After earning his M.A. Tyndale sought "the brighter air of Cambridge, where Erasmus had recently taught Greek (1511–1514)."[121] At Cambridge Tyndale had the desire to translate the bible into the vernacular, having been inspired by Erasmus' Latin translation of the Greek New Testament and Luther's German translation of the bible. Tyndale sought the permission of the bishop of London, Cuthbert Tunstall, to translate the bible into English. His initial attempt was rejected by the bishop, who was reputed to have said "we must root out printing or printing will root out us."[122]

---

115. Thompson, *The Bible in English* 1525–1611, 2.

116. Ibid.

117. Ibid.

118. Ibid.

119. The actual year of Tyndale's birth seems to be in dispute. A newly discovered record of his ordination to the priesthood in 1515 suggests that he was born in 1491, not 1493. See Day, Lund, & O'Donnell, eds., *Word, Church, and State*, ix. See also Brown, *William Tyndale on Priest and Preachers*.

120. Holmes & Bickers, *A Short History of the Catholic Church*, 149. Although the Vulgate was in use in the medieval church it was not made official until the sixteenth century, when the Council of Trent declared it the authentic Bible (1546), and in 1592 Pope Clement VIII issued a revised and official text.

121. Day, Lund, & O'Donnell, *Word, Church, and State*, ix.

122. Lindberg, *The European Reformations*, 313–14.

Tyndale was thought to be a linguistic genius who spoke so many languages: Hebrew, Greek, Latin, Italian, Spanish, English, French, and German.[123] Tyndale needed the authorization of his bishop to proceed because the Constitutions of Oxford (1407–1409) against Wycliffe's translations of the Vulgate were still in force.[124] When he could not obtain the support of the bishop of London for this task he accepted the financial assistance of a London merchant,[125] and fled to Germany where he could more freely publish his translations and get them smuggled back home.[126] In 1525 he translated the New Testament into English.

> Just as Luther had pointed out in the first of the Ninety-Five Theses that the sacrament of penance rested on a mistranslation of the Greek, so too did Tyndale translate the Greek metanoeite by "repent" instead of the Vulgate's "do penance" (*poenitentiam agite*). Likewise, just as Luther consistently used "congregation" or "community" instead of "church," so Tyndale translated the Greek ekklesia as "congregation." The Catholic establishment was further undermined by Tyndale's translation of the Greek *presbyteros* as "elder" rather than as "priest."[127].

Tyndale also translated Luther's works (which had been banned) and made them available in English. He was arrested on October 6, 1536 and burned at stake. He was accused, among other things, of rejecting papal authority. A good number of his works, however, especially the first half of the Old Testament and the entire New Testament, was incorporated into the King James Bible.[128]

Miles Coverdale (1488–1568)

Miles Coverdale was originally an Augustinian friar at Cambridge. He worked with Tyndale to translate the Old Testament and was responsible for the first complete translation of the Bible in 1535.[129] He was born in either 1487 or 1488 in or very near the city of York.[130] It is not clear why Coverdale

---

123. Ibid., 314.
124. Day, Lund, & O'Donnell, *Word, Church, and State*, ix.
125. Grimm, *The Reformation Era*, 290.
126. Day, Lund, &O'Donnell, *Word, Church, and State*, ix-x.
127. Lindberg, *The European Reformation*, 314.
128. Day, Lund, &O'Donnell, *Word, Church, and State*, x.
129. Ibid., 315.
130. Worthy, *Church, Monarch and Bible in Sixteenth Century England* 43.

chose to join the Augustinians. But "in light of his youthful attitude toward learning, quite possibly the order's well known respect for scholarly studies played a significant role in his choice."[131] He was ordained a priest in 1514 and was assigned to Cambridge. It was probably at this time that Coverdale came into contact with Tyndale.[132]

THE CATHOLIC REFORM

By the middle of the 16th century the reformers were beginning to win more and more converts and the Catholic Church was increasingly becoming disillusioning to many. In spite of Pope Leo X's initial dismissal of the Reformation as "nothing other than a drunken brawl among German Monks," there was a growing realization even among the hierarchy that the church was in need of renewal and reform.[133] The Catholics knew it was time to put their house in order. Historians refer to the Catholic reform movement as Catholic Reformation or Catholic Counter-Reformation. Perhaps it should be pointed out that the Catholic renewal movement was not necessarily a reaction, a Counter-Reformation,[134] for the fact that even before Luther the Church had produced reform-minded individuals who had set in motion the Catholic renewal movement. Giles of Viterbo, for instance, at the opening of the fifth Lateran Council, candidly addressed Pope Julius II and the other prelates present with the words: "Unless by this Council or by some other means we place a limit on our morals, unless we force our greedy desire for human things, the source of evils, to yield to the love of divine things, it is all over with Christendom."[135] This appeal for personal renewal as the key to reform and renewal in the Church was characteristic of the Catholic reform efforts both before and after Luther.[136]

The first reform movement in the Catholic Church began with the religious orders. The old Orders, the mendicants in particular, began to reform. The reform among the Franciscans, for instance, led to the emergence of the Capuchins. In 1574 the Capuchins received papal permission to establish houses outside Italy and in 1619 were recognized as a separate order distinct from the Franciscans. The French Cistercians also reformed in 1580 as well as the Benedictines. In Spain John of the Cross (1542–91) and Teresa of

---

131. Ibid.

132. Ibid.

133. Lindberg, *The European Reformations*, 335.

134. Ibid.

135. Olin, *Catholic Reform*, 57. See also Lindberg, *The European Reformations*, 335.

136. Lindberg, *The European Reformations*, 336.

Avila (1515–82) led the reform of the Carmelites. New religious orders and congregations emerged at the end of the 15th century, mostly in Latin (as against Germanic) countries. They engaged in active, rather than contemplative, apostolate, devoting their attention to preaching, teaching and the needs of the poor. The most influential of the religious orders at this time was the newly formed Society of Jesus or the Jesuits who became the agent of Catholic-Reformation.[137]

The Society of Jesus was founded by St. Ignatius of Loyola (1491–1556). Ignatius was born in 1491 into a noble family in the Basque region of Spain. While fighting in the siege of Pamplona in 1521 he was severely injured. He went to Monserrat after recovering from his illness and began writing the *Spiritual Exercises* in 1522, which was to be the central core of Jesuit spirituality. His idea was to form soldiers who would find God in all things and do all things for the greater glory of God i.e. people who would not acquiesce to the temptations and conflicting attractions of world culture.[138] The Society of Jesus was formally recognized in 1540. Their numbers increased in leaps and bounds and they sent members to such places as India, Brazil, Japan and China. The Jesuits supported the papacy, founded colleges in Rome (1551) and France (1556) for the training of the clergy. They preached, often using the same methods as the Protestants, and became valuable instrument for the reform movement in the Church.[139]

The Catholic Church also responded to the Protestant Reformation by some controversial means. Pope Paul IV, who has been termed the first of the Counter-Reformation Popes and in whose pontificate the Catholic renewal movement centered on repression and earned the label, "Counter-Reformation," introduced the *Index Librorum Prohibitorium* (Index of Prohibited Books) in addition to the Inquisition, the juridical persecution of heresy by special ecclesiastical courts whose roots go back to the 13th century proceedings against the Catharist heresy.[140] Paul IV was convinced that effective thought control included not only burning the authors who propagated heresies, but their writings as well.[141] The *Index*, which was first published in 1559 under Paul IV and modified in 1564 by the Council of Trent, was to be an essential feature of Catholic Counter-Reformation until its final abolition in 1966. In 1571 Pius V established the Congregation of the Doctrine of Faith and transferred the duties of the Index to this newly

---

137. Homes & Bickers, *A Short History of the Catholic Church*, 162.

138. Olsen, *Beginning At Jerusalem*, 134.

139. Homes and Bickers, *A Short History of the Catholic Church*, 163.

140. Lindberg, *The European Reformations*, 341.

141. Ibid., 342.

found congregation.[142] The effect of the *Index* on culture, especially in Europe, is still debated to this day. Some have argued that it stymied exchange of cultural ideas, especially in Catholic countries, where its devastating effect was more apparent.

The other essential element of Catholic reform was by way of a General Council, the Council of Trent, which met in three major periods over the course of eighteen years. The Council first met from 1545–1547 and dealt with doctrinal and disciplinary matters. They dealt with such doctrinal matters as the sources of revelation, the role of the Church as interpreter of Scripture, the Canon of Scripture, Original Sin and Justification (Joint Lutheran-Catholic Declaration on Justification, 1999, resolved this issue). The disciplinary issues they discussed include "pluralism" (holding several benefices), raising the standards of the clergy, importance of preaching, episcopal residence. The Second period of the Council was from 1551–52. They dealt with such doctrinal issues as the Eucharist, Penance, Extreme Unction (Anointing of the Sick). War broke out in Germany 1552 which led to the suspension of the Council. It did not reconvene until ten years later. The Third period of the Council was held in 1562–3. The Council then issued teachings on the Eucharist, the Cult of the Saints, the veneration of relics, the use of Indulgences and the doctrine of purgatory.[143]

142. Ibid.

143. Holmes and Bickers, 167–70.

10

Islam

LIKE JUDAISM AND CHRISTIANITY, Islam traces its roots to Abraham and like these religions is known as an Abrahamic religion. Islam's historic religious and political ties to Judaism and Christianity has "been the source of mutual benefit and borrowing as well as misunderstanding and conflict."[1] Islam is the second largest religion in the world, second only to Christianity. There are over 900 million and counting Muslims all over the world. There are also sizeable Muslim populations living in more than forty-four countries spread across Europe, Asia, Middle East, and Africa.[2] Although Muslims the world over belong to one community of believers and share a unity of faith in the one God, Allah, the guidance and message of Prophet Muhammad (PBUH),[3] and the divinely revealed Scripture, the Quran, there are two broad divisions in Islam: Sunni Muslims who constitute about 85 percent and Shia Muslims who constitute about 15 percent of Muslims.[4] This chapter will focus only on the shared beliefs of all Muslims.

---

1. See Esposito, *Islam*, 2.

2. Ibid., 1.

3. According to the Hadith, there are numerous benefits to be derived in bestowing "salaam" (peace) on the Prophets of Allah. As a mark of respect, Muslims traditionally invoke this blessing by saying *sal Allahu allayhi wa sallam* (peace be upon him) each time the name of Prophet Mohammad is mentioned. The honorific blessing, abbreviated "PBUH" will follow in parenthesis each time the Prophet's name is mentioned.

4. Esposito, *Islam*, 2.

PRE-ISLAMIC ARABIAN PENINSULA

The religion of Islam emerged in some ways as a response to the chaotic social, political, religious, and economic climate of 7th century CE Arabian Peninsula. Jews, Christians, people who practiced ancient Egyptian and Mesopotamian religions, and people of no faith lived in the Arabian Peninsula at the time. The expansionist policy of Roman emperors, which brought political and economic growth to the empire, had begun to weigh heavily on the empire which was becoming too large and too big to be efficiently governed by the central government in Rome. For practical purposes the empire was divided into two halves: East and West. The Eastern half, known as the Byzantine Empire, extended to far places like Egypt, Palestine, and Syria, up to the region of the Tigris— modern day Iran. It shared close boarders with the Persian Empire, which was always at war with the Roman Empire. What was then Arabia was an isolated and poor region, mostly desert wasteland that enjoyed complete autonomy because neither of the two superpowers that shared its boarder (i.e., Byzantine to the north and Persia to the north-west) was interested in controlling it.[5] What was then Arabia was a region of about 1 million square miles (about a third of the United States), mostly desert area and landscapes "dotted with oasis towns and cities."[6] Nomadic Bedouin tribes controlled a large portion of agriculture and commerce that took place in the desert.

The 7th century CE Arabia was also an important trade center for the Silk Road (a trade network that connected the West to China and the Far East). The city of Mecca was particularly an important commercial center of this trading activity. Merchants who controlled the trade became enormously rich and often at the expense of the poor whom they exploited. Rich merchants used camel and caravans to gain upper hand. The Byzantine Empire also had a great influence on the trading activities that took place as they controlled most of the centers that link the Silk Road to the Far East. Local tribes fought for control over trade. The rivalry was fierce and often led to banditry and armed robbery.

The Silk Road brought people of different ethnicities and religions to the Arabian Peninsula. Jews and Christians lived in the desert spots and in the Byzantine Empire. There were also Buddhists and Hindus who brought their religions from the Far East. But the predominant religion in Arabia was animism (worship of spirits and lesser deities). So there was animism on the one hand and polytheism (deriving from Hinduism) on the other

5. Foad, *The Seerah of Prophet Muhammad*, 4.

6. Esposito, *Islam*, 2.

hand. Those who worshipped other deities relied on these deities for protection from armed robbers and gangs who laid siege to the trade routes. The city of Mecca was a center of activity for the worship of different deities. There was a large black stone (cubic-shaped building) known as the Kaaba that held a special status in the city as a place where people came for worship of deities and annual pilgrimage. A powerful myth or legend developed around the Kaaba. One legend tells that the Kaaba was consecrated by Abraham and his son Ishmael (who according to the Christian Bible was the son of Abraham by a slave woman Hagar) for the worship of the one God, Allah. Arabs consider Ishmael, who for them was the legitimate son and heir of Abraham, to be the father of all Arabs (not Isaac as Christians think). The ritual pilgrimage that developed around Kaaba brought Arabs and people from all works of life to Mecca. Most Arabs followed the religion of their forefathers Abraham and Ishmael before they deviated and started worshiping idols they themselves had crafted. Merchants made a business out of the pilgrimage and exploited it for economic gains. Because the Arabs had lapsed into polytheism and deviated from the worship of the one true God that Abraham and Ishmael worshiped, the question of reform was just a matter of time.

The peoples of Arabia lived in tribal groups. "Social organization and identity were rooted in membership in an extended family. A grouping of several related families comprised a clan. A cluster of several clans constituted a tribe."[7] Emphases were placed on tribal ties and group solidarity, which provided identity, power, and protection in a society that had no central political authority or law.[8] Politically, Arabian society was hierarchically structured. There were three classes in the society: the nobles or "Ashraf," the allies who were under the protection of the nobles, and the servants or "Al-Abeed" who were poor and oppressed.[9] The tribe was the basic unity of society. The most famous of the tribes was the Quraish (sometimes spelt Koraish), which was in Mecca. They were the guardians of the Kaaba.[10]

---

7. Esposito, *Islam*, 3.

8. Ibid.

9. Foad, *The Seerah of Prophet Muhammad*, 4.

10. Ibid., 3.

Birth and Early Life of Muhammad Ibn Abdallah (PBUH)

It was under this social and political situation, i.e., of an Arabian tribal society with a Bedouin polytheistic ethos,[11] that Prophet Muhammad (PBUH) was born and reared. Not much is known about the early life of Prophet Muhammad (PBUH). But we do know that his father, Abdallah, died when his mother Amina, was about two months pregnant with him. Muhammad (PBUH) was born in Mecca in 570 CE. His mother died when he was about six years old. According to the Quran (93:6), Muhammad (PBUH) was born an orphan, but Allah took care of him. Muhammad (PBUH) was born into a noble tribe, the Quraish. The Quraish trace their lineage to Ishmael and Abraham.

A Tradition about the Birth of Prophet Muhammad

Abdallah came into the house of another wife he had besides Amina, and he was stained with the clay he had been working in. He asked her to have sex, but she put him off because he was dirty. So he left her and bathed, washing away the clay that was on him. Then he went out intending to go to Amina. As he passed the other wife she invited him to come to her. He refused, since he wanted Amina. He went into her, had intercourse and she conceived Muhammad. When he passed the other wife again he asked if she still wanted him. She said, "No. When you just passed me there was a shining white spot between your eyes and I invited you, but you refused me and went to Amina instead, and she has taken it away."

Muhammad's grandfather raised him after his mother's death and when the grandfather passed away he was raised by his uncle Abou Talib. Abou Talib took him on several of his trading trips. Muhammad (PBUH) had to work as a driver in some of the trading caravans. It was while working in one of such caravans to Syria that he met a wealthy widow from Mecca by name Khadija who hired him to work in her caravan. Impressed by Muhammad's honesty and spiritual qualities, Khadija proposed Marriage to Muhammad (PBUH) when he was 25 years old. She at this time was, at least, 10 years older than Muhammad. Khadijah provided him a much-needed economic stability. Together they had two sons (Al-Qasim and Abdallah) and four daughters (Zaynab, Ruqaya, Umkulthum, and Fatima). Al-Quasim and Abdallah died young, but the four daughters all survived. Of the four daughters Fatima seemed to have lived longer. She was the only one that provided Muhammad (PBUH) much-needed grandchildren, even though there were no boys among them.

11. Esposito, *Islam*, 3.

Muhammad's marriage to Khadijah was a monogamous one and lasted for twenty-four years.[12] When Khadijah died Muhammad (PBUH) was 49 years old. He married Sawda bint Zam'a, the widow of one of his companions when Khadijah died. He married nine other women after emigrating to Medina.[13] Most of his wives were "widows of his Companions or of enemies killed in battle, and he seems to have married them primarily in order to give them protection."[14] Muhammad (PBUH) also had concubines, which he took for political reasons. There was Rayhana, a Jewish prisoner of war, and Mariya, a Coptic Christian that was given to him by the Byzantine governor of Egypt.[15] Muhammad's marriage to Zaynab, the divorced wife of his adopted son Zayd, has sometimes fuelled anti-Muslim polemic because non-Muslims wrongly think Zayd divorced Zaynab so Muhammad (PBUH) could marry her.[16] An account of the story is found in Quran 33:37. Some Muslim scholars who know more about the circumstances that led to the marriage between Zyad and Zaynad and who know more about the mismatch between the two when they were married interpret the revelation that Muhammad (PBUH) marries Zaynab to mean that God gave Zaynab to Muhammad (PBUH) in marriage "in order to establish an important social reform, the abolition of adoption."[17] The full explanation of this episode is beyond our scope here. Nevertheless, it is important to keep in mind these key points offered by John Esposito when addressing the issue of Muhammad's polygamous marriages: .

i. Semitic culture in which Muhammad (PBUH) lived permitted polygyny.

ii. Muhammad (PBUH) remained married to only one wife throughout the prime of his life.

iii. It was only after the death of his wife, Khadija, that Muhammad (PBUH) took a number of wives.

iv. Most of Muhammad's eleven marriages, as was customary for Arab chiefs at the time, were political marriages meant to cement alliances.

v. Some of Muhammad's marriages were marriages to widows of his companions who had fallen in combat and in need of protection.

12. Robinson, *Islam*, 92.

13. Ibid.

14. Ibid.

15. Ibid.

16. Ibid.

17. Ibid.

vi. Remarriage was difficult in the society in which Muhammad (PBUH) lived because the society emphasized virgin marriages. Aisha was the only virgin that Muhammad married.

vii. Muhammad's teachings and actions improved the status and lots of women.[18] .

Piecing together the events of the early life of Muhammad (PBUH) is not easy to do because there were no many written accounts of his life. The earliest written account of the events of his early life was the *Sira* (biography) by Ibn-Ishaq (d 768 CE), written about 125 years after the Prophet's death. The most definitive authority remains the Quran. But the Quran does not offer much either by way of biography, except for scattered references. In fact, the Quran only mentions Muhammad (PBUH) by name four times (Quran 3:144, 33:40, 47:2, and 48:29). But in spite of the paucity of biographical information a lot is said or implied about Muhammad's status in the Quran.[19] We do know that he was a righteous man who Muslims believe to be the perfect example of men. They regard him as the last and the greatest of the messengers and prophet of God. The Quran addresses him as Prophet (Quran 8:64) and Messenger of Allah (Quran 5:41). It also mentions him in the same breath as Noah, Abraham, Moses, and Jesus (Quran 42:13) and describes him as "the seal of the prophets" (Quran 33:40).[20]

Another reliable sources for the life of the Prophet, apart from the Quran, are the compilations of the sayings of the Prophet put together by some of his companions and successors. The individual compilations of the sayings are called hadiths. Taken together collectively they are called Hadith. There are two main kinds of Hadith: the *musnad*—hadiths compiled on the basis of individual persons who compiled them and the *musannaf*—hadiths that are arranged according to the subject matter discussed.[21] Traditional Islamic societies, i.e., the way Muslims in traditional Islamic societies, "pray, conduct business, wage war, marry and divorce, rear their children, dress, greet one another, eat and drink, or attend to matters of personal hygiene, are all largely determined by what the Prophet is deemed to have said and done, or tacitly approved or disapproved."[22] Muslims also look to Muhammad's example for guidance in other aspects of life like what to eat or drink, what to wear, how to treat one's friends and enemies. These are called the Sunna (the trodden path)—the examples of the prophets that

18. Esposito, *Islam*, 16–17.

19. Robinson, *Islam*, 85.

20. Ibid.

21. Ibid., 86.

22. Ibid., 88.

have been handed down by oral traditions and customs from generation to generation.[23]

The Beginnings of Revelations

Muhammad (PBUH) began to receive revelations about 610 CE, when he was about 40 years old. There are different accounts of the nature of these revelations. Some depict the revelations as visions that came to Muhammad (PBUH) "like the brightness of daybreak" at his home in Mecca, while other accounts suggest that these events took place at Mount Hira, a secluded place outside of Mecca where the Prophet used to go and repair for solitude and prayer. Angel Gabriel would bring him revelations. The first revelation occurred in the month of Ramadan (Quran 2: 185), probably on the 27th or somewhere within the last ten days of the month of Ramadan. The night on which the first revelation occurred is referred to as *Lai lat al-Quadri* (the night of power or night of majesty, see Quran 97:1). "The revelations are explained by Islamic doctrine as the text of a divine book written by God in heaven, brought by the angel Gabriel, and recited by Muhammad."[24] The first revelation which Gabriel gave the Prophet is recorded in Quran 96: 1–3: "Read in the name of your Lord who created man out of clot. Read and your Lord is the most generous." Muhammad (PBUH) was not a lettered man yet the angel urged him to read (Quran 29:48). Muhammad was alone when he had this awesome experience which terrified him greatly. When he returned home trembling the Prophet narrated the experience which caused him "great dread and anxiety" to his wife Khadijah who assured him that he is the prophet of God.

Muhammad (PBUH) received these revelations for 23 years. The first person to believe in Muhammad as God's Prophet and accept Islam was Khadijah his wife. Then there was his companion Abou Bakr, his cousin Ali (the son of Abou Talib), his children, and other companions and servants like Belal who all believed and accepted Islam. These early Muslims met privately with Prophet Muhammad (PBUH), learned from him, and prayed with him before the order came from Allah to Prophet Muhammad (PBUH) to openly proclaim Allah's message and warn his nearest of kin.[25] The revelation was for Muhammad (PBUH) to remind his people about the oneness and greatness of God and also to warn them of the judgment that will take place on the last day (Quran 74:2; 87:9). Prophet Muham-

23. Esposito, *Islam*, 11.

24. Carmody and Brink, *Ways to the Center*, 300.

25. Foad, *The Seerah of Prophet Muhammad*, 15.

mad (PBUH) "climbed to the top of Safa (a hill in Mecca) and called on the various branches of Quraish to invite them to worship Allah alone and to believe in him as Allah's messenger."[26]

Open Dawa and Hejira

In the first three years of his call to serve Allah Prophet Muhammad (PBUH) proclaimed the Dawa (call to serve Allah) in secret and only his family and close associates became Muslims. After three years he was instructed to proclaim the Dawa publicly to the people of Mecca. Muhammad's preaching was initially not well received by the Meccans because it threatened both their polytheism and economic activities around the Kaaba. They feared that destroying their idols would put an end to the flood of pilgrims that came to Mecca and cripple their businesses. The leaders of the Quraish went to Abou Talib, the Prophet's uncle, and pleaded with him to intervene and stop his nephew from ridiculing their idols. They even tried to bribe Prophet Muhammad (PBUH) with money and promise of power and leadership. But Prophet Muhammad (PBUH) was not after money or fame, but only to steadfastly proclaim God's message.

When they could not stop the Prophet by bribe the people of Mecca began to persecute Muslims. In the fifth year of his revelations Prophet Muhammad (PBUH) encouraged some of his followers to emigrate to Habash (Ethiopia). Twelve men and four women, including Prophet Muhammad's daughter, emigrated to Ethiopia where they were offered protection by the king of Ethiopia. The King of Ethiopia was a Christian. The enemies of the Muslims, many of whom were from the Quraish tribe, sent delegates bearing gifts to the king of Ethiopia to repatriate the Muslims back to Mecca. But the King would not acquiesce. The King was so impressed with the Muslims when he heard their account of the state of decadence of Mecca before Islam and how Prophet Muhammad (PBUH) was turning things around by preaching belief in one God, Allah, prayer, and charity to the poor. The King turned down the Quraish delegations and told them that the Muslims were free to stay in his kingdom. The king's gesture encouraged more Muslims to emigrate to Habash. There were about eighty three men and eleven women in the second emigration to Habash.[27]

The Meccan leaders did everything they could to discredit Prophet Muhammad (PBUH) and levelled all kinds of accusations against him. They claimed he was destroying their traditional religion and customs. They also

26. Ibid., 16.

27. Ibid., 24–25.

accused the Prophet of sorcery, a baseless allegation particularly when one considers the fact that Prophet Muhammad's whole point in the first place was to wipe out diviners and sorcerers. They also alleged that his revelations were a forgery (see Quran 25:4–5; 68:15) and that the Quran need not be taken seriously because it came, according to them, from the devil (See Quran 7:184; 15:6; 68:42). Muhammad (PBUH) responded to these charges by challenging his critics who claimed that he invented the Quran to produce something similar if the Quran was invented. Muslims hold that the Quran is sui generis and incapable of being imitated.[28] We shall discuss more on this point in the next section.

In spite of persecution from the Meccans, Prophet Muhammad's message gained much ground. Some warring groups from a nearby town called Yathrib accepted Islam and pledged their allegiance to the Prophet. In 622 CE Prophet Muhammad (PBUH) left Mecca for Yathrib to arbitrate a long standing dispute between two of the warring tribes. After the Prophet settled their dispute with revelation he received from Allah the people of Yathrib enjoined on him to stay. Muhammad (PBUH) stayed and became the religious and political leader of Yathrib. Later the name of the town was changed to Medina, meaning the city of the prophet. Muhammad's journey from Mecca to Yathrib (Medina) is known in Islamic history as the Hejira, a significant and turning point in Islamic history. Muslims call their calendar the *Hijri* calendar and use the designation *Anno Hejira* (AH), meaning "in the year of the Hejira. Since the emigration to Medina occurred in 622 CE, most likely the 20th of September (according to the Gregorian calendar), that year is considered 1AH in Islamic calendar. The Islamic calendar is a lunar based calendar, consisting of 12 lunar months. Length wise, lunar months alternate between 29 and 30 days, which means that the Islamic calendar has approximately 354 days, about 11 or 12 days short of the solar based Gregorian calendar. Muslims today use both the Gregorian calendar (for civic purposes) and the Islamic calendar (for religious purposes) to determine when to kick start their annual fast, begin their annual pilgrimage, and celebrate Islamic festivals.

28. Kaltner, *Introducing the Quran*, 14.

Islamic Calendar Month	Meaning	Activity/Significance
1. Muharram	Muharram is derived from the term "haram," meaning "forbidden."	• Considered unlawful to fight in this month. • Believed to be the month in which Allah created the heavens and earth. • Believed to be the month Allah created Adam and pardoned Adam and Eve for their transgressions. • Believed to be the month Noah's Ark landed safely on Mount Judi. • It is this month (680 CE/61 AH) that Prophet Muhammad's grandson, Imam Husain, together with his family and friends, were massacred in the battle of Karbala.
2. Safar	Means "empty" or "void"	• Shia Muslims, who consider Imam Husain the third Imam, remember both the heroism and brutal murder of Imam Husain at Karbala on the 10th of Muharram. • Muslims hold mourning ceremonies/prayer throughout the month of Muharram and Safar.
3. 1st Rabi or Rabi-Ul-Awwal	The first month of Spring	• Prophet Muhammad (PBUH) was born in this month. • Emigration to Mecca occurred this month.
4. 2nd Rabi or Rabi-Ul-Akhir	The second month of Spring	
5. 1st Jumaada or Jumaada-Al-Oola	1st of Parched land	• Prophet Muhammad (PBUH) married Khadijah in this month. • Considered summer in pre-Islamic Arabia.
6. 2nd Jumaada or Jumaada-Ath-Thani	2nd of Parched land	

7. Rajabi	Honor or Respect	• The Miraj (Muhammad's night journey to heaven) took place on the 27th of Rajab. • Sacred month in which fighting is forbidden.
8. Sha'ban	Scattered	• Quibla (direction of prayer facing Mecca) was adopted in the 15th of Sha'ban, two months after Hejira. • Fasting in the month of Ramadan was made compulsory on the 25th of Sha'ban, two years after Hejira.
9. Ramadan	Literally means "intense heat" or "burning"	• The Quran was revealed on the 27th night of this month. • Hasan, the grandson of Prophet Muhammad (PBUH) was born on the 15th of Ramadan, three years after Hejira. • The Battle of Badr took place on the 12th of Ramadan, two years into the Hejira.
10. Shawwaal	Means "breakage: or "raised." The name derives from a superstition among pre-Islamic Arabs who believed that any marriage that takes place in this month will in the end be unsuccessful.	• Fasting month for Muslims. • The month of Hajj (pilgrimage). • The first day of Shawwaal is Muslim festival of Eid-Ul-Fitri, a day when sins are forgiven. • The Prophet's grandson, Husain (son of Fatimah) was born this month, four years after Hejira. • The Battle of Uhud took place this month, three years after Hejira.
11. Dhul-Qu'da or Zul-Qa'dah	The one of Truce	• One of the months of Hajj (pilgrimage). • Another month in which war is forbidden.

12. Dhul-Hijja or Zul Hijjah	The one Pilgrimage or month of Hajj.	• Another month in which war is forbidden.
		• First ten days of this month are considered most virtuous days of the month. Hajj is performed within those ten days.
		• Prophet Muhammad (PBUH) performed his "Farewell Hajj" and gave his "Farewell Sermon" this month.
		• Umar, the second caliph, was killed 27th of this month, 26 AH.
		• Uthman appointed third caliph this month.
		• Uthman was killed 18th day of this month, 35 AH.

The people of Medina were by no means monolithic. They were diverse groups with diverse interests that can be subdivided into four interest groups: .

1. Muslims who emigrated from Mecca, known as the Muhajereen.

2. Muslims resident in Medina, known as the Ansar.

3. Arab groups resident in Medina who were yet to accept Islam and

4. Jewish groups resident in Medina. Three Jewish groups (Bani Quinuq'a, Bani An-adeer, and Bani Qoraiza) lived in Medina by the time of the Hejira. These Jewish groups, which had Arab names and cultures similar to those of Arabs, must have emigrated to Medina from Palestine to escape persecution. They maintained their Jewish identity and controlled the commerce in Medina.[29]

Economically, Medina was poor. The continued influx of Muslims from Mecca was a drain on the economy of this poor town that was decimated by the two warring tribes of the Ansars—the Aws and Khazraj that fought each other for years with regularity.[30] Religiously, the Mosque built by Prophet Muhammad (PBUH) at Medina would serve as a symbol of unity for all the warring groups. Prophet Muhammad (PBUH) united the Muhajereen and the Ansar and they all saw one another as brothers and sis-

29. Foad, *The Seerah of Prophet Muhammad*, 74.

30. Ibid., 65.

ters in the faith. The Muslims met there regularly to worship and learn from Prophet Muhammad (PBUH). "The mosque united the hearts of Muslims and served as the focal point in their lives. If one or more people did not show up, they were missed and the others would go and find why they had stayed away from the mosque or offer help if they were in need."[31] According to Salem Foad, Prophet Muhammad (PBUH) signed a non-aggression treaty and pact of cooperation between Muslims and non-Muslims in Medina and established there a Muslim state. The principal element of the agreement include the following 5 points: .

1. All Muslims are equal in their rights and privileges. A believer also must not only help a believer, but must not help an unbeliever against a believer.

2. Prophet Muhammad (PBUH) settled all disputes between the believers.

3. The Muslim state was built on the best principles and rules that guaranteed peace. Every citizen had the right to travel inside and outside of the state.

4. Non-Muslims who wanted to live in peace with their Muslim counterparts were protected by the state. Their property was safeguarded and guaranteed and no one was forced to accept Islam.

5. The authority that safeguarded these rules was based on the belief in Allah and obedience to Prophet Muhammad (PBUH).[32] .

AL QUR'AN

Muslims believe that the Quran contain the same divine message that was revealed to previous prophets and messengers of God. Muhammad (PBUH) is the last in this chain of prophetic figures that goes back to Jesus, Moses, Abraham, and Adam. Muhammad (PBUH) is the last of these prophets, a reason for which he is called "the seal of the prophets." The Quran is, for Muslims, "the guarded tablet" (Quran 85:22) and "the mother of the Book" (Quran 43:4). Belief in the preexistence of the Quran as "the guarded tablet" should be understood against the backdrop of beliefs in Ancient Near East about the pre-existence of divinely revealed books, as in the example

31. Ibid., 67.
32. Ibid., 73.

of Moses ascending the Mountain to receive from Yahweh Ten divinely revealed Commandments that were inscribed on tablets.[33]

When the Quran was revealed the enemies of Islam who opposed the
Prophet claimed it was a forgery. Muslims responded by urging them to
produce something similar (Quran 28:49; 11:13). Their inability to do so
reinforced Muslim believers' belief that the Quran is inimitable and that
the inimitability (i.e., that the language, ideas, and style of the Quran cannot be reproduced) speaks to its divine origin.[34] For Muslims, the Quran
is perfect, eternal, and unchangeable. In this regard it is the only miracle
brought about by Prophet Muhammad (PBUH).[35] Some Muslim scholars
also believe that the Quran is a copy of a heavenly original or urtext that resides with God in heaven and that God sent the Quran down to the prophet
who in turn transmitted the words he heard. Muslims greatly revered the
Quran for these reasons.

Thus, Muslims believe that the Quran is the divine message that was
delivered orally to Prophet Muhammad (PBUH) by the angel Gabriel over
a period of twenty three years. The Prophet and his companions committed
the message to memory and recited them during prayers. The first revelation occurred on "the night of power," in the month of Ramadan. The Quran
does not say anything about what the experience of receiving revelations had
on Prophet Muhammad (PBUH). "The matter is treated in non-scriptural
sources that refer to various consequences of the revelatory state. Among
the most commonly mentioned are that revelation was accompanied by
the ringing of a bell and that Muhammad experienced physical symptoms,
including a trance-like state, loss of consciousness, fatigue, perspiration, a
change in skin complexion, and general physical discomfort."[36]

The Quran, at least in its Arabic form, is "primarily an aural-oral phenomenon. It exhibits rhyme, rhythm, assonance, alliteration and other poetic qualities which are lost when it is rendered into English."[37] The divine
message that was revealed over a twenty three year period was revealed in
stages: ten years of revelations in Mecca and thirteen years of revelations
in Medina. During the Mecca revelations the Prophet repeated what was
revealed to him to his companions who "jotted them down on loose leaves
as aide memoire."[38] But in the Medinan period the Prophet "deliberately

33. Robinson, Islam, 91–92.

34. Ibid., 59.

35. Esposito, Islam, 19.

36. Kaltner, Introducing the Quran, 13.

37. Robinson, Islam, 59.

38. Ibid., 60.

employed scribes" such that by the time the Prophet died in 632 CE "all the revelations had been memorized and were also available in written form."[39]

The Quran in its present form consists of 114 Suras (chapters) of approximately 6000 verses. The Suras are not arranged in chronological order. The first revelation, for example, that was revealed to Prophet Muhammad (PBUH) is placed in Surah 96 and the final revelation is to be found in Surah 5. This last divine message was revealed in 632 CE and was the subject of a sermon the Prophet preached at Arafat while performing his last pilgrimage there.[40] The first Surah of the Quran, the Al-Fatiha (the Opening), is often treated as a standard prayer, while the last Surah, for Muslims, is a clear testimony to the perfection of the religion of Islam: "This day have I perfected for you your religion and completed my favor to you and chosen for you Islam as a religion" (Quran 5:3). The Prophet probably died shortly after this verse was revealed (about eighty-one or eighty-two days after). Mohammad (PBUH) is considered the last of the prophets because of this testimony of the perfection of the religion of Islam. The logic here is that if the religion has been perfected there is no need for a prophet after him.

Generally speaking, the Quran is arranged from the longest to the shortest chapters. From the arrangement of the Quran one cannot gain any certainty regarding the precise order in which all the Suras were revealed. But "in most instances it is usually fairly clear from the contents of a given Surah whether it was revealed during the Meccan or the Medinan period."[41] There are some differences between Meccan and Medinan Suras: .

1. Generally speaking, the Meccan Suras tend to be shorter than the Medinan Suras.

2. The Meccan Suras tend to have short verses (called Ayas).

3. According to Neal Robinson, Meccan Suras contain six principal types of material:

    i. Messenger Sections: addressed primarily to Muhammad the messenger of God, as message of comfort, rebuke, and encouragement.

    ii. Sign Sections: that points to the wonders of God's creation, which should elicit gratitude on the part of the believer.

    iii. Polemical Sections: that rebuke Arab pagans for worshipping false deities, rebukes them for their inordinate desire for

39. Ibid.
40. Ibid., 63.
41. Ibid., 63.

material things, and chastises them for not caring for vulnerable members of the society.

iv. Narrative Section: describes exemplary lives of believers like Joseph and Mary mother of Jesus and also describes how people who previously rejected God's divine message were punished.

v. Eschatological Sections: describes last judgment—the pleasures of Paradise and torments of Hell.

vi. Revelation sections: describes the authenticity of the divine message revealed to Muhammad and rebuts accusations against the Prophet.[42]

4. Medinan Suras often tend to be long and intricate, perhaps because they have universal significance. According to Robinson, the Medinan Suras contain the same six types of materials that are in the Meccan Suras but in a modified form:

i. Messenger Sections: often begin with the words "O Prophet. . .," suggesting that Muhammad is not the author of the message but a transmitter of the message.[43]

ii. Sign Sections: because the Medinan revelations are addressed primarily to Muslims, Jews, and Christians who share similar belief in the creative acts of God the sign sections are rare because they are no longer necessary.[44] Nevertheless, the sign sections still "affirm that God is the sole Creator and that all around us there are abundant signs of His beneficence and power which should evoke our gratitude and awe."[45]

iii. Polemical Sections: polemic against Arabs gradually gives way to tirade against unbelievers. The section takes "human beings to task for their inclination to worship false gods who leave them free to indulge their selfishness and greed to the detriment of the weaker members of society."[46]

iv. Narrative Section: "the narrative sections are no longer dominated by punishment stories about peoples who were utterly destroyed for their unbelief, but rather by stories of how God repeatedly forgave the children of Israel in Moses' time after

42. Ibid., 63–64.
43. Ibid., 65.
44. Ibid., 64.
45. Ibid., 65.
46. Ibid.

chastising them."[47] It is also a "salutary reminder that past civilizations which sank to that level of degradation, and which rejected the upright prophets and messengers who tried to call the people to their senses, have vanished almost without trace."[48]

v. Eschatological Sections: the long eschatological section is now replaced "by much simpler stereotyped allusions to Paradise and Hell which are addressed to the believers."[49] Prophet Muhammad (PBUH) is also portrayed as having the same status as the other Hebrew prophets like Moses. The eschatological sections offer a dire warning that our society is heading the same way as that of the past civilization who rejected the message of the prophets.

vi. Revelation sections: the revelation sections are relatively rare. But it does "reinforce the Messenger sections by indicating that the message originated with none other than the Creator."[50]

5. The Medinan Suras "contain a profusion of legal precepts and exhortations intended specifically for the believing community."[51]

6. Unlike Mecca where the Prophet had only a small group of followers in the early beginnings of the religion, in Medina the Prophet was an established religious and political leader and had to attend to matters of law and order as a religious and political leader. The Medinan revelations tend to reflect these hands-on useful matters, which for all practical purposes are the seeds of Islamic laws on social justice (inheritance, divorce, war, almsgiving, etc.). For example, the Medinan revelations prohibit gambling and usury (charging of interest on loans). The Medinan revelations also command the payment of compulsory charity (zakat) and institute the Ramadan fast as a way of mortification and inculcating self-discipline, and self-restraint.[52].

In terms of arrangement of the Quran, in some places some Meccan passages are interspersed with Medinan passages. But the central message of both the Meccan and Medinan revelations remain the same: that there is no God but Allah. Both the Meccan and Medinan messages were framed in a way that would appeal to Muhammad's contemporaries: "Hell is depicted

47. Ibid., 64.
48. Ibid., 65.
49. Ibid
50. Ibid., 65.
51. Ibid., 65.
52. Ibid., 66.

as worse than a tropical desert in the heat of summer, with neither water nor shade, whereas Paradise sounds more enticing and refreshing than any earthly oasis."[53] Most scholars agree that the Quran went through an editing process, which may have been responsible for the arrangement of the book. The standard Egyptian edition of the Quran follows ancient traditions whereby each Surah comes with a heading that states whether the message was revealed in Mecca or Medina. Some English translations of the Quran have also copied this idea of giving a standard heading to each Surah.[54]

THE FIVE PILLARS OF FAITH

So far we have seen that the Islam that emerged in the seventh century CE in Arabia "was not an isolated, totally new monotheistic religion."[55] Before Islam, Zoroastrianism, Judaism, and Christianity all preached monotheistic faith. These three religions "had been flourishing in Semitic and Iranian cultures for centuries preceding Muhammad's ministry."[56] Although these religions preached monotheism, community, fidelity, final judgment, etc., one of their main problems was that they had all, to some degree, "become associated with political power, that is, had become an official state religion: Judaism in the kingdoms of Judea and Israel, Christianity in the Roman (Byzantine) empire, Zoroastrianism in the Persian (Sassanid) empire."[57] Muhammad's essential claim was that he did not start a new religion but rather that his message was to call people back to the original message of the God that the people had deviated from. He thought that "majority of Arabs lived in ignorance (*jahiliyya*) of Allah and His will as revealed to the prophets Adam, Abraham, Moses, and Jesus. Moreover, he believed that both the Jewish and the Christian communities had distorted God's original revelation to Moses and later to Jesus."[58] Thus, what Muhammad brought was not a new religion, but Islam (total self-surrender) to the will of Allah. This requires turning from unbelief to the straight path or law (sharia) of God.[59] For the sake of simplification it is not unusual to speak of Muhammad's message as the Five Pillars of Faith. These "pillars" are the bedrock on which Islam is built: .

53. Ibid., 65.
54. Ibid., 63.
55. Esposito, *Islam*, 4.
56. Ibid.
57. Ibid.
58. Esposito, *Islam*, 12.
59. Ibid.

1. The Witness of Faith or *Shahada*

Pre-Islamic Arabia recognized the existence of God whom they called *alilah*, meaning "the god." They thought of this god as a high god or a remote deity who had little or no relevance to their everyday life. He was not, in their view, the sole deity, but one of many. They also thought this deity, *alilah*, had daughters (like the goddesses "Lat Manat" and "al-Uzza) and associates that could be appealed to for help.[60] But not all inhabitants of pre-Islamic Arabia were pagans. There were some Arab-speaking Jews and Christians who recognized the moral demands God makes of us and know God properly as Allah. They are recognized by the Quran as the "People of the Book." There were also others who practiced Zoroastrianism, a religion that the Quran finds repugnant. Zoroastrianism was established in Persia around the sixth century BCE. It was founded by Zoroaster who lived from 628–551 BCE. Zoroaster taught a monotheistic doctrine. The name of the one supreme God is Ahura Mazdah. But Zoroaster's doctrine was dualistic—that there are two powerful and competing forces in the world. Zoroastrianism was the official religion of Persia (modern day Iran) in pre-Islam Arabia. Under the threat of Islam Zoroastrians began to leave Persia and headed towards India where they founded a community. They were known as the Parsis in India. The remnants of the group who are still in Iran are referred to as the Gabars.

Although all these religious groups recognized the majesty of God, "some of them had unorthodox beliefs about Him."[61] The Christian belief in the Trinitarian Persons was considered one of these "unorthodox beliefs" about Allah. Islam explicitly condemns the thought of setting up a partner with God. This is called shirk or association, an offense the Quran says will not be forgiven (Quran 4:48, 116).[62] A person who engages in the sin of shirk is called a *mushrik*, meaning he or she associates something with God and violates the essential oneness of God.[63] It is good to be clear though that the Quran never considers Jews and Christians to be *mushrikun* because Jews and Christians, like Muslims, believe in one God and have God's word transmitted to them through the *Tawrat* (Torah) and the *Injil* (Gospels). This is why the

60. Robinson, *Islam*, 75.

61. Ibid., 76.

62. Kaltner, *Introducing the Quran*, 44.

63. Ibid., 210.

Quran repeatedly refers to Jews and Christians as "People of the Book," meaning that they are the recipients of revealed texts.[64]

The Quran explicitly teaches God's unity (*tawhid*) or oneness of God. This explicit teaching about the oneness of God was preached by Adam, the first prophet, and continued down to the other prophets of Allah like Abraham, Moses, Noah, etc. "An uncompromising belief in the monotheistic nature of God is therefore not only the foundation of Islam, but also the first and foremost condition of being a Muslim."[65] The *Shahada* or the Muslim testimony that there is no god but the one God and that Muhammad is His prophet is the most devoted testimony to the absolute oneness of God.[66] "It is a grave sin to generate or worship the images of God in any shape or form. It is unthinkable for a Muslim to conceptualize God as a figure with any biological or physical features."[67] The Quran ascribes different names to God to stress both the unity and eternity of God: beneficence, merciful, Self-sufficient, omnipotence, and omniscience, etc. The Quran teaches that this one God is Creator and that this Creator-God participates in human history. "The blind fatalism of the pre-Islamic Arabs is countered by the Quran's assertion that Allah determines when we are born, what calamities will befall us, and when we shall die. He knows everything we do and not even our innermost thoughts escape Him."[68]

2. Prayer or *Salat*

The second pillar of faith is *salat* (prayer). Islam recognizes that every religion practices some forms of ritual prayer. Islamic tradition believes that the purest form of ritual prayer was practiced by Abraham, Ishmael, Moses, and Jesus, but that generations after them watered down the ritual prayer which these prophets held in their sublime form. The Quran specifically denounces these watered down prayer, particularly the one that was practiced by the Arabs at Kaaba before Islam, describing it as "nothing but whistling and clapping of hands" (Quran 8:35).[69] Prayer in Islam is a way of reaffirming the majesty of God and seeking from God his help in walking the straight path of virtue, as against choosing the path of wrath and destruction.[70]

64. Ibid., 211.

65. Nawaz, *Islam*, 10.

66. Ibid., 12.

67. Ibid.

68. Robinson, *Islam*, 77.

69. See Robinson, *Islam*, 96.

70. Nawaz, *Islam*, 14.

According to tradition, Muhammad (PBUH) received revelation that he and his followers must pray fifty times a day but because this would prove too arduous Muhammad (PBUH) pleaded and bargained with God until the number was reduced to five.[71] Following a Muslim's testimony to the oneness of God (the *Shahada*), "prayer constitutes the second of the obligatory duties that a believer must perform five times a day."[72] Prayer times are determined by the position of the sun and may vary depending on the season. In Muslim countries prayer times are followed by an announcement that is broadcast from the minaret of the mosque by the adhan (call to prayer).[73] More important however is that the daily prayers be spread out throughout the day:

1. Fajr: the first of the five daily prayers performed at dawn or day break.

2. Zhuhr: the second of the five daily prayers performed at midday (see Quran 62:9–11).

3. Asr: the third of the five daily prayers performed late afternoon.

4. Maghrib: the fourth of the five daily prayers performed at sunset.

5. Isha: the fifth of the five daily prayers performed at night.

The proper place for obligatory prayer is the Masjid (mosque). Prayer can be performed individually or as a group. Group prayer is preferred because it shows the unity of the Muslim community. Muslims pray facing the Quibla—direction of the holy Mosque at Mecca. But a working or travelling Muslim can pray anywhere. All they need to do is find a clean place and make the place a suitable place for prayer. Sunni Muslims usually pray on a mat while it is customary for Shia Muslims to pray on bare earth.[74] "In addition to finding a suitable place for prayer, a Muslim must be appropriately dressed. A man's clothing should cover his shoulders and the area between the navel and the knees. According to some authorities his head should also be covered. A woman must cover her whole body apart from her face and hands. Men and women alike remove their shoes."[75]

Prayer, for a Muslim, is not a mechanical or ceremonial act. The mechanical form is not as important as the spirit of righteousness.[76]

71. Robinson, *Islam*, 97.

72. Nawaz, *Islam*, 15.

73. Robinson, *Islam*, 98.

74. Ibid., 99.

75. Ibid.

76. Nawaz, *Islam*, 18.

One of the requisites demand for prayer is a clean state of mind. This means that a Muslim performing prayer must carry out prayer with a clear mind such that he or she understands the recitation and actions involved in prayer.[77] If a Muslim performs prayer without being pure and clean that prayer is not valid. The Quran lists some things that render a person unclean for prayer. If a person, for instance, has just had urination, defecation, and sexual intercourse they are considered ritually unclean (see Quran 4:43; 5:6). These require some ritual purification known as *At-taharah*, which in itself is of two kinds: Wudu (ablution) and Ghusl (full ablution). Ablution is not done randomly. Rather, it is performed diligently according to a set of rules by washing one's hands, feet, mouth, nose, face, forearms, and head. If a woman, for example, have just completed menstruation or is within forty days of child birth she is required to perform ghusl (ritual washing of the whole body).[78]

How to Perform Wudu	How to Perform Ghusl
1. Must have the intention of performing Wudu.	1. Must have the intention of performing Ghusl.
2. Say: "Bismilahi Rahmani Rahim" (in the name of Allah, Most Gracious, Most Merciful).	2. Take full shower.
3. Wash hands, rinse mouth and clean inside of the nose with water.	
4. Wash face.	
5. Wash arms up to the elbows, starting with the right arm.	
6. Rub the head and ears with wet arms.	
7. Wash feet up to the ankle, starting with the right foot.	
8. Say the *Shahada*.	

Friday is to Muslims what Sunday is to Christians. The Friday congregational or juma prayer has a special significance for Muslims.[79] All adult males are encouraged to attend the Friday congregational prayer. Women are also encouraged to attend, but their attendance is not obligatory. The mode of prayer, in general, consists of a sequence of movements called a raka, "standing upright, bowing from the waist, standing upright again, prostrating, sitting on the left hell, prostrat-

77. Nawaz, *Islam*, 16.

78. Robinson, *Islam*, 99–100.

79. Nawaz, *Islam*, 17.

ing again, and then returning to the sitting position- accompanied by Qur'anic recitations and the utterance of set of expressions in Arabic."[80] The number of rakas to be performed vary according to the prayer time, i.e., whether it is morning prayer, afternoon prayer, or evening prayer.

3. Fasting or *Sawm*

Muslims are required to fast all year round, particularly in the month of Ramadan (the ninth month of the Islamic lunar calendar). The holy month of Ramadan is to the Islamic calendar year what prayer is to the daily life of a Muslim because the celebration of the Ramadan fast gives "the year its rhythmic turning around God."[81] Ramadan holds special significance because it is the month in which the Quran was revealed. Fasting attunes the Muslim to God, making him or her aware of God's ever presence. As a way of showing gratitude to God the Muslim refrains from evil thoughts and evil actions. Fasting also helps the Muslim learn and practice self-denial and self-control. The Quran also prescribes fasting as a means of expiating one's sins (Quran 33:35).[82]

The Quran prescribes the fixed number of days of fasting, what is to be done and what is to be avoided during fast (Quran 2:183–185, 187). Fasting begins from sunset and lasts till sundown. No food, drink, or sexual activities are permitted during fast. Fasting is compulsory for all adult male and female Muslim in sound health. People with serious illness and elderly people are exempted from fasting. Children who have reached the age of puberty are encouraged to fast, but not compulsory.[83] "Those who are traveling or suffering from an ailment are allowed to make up for the missed days when they have completed their journeys and recovered from sickness."[84]

Before fasting in the month of Ramadan was made compulsory Muslims who were with Prophet Muhammad (PBUH) in Medina used to fast with Jews, as a show of solidarity, on the day of Ashura (the tenth day of Muharram, the first month of the Muslim calendar), the Jewish Day of Atonement, and a day that Jews commemorate their liberation from Egypt. The Jewish Day of Atonement is commemorated on the ninth day after Rosh Hashanah (Jewish New Year). It was Jewish belief that God was closer to them on the Day of Atonement

---

80. Robinson, *Islam*, 100.

81. Carmody and Brink, *Ways to the Center*, 303–4.

82. Robinson, *Islam*, 117.

83. Nawaz, *Islam*, 36.

84. Ibid.

than on any other day.[85] When the practice of fasting in the month of Ramadan became mandatory after Muslim break with the Jews fasting on the day of Ashura became optional. But the idea of the nearness of God to the Muslim on this month is retained. Apart from the moral and spiritual significance of fasting in the month of Ramadan, there is also a socio-religious significance. "The method and timing of the fast distinguishes Muslims from Jews and Christians, marking them off as a distinct community. The fact that all Muslims fast during the same period and break the fast at the same time increases their sense of solidarity with each other at both the local and the international level."[86]

When does fasting in the month of Ramadan begin? The Islamic calendar, a lunar based calendar has twelve lunar months of 29 or 30 days, which totals about 355 days (11 days short of the Gregorian calendar). The month before Ramadan is called the *Shaban*. Muslims begin to look for the thin crescent of the new moon from the twenty-ninth day of *Shaban*. When the *qadi* (Islamic judge) determines that the new moon is out Muslims are informed to begin fasting the following day.[87] This means that the beginning of Ramadan fast varies from country to country. Neal Robinson points out three potential problems this variation of the start of Ramadan fast poses for Muslims living in northern Europe and North America in contemporary world. First, the marked seasonal variation in number of daylight hours means "that when Ramadan falls in summer, the fasting period is far longer than it would be in Arabia, but that when it falls in winter it is far shorter."[88] Second, regarding the beginning and ending of the Ramadan fast, "because northern skies are often occluded at night, local Muslim communities usually take their cue from religious authorities in Saudi Arabia, Iran or Pakistan, rather than rely on local sightings of the new moon. Unfortunately this often results in different ethnic groups being out of step with each other by twenty-four hours, despite living in the same city."[89] Third, "against the clear skies of Arabia, the moon is visible night after night, and Muslims watch it wax and wane. They know for example that when there is a full moon they are half way through the month. In northern cities, however, the moon may be visible for as few as two or three days. For their inhabitants,

85. Robinson, *Islam*, 123.
86. Ibid., 124.
87. Robinson, *Islam*, 119
88. Ibid., 126.
89. Ibid.

the link between Ramadan and the lunar cycle is thus almost entirely severed."[90]

The Ramadan fast ends with the feast of *Eid-el-Fitr* that is celebrated on the first day of *Shawwal* (the tenth month of the Islamic calendar). *Eid* celebrations hold special significance for Muslims all over the world because it symbolizes their unity, brotherhood, and solidarity. "Every household with financial capabilities is required to donate a specific amount of money or its equivalent in kind (called 'Fitra') for charitable causes. In addition, people with ample monetary resources contribute generously to help the poor and the needy."[91]

4. Almsgiving or *Zakat*

Zakat is obligatory charity expected of a Muslim. The Quran prescribes prayer and charity, not as options, but as duties that help a Muslim purify his or her life. The word "zakat" originally meant "purity."[92] When *Zakat* was first revealed it was intended as a voluntary charity (Quran 73:20) but was later extended to mean an obligatory duty because it serves as "a source of purification and sanctification of human soul, a vehicle of inner security, and a means of repentance from one's sinful actions (Quran 9:104)."[93] The obligation to do *zakat* is an obligation to donate a fixed percentage of one's income or wealth. *Zakat* is distributed to the poor and needy; never to be given to the rich or one's dependents. If a person is too poor to pay the obligatory zakat he or she is still expected to act charitably.[94] At its root *zakat* has a spiritual significance in that it binds the giver and receiver in mutual respect and affection.[95] Giving a certain percentage of one's wealth helps one fulfill an important religious obligation and by so doing purifies one from greed and selfishness. In similar fashion, the one who receives zakat is purified because zakat saves the person from humiliation that comes from begging.[96] There is also the socio-economic function of zakat. "Together with the prohibition of usury, *zakat* discourages the hoarding of capital and stimulates investment in the means of production or merchandise, neither of which is usually regarded as zakatable."[97]

90. Ibid.

91. Nawaz, *Islam*, 38.

92. Robinson, *Islam*, 111.

93. Nawaz, *Islam*, 39.

94. Robinson, *Islam*, 113.

95. Ibid., 115.

96. Ibid.

97. Ibid.

Besides *zakat*, Islam also encourages voluntary almsgiving known as *sadaqa*. Quran 9:60 lists eight categories of people that are eligible to receive *sadaqa*: the poor, destitute, captives who need to obtain their freedom, debtors, wayfarers, those employed to collect funds, those whose hearts are to be reconciled (perhaps may be referring to inhabitants of Mecca who were at first hostile to Islam but later converted when Mecca was conquered by Muslims), and those engage in holy war.[98]

5. Pilgrimage or *Hajj*

Muslims pray facing Mecca because for Muslims Mecca is "the center, the omphalos (navel) where the world was born."[99] The same inner logic is present in the obligation to make pilgrimage to Mecca at least once in one's life time.[100] The obligation to make pilgrimage to Mecca was instituted in the ninth year of the *Hejira* (Muhammad's flight from Mecca to Medina). Pre-Islamic Arabs made pilgrimage to the Kaaba in Mecca where they worshipped idols, particularly the three idols Al-Lat, Al-Manat, and Al-Uzza that were designated by the Koraish as daughters of Allah. The Quran denounces this idol worship as blasphemy. When obligatory pilgrimage was mandated for Muslims, Abou Bakr, one of the closest companions to Prophet Muhammad (PBUH), on the orders of the Prophet made a public announcement that "no polytheist shall be allowed to perform Hajj (pilgrimage) after that year."[101] This prohibition forbidden pagans and polytheists from performing pilgrimage to Mecca came approximately 631 CE. Prophet Muhammad (PBUH) led an exclusively Muslim Hajj in 632 CE. Today the area in Mecca known as the haram (sanctuary or sacred precinct) are clearly marked and non-Muslims are not allowed anywhere near the area. In this area is located the sacred mosque known as al-masjid al-haram. To the east of the sacred mosque are two hills Safa and Marwa that pilgrims have to pass through. At the center of the sacred mosque is the Kaaba (a cube shaped building that pilgrims circumambulate counter-clockwise).

Muslims usually trace the origin of pilgrimage to Mecca to Abraham and Ishmael who performed true worship of Allah at the Kaaba. The Quran explicitly states that it was Abraham and his son Ishmael who erected the Kaaba and God ordained it to be a sanctuary

---

98. Robinson, *Islam*, 112–13.

99. Carmody and Brink, *Ways to the Center*, 304.

100. Ibid.

101. Nawaz, *Islam*, 47.

or place of prayer (see Quran 2:124–9).[102] But with passage of time the followers of Abraham and Ishmael relapsed into idol worship.[103] Thus, Muslims perform pilgrimage to Mecca "to sanctify their true faith in Allah, the one and Absolutely One God without any partners or associates."[104] The Hajj is performed the second week of *Dhul-hijja* (the twelfth month of the Muslim calendar) and lasts for five days. The Hajj consists of series of rituals. Muslims performing the hajj dress modestly to signify their renunciation of worldly vanities. The simple dress of all the pilgrims also signify the unity of the believers—that there is no socio-economic or racial distinction. The Quran mentions that Safa and Marwa are among the places ordained by God for sacred rites (Quran 2:18).[105] The pilgrims run seven times between the hills of Safa and Marwa to "commemorate the agony of Hagar, wife of Abraham, running between the hills of find water for her son Ishmael. It also symbolizes the struggle of life which prompts human beings to enhance their efforts in seeking divine support."[106] There is the other ritual of throwing stones at the three pillars, which symbolizes Muslim rejection of the devil—the same devil who tried to dissuade Abraham from sacrificing his son as commanded by God.[107] At the conclusion of the Hajj Muslims shave their head and slaughter an animal in imitation of Prophet Muhammad and his companions who shaved their head and slaughtered a sacrificial animal at the conclusion of their hajj. The slaughtering of animal takes place on the third day of the Hajj when Muslims celebrate *Eid ul-Adha* (Festival of the Sacrifice). At the conclusion of the Hajj those Muslims who could afford it are encouraged to visit the Prophet's burial place in Medina, the second holiest city for Muslims.

Related to the Hajj is a lesser pilgrimage known as the *Umra*. The *Umra* is not an obligation, but is encouraged. It can be performed at any time of the year. Pagan Arabs who performed Hajj also performed the *Umra* until they were forbidden to do these in 631 by the prophet. The series of rituals involved in *Umra* is about the same as that of Hajj.

102. Robinson, *Islam*, 129–30.

103. Nawaz, *Islam*, 47.

104. Nawaz, *Islam*, 47–48.

105. Robinson, *Islam*, 130.

106. Nawaz, *Islam*, 51.

107. Ibid.

Islam in the United States of America

Often neglected in the history of the Atlantic Slave Trade is the fact that Slave Trade brought significant number of black Muslims to the United States of America and the so called New World. Before the Atlantic Slave Trade Islam flourished in many African Kingdoms, particularly in the Old Ghana Empire that reached its peak in the 13th century, the Old Mali Empire that reached its peak in the late 15th/16th century CE, and the late Songhai Empire that thrived in the 16th century. Islam was introduced to these kingdoms in the ninth and tenth century CE. Africa was connected to the Muslim world through the Trans Saharan Trade routes that were controlled by Berbers from North Africa and Muslim traders from Tunisia, Morocco, Egypt, and Algeria. These Muslim traders traded in salt and gold with their sub-Saharan African counterparts. Trade brought a lot of cultural exchanges between the different trading partners. Islamic art, calligraphy, music, and ways of life were introduced to sub-Saharan Africa. One of the reasons for the growth of the early African kingdoms was Islam, which served as a means of unity and also provided social and political privileges. Many of the rulers, like Mansa Musa of Ghana, were devout Muslims who saw Islam as an opportunity to trade and connect with the Muslim world. Following the mandate that the religion of the king was the religion of the state, many Africans converted to Islam as soon as their leader became a Muslim. Timbuktu became a great center of Islamic learning. About 3 million of the African slaves that were brought to the Americas and the Caribbean islands in the seventeenth and eighteenth century were Muslims. About one million of these Muslim slaves made it to the United States. Many of the Muslim slaves captured in what is now Mali, Nigeria, Ghana, Senegal, Guinea, and Gambia were literate and learned. They kept aspects of their culture and Islamic religion when they were brought to the United States. From police records, plantation logs, and runaway notices that were kept by the courts and slave owners we know that some of these slaves practiced their Islamic religion openly while others practiced them secretly. For example, many of the slaves said their five daily prayers, fasted during the holy month of Ramadan, abstained from eating pork, bore Muslim names, and made Islamic calligraphy (artistic representation of Islamic faith). Some of the Muslim slaves even left journals.

The second wave of Muslim immigration into the United States was in the mid-twentieth century when Palestinian refugees began emigrating to Europe and the United States following the creation of the state of Israel by the United Nations in 1948. The Immigration and Nationality Act of 1952 (also known as the Mc-Carran-Walter Act) also helped to accelerate the wave of Muslim immigration to the United States. The Mc-Carran-Walter

Act was put in place as a post-World War II and Cold War measure to check the influx of communists from Japan and the former Soviet Union (USSR) into the United States. While the goal of the Act was to reward notable Asian countries, like China, and assimilate them into the mainstream of US life, the Act was also an exclusionary measure meant to deny entry to the United States to people who refuse to be assimilated into the US economic and political structures. The Mc-Carran-Walter Act was deemed exclusionary by critics and the controversy surrounding the Act, together with other factors, led to a revision of the US immigration laws in 1965. The 1965 Immigration and Nationality Act (also known as the Hart-Celler Act) abolished the national origins formula of the Mc-Carran-Walter Act and instituted a new formula based on skill sets of immigrants. This new policy open the flood gate of immigration for Muslims fleeing political and economic oppression in places like Palestine, Syria, Jordan, Pakistan, and Egypt. They established mosques in cities like Detroit, New York, New Jersey, and Chicago.

Wallace D. Farad, one of the immigrants from the Middle East, established a mosque in Detroit that attracted African-Americans. His message was a mixture of Islam and Black Nationalism. The movement thrived under his disciple Elijah Mohammed who made Chicago the capital of movement. Many African-Americans saw this movement, which preached black pride and black emancipation from white rule, as a way to liberate themselves from poverty and racism. For these reasons they converted in droves. This group got the attention of the world during the 1960s civil rights movement. They were popularly referred to as Black Muslims. Malcolm X (formerly Malcolm Little), a student and disciple of Elijah Muhammad's, exemplified what the movement represents with the credo "the white man hates us, so we should hate the white man back."[108] Malcolm denounced Christianity as a religion designed for slaves and defended Islam as the only religion that was not fixated on color differences or race. Malcolm argued, therefore, that black people have to be separated (not integrated) with white America and that it was only through separation that black people in America will discover their self-identity.

108. See Haley, *The Autobiography of Malcolm X*, xvi.

11

Religious Rapprochement and African Traditional Religions

ACCORDING TO THE EVOLUTIONARY science of religion, religion is not a term with a fixed meaning, but a word whose meaning is always evolving and adapting. In its evolutionary sense, the word religion can convey different meanings to different people and can also represent totally different realities.[1] Most people who consider themselves religious accept the particular religion that they are born into. There are also those who self-consciously choose their own religion later on in life. But that is not to say that the two are mutually exclusive. A person can be born into a particular religion and still self-consciously choose it, making it a life-vision. In this final chapter we shall examine the Tribal religions, with particular attention to African Traditional Religions (ATRs), and with a view to highlighting the differences between "religion as clan-solidarity" and "religion as life-vision."[2] But before delving into this distinction it is important to highlight some key common features of the religions of the world, many of which we did not examine in this book because they do not fall within our Abrahamic religions.

1. Fernando, "An Asian's View of Jesus' Uniqueness," 70.
2. Ibid.

WORLD RELIGIONS: COMMON THEMES

The three Abrahamic religions we examined, i.e., Judaism, Christianity, and Islam, are religions that the British historian, Arnold Toynbee (1889–1975), characterized as the religions of revelation, According to Toynbee, in spite of their common historical root, these three religions have a tendency towards exclusivism and intolerance.[3] Toynbee also described these three Abrahamic religions as religions that ascribe to themselves ultimate validity. Building on this idea, the German theologian, Friedrich Heiler (1892–1967), suggested that what these religions in fact do is "transfer the absoluteness which is an attribute alone of the divine and eternal to their own system of faith without seeing that this divine absolute can also be comprehended in entirely different forms of thought and devotion."[4] The logical outcome of this is to fall into the danger of thinking of religions other than the Abrahamic ones as "second class" religions or not even religions in the proper sense. To help correct this mistaken notion that the non-Abrahamic religions may have emerged as an "outgrowth of error, sin, and malice,"[5] it is good that we end this work by examining some common threads that hold the religions of the world (i.e., World Religions) together—Judaism, Christianity, Islam, Zoroastrianism, Hinduism, Buddhism, and Taoism.

World Religions differ from Tribal religions. Unlike tribal religions, the World Religions are more global and spread out. They are not concentrated in one region or place. The World Religions are also proselytizing religions—they are given to making converts. Another distinguishing factor is that World Religions usually have a founder and a written text that serve as scripture. The only exception to this is Hinduism, which has no founder, no divinely revealed scriptures, no creed or dogmas, no ecclesiastical organization or 'church,' and, in many of its forms, does not give importance to the concept of a personal divinity.[6] In general, however, all the World Religions have a common concern for cosmic harmony, inner peace, oneness with nature, the art of meditation as a way to the divine, asceticism and self-denial, the full use of higher human faculties, communication with the spirit world, and loyalty to one's family, community, and tradition.[7] Seven principal areas of agreement are worthy of attention.[8] .

3. See Toynbee, *An Historian Approach to Religion.*

4. See Heiler, "The History of Religions as a Preparation for the Cooperation of Religions."

5. Ibid.

6. Kessler, *Eastern Ways of Being Religious*, 39.

7. Hellwig, "Rethinking Uniqueness," 77–78.

8. See Lonergan, "The Future of Christianity," 149–63.

1. Reality of the Transcendent.

   All the World Religions acknowledge "the reality of the transcendent, the holy, the divine, the Other," who is assumed to be the eternal truth or "one without counterpart."[9] In Judaism this eternal truth is Yahweh. In Christianity, it is the Trinitarian Godhead—Father, Son, and Holy Spirit. In Islam it is the one God, Allah. Hinduism has an evolving polytheism that recognizes about 330 million gods, like Brahma (creator god), Vishnu (preserver), and Shiva (the destroyer). In Buddhism although divinities of one kind or the other may play some role in stories and practices that shape the peoples' life, "the divine is essentially unimportant when it comes to understanding life, suffering, and the way to overcome suffering."[10] Taoism recognizes the Highest Venerable Lord—the manifestation of Tao or Way of Reality.[11] Zoroastrianism speaks of the one supreme God, Ahura Mazda who is called the Wise Lord.[12]

2. The Divine Transcendent is Immanent in Human Hearts.

   All the World Religions find a creative balance for the tension between the transcendence and immanence of God. Jewish Scripture speaks of God in terms of both of God's transcendent and immanent qualities: "Am I a God nearby, says the Lord, and not a God far off? Who can hide in secret places so that I cannot see them? Says the Lord. Do I not fill heaven and earth? Says the Lord" (Jer. 23: 23–24). Christian Scripture speaks of the indwelling of the Holy Spirit among humans: "do you not know that your body is a temple of the Holy Spirit within you, which you have from God, and that you are not your own?" (I Cor. 6:19). Islam's distinctive virtue is to recognize the indwelling place of God in human hearts: "O you who believe! Answer (the call of) Allah and His Messenger when he calls you to that which gives you life; and know that Allah intervenes between man and his heart, and that to Him you shall be gathered" (Al-Anfal 8:24). In the Hindu pantheistic conception of God in the Upanishads, God is everything and everything is God. A person's goal is to be one with God (Brahma). In Taoism, humans are part of the cosmic process known as the Tao and the goal of human life, like that of all created reality, is harmony with the Tao.[13]

9. Ibid., 149–50.

10. Kessler, *Eastern Ways of Being Religious*, 99.

11. Ibid., 227.

12. Carmody and Brink, *Ways to the Center*, 74.

13. Young, *The World Religions*, 118.

3. The Highest Good is the Final Goal.

All the World Religions teach that the highest good is the final goal of all human striving.[14] Judaism, Christianity, and Islam all describe God as the ultimate and supreme good to whom all things tend and towards whom all humans strive. It is akin to the notion of *moksha* (liberation or release) from the world of suffering and cycles of life, death, and re-birth in Hinduism. In Buddhism it is nirvana—liberation from the cycle of suffering, birth, death, and re-birth. In Taoism it is transformation occurring within this life on earth.

4. The Reality of the Divine is Ultimate Love.

All the World Religions treat love as both the way of God and the way to God. In Judaism Yahweh's mercy is the same as Yahweh's justice and love. Christianity is a religion of love: "Beloved, let us love one another, because love is from God" (I John 4:7). Love is the basis of relationship in Islam: "And among His Signs is this, that He created for you mates from among yourselves, that ye may dwell in tranquility with them, and He has put love and mercy between your [hearts]: Verily in that are Signs for those who reflect" (Al-Rum 30:21). Love is at the root of the Hindu ethic of *ahimsa* (non-injury to animals and all life forms) and Buddhist asceticism.

5. The Way to God is through Sacrifice.

All the World's Religions teach that the way to reach God is through sacrifice. The Jewish *Yom Kippur* (Day of Atonement) is a subdued and solemn celebration of fasting and reconciliation—a period in which one makes effort to reach out and reconcile with estranged members of one's family or community. Islam recommends fasting, especially in the holy month of Ramadan. Christians fast for forty days in Lent. Hindu gurus practice self-discipline. Many of them flock to Varanasi at old age, the site of the Hindu sacred river Ganges, to die and reflect the Hindu belief "that death in or near the Ganges at Varanasi results in Moksha, the final liberation from the endless cycles of birth and re-birth that is the ultimate spiritual goal of most Hindus."[15] Buddhism is called the Middle Way because Buddhists seek a middle way between excesses of sensuality and extreme asceticism.

6. Love of Neighbor.

The World Religions teach, not only love of God, but also love of one's neighbor. "All preach brotherly love, a love on which there are no

14. Lonergan, "The Future of Christianity," 150.
15. Kessler, *Eastern Ways of Being Religious*, 41.

limitations, a love that is to be extended even to enemies, a love that has its origin and source not in man himself but in God operating on man."[16] Christianity, Islam, and Judaism are religions that emphasize personal and communal salvation. The Hindu, Buddhist, and Taoist do not think of self in isolation from nature and society. Karma, which Hinduism and Buddhism preach, shows that what a person does or fails to do in this present life is going to determine his or her fate in this life or next. In other words, one's advancement or regression is going to be determined by the extent to which one has loved one's neighbor.

7. Love is the Ultimate and Supreme Way to God.

All the World Religions preach an ethic of love, i.e., love that has no limits, no qualifications. Jesus showed that love by dying on the cross. Love is at the heart of Gandhi's doctrine of non-violence resistance. Buddha showed it through the enlightenment that earned him nirvana.

TRIBAL RELIGIONS

Tribal religions are the religious systems of indigenous peoples—African Traditional Religions (ATRs), Native American Religions, Australian Aborigines, and the Arctic peoples who inhabit the regions of Siberia to Alaska, to Canada, i.e., the Eskimos, Inuits, and Aleuts, etc. Tribal religions differ from the World Religions in many respects. The designation "tribal" is used to capture their form of social organization, which was usually a small band of hunters and gatherers who lived in an extended family structure or clan.[17] Hunting and gathering, their main economic activity, varied according to geographical and historical peculiarities.[18] Some anthropologists have taken to referring to tribal religions as prehistoric, pre-literate, and oral. These designations are meant to capture the fact that tribal peoples have no written records.

Modern mentality is far different from that of ancient cultures where history and culture were transmitted orally from generation to generation. But modern mentality requires writing "for a critical, objective, factual, trustworthy account of what happened."[19] It is helpful to understand that what makes these cultures tribal is their social organizations, which are based on tribes or clan. They are by no means "primitive" or "pagan" as

16. Lonergan, "The Future of Christianity," 151.

17. Carmody and Brink, *Ways to the Center*, 27.

18. Ibid.

19. Carmody and Brink, *Ways to the Center*, 25.

some Western anthropologists sometimes pejoratively describe them. They may not have had technology in the modern understanding of the term, but they had a well-developed religious organization that addressed their most absorbing issues—those relating to survival, like birth, subsistence, and death.[20] They pondered life mysteries in terms of its implications to hunting. Hunting and gathering were, for them, sacred affairs that deal with nature's awesome powers concerning life and death.[21]

Common Areas

When a person is born and socialized into a religion, that religion can become for that person a form of "clan solidarity." Religion as "clan solidarity" is quite different from religion as "life-vision." The latter is a religion a person is "re-born to."[22] Tribal religions are good examples of "religion as clan solidarity." As a constituent element of culture, tribal religions fulfill an important sociological function that is vital for human existence.[23] Tribal religions, like culture's other constitutive elements —history of the clan, the geography of the clan, and the language of the clan— ensure clan solidarity.[24]

Like the World Religions, tribal religions have their own core common characteristics. As oral cultures, their sacred texts are not recorded in what may amount to holy books or scripture, but are contained in the memory of the people, particularly the elders of the community, and are transmitted through their traditional symbols, rituals, myths, and practices. Tribal religions are essentially religion as clan solidarity. As a form of clan solidarity, tribal religions are more provincial in their concerns. In other words, the characteristics that make them tribal are simply virtues that are culturally conditioned.[25] .

1. The Sacred.

   In his book, *The Idea of the Holy*, the German Lutheran theologian, Rudolph Otto (1869–1937) analyzes the experience that underlies all religions. He calls this experience "numinous" and suggests that there are three components of this experience: *mysterium tremendum et*

---

20. Ibid., 27.
21. Ibid., 28.
22. Fernando, "An Asian's View of Jesus' Uniqueness," 70.
23. Ibid.
24. Ibid., 70–71.
25. Ibid., 71.

fascinans (mystery that is tremendous and fascinating). The mystery that is experienced, according to Otto, is unlike anything one experiences in ordinary life and because this mystery is "wholly other" it evokes silence and provokes awe or fear. The other part of this mystery or "awe" is that when provoked it does not dispel but attracts (fascinans).[26] Tribal religions experience the sacred in the Otto sense of *mysterium tremendum et fascinans.* The Pacific island people of Papua New Guinea (known as Melanasians), for example, consider their deity to be sacred. They also consider their land to be sacred because it was given to them by their deity who created it from the remains of the sun and the moon.[27] This idea that certain things are set apart to be revered as sacred is common among tribal cultures. Emile Durkheim's (1858–1917) definition of religion as "a unified system of beliefs and practices relative to sacred things, that is to say, things set apart and forbidden"[28] captures the essence of tribal religions.

2. Animism

   Animism is the belief that all things, whether animals, plants, vegetation, seas, rivers, etc. have spirits or soul. Tribal cultures believe that there is a wide array of spirits out there with vested interests in human affairs and that the way one relates to the spirit world enhances or undermines one's life activities. This belief in spirits inform their worldview that spirits have to be worshiped or venerated. There are good spirits and bad spirits. Good spirits bring good fortune. Bad spirits bring bad fortune. Some cultures venerate the spirits of their dead ancestors, believing that such veneration will bring them good fortune. In Shintoism (the ancient religion of Japan) spirits are called "kami." Because they believe that "kami" exists in all natural things like lakes, rivers, mountains, oceans, animals, and plants, Shintos have shrines in several places for the worship of "kami." The British anthropologist, Sir Edward Burnett Tylor (1832–1917), developed the idea that religion at its core was animistic—that religion began as an attempt to explain ghosts.[29]

3. Exorcism.

   The belief in animism is related to the idea of exorcism—that bad spirits, which possess a person, need to be cast out. The duty of casting out evil spirit is not for everyone. It is usually the task of the high priest or

26. See Otto, *The Idea of the Holy.*

27. Carmody and Brink, *Ways to the Center,* 52.

28. Durkheim, "Ritual, Magic, and the Sacred," 193.

29. Carmody and Brink, *Ways to the Center,* 21.

shaman. The shaman is the medicine man who has good knowledge of the religious and cultural traditions of the people. Many indigenous cultures have women shamans. They ward off evil spirits through various means, like incantations and herbal medicine.

4. Healing.

Exorcism is one way of procuring healing. But it is not only the one possessed by evil spirit that needs healing. There is a wide range of activities in tribal cultures that require healing. A person who has committed a taboo, for example, or one who has fractured his or her relationship with the community, is brought back to the community only after going through a ritual sacrifice intended to heal or make whole.

5. Sacrifice.

Sacrifice is a ritual performed to appease deity in tribal cultures. Sacrifices usually take the form of ritual offerings, like animal sacrifice, and in some societies, human sacrifice. The purpose of sacrifice is to restore harmony where the social fabric of society or community has been broken.[30] According to the French-born American philosopher of history and literary critic, Rene Girard (1923—), human beings are prone to violence because violence is at the core of human nature. Human propensity towards violence is a conundrum for which human beings have to find a solution. From the beginning of human history, according to Girard, cultures have developed different methods of dealing with violence and one of this mechanism is religion. Religion, for Girard, therefore, is a mechanism which humans have developed to defend themselves against their own violent nature. The logic of Girard's argument is that tribal cultures lack a well-developed judicial system to deal with violence. Since each act of violence evokes another, "to prevent this sequence, a victim—often a slave, king, or animal—is chosen. On this victim violence may be practiced without fear of reprisal."[31] Sacrifice, in the Girard sense, may be understood as a "regular exercise of good violence," which is used to overcome "bad violence."[32]

6. Taboo.

A taboo, as understood in tribal societies, is a violation of prescribed action. It is also a morally reprehensible act. A person who commits

---

30. Girard, "Violence and the Sacred," 244.

31. Ibid. 239.

32. Ibid.

a taboo incurs automatic punishment. Taboos are social mechanisms designed to establish some fundamental social values that are vital to society.[33] There are many types of taboos in tribal societies. Some taboos are designed for some specific occasions. Some cultures have taboos that are associated with farming or cultivation, for example. There are also taboos associated with harvesting, taboos for certain festivals, taboos to protect religious persons and places of worship, and taboos designed to keep women and children in certain places and at certain times. Like all religions (not excluding Judaism, Christianity, Islam, Hinduism, and Buddhism), tribal cultures have taboos that place restrictions on menstruating women. Prohibitions on menstruating women lead to prohibitions on "physical intimacy, cooking, attending places of worship, and sometimes requiring women to live separately from men" throughout their menstrual period.[34] In general, the sanctity of taboo is inspired by the idea that when a taboo is violated it may lead to disaster, not only for the individual violator, but for the society at large. The socio-cultural significance of taboo, therefore, is to confine the individual to the norms of society.[35]

7. Magic.

As we saw already, sanctions always inevitably follow the breaking of taboos. When taboos are broken some tribal people turn to religious rituals to mitigate the wrong committed. Others at times turn to magic. Magic is an attempt to manipulate spiritual forces.[36] Unlike religious rituals, which usually take place in public and are often characterized by adoration and obeisance to the spirits, magical rites are often private, and like religious rituals acknowledge that all reality has some spiritual components.[37] Magic then is an attempt to interfere with the spiritual and make the spirits do human biddings. The Polish and British anthropologist, Bronislaw Malinowski (1884–1942) who was considered the father of Functionalism branch of anthropology (i.e., the idea that all parts of society work together to form a coherent meaningful whole) considered magic to be a precursor to religion. In other words, magic, for what he called "primitive" cultures, played the

---

33. Barnerjee, "Religious Beliefs and Practices among the Bokars of Arunachel Prandesh," 155.

34. See Guterman, Mehta, and Gibbs, "Menstrual Taboos among Major Religions."

35. Barnerjee, "Religious Beliefs and Practices among the Bokars of Arunachel Prandesh," 155.

36. Carmody and Brink, *Ways to the Center*, 33.

37. Ibid.

role technology plays for us moderns. According to him, "all peoples use the best technology available to them but turn to magic and religion when the problems they confront exceed that technology."[38]

8. The Profane.

In the United States, like most of the Industrialized West, we are used to separation of Church and State and hold the two realms in creative tension. Not so with indigenous societies. For them, religion and society are not two separate orders, but one and the same reality. The profane, for them, is the social order, i.e., the opposite of the sacred. But they do not understand the profane to be in opposition to the sacred. The distinction between the sacred and profane is, for them, just a way of speaking and demarcating two realms that are by no means opposed.

9. Rites of Passage.

Tribal cultures have well developed rites of passage. A rite of passage is a stage in life in which a person moves from one socially constructed role to another. Arnold Van Gennep (1873–1957) was the first to provide a scholarly definition of a rite of passage in 1960.[39] He defined rite of passage as "rites which accompany every change of place, state, social position, and age."[40] Rites of passage cuts across all religions. Judaism is a good example of a World Religion with three well-defined rites of passage: Bris (infant circumcision), Bar Mitzvah (the coming of age ceremony for teen-age boys), and Kadish (funeral ceremony). Tribal cultures have rites of passage with striking similarities to those of the World Religions. There are basically four main rites of passage in tribal societies: birth (a ceremony initiates a child into the tribe), adolescence (ceremony that shows a person has moved from childhood to adulthood), marriage (a person becomes a responsible parent), and death (passage from this life to the next). "For every one of these events," Van Gennep wrote, "there are ceremonies whose essential purpose is to enable the individual to pass from one defined position to another which is equally well-defined."[41] Van Gennep went on to suggest that all rites of passage exhibit a pattern (or schema), which vary in importance, depending on the degree or the transitional phase that is being celebrated. The three patterns or schema are: separation, margin, and aggregation. The separation phase "comprises symbolic

---

38. Ibid., 21.

39. See Van Gennep, *The Rites of Passage*.

40. See Turner, "Liminality and Communitas," 512.

41. Van Gennep, *The Rites of Passage*, 3.

behavior signifying detachment of the individual or group either from an earlier fixed point in the social structure, from the set of cultural conditions or from both."[42] The rite of circumcision of a child will be an example of Van Gennep's separation phase. In the margin phase the person going through the ritual is in a liminal situation and because of this he or she manifests characteristics that are ambiguous.[43] The rites of adolescence or puberty will be a good example of the liminal stage. Finally, in the third phase, the one going through the ritual is in a relatively stable state and now same rights and obligations as others. He or she "is expected to behave in accordance with certain customary norms and ethical standards binding on incumbents of social position in a system of such positions."[44] An example here would be the rites of marriage.

Rites of passage in tribal societies are encoded in symbols. Symbols of course have different layers of meanings. The American Anthropologist-linguist, Edward Sapir (1834–1939) spoke of two main classes of symbols. The first kind, Referential symbols, are for the most part cognitive in the sense that they refer to facts that are already known to the community or society. Examples of this are oral speech or flag or code of arms of a community. The other class of symbol he called Condensation symbol. Ritual symbols in tribal societies are a good example of Condensation symbol.[45] The British cultural anthropologist whose work on symbols revolutionized contemporary understanding of symbols, particularly as it pertains to our understanding of tribal societies, Victor Turner (1920–1983), brings to our awareness the fact that symbols are polysemy (have many senses). Turner distinguishes three levels of symbolic meanings, which are important for understanding tribal ritual rites of passage. Turner calls the first level Exegetical meaning (understanding how the locals interpret their symbols). The second level is Operation meaning (understanding not only what the people say about their symbols, but also understanding what they do with their symbols). The third level is Positional meaning (understanding the meaning of the symbol in question in relationship to other system of symbols.[46] To understand tribal rites of passage one needs to investigate their ritual following these three levels.

42. Turner, "Liminality and Communitas," 512.

43. Ibid.

44. Ibid.

45. Sapir, "Symbols," 492–93.

46. Turner, "Symbols in Ndembu Ritual," 526.

10. Divination.

Divination is an attempt to discern the will of deity or oracle for a particular course of action. It is also the practice of predicting or foretelling the future. Divination, in contemporary society, is akin to psychic hotline. Many people go to psychics today to get "answers" to their troubles, say marriage, illness, poverty, etc. In tribal societies divination "is similar to magic in that it is an occult, non-technological solution to life's problems, but whereas magic tries to manipulate future events, divination is the mere attempt to predict those events."[47] In many tribal societies, when someone is chronically ill and return to health of the sick person is hard to come by, many people take their sick ones to a shrine or oracle to meet a diviner for diagnosis and prognosis. Diviners use different methods, like looking at the entrails of animals (say sheep or goat), examining the flight path of birds, or reading cracks in the shell of tortoise.[48] Among the Yoruba people of southwest Nigeria Ifa divination is very common. Ifa priests are well revered and respected by both the Yoruba and non-Yoruba people alike.

11. Creation Myths.

According to a recent study in neurobiology, due to the structure of the brain, human beings inevitably construct myths to explain their world.[49] A myth is usually a traditional storied form of explanation.[50] "A myth is an explanation of what has happened, and it is repeated because it expresses the tribe's identity and values. Peoples tell myths explaining how they came to be where and what they were."[51] According to the American mythologist, Joseph Campbell (1904–1987), there are four main functions of myth: (i) metaphysical function: to express a people's sense of awe before the absolute mystery (ii) cosmological function: to account for the origin of the universe (iii) sociological function: to provide support for the existing social order and integrate the individual into it and (iv) pedagogical: to teach and guide the individual on how to attain spiritual growth and human flourishing.[52]

---

47. Carmody and Brink, *Ways to the Center*, 34–35.

48. Ibid., 35.

49. See D'Aquili and Laughlin, "The Neurobiology of Myth and Ritual."

50. Carmody and Brink, *Ways to the Center*, 35.

51. Ibid.

52. See Campbell, *Occidental Mythology*.

Myths essentially help establish models of behavior,[53] and as narrative accounts of the acts of creation serve as models for ritual.[54]

12. Totems.

Totem is an object that is considered sacred, which is used as the symbol of the family, clan or tribe. It is usually made of an animal or plant that is revered by the family, clan or tribe. The totem serves as an emblem on which the people rally together. It gives them a sense of pride and identity. The idea of using plant or animal objects is also to show the interconnectedness of all beings.

13. High God.

Most tribal societies believe in deity and locate the heavens or sky as the abode of the high God. The location of sky as the abode of deity conveys the idea that the high God is centrally located. It also shows the power of this deity who is usually conceived in masculine terms. He resides in heaven and is control of the galaxies—the moon, the stars, the planet— and all created realities. He is everywhere and oversees all things. Deity is addressed by a great variety of names. The Massai of East Africa, for example, address divinity "directly with a great variety of names which are metaphorical masks for the incomprehensible ground of all reality, the inscrutable mystery of life behind the visible universe."[55]

14. Afterlife.

Belief in afterlife is a common feature of tribal religions. Life on earth is just the beginning of the life that is yet to come. The way a person lives and acts in this life will determine one's eschatological future. Tribal religions, more than all other religions, stress the importance of interwoven solidarity with one's kinsmen and women both past and present. Deceased relatives are not considered dead, but as having gone to take their place with the ancestors. The ancestors look after the tribe or clan from heaven.

15. Megaliths.

Megaliths, in ancient times, particularly in Neo-lithic cultures (New-Stone Age), were carefully constructed centers of ritual, usually made of large stones. The notion of Megalith in tribal cultures is related to the reverence they have for their dead and ancestors. Stone in ancient times was a sign of fortress. People always sought refuge from

---

53. Eliade, *Myth and Reality*, 8.
54. See Eliade, "The Symbolism of the Center."
55. Hillman, *Toward an African Christianity*, 51.

life troubles by maintaining contact with ancestors and seeking from them strength and succor. Those who sought close communion with their dead ones often came to these ritual centers for both security and strength. Megalith then served as a "symbol of permanence—of resistance to change, decay, or death."[56] The Stonehenge in England is one of the world's famous megaliths.

16. Shaman.

The Shaman is akin to a priest in contemporary society. The shaman is entrusted with cultic duties. He or she is essentially at the center of divination, healing, sacrifice, and even rites of passage. In many societies the shaman is reputed to have clairvoyance and clairaudience, i.e., has the ability to see and hear beyond the normal range.[57] According to Mircea Eliade, shamans play a great role in the defense of psychic integrity of the community. They champion anti-demonism by combating demons and diseases.[58] They uphold life, health, fertility and wage war against death, disease, sterility, disaster, and as well as all forces of darkness.[59] They play these role so well because of their ability to travel to the supernatural world where they encounter superhuman beings (gods, demons, spirits of the dead, etc.).[60] Tribal people find it very comforting to know that their shaman has the uncanny ability to fight the forces of evil. The also find it reassuring to know that a member of their community, i.e., the shaman, is not only able to see what is hidden and invisible to others, but can also bring back direct and reliable information from the spirit world.[61]

AFRICAN TRADITIONAL RELIGIONS

The word "religion," as we have pointed out repeatedly, is western in origin. Although Africans have strong beliefs about God and the supernatural world, they do not have a word for religion in its Western sense. In traditional African society, like in all tribal religions, there was no wall of separation between church and state or religion and society. What religion accepted or forbade was accepted or forbidden by society. In a sense there

56. Carmody and Brink, *Ways to the Center*, 37.

57. Ibid., 38

58. Eliade, *Archaic Techniques of Ecstasy*, 508.

59. Ibid., 509.

60. Ibid.

61. Ibid., 508

was an overlap between the state and religion in matters of politics and morals. But if we are to speak of religion in the Western sense of the word *religio* (to perform ritual with care) or *religare* (to bind), it is safe to say that Africans have different activities and practices they do that parallel what the West means by religion. The African sense of Supreme Being, the spirit world, the relationship of ancestors to the spirit world, relationship of the person or individual to his or her clan, village, tribe, ethnicity, and culture, and belief in after life, are activities and practices that parallel activities we mean by religion in the western use of the term.

Since religion permeates all aspects of African life, it is best to speak rather of African Traditional Religions (ATRs). We speak of African Traditional Religions (ATRs) in the plural because each ethnic group has its own traditional beliefs and practices. Ritual practices also vary from place to place and from one tribe to another. In sub-Saharan Africa alone there are hundreds of tribes and language groups. Sometimes it is easy to forget that there are stark differences in the religious practices and belief systems of the multitudinous religions we call ATRs. Sometimes these differences can be very significant and well pronounced as in the differences between, say Christianity and Islam or differences between Judaism and Hinduism.

In spite of their differences, there are also common elements among ATRs. Like Islam and Christianity, all religions under the umbrella of ATRs ask questions that are fundamental to human existence: what is the meaning of human life? What does it mean to be human? Why do people suffer? Why sickness? Why do bad things happen to good people? Why afterlife? What will happen to people who live good life at the end of time and what will happen to people who live bad lives at the end of time? The questions of human origins, eschatology, and practical guides on how to survive the brutalities of life are contained in folklores, songs, hymns, and proverbs that are transmitted orally from generation to generation. Although ATRs are similar in the manner in which they pose these questions, they however do not answer them in exact same way and their ritual prescriptions also vary significantly. Take the example of Christianity in the United States, in the early 1920s up to the 1960s when US Catholicism was still very much an ethnic immigrant Church, it was common to see in the same locale a Polish Catholic Church, an Italian Catholic Church, an Irish Catholic Church, and a German Catholic Church, etc. Even though they shared the same Catholic identity, the Irish expressions of Catholicism were in some ways different from the Polish expressions of Catholicism, just as the German and Italian expressions of Catholicism were different from other ethnic expressions of Catholicism. Or take the example of Islam where in one city you can have some Sunni or Shia Muslims or even Ahmmadiya Muslims. Even though they all share the same fundamental beliefs of Islam, there may be slight differences in their ritual practices or differences in allegiance to authority. The same thing is true of ATRs. The differences in religious practices and belief systems of ATRs do vary according to tribes, ethnicity, and language. It is therefore helpful to examine some common practices/belief systems of ATRs.

NINE CORE SET OF BELIEFS

There are as many brands of local religions in Africa as there are tribes, as we have pointed out. Each local religion, as we have pointed out also, has its own specific religious beliefs and practices. But in general they have some common features, which unify them and make it possible for us to speak of them as ATRs. In Islam it is common to speak of belief in Allah, fasting, praying five times a day, almsgiving, and pilgrimage to Mecca as five pillars of faith. This is a way of identifying the core beliefs of the followers of Prophet Muhammad (PBUH). ATRs do not have five pillars, but several pillars. Here we approximate nine of as core set of beliefs. .

1. Belief in Supreme Being.

   In the Western world it is not uncommon to find people who proudly self-identify as atheists. These people claim that they do not believe in any deity or Supreme Being. There may also be those who call themselves agnostics. Those who call themselves agnostics claim that it is not possible to prove whether or not there is God or deity and therefore we should doubt. In African society in general it is difficult to find any atheists or agnostics because Africans take the existence of God as a given. There is an African proverb that says you cannot show a child the palm of his hands. The palm of a child's hand is taken for granted because the child sees it every day and knows that it is there. The same idea is applicable when it comes to the existence of God—that God is a reality that the African sees every day. The African does not need a rational proof of God's existence in the face of empirical evidence. Religion in traditional Africa was a way of life that involved the whole community. Even if there were to be antireligious persons they still had to be "involved in the lives of their religious communities, because in terms of African thought, life can be meaningful only in community, not in isolation."[62]

---

62. Moyo, "Religion in Africa," 317.

ATRs notion of God is that of a supreme being who is transcendent and distant. God is also a spirit and active force that is immanent in the world. Following the idea that God is an active force, Africans conceive the nature or essence of anything in the universe as "force." There are different categories of force, which Africans maintain follow a hierarchical order "such that God precedes the spirits; then come the founding fathers and the living-dead, according to the order of primogeniture; then the living according to their rank in terms of seniority."[63] God is called by various names in traditional Africa religions. The variety of names are "metaphorical masks for the incomprehensible ground of all reality, the inscrutable mystery of life behind the visible universe."[64] The name for God among the Massai of East Africa, for example, is "Enkai," meaning "the Originator." "Enkai" is neither male nor female, but still a personal helpful reality that is immanent and transcendent and with whom the people can and do enter into relationships.[65] There are those who want to claim that Africans believe in plurality of gods and that they are polytheistic. This is not true across the board. Although Africans believe in the existence of other deities, they clearly distinguish these deities from the one supreme God who created and sustains all creation.

2. Belief in Spirit World

ATRs attribute the creation of the world to God, the Supreme Being. God's creation is two-fold: the visible world of the physical universe made up of humans, plants, and animals and the invisible world of spirits and deceased ancestors. There is interaction between the physical world of humans and the invisible world of spirits. This network of relationship is marked by cooperation and respect. Humans respect the spirit world by living in accord with deity's commands and in harmony with nature. The spirit world cooperates the humans by looking after them and protecting them from the forces of nature and the harsh realities of life. Humans interact with the spirit world through worship, sacrifice, and divination. Prohibited acts called taboos are assumed to be criminal acts against society (lying, murder, sodomy, adultery, theft, etc.) and are punishable by communal sanctions. There are no written legal codes specifying what is permitted or forbidden. ATRs have no sacred books and no founder. Values, together with what is believed,

63. See Onyewuenyi, "Reincarnation."

64. Hillman, *Toward an African Christianity*, 51.

65. Ibid.

are transmitted orally from generation to generation and for the most part everyone knows them.

3. Community

A person is a union of two forces: material and spirit. At death the spirit returns to the spirit world to join the company of the ancestors. For this reason a person is also not an individual alone, but a being in community—a community with a network of relationships to the ancestors and the spirit world. Community is the basis of morality. The community is hierarchically structured. The order of importance is determined by age—from the oldest to the youngest. Older people in the community are closer to the ancestors by virtue of their age and are accorded respect. They are also thought to be wiser than anyone else. Their role is to teach and mentor the young. Just as the community occupies a center stage in the tribe or clan, the family is also at the center of the community. The family, like society, is also hierarchically structured and almost always patriarchal. In every family the first born, especially if he is male, occupies a central role and is a chief decision maker in family matters. Men rule the family and have rights of inheritance.

4. Belief in a Personal God or "Chi."

In Christian teaching there is the belief in guardian angels. The concept of personal god or "chi" in ATRs comes closest to the Christian idea of guardian angels. Most Africans believe that everyone has a personal god, which is called "chi" among the Igbos of Southeast Nigeria. The general idea is that a person works in cooperation with his or her "chi." This is captured in the Igbo proverb that when a man says yes his chi says yes. But there is also the idea that a person's fortune, whether good or bad, is determined by his or her personal god. Some people believe that one's personal god, "chi," sets one's destiny and that one's destiny is always pre-determined because a person cannot rise above the destiny of his or her "chi." This idea that a person's "chi" sets one's destiny is always in dialectical tension with the individual quest to shape his or her own destiny. Chinua Achebe gives us a good example in his epic novel, *Things Fall Apart*:

> [Okonkwo's] life had been ruled by great passion—to become one of the lords of the clan. That had been his life-spring. And he had all but achieved it. Then everything had been broken. He had been cast out his clan like a fish not a dry, sand beach, panting. Clearly his personal god or chi was not made of great things. A man could not rise beyond the destiny of his chi. The

saying of the elders was not true—that if a man said yea his chi also affirmed. Here was a man whose chi said nay despite his own affirmation.[66] .

The idea that one cannot rise above the destiny of his or her "chi" can also be problematic. It seems to make "chi" the sole determinant and the one responsible for one's fortune. When things go well one can easily take responsibility or attribute it to the good fortune of one's "chi." But what happens when a person's bad fortune is as a result of one's obvious bad decisions and choices? Does the person lay it squarely on the feet of his or her "chi?" The consensus would be that every one's "chi" helps him or her to work out his or her destiny.

5. Ancestors.

   Africans accord a lot of respect to the ancestors. Respect for ancestors is the African way of expressing "fellowship, hospitality, and family continuity."[67] In many places ancestor worship is part and parcel of the people's folklore and mythologies. In some places people pray to the spirit of their dead ancestors for favors, like good health and good fortune.

6. Afterlife

   Belief in ancestors is tied to the notion of afterlife. Traditional Africans are reminded every day about afterlife. A person's life is marked by a series of birth, death, and re-birth. We see a good example at the burial ceremony of a revered elderly man, Ogbuefi Ezeudu, in Chinua Achebe's *Things Fall Apart*. In the story, the one officiating at the funeral ceremony yelled to the dead man: "If you had been poor in your last life I would have asked you to be rich when you come again. But you were rich. If you had been a coward, I would have asked you to bring courage. But you were a fearless warrior. If you had died young, I would have asked you to get life. But you lived long. So I shall ask you to come again the way you came before."[68]

7. Elders.

   The elders are the closest to the ancestors. Traditional African society was theocratic in nature. The elders are considered human representatives of deity and the moral conscience of the community. Where problems arise in the community it is the role of the elders to adjudicate and establish order. They also establish what is right and what is

66. Achebe, *Things Fall Apart*, 131.
67. See Onyewuenyi, "Reincarnation."
68. Achebe, *Things Fall Apart*, 123.

wrong. In the following verse, an oracle, the Odu Obara Meji oracle of the Yorubas of southwest Nigeria, condemns disrespect for elders:

> If a child indulges in stubborn acts,
> if he sees an aged priest and slaps him,
> if he comes across an aged physician and beats him mercilessly,
> if he goes on and meets an aged priest and knocks him down,
> thus declares the oracle to the disobedient child,
> "who says nobody could control him?"
> Orunmila says: "Don't you know that there is no long life for any child who beats
> the elderly priest, no long life for any child who slaps an aged physician. Any child
> who flogs an aged priest is seeking his own death. Respect for elders means long life."[69]

8. Rituals.

   The African worldview is permeated by rituals. "A man's life from birth to death was a series of transition rites which brought him nearer and nearer to his ancestors."[70] Ritual practices are used to offer logical explanations of phenomena. Ritual practices vary according to place and convention. There are rituals that pertain to worship. There are also rituals pertaining to festivals, marriage, death of a loved one, and birth of a new child. There are also rituals pertaining to the way to farm, the way to eat, and the way to treat one's guests or strangers. If a member of the community steals, for example, there is a ritual sacrifice to be performed to find out who the thief is and, if possible, recover the stolen property.

9. Theophoric Names

   African names are loaded with messages and carry a lot of meanings and symbolism. By the time you know somebody's names you get to know practically their family history. In conferring names Africans also show the God-centeredness of ATRs by bringing God into the picture and making fundamental statements about themselves and their place in the world. Many African names are theophoric (God-bearing names) in that they either have "God" as a prefix or suffix. According to the African writer Theophilus Okere, Africans use the occasion of conferring names to tell their life story, make their profession of faith, pronounce judgment on the world, make fundamental

---

69. See Adewale, "Crime and African Traditional Religion."

70. Achebe, *Things Fall Apart*, 122.

statement about the meaning of life, celebrate their moral victories over their enemies, express their optimism for the future, and reassure themselves about the truth of things. They also use the occasion of conferring names to praise and lament, taunt and defy, dare, fawn, and pray.[71] The Igbos of southeast Nigeria, for example, have variety of names that entreat God for favor or affirm their belief in God. God, for them is "Chukwu" or "Chineke." Some use the shortened form "Chi" to refer to this creator God. Name like *Chidi* means "there is God;" *Chinwe* means "I am owned by God;" *Chima* means "God knows the hidden secrets and mysteries of life;" *Chinua* means "God fights on my behalf;" *Ogechi* means "God's time is the best;" and *Onyeberechiya* means "bring your complaints to God."[72] The Yoruba of south-west Nigeria have similar ways of conferring names. They have a class of names they call *Oruko Amutorunwa* (literally= names a person brings from heaven). These names would depict all special events or unusual circumstances surrounding the birth of the child. For example, all twin-born children have specially designated names as the first of twins is called "Taiwo" and the second "Kehinde." A child born immediately after a set of twins is called "Idowu" and the one after "Idowu" is called "Alaba." They also have other classification of names. For example, a male child born after the father is recently deceased is called "Babatunde" (literally "father has made a come-back"). A girl who is born to a family where the mother has recently been deceased is called "Iyabode" (literally "mother has made a come-back"). In all, the invocations in African names "offer infinite possibilities of prayer and communion with a God who is both Lord and master, friend and companion, judge and witness."[73]

ATRS IN POST-COLONIAL AFRICA

Colonialism brought a lot of material benefits to Africa. It brought Western style education, Western clothing, economic development, and Western religions and ways of life. Colonialism also brought Africa to the realities of modern world. Today a large number of Africans speak European languages, like English, French, and Portuguese, in addition to their own local languages. Those who receive formal Western education are more likely to speak either of these languages while the uneducated ones are more likely

71. Okere, "African Thought, Philosophy, and Spirituality."

72. Ibid.

73. Ibid.

to speak an adulterated version of these languages. For the sake of simplification local languages spoken in Africa can be grouped into five family groups: .

(1).the Niger-Kordofanian family, which includes over 300 Bantu languages (like Swahili, Ganda, Kongo, Sesotho, and Zulu. These Bantu languages are spoken by Bantu people who live in central, eastern, and southern Africa. The Niger-Kordofanian language family also includes some non-Bantu languages, like Igbo, Yoruba, and Akan, that are spoken in West Africa.[74]

(2). Nilo-Saharan family language (like Dinka, Nuer, Kanuri, and Massia) spoken by people who live in countries like Chad, Niger, Mali, Tanzania, Uganda, Kenya.

(3). Khoihoi language family group (like San and Khoihoi), sometimes called click-languages because of the click-like sound of the language, spoken in Tanzania and South Africa.

(4). Afro-Asian languages like Berber, Arabic, Amharic, Gall, Somali, and Hausa spoken in northern Africa and parts of West Africa.

(5). Indo-European languages, like Afrikaans that was developed by Dutch settlers in South Africa.

But the benefits of colonialism came with a price. The feeling among Africans in general is that colonialism brought a lot of exploitation and instability to the continent. Many of the nation-states created under colonialism are still politically and economic unstable. The general feeling is that these nations only received paper independence, not real independence. Many of them still depend on their colonial rulers for economic sustenance. Some who see colonialism as a massive failure have called for a return to traditional African belief systems and values. One of these was the Nigerian writer, Chinua Achebe, who expressed the clash between western civilization and African belief systems in his novel, *Things Fall Apart*. Achebe meant his work as a response to Georg F. Hegel (1770–1831) and Joseph Conrad's Heart of Darkness that depicted Africa as barbaric, cultureless, and uncivilized. In the novel Achebe shows how culturally superior Africans were before the contact with the West and how social institutions in Africa prior to European contact was solid and well organized. On the political front, in the wake of independence some African political leaders started urging Africans to desert the colonial project and re-discover their humanity has been taken from them and return to the African value systems, particularly

---

74. See The World Book Encyclopedia.

the African sense of family. Some of these leaders attempted to build a political system that draws from traditional African values. .

1. Kenneth Kaunda's African Humanism (1924—): Kenneth Kaunda who ruled Zambia from 1964–1991 developed a socio-political and economic ideology he called African Humanism. Kaunda called on Africa to exercise caution in matters pertaining to western technology and discover and cherish African ways of being human. Kaunda thought that the two competing ideologies of the West (communism and capitalism), not only encourage violence but also dehumanizes the African. Thus, Kaunda wanted to recover the African sense of community and the African sense of personhood.

2. Kwame Nkrumah (1909–1972): Nkrumah ruled Ghana (then known as Gold Coast) from 1951–1966. He developed a philosophy of African personality he called "Consciencism." Nkrumah also thought that Western ideologies were dehumanizing and secularizing. He argued that the African sense of personhood is very spiritual and ennobling and therefore need to be re-discovered.

3. Leopold Senghor (1906–2001): Senghor was a poet and cultural theorist who ruled Senegal from 1960–1980. He developed a philosophy he called "Negritude." Senghor thought that the colonial system has produced in the African a split personality and an African who has lost true worth of self. Negritude will make the African appreciate his or her blackness and be a proud African.

4. Julius Nyerere (1922–1999): Nyerere ruled what was then known as Tanganyika and later Tanzania from 9161–1985. He developed a socio-economic system he called "ujamaa," a Swahili word meaning "familyhood." *Ujamaa* is a brand of African socialism that takes the family as its centerpiece. Nyerere wanted to build a society in which the yardstick would be, not material things, but the progress of the people. What he calls *Ujamma* is different from the Marxist inspired communism because it deplores violence and rejects class struggle. It is also different from liberal capitalism because it rejects exploitation of people. .

These calls for return to traditional African values were greeted with enthusiasm by some and skepticism by others. In Zaire, for example, Mobutu Sese Seko abandoned his Christian name Joseph Desire and opted instead for an African name. Mobutu also renamed his country from the Belgian Congo to Zaire and renamed what was then Leopoldville Kinshasa and Elizabethville Lubumbashi.[75] Some countries, like Upper Volta, which became Burkina Faso, changed their names to more indigenous ones as part of this spirit of African nationalism or personhood. In the end however, the call for rediscovery of African traditional values was met with stiff opposition. The project failed mainly for two reasons. First, the political leaders who advocated return to traditional African values were themselves corrupt. Some of them run a one-party state and looted state treasuries. Second, some of these ideologies, like the *ujamma* project of Nyerere, suffered from lack of organization and poor funding. All these made the philosophies expounded by these leaders seem like an empty slogan.[76]

There were also those who opposed the return to African traditional roots on academic grounds. These people argued that ironically it was the traditional African sense of familyhood and hospitality that made Africa vulnerable to foreign exploitation. These people "have no regrets about the loss of the African root, or its humane values, for they think that technologization, urbanization, and modernization cannot co-exist with those values."[77] They think that rather than return to traditional roots, Africa needs to fully embrace the modern world and catch up with the rest of the world in politics, economy, and technology. Some also dismiss the call to return to traditional African roots as amounting to nothing other than romanticization of the past. According to them, "the African past is characterized by such social habits and loyalties that are suspicious of innovation and hardened against change."[78] A return to such a society, while romantically desirable, is unrealistic and practically impossible.[79]

ATRs and Dialogue with Christianity

The Pontifical Council for Interreligious Dialogue underscored the importance of ATRs and called for greater pastoral attention to these religions for the following reasons. .

1. ATRs is the religious and cultural context from which most Africans come and in which many of them still live.

---

75. Hillman, *Toward an African Christianity,* 15.

76. Ehusani, *An Afro-Christian Vision,* 25–26.

77. Ibid.25.

78. Ibid., 26.

79. Ibid.

2. ATRs is dynamic and ever evolving. "Its vitality varies from country to country. In some African countries, some of the intellectual elite are declaring themselves to be adherents of ATR."[80]

3. Because of the Church's respect for religions and cultures of other people the Church wants to preserve what is noble, true, and good in those religions.

4. By understanding ATRs the Church would better meet the needs of African Christians so that "the Church will be more and more at home in Africa, and Africans will be more and more at home in the Church."[81]

---

80. See Pontifical Council for Interreligious Dialogue, "Pastoral Attention to African Traditional Religion."

81. Ibid.

Bibliography

Achebe, Chinua. *Things Fall Apart*, 50th Anniversary Edition. New York: Anchor, 1994.

Adewale, A. S. "Crime and African Traditional Religion." Online: http://users.iol.it/osorio/atr-crime.htm.

Amiot, Francois. "Jesus, an Historical Person." In *The Sources for the Life of Christ*, edited by Francois Amiot, et al. New York: Hawthorne, 1962.

Anderson, J. C. and Moore, S. D. "Introduction: The Lives of Mark." In *Mark and Method: New Approaches in Biblical Studies* ed. Minneapolis: Fortress, 1992.

Anderson, Bernhard W. *Understanding the Old Testament*, 4th ed. New Jersey: Prentice Hall, 1986.

Anselm of Canterbury. "Proslogion," In *Anselm of Canterbury*, edited and translated by JasperHopkins and Herbert Richardson. New York: Edwin Mellen Press, 1974.

Anderson J.C. and Moore, S.D. "Introduction: The Lives of Mark." In *Mark and Method: New Approaches in Biblical Studies* ed. J. C. Anderson and S.D. Moore. Minneapolis: Fortress Press, 1992.

Arbuckle, Gerald A. *Culture, Inculturation, and Theologians: A Postmodern Critique.* Collegeville: Liturgical Press, 2010.

Bailey, Lloyd R and Furnish, Victor P., eds. The *Pentateuch: Interpreting Biblical Texts.* Nashville: Abingdon, 1981.

Bainton, Roland H. *Christianity*. Boston: Haughton Mifflin, 1987.

Bandstra, Barry L. *Reading the Old Testament: An Introduction to the Hebrew Bible*, 2nd ed. Belmont: Wadsworth, 1999.

Banerjee, Bikash. "Religious Beliefs and Practices among the Bokars of Arunachel Prandesh." In *Understanding Tribal Religion*, edited by Tamo Mibang & Sarit Kumar Chandhuri, 143–158. New Delhi: Mittal Publications, 2004.

Barton, J. *Isaiah 1–39: Old Testament Guides*. Sheffield: Sheffield Academic Press, 1995.

Beardslee, W.A. *Literary Criticism of the New Testament*. Philadelphia, 1970.

Bejczy, Istvan. *Erasmus and the Middle Ages: The Historical Consciousness of a Christian Humanist*. Brill, 2001.

Benjamin, Don C. *The Old Testament Story: An Introduction*. Minneapolis: Fortress, Press, 2004.

Blake, H. *Caxton and His World*. London: Andre Deutsch, 1969.

Blenkinsopp, Joseph. *A History of Prophecy in Israel*. Louisville: John Knox, 1996.

———. *The Pentateuch: An Introduction to the First Five Books of the Bible*. New York: Doubleday, 1992.

Boadt, Lawrence. *Reading the Old Testament: An Introduction.* New York: Paulist Press, 1984.

Brown, Raymond, E. *An Introduction to the New Testament.* New York: Doubleday. 1997.

Brown, Raymond, et.al. eds. *The New Jerome Biblical Commentary.* New Jersey: Prentice Hall. 1990.

Brown, Andrew J. *William Tyndale on Priest and Preachers.* London: Inscriptor Imprints, 1996.

Brueggemann, Walter. *The Creative Word: Canon as a Model for Biblical Education.* Philadelphia: Fortress Press, 1982.

————. *Hopeful Imagination: Prophetic Voices in Exile.* Philadelphia: Fortress Press, 1986.

————. *Isaiah 40–66.* Louisville: John Knox Press, 1998.

————. *Theology of the Old Testament: Testimony, Dispute, Advocacy.* Minneapolis: Fortress Press, 1997.

Caird, G.B. *The Language and Imagery of the Bible.* Philadelphia: Westminster, 1980.

Campbell, Joseph. *The Mythic Image.* Princeton: Princeton University Press, 1974.

————. *Occidental Mythology.* New York: Penguin Books, 1991.

Carmody, D. L. and Brink, T.L. *Ways to the Center: An Introduction to World Religions,* 6th ed. Belmont: Wadsworth, 2006.

Carson, D.A. et. al., *An Introduction to the New Testament.* Grand Rapids: Zondervan, 1992.

Carter, Stephen L. *The Culture of Disbelief: How American Law and Politics Trivialize Religious Devotion.* New York: Anchor Books, 1993.

Catechism of the Catholic Church 2nd ed. New York: Doubleday, 1995.

Catholic Study Bible. New York: Oxford University Press, 1990.

Cohn-Sherbok, Dan. *The Hebrew Bible.* London: Wellington House, 1996.

Conzelmann, Hans and Lindemann, Andreas. *Interpreting the New Testament.* Peabody: Hendrickson, 1988.

Copeland, Shawn. "Guest Editorial," *Theological Studies* 61 (2000): 604–05.

Cunningham, Lawrence. *The Catholic Heritage.* Eugene: Wipf and Stock, 1995.

Davis, Philip G. "Mark's Christological Paradox." In *The Synoptic Gospels: A Sheffield Reader,* edited by Craig Evans and Stanley Porter. Sheffield: Sheffield Academic Press, 1995.

Davis, Stevan L. *The New Testament: A Contemporary Introduction.* San Francisco: Harper and Row, 1980.

D'Aquili, Eugene and Laughlin, Charles. "The Neurobiology of Myth and Ritual." In *The Spectrum of Ritual: A Biogenetic Structural Analysis* by Eugene D'Aquili, Charles Laughlin, and John McManus, 153–182. New York: Columbia University Press, 1979.

Day, John T., Lund, Eric, & O'Donnell, Anne, M. eds., *Word, Church, and State: Tyndale Quincentenary Essays.* Washington DC: Catholic University of America Press, 1998.

Dempsey, Deidre, A. "2 Samuel 7." In *Introduction to Theology,* edited by John Laurance, 7–10. Boston: Pearson Custom Publishing. 2000.

Dines, Jennifer. "Imaging Creation: The Septuagint Translation of Genesis 1: 2" *The Heythrop Journal* 36 (1995) 439.

Doyle, Dennis. *Communion Ecclesiology.* Maryknoll, NY: Orbis, 2000.

Douglas, Mary. *Leviticus as Literature.* Oxford: Oxford University Press, 1999.

————. *Purity and Danger: An Analysis of the Concepts of Pollution and Taboo*. New York: Pantheon Books, 1966.

Duling Dennis, and Norman Perrin. *The New Testament: Proclamation and Parenesis, Myth and History* 3rd ed. Philadelphia: Harcourt Brace College Publishers, 1994.

Dulles, Avery Dulles. *Models of the Church*. Garden City: New York, 1974.

Dumbrell, William. *The Faith of Israel: A Theological Survey of the Old Testament*, 2nd ed. Grand Rapids: Baker Books, 2002.

Durkheim, Emile. "Ritual, Magic, and the Sacred." In *Readings in Ritual Studies*, edited by Ronald L. Grimes, 188–193. Upper Saddle River: Prentice Hall, 1996.

Eckhart, Meister. *Selected Writings* translated by Oliver Davis. London: Penguin, 1994.

Ehrman, Bart. *The New Testament: A Historical Introduction to the Early Christian Writings* 3rd ed. Oxford: Oxford University Press, 2004.

Ehusani, George Omaku. *An Afro-Christian Vision: "Ozovehe" Toward a more Humanized World*. Lanham: University Press of America, 1991.

Eliade, Mircea. *Archaic Techniques of Ecstasy*. Translated by Willard R. Trask. Princeton: Princeton University Press, 2004.

————. *Myths and Reality*. New York: Harper and Row, 1963.

————. "The Symbolism of the Center." In *Cosmos and History: The Myth of the Eternal Return*, 12–27. New York: Harper and Row, 1953.

Enchiridion Biblicum, Online: http://www.catholicscripture.net/enchiridion/

Esposito, John L. *Islam: The Straight Path*, 3rd ed. Oxford: Oxford University Press, 1998.

Farmer, W.R. *The Synoptic Problem: A Critical Analysis* 2nd ed. Macon: Mercer University Press, 1976.

Fanning, Steven. *Mystics of the Christian Tradition*. New York: Routledge, 2001.

Fee, Gordon. "A Text-Critical Look at the Synoptic Problem." In *The Synoptic Problem and Q: Selected Studies from Novum Testamentum* vol.4, compiled by David Orton. Leiden: Brill, 1999.

Feldman, Stephen M. *Please Don't Wish Me A Merry Christmas: A Critical History of the Separation of Church and State*. New York: New York University Press, 1997.

Fenton, Terry. "Israelite Prophecy: Characteristics of the First Protest Movement." In *The Elusive Prophet: The Prophet as a Historical Person, Literary Character and Anonymous Artist*, edited by Johannes C. De Moor. Leiden: Brill, 2001.

Fernando, "An Asian's View of Jesus' Uniqueness." In *The Uniqueness of Jesus: A Dialogue with Paul F. Knitter*, edited by Leonard Swidler and Paul Mojzes, 68–73. Eugene: Wipf & Stock, 2007.

Fink, K.A. *History of the Church* vol.4, ed. H. Jedin and J. Dolan. New York: Crossroad, 1986.

Fitzgerald, Allan, O.S.A., ed. *An Encyclopedia through the Ages*. Grand Rapids: Eerdmans, 1999.

————. "Church of North Africa." In *Encyclopedia through the Ages*. Grand Rapids: Eerdmans, 1999.

Foad, Salem M. *The Seerah of Prophet Muhammad*. New York: Vantage Press, 2001.

Francisco, Clyde. "The Moral Message of the Hebrew Prophets" *Review and Expositor* 45 (1948), 435.

Frankl, Viktor. *Man's Search for Meaning*. New York: Pocket Books, 1984.

————. *The Will to Meaning: Foundations and Applications of Logotherapy*. New York: Penguin Books, 1988.

Freed, Edwin, D. *The New Testament: A Critical Introduction*. Belmont: Wardsworth, 1986.

Gamble, Harry Y. *The New testament Canon: Its Making and Meaning*. Philadelphia: Fortress Press, 1985.

Girard, Rene. "Violence and the Sacred: Sacrifice." In *Readings in Ritual Studies*, edited by Ronald L. Grimes, 239–256. Upper Saddle River: Prentice Hall, 1996.

Goldingay, John. *Old Testament Theology: Israel's Gospel*. Downers Grove: Inter Varsity Press, 2003.

Goodacre, Mark. *The Synoptic Problem: A Way through the Maze*. London: Sheffield Academic Press, 2001.

Gonzalez, Justo L. *Church History: An Essential Guide*. Nashville: Abingdon Press, 1996.

———. *A History of Christian Thought: From the Protestant Reformation to the Twentieth*
Century vol. III, Revised Edition. Nashville: Abingdon Press, 1987.

Grabbe, Lester L. *Priests, Prophets, Diviners, Sages: A Socio-Historical Study of Religious Specialists in Ancient Israel*. Valley Forge: Trinity Press, 1995.

Grimm, Harold J. *The Reformation Era: 1500–1650*. New York: The Macmillan Company, 1954.

Groohans, Hans-Peter. *Luther*. London: Collins Publishers, 1997.

Gunkel, H. "Fundamental Problems of Hebrew Literary History." In *What Remains of the Old Testament*. London: George, Allen and Unwin, 1928.

Guterman, M., Mehta, P., and Gibbs, M. Menstrual Taboos Among Major Religions. TheInternet Journal of World Health and Societal Politics 5 2007. Online: https://ispub.com/IJWH/5/2/8213.

Haley, Alex. *The Autobiography of Malcolm X*. New York: Ballantine Books, 1999.

Halivni, David. "Aspects of Classical Jewish Hermeneutics." In *Holy Scriptures in Judaism, Christianity and Islam: Hermeneutics, Values and Society*, edited by Hendrik Vroom andJerald Gort. Amsterdam: Rodopi, 1997.

Heiler, Friedrich. "The History of Religions as a Preparation for the Cooperation of Religions."In *The History of Religions: Essays in Methodology*, edited by M. Eliade & J. Kitagawa. Chicago: University of Chicago Press, 1958. Online: http://www.religion-online.org/showchapter.asp?title=580&C=767.

Helms, Randel McCraw. *Who Wrote the Gospels?* Altadena: Millennium Press, 1997.

Henn, William. "Hermeneutics and Ecumenical Dialogue: BEM and Its Responses on "Apostolicity."" In *Interpreting Together: Essays in Hermeneutics*, edited by PeterBouteneff and Gagmar Heller. Geneva: WCC Publications, 2001.

Hillman, Eugene, C.S.Sp. *Toward an African Christianity: Inculturation Applied*. Mahwah: Paulist, 1993.

Hogan, Richard. *Dissent from the Creed: Heresies Past and Present*. Huntington: Our Sunday Visitor Publishing, 2001.

Holmes, Derek, J. and Bickers, Bernard W. *A Short History of the Catholic Church*. New York: Continuum, 2002.

Honore, A.M. "A Statistical Study of the Synoptic Problem." In *The Synoptic Problem and Q: Selected Studies from Novum Testamentum* vol.4, compiled by David Orton. Leiden: Brill, 1999.

Houtepen, Anton. "Hermeneutics and Ecumenism: The Art of Understanding a CommunicativeGod." In *Interpreting Together: Essays in Hermeneutics*, edited by Peter Bouteneff andGagmar Heller. Geneva: WCC Publications, 2001.

Huff, Margaret C. and Wetherilt, Ann, K. *Religion: A Search for Meaning.* New York: McGraw Hill, 2005.

Isichei, Elizabeth. *A History of Christianity in Africa: From Antiquity to the Present.* Grand Rapids: Eerdmans, 1995.

Jeanrond, Werner. *Theological Hermeneutics: Development and Significance.* New York: Crossroad, 1991.

Johnson, Luke Timothy. *The Writings of the New Testament: An Interpretation* revised edition. Minneapolis: Fortress Press, 1999.

Jones, A.H.M. *Constantine and the Conversion of Europe.* Toronto: University of Toronto Press, 1978.

Kaltner, John. *Introducing the Qur'an.* Minneapolis: Fortress Press, 2011.

Kapr, Albert. *Johann Gutenberg: The Man and his Invention* translated from the German by Douglas Martin. Brookfield: Ashgate Publishing Co., 1996.

Kessler, Gary. *Eastern Ways of Being Religious.* Mountain View: Mayfield Publishing, 2002.

Klein, William, et. al., *Introduction to Biblical Interpretation* Revised and Updated. Nashville: Thomas Nelson Publishers, 2004.

Knitter, Paul. "Five Theses on the Uniqueness of Jesus." In *The Uniqueness of Jesus: A Dialogue with Paul F. Knitter,* edited by Leonard Swidler and Paul Mojzes. Eugene: Wipf and Stock, 2007.

La Due, William. *The Chair of Saint Peter: A History of the Papacy.* Maryknoll: Orbis Books, 1999.

Landry, D and Penchansky, D. "The Primeval Story." In *The Christian Tradition,* Second Edition, edited by Catherine Cory and David Landry. New Jersey: Prentice Hall, 2003.

Laurance, John, ed. *Introduction to Theology.* Boston: Pearson Custom Publishing, 2000.

Leo XIII. Encyclical Letter *Aeterni Patris* (1879) [On the Restoration of Christian PhilosophyAccording to the Mind of St. Thomas Aquinas, the Angelic Doctor]. In *St. ThomasAquinas Summa Theologica* vol.1, translated by the Fathers of the English DominicanProvince. Allen: Christian Classics, 1981).

Lemche, Niels Peter. "Hebrew." In *The Anchor Bible Dictionary* vol.3, ed. David Freedman, et.al. New York: Doubleday, 1992.

Lindberg, Carter. *The European Reformations.* Oxford: Blackwell Publishers, 1996.

Lonergan, Bernard. *Insight,* Collected Works of Bernard Lonergan, vol. 3, edited by F. Crowe and R. Doran. Toronto: University of Toronto Press, 1997.

———. "The Future of Christianity." In *A Second Collection,* edited by William F.J. Ryan, S.J. and Bernard J. Tyrell, S.J. Toronto: University of Toronto Press, 1974.

———. *Method in Theology.* Toronto: University of Toronto Press, 1971.

———. *Philosophy of God and Theology.* Philadelphia: Westminster Press, 1973.

Lowe, Mary Elise. "Woman Oriented Hamarthologies: A Survey of the Shift from Powerlessness to Right Relationship." *Dialog: A Journal of Theology* 39 (2000) 128.

Luhrmann, Dieter. "Q: Sayings of Jesus or Logia." In *The Gospel behind the Gospels: Current Studies on Q,* edited by Ronal A. Piper. Leiden: Brill, 1995.

Machiavelli, Niccolo. *The Prince* reprinted in *The Prince and the Discourses* 2. Translated by Luigi Ricci Modern Library ed. 1950.

Macquarie, John. *Principles of Christian Theology.* New York: Charles Scribner's Sons, 1977.

McDermott, Timothy, ed. *St. Thomas Aquinas Summa Theologiae: A Concise Translation*. Westminster: Christian Classics, 1989.

McEnhill, Peter and Newlands, George. *Fifty Key Christian Thinkers*. London: Routledge, 2004.

McGonigle Thomas, D. and Quigley, James, F. *A History of Christian Tradition: From its Jewish Origins to the Reformation*. New York: Paulist Press, 1988.

Malina, Bruce and Rohrbaugh, Richard. *Social Science Commentary on the Synoptic Gospels* 2nd ed. Minneapolis: Fortress Press, 2003.

Masson, Robert. *The Charmed Circle: Theology for the Head, Heart, Hands and Feet*. Kansas City: Sheed & Ward, 1987.

McBrien, Richard P. *Catholicism*. New York: Harper Collins, 1994.

McEnhill, Peter & Newlands, George. *Fifty Key Christian Thinkers*. New York: Routledge, 2004.

McGrath, Allister E. *Theology: The Basics*. Oxford: Blackwell, 2004.

McKnight, Edgar. *Jesus Christ in History and Scripture: A Poetic and Sectarian Perspective*. Macon: Mercer University Press, 1999.

Miller, J. W. Miller. Meet the Prophets: A Beginner's Guide to the Books of the Biblical Prophets. New York: Paulist Press, 1987.

Moyo, Ambrose. "Religion in Africa." In *Understanding Contemporary Africa*, 4th ed., eds., April and Donald Gordon. Boulder: Lyne Reiner Publishers, 2007.

Nawaz, Muhammad. *Islam: Religion of Peace*. Bloomington: 1st Books, 2003.

Nissinen, Martti. "What Is Prophecy? An Ancient Near Eastern Perspective." In *Inspired Speech: Prophecy in the Ancient Near East: Essays in Honor or Herbert B. Huffmon*, edited by John Kaltner and Louis Stulman. London: T and T Clark, 2004.

Oakes, Edward T. *Pattern of Redemption: The Theology of Hans Urs von Balthasar*. New York: Continuum, 2005.

Okere, Theophilus., "African Thought, Philosophy, and Spirituality." Unpublished Paper.

Olin, John. *Catholic Reform: From Cardinal Ximenes to the Council of Trent 1495–1563*. New York: Fordham University Press, 1990.

Olsen, Glenn. *Beginning At Jerusalem: Five Reflections on the History of the Church*. San Francisco: Ignatius Press, 2004.

O'Meara, Thomas. *Thomas Aquinas Theologian*. Notre Dame: University of Notre Dame Press, 1997.

Onyewuenyi, Innocent. "Reincarnation: An Impossible Concept in the Framework of African Ontology." Online: http://users.iol.it/osorio/atr-reincarnation.htm.

Orji, Cyril. *A Semiotic Approach to the Theology of Inculturation*. (Eugene, OR: Pickwick, 2015.

————. *The Catholic University and the Search for Truth*. Winona, MN: Anselm Academic, 2013.

Orlandis, Jose. *A Short History of the Catholic Church*. Dublin: Four Courts Press, 1994.

Otto, Rudolph. *The Idea of the Holy*, 2nd ed. Oxford: Oxford University Press, 1950.

Panikkar, Raimon. "The Invisible Harmony: A Universal Theory of Religion or a Cosmic Confidence in Reality?" In *Toward a Universal Theology of Religion*, edited by Leonard Swinder. Maryknoll: Orbis Books, 1987.

Pontifical Biblical Commission. "Instruction on the Historical Truth of the Gospels." *The Catholic Biblical Quarterly* 26 (1964) 299–312.

———. *The Interpretation of the Bible in the Church*. Boston: St. Paul's Books & Media, 1993.

Pontifical Council for Justice and Peace. *Compendium of the Social Doctrine of the Catholic Church*. Washington DC: USCCB, 2004.

Pontifical Council for Interreligious Dialogue. "Pastoral Attention to African Traditional Religion." Online: http://users.iol.it/cdi/meeting/xtianity/vatican.html.

Portier, William L. *Tradition and Incarnation: Foundations of Christian Theology*. New York: Paulist Press, 1994.

Schweitzer, Don. *Contemporary Christologies*. Minneapolis: Fortress Press, 2010.

Rahner, Karl. *Foundations of Christian Faith: An Introduction to the Idea of Christianity*. New York: Crossroads, 1997.

Rhoads, D. Dewey, J. and Michie, D. *Mark As Story: An Introduction to the Narrative of a Gospel* 2nd ed. Minneapolis: Fortress Press, 1999.

Robinson, Neal. *Islam: A Concise Introduction*. Washington DC: Georgetown University Press, 2007.

Rolle, Richard. *The Fire of Love* translated F.M. Compar. London: 1914.

———. "The Form of Living." In *The English Writings of Richard Rolle* ed. Rosemary Allen. London: SPCK, 1989.

Sanneh, Lamin. *West African Christianity: The Religious Impact*. Maryknoll: Orbis Books, 1983.

Sapir, Edward. "Symbols." In *Encyclopedia of the Social Science* XIV, 155–169. New York: McMillan, 1933.

Schwarz, Hans. *Theology in a Global Context: The Last Two Hundred Years*. Grand Rapids: Eerdmans, 2005.

Schweitzer, Albert. *The Quest of the Historical Jesus*, edited by John Bowden. Minneapolis: Fortress Press, 2001.

Shannon, Thomas A. "Grounding Human Dignity." *Dialog: A Journal of Theology* 43 (2004), 114–117.

Sigmund, Paul E., ed., *St. Thomas Aquinas on Politics and Ethics: A New Translation, Backgrounds, Interpretations*. London: W.W. Norton & Co., 1988.

Smith, MacDonald J. "Can Science Prove That God Exists?" *The Heythrop Journal* 3 (1962), 126–138.

Sparks, Kenton. *Ancient Texts for the Study of the Hebrew Bible: A Guide to the Background Literature*. Peabody: Hendrickson, 2005.

Swanston, Hamish. *The Kings and the Covenant*. London: Burns and Oates, 1968.

Swartley, William. *Israel's Scripture Traditions and the Synoptic Gospels: Story Shaping Story*. Peabody: Hendrickson, 1994.

Talbert, Charles, ed., *Reimarus: Fragments*, translated by Ralph Fraser. Chico: Scholars Press, 1985.

Tatum, Barnes, W. *In Quest of Jesus*, revised and enlarged. Nashville: Abingdon Press, 1999.

Thomas Aquinas, *Summa Theologica*, translated by the Fathers of the English Dominican Province. Allen: Christian Classics, 1981.

Thompson, L.A. and Ferguson, J. *Africa in Antiquity*. Ibadan: Ibadan University Press, 1969.

Thompson, Craig R. *The Bible in English* 1525–1611. Washington: The Folger Shakespeare Library, 1958.

Torell, Jean-Pierre. *St. Thomas Aquinas: The Person and his Work* vol.1 trans. Robert Royal. Washington DC: Catholic University of America Press, 1996.

Toynbee, Arnold. *An Historian's Approach to Religion*. Oxford: Oxford University Press, 1956.

Tuohey, John F. "The Gender Distinctions of Primeval History and a Christian Sexual Ethic." *The Heythrop Journal* 36 (1995) 175.

Turner, Victor. "Liminality and Communitas." In *Readings in Ritual Studies*, edited by Ronald L. Grimes, 511–519. Upper Saddle River: Prentice Hall, 1996.

————. "Symbols in Ndembu Ritual." In *Readings in Ritual Studies*, edited by Ronald L. Grimes, 520–529. Upper Saddle River: Prentice Hall, 1996.

Ullmann, Walter. *The Origins of the Great Schism*. London: Burns & Oates, 1948.

Vassiliadis, Petros. "The Nature and Extent of the Q-Document." In *The Synoptic Problem and Q: Selected Studies from Novum Testamentum* vol.4, compiled by David Orton. Leiden:Brill, 1999.

Van Gennep, Arnold. *The Rites of Passage*. Chicago: University of Chicago Press, 1960.

Vatican II, "Nostra Aetate." Online: http://www.vatican.va/archive/hist_councils/ii_vatican_council/documents/vat-ii_decl_19651028_nostra-aetate_en.html.

Waller & Benedicta Ward. Trowbridge: The Cromwell Press, 1999.

Ward, Benedicta. "The English Mystics." In *An Introduction to Christian Spirituality* edited by Ralph Waller and Benedicta Ward. London: SPCK, 1999.

Walsh, James, ed. *Cloud of Unknowing*. London: SPCK, 1981.

Weaver, Walter P. *The Historical Jesus in the Twentieth Century* 1900–1950. Harrisburg: Trinity Press, 1999.

Westermann, Claus. *Isaiah 40–66: A Commentary*. Philadelphia: Westminster Press, 1969.

Widyapranawa, S.W. *Isaiah 1–39: The Lord Is Savior: Faith in National Crisis*. Grand Rapids: Eerdmanns, 1990.

Wilson, Robert. *Prophecy and Society in Ancient Israel*. Philadelphia: Fortress Press, 1984.

Worthy, Roland H. *Church, Monarch and Bible in Sixteenth Century England: The Political Context of Biblical Translation*. London: McFarland & Company, 2000.

Wrede, William. *The Messianic Secret*, trans. J.C. G. Greig. Greenwood: Attic Press, 1971.

Wright, Addison, Murphy, Roland, and Fitzmyer, Joseph. "A History of Israel." In *The New Jerome Biblical Commentary*, edited by Raymond Brown, Joseph Fitzmyer, and Roland Murphy. New Jersey: Prentice Hall, 1990.

Wright, N.T. *The Challenge of Jesus: Rediscovering Who Jesus Was and Is*. Downers Grove: Intervarsity Press, 1999.

————. *The Contemporary Quest for Jesus*. Minneapolis: Fortress Press, 2002.

Young, Walter A. *The World's Religions: Worldviews and Contemporary Issues*, 2nd ed. Upper Saddle River: Prentice Hall, 2005.

Index

A

Abdallah Ibn, 223
Abel, 38, 40
Aborigines, 253
Abraham, 8, 11, 39–40, 46–47, 51, 54,
    81, 89, 220, 222–23, 225, 232,
    237, 239, 245–46
Abrahamic monotheistic religions, 4,
    26–29, 220, 249–50
Acts of the Apostles, 87, 157
Africa/Africans, viii, xi, 1, 128, 129,
    131, 133, 149, 155, 167, 186–90,
    205, 220, 247, 261–73, 275,
    278–81
African church (North African
    church) 129, 130, 132, 142, 151,
    170, 187–89, 247, 278
African Traditional Religions (ATR),
    ix, 4, 9, 249, 253, 262–63,
    267–273
Agnostic, 4, 264
Ahimsa, 252
Ahura Mazda, 238, 251
Akhenaton, 4, 7
Alexander the Great, 119
Allah, 35, 38, 220, 222–23, 225–29,
    232, 239, 241, 245–46, 251, 264
Allport Gordon, 152,
Almsgiving, 236, 245, 264
Angel [Gabriel], 226, 233
Angels, 3, 36–38, 141, 145–46, 148
    [Guardian Angels], 226
Angelic [St. Thomas], 237, 140
Angelicus [doctor], 141, 145, 279

Anglican, 21, 190
Animism, 8, 221, 255
Anointing of the Sick, 145, 161–62,
    219
Anselm of Canterbury, 16–17, 24, 275
Anthropomorphism, 8, 91
Anti-Semitism, 153
Apocalypse, 87
Apocrypha Books, 84, 87, [Apocry-
    phal Gospels] 112
Apodictic law, 56, 78
Apollo, 63
Apostasy, 132
Apostles, 98–99, 114, 116, 157, 166,
    171–73, 177, 187
Apollinarius, 184–85
Aquinas St. Thomas, viii, 17–19, 22,
    25, 128, 135, 137–38, 140–151,
    195, 279–82
Arius/Arianism, 160, 182–83
Aristotle, 17–18, 25, 136–37, 139–40,
    143, 149
Aryan, 4, 6
Asceticism, 181–82, 188–89, 250, 252
Athanasius, 20, 131, 141, 181, 183,
    187
Atheism, 4, 173
Atonement, 51, 93, 110, 242, 252
Augustine, viii, 19–20, 22, 101, 107,
    122, 128–37, 141, 150–51, 162,
    182, 187
Avicebron, 136,
Avicenna (Ib'n Cina), 136, 140
Averroes Ibn Rushed, 136–37, 140,
    143

B

Babylon/Babylonia, 9, 27, 52, 55–56, 58, 60, 62, 67–69, 73–76, 81, 84, 88, 118 [Babylonian creation epic], 34, 40–42 [Babylonian captivity], 209

Baptism, 117, 131, 133–35, 145, 161–62, 175 [rebaptism of lapsed Christians], 133

Baptist [John], 86, 102, 110 [Baptist Church], 163

Bar Mitzvah, 58, 258

Belief, ix, 3–5, 8, 12, 20–21, 23, 83, 109, 154–56, 167–68, 201, 204, 220, 227, 232–33, 235, 238–39, 242, 252, 255, 261–67, 269–70, 275 [unbelief/disbelief], 5, 161, 235, 237, 276

Beneficent [God is], 36, 235, 239

Benefices, 194, 211, 219

Berith, 51

Bible, 8, 20, 57, 61, 65, 82, 118, 120, 122–23, 125, 156, 166, 187, 211, 214–16, 222, 276, 279, 281–82 [Christian Bible], vii, 82 [Gutenberg Bible, 196 [Hebrew Bible/Tanak] 27–28, 46, 53, 56, 61, 65–66, 80–81, 83–91, 93–94, 97, 275

Bishop 15, 98–99, 129, 131–32, 143, 155, 157–58, 162, 177, 180–81, 183, 185, 189, 192, 200, 203, 206, 211, 215–16 [Archbishop of Canterbury],16, 214 [Archbishop of Cologne], 200 [Archbishop of Milan], 192 [Archbishop of Mainz], 208

Black Muslims, 186, 247–48

Blasphemy, 245

Booths, 51

Brahman, 8

Bris, 58, 258

Buddha, 253

Buddhism, 9, 13, 155, 200, 250–53, 257

Bultmann, Rudolf, 21, 121, 123, 125

C

Calvin John, 211–13 [Calvinists], 21

Canon [of Scripture], vii, 27, 59, 80–91, 96–97, 108, 111–12, 126, 179, 219, 276, 278 [Canon Law], 140 [Muratorian Canon], 98

Canonicity (criteria of), 83, 97

Canonists, 193

Canonize, 136, 141

Case law (casuistic law), 52, 56, 78

Cassisiacum, 135

Catechism, 87n13, 276

Catharist heresy, 218

Cathedral, 157, 189, 211

Catholic, 162–63 [Catholic Church], vii-viii, 8, 12, 15, 17, 20–21, 23–24, 80, 83–4, 86–7, 93, 97, 113, 119–20, 125, 128, 132–33, 135–41, 143, 145, 147–48, 150, 155, 158, 161–66, 190, 212–19, 276–77, 280–82

Catholicism, viii, 162–68, 263, 280

Catholicity, 98

Celibacy, 210

Chiasm, 48

Christ, Jesus, 82, 85–86, 96–97, 100, 108, 112, 114, 117, 122, 124, 136, 145–47, 158, 160–62, 164, 167–68, 175, 191, 193

Christendom, 138, 193, 206–7, 217

Christians, 80–150, 161–64, 169, 171–75

Christianity, 85, 110–17, 128, 131–32, 169, 171–72, 174–90

Christology, 152–60, 163 [Christo-logical Controversies], 160–61, 168, 179, 184, 186, 276

Church [Eastern/Orthodox], 141, 163

Circumcision, 54, 173, 258–59

Civilizations, vii, 9, 27–28, 80–81, 128, 140, 236, 270

Clairvoyance, 262

Clergy, 133, 136, 140, 194, 197–99, 206, 213, 218–19

Clerical, 197, 211

Cognitive, 259

Communion Holy (see Eucharist), 199

Confession, 34, 207, 130 [confessional
    statement], 108, 212-3, 28[Con-
    fessions of St. Augustine], 20,
    129, 131, 134
Confirmation, 161
Conscience, 207, 210, 267
Conscious/consciousness, 108-9,
    110-11, 118, 148, 159, 205-6,
    233, 275 [Self-consciously], 249
    [Unconscious], 3, 5-6, 24-25
Constantine, 176, 180-83, 203, 279
Contrition, 207
Conversion, 131, 157, 171, 176,
    181-82, 203, 279
Coptic, 163, 186, 189, 224
Cosmological, 26, 260-61
Council [Ecumenical], viii, 138,
    160-62, 172-73, 179, 182-86,
    192-94, 209, 211, 217-19, 272,
    281-82 [Council of Jamnia], 86
    [Council of Trent], 86, 140, 147,
    215n20, 280 [Second Vatican
    Council], 119
Covenant, vii, 39, 47, 51-56, 58-60,
    77-8, 84-6, 88-9, 92, 97, 281
Creed, 179, 182-85, 250, 278
Cross, 10, 154, 156, 201, 217, 252,
Crucifix, 202 [Crucifixion] 109
Cult/cultic, 33, 62, 71, 93, 202, 206,
    219, 262 [Occult], 260
Culture, 1-4, 8-9, 14-15, 22-23, 27,
    39, 55, 62-63, 81, 119, 123, 129,
    131, 143, 148, 151, 165, 167, 169,
    186, 196, 206, 218-19, 224, 231,
    237, 247, 253-58, 261, 263, 273,
    275-76
Cuneiform, 52, 81
Curia, 194, 206, 208-9

D

Deacon, 157-58, 172
Deism, 4, 109
Deity/deities, 3-5, 8-9, 12, 42, 64-65,
    129, 221-22, 224, 234, 238,
    255-56, 260-61, 264-65, 267
Demon/Devil, 101, 103, 161, 182, 228,
    246, 262

Demythologization, 125
Denomination (see sect/sectarian)
Detachment, 259
Devil (see demon)
Devotion, 12, 141, 195-96, 199,
    202-3, 250, 276
Diaspora, 170, 172
Dietary laws, 56-57
Dilthey Wilhelm, 120-21
Diocese, 208
Disciple/Discipleship, 67-9, 76,
    101-2, 110, 114-15, 141, 145,
    157, 159, 170-71, 177, 180, 200,
    248
Divination, 62, 260, 262, 265
Divine, 3, 13, 15, 17-19, 25, 33-36,
    39-40, 43, 51, 54, 58, 60, 63-67,
    71, 75, 82, 85, 116-17, 120, 130,
    133, 140, 145-56, 159-61, 164,
    166-67, 180, 184-85, 201, 217,
    220, 226, 232-35, 246, 250-52,
    260, 278
Diviner/Sorcerer, 67n87, 228, 260,
    278
Doctrine, viii, 9, 13, 17-21, 23, 42-43,
    114, 128, 130, 137, 140-41,
    145-46, 148, 150, 152, 155, 158,
    163, 169, 171, 173-89, 192,
    209-10, 212, 218-19, 226, 238,
    253, 281
Dogma, 20, 109, 111, 250
Dominicans, 136,-43, 150-51,
    199-200, 202, 208, 279, 281
Donatism, 132, 150
Dualism/Dualist, 34, 130, 178-79, 238
Durkheim Emile, 255, 277

E

Easter, 131
Eastern, 27, 40, 55, 61-63, 65-66, 79,
    141, 162, 178, 184, 186, 199, 205,
    221, 270, 279-80
Eastern Orthodox (see Church)
Ecclesiastical, 99, 138, 143, 198,
    211-12, 214, 218, 250
Ecclesiasticus, 84-5, 87
Eckhart Meister, 199-200, 277

Ecumenical, viii, 160, 163, 179, 182–84, 278

Egypt/Egyptians, vii, 4, 8–9, 27, 40, 42, 46–50, 57–58, 62, 73, 77, 78, 81, 85, 89, 98, 128, 130–31, 172, 181–82, 186–89, 221, 224, 237, 242, 247–48

Eightfold path, 13

Eliade Mircea, 262, 277–78

Elijah (Prophet), 63

Elisha, 63

Elijah Muhammad, 248

Elohim, 28–9, 44, 57, 88, 90, 92

Enlightenment, 109, 253

Episcopal, 189, 219

Epistle, 97, 118, 141, 211

Erasmus Desiderius, 197–98, 208, 210, 215, 275

Esau, 47

Eschatology, 61, 263

Eskimo, 253

Ethics, 9, 12, 21, 80, 281

Ethnic, 2, 46, 95, 158, 170, 172, 221, 243, 263–64

Eucharist (see Communion, Holy), 145, 157, 161–63, 203, 209, 219

Evangelical, 136, 139

Evangelist, 95, 104–5, 109, 115–16, 126, 171, 187

Evolution, 5, 249

Excommunication, 209

Exegesis, viii, 113, 118, 121, 128, 148–49, 195

Exile, 33, 60, 68–70, 74–77, 88, 93, 118, 213, 276

Exodus, vii, 28–29, 46–54, 56–58, 75–78, 83, 87, 89, 118

Exorcism, 255–56

F

Faith, viii, 5, 15–16, 18–22, 34, 40, 64, 69, 75–6, 81, 91, 94, 96, 98, 101–2, 108–11, 114–16, 119, 124, 128, 131–32, 134–36, 139, 143, 147–48, 157, 159–63, 165–67, 170–71, 174–77, 181–83, 187–88, 192–93, 197, 208–10, 213, 218, 220–21, 232, 237–39, 246–47, 250, 264, 268, 277, 281–82

Fasting, 12, 171, 179, 182, 210, 230, 242–43, 252, 264,

Father, 4, 6, 8, 16, 21, 28, 30, 46–7, 49, 54, 69, 73, 85, 129, 138, 180, 194, 207, 211–12, 222–23, 257, 265, 269, 279, 281 [Apostolic Fathers], 177 [God as Father], 158, 160–61, 183, 202, 251 [Fathers of the Church], 19–20,113, 119, 125, 137, 140, 148, 162, 184, 187

Fertility, 262

Five pillars, viii, 237, 264

Form criticism, 66, 123

Four Noble Truths, 13, 155

Francis of Assisi, 136

Frankl Viktor, 5–7, 9, 24–25, 59, 152–53, 156, 168, 277

Free-will, 128, 146

Freud Sigmund, 6

Friends, 58, 101, 131, 139, 191, 202, 212, 225, 229, 269

Functionalism, 257

G

Gabriel, 226, 233

Galilee, 100, 109, 111, 114

Gandhi Mohandas, 253

Gentile, 15, 57, 90, 100–1, 171, 173

Gilgamesh, 41, 58

Gnostic/Gnosticism, 178–79, 182–83

Gospel, viii, 14, 57, 77, 87, 95–116, 122–23, 126, 139, 141, 159, 167, 169, 171–72, 176, 179, 186, 202, 239, 276, 278, 280–81

Grace, 22, 43, 47, 78, 128, 133–34, 145, 147–48, 158–59, 161, 163–66, 199, 207

Gunkel, H, 66, 278

Guru, 252

H

Hadith, 36, 220n3, 225

Hajj, 230–31, 245–46

Hammurabi, 9, 52, 56

Hanukkah, 51

Harappan, 4

Heaven, 5, 11, 29, 31, 35–40, 42, 65,
    117, 132, 202, 226, 229–30, 233,
    251, 261, 269

Hebrew, 46, 49, 61, 63–65, 77–78
    [Hebrew Scriptures], see Bible/
    Tanak

Hell, 133, 202, 235–36, 241

Hellenist/Hellenistic, 8, 27, 99, 116,
    119, 123, 169, 172

Henotheism, 8

Henry Suso, 200

Henry VIII, 211, 213–14

Hermeneutics, viii, 113, 117–22,
    125–26, 278–79

Heresy, 177, 185–86, 193–94,
    199–200, 215, 218

Hesed, 51

Heterodox, 113

Hinduism, 4–5, 8–9, 200, 221,
    250–53, 257, 263

History, vii, 3, 9, 14–15, 20, 22–24,
    27–29, 34–35, 40, 44, 46–47,
    50, 52, 58–59–60, 65–66, 73,
    78,80–82, 88–9, 91, 93–4, 98–99,
    101, 104, 106–7, 109–12, 118,
    121, 125, 132–36, 138, 140,
    148–49, 153, 157, 159, 161,
    164–66, 169, 186–87, 191–92,
    197, 210, 228, 239, 247, 253–54,
    256, 268, 275–80, 285

Holocaust, 152–53, 6,

Holy, 33, 42, 45, 57, 63, 72, 95, 101,
    131, 133, 137–38, 140, 189, 195,
    212, 242, 245, 247, 251, 254, 278,
    280 [Holy Mosque at Mecca],
    240

Holy Communion, 199

Holy Orders, 145, 161–62,

Holy Spirit, 82–3, 104, 116, 157–58,
    160–61, 166, 171–72, 179, 184,
    251

Human sacrifice, 256

Humanism 194, 210 [African Hu-
    manism], 271

Humanist, 122, 194–98, 204, 210,
    212, 275

I

Icon, 10

Idolatry, 76, 88

Ignatius of Loyola, 218 (see Society
    of Jesus)

Imam, 229

Incarnation, 147, 163, 175, 281

Indulgences. 197, 203, 208, 219

Initiation rites, 130, 161, 213

Inquisition, 218

Inuit, 253

Iran, 73n108, 221, 237–38, 243

Isaac, 28, 46–7, 54, 222

Islam, viii, 3–4, 8–9, 14, 22, 27, 36,
    40, 54, 138, 153, 186, 188–89,
    220–21, 225–48, 250–53, 257,
    263–64, 277–78, 280–81

Israel, vii, 13, 28–29, 33–34, 40, 42,
    44, 46–96, 153, 157, 160, 235,
    237, 247, 275, 277–78, 282

J

Jacob, 28, 46–8, 54

Jehovah Witnesses, 164, 167

Jesuit, 7, 21–22, 157, 218

Jethro, 49

Jew/Jewish, 4, 6, 10, 12–15, 28, 46,
    50–51, 56–8, 63, 69, 76, 78,
    81–4, 86–7, 89–90, 97–100, 109,
    111–12, 114, 116, 118, 136, 153,
    157, 169–75, 187, 221, 224, 231,
    235, 237–39, 242–43, 251–52,
    278, 280

John, Gospel of, 159 [Fourth Gospel]
    14

John the Baptist, 86, 102, 110

Joseph, 28, 47–48, 77–78, 81, 126,
    235, 260, 270–71, 275–76, 282

Josephus, Flavius, 89, 112

Judaism, vii, 4, 8, 27, 46–79, 87, 95,
    111, 119, 128, 153, 169, 170–71,
    173, 220, 237, 250–53, 257–58,
    263, 278

Judea, 70–71, 100, 103, 169, 173, 237

Justification, 20, 208–9, 219

Justin Martyr, 174

K

Kami, 8, 255
Kant Immanuel, 120
Kaddish, 58
Khadijah, 223–24, 226
Karma, 253
Koran (see Quran)
Kosher, 56

L

Laity, 129, 136, 203, 206, 209
Lapsed, 210, 222 [Lapsed Christian],
    133
Lent, 12, 211, 252
Liberation Theology, 22, 122, 155
Liturgy, 87–88, 124, 141, 203–4
Logos, 14, 123, 175, 183–84
Lonergan, Bernard, 20–25, 155, 279
Lord's Supper (see Eucharist), 211
Luther, Martin, 19–20, 25, 97, 128,
    206–211, 213, 215–17, 278
Lutheran, 163, 190, 212, 219, 244

M

Maccabees, 51, 84, 87
Magic, 62, 158, 257–58, 260, 277
Malcom X, 248, 278
Malinowski Bronislaw, 257
Manichean(ism), 130, 135
Marcel, Gabriel, 121
Marcion/Marcionism, 85, 178–79, 182
Marduk, 34, 41–42, 52, 58
Martyr, 129, 132, 154, 170, 175,
    179–81, 187–88, 190, 203
Mary, 99, 156, 165, 171, 185, 202,
    213–14, 235
Masjid (see Mosque), 240, 245
Mass (see Eucharist), 203–4, 206,
    209–10, 213
Mecca, 10–11, 221–23, 226–31,
    233–37, 240, 245–46, 264
Medicine man, 256
Meditation, 198, 200, 250
Megaliths, 261–62
Mesopotamia, 9, 27, 34, 41–2, 44, 62,
    81, 221

Messiah, 14, 70, 77, 101–3, 108,
    110–11, 126, 160, 170
Middle Way, 13, 252
Minister, 48, 133
Miracle, 49, 102, 110, 114, 233
Mohammad, 220n3, 234, 248
Monastery, 138–39, 186, 201, 207–8
Monasticism, viii, 181–82, 188, 210,
Monk, 15–16, 20, 131, 133, 138, 182,
    198, 207, 217
Monolatry, 8
Monotheism, 4, 237, 171
Montanism, 178–79, 182
Morphology, 8
Mortification, 132, 236
Moses, 9, 11, 14, 46, 49–52, 54–56, 60,
    77–8, 83, 89–90, 92–4, 122, 136,
    225, 232–33, 235–37, 239
Mosque, 12, 189, 231–32, 240, 245,
    248
Muratorian canon, 98
Muslim, 2, 10–12, 36, 142–43, 186,
    188–89, 220n3, 224–35, 238–48,
    263
Mystic/Mystical, 140, 151, 188, 198,
    200–2, 277, 282
Mysticism, 198, 200
Myth, 9, 11–12, 27–8, 40, 44, 110,
    115, 117, 130, 187, 222, 254,
    260–61, 267, 276–77

N

Names, 30, 36–7, 60, 63, 67, 99, 120,
    172, 231, 239, 247, 261, 265,
    268–69, 272
Nation of Islam, 186
Nazis, 6, 152
Nestorians, 185
New Testament, viii, 15, 20, 54, 77, 82,
    85–7, 90, 93, 95–127, 131, 159,
    171, 179, 215–16, 275–79
Nicaea, 160, 162, 182–84
Noah, 39, 51, 53–4, 225, 229, 239
Noble truths, 13, 155
North America, 205, 243
Old Testament, vii, 20, 77, 80, 84–7,
    93–94, 96–7, 119, 160, 175, 179,
    187, 215–16, 275–78

Ontological argument, 16
Oracles, 60, 63–4, 67–8, 70–2, 74n118, 76, 99, 117, 260. 268
Oral cultures, 254
Origen, 85, 122, 160, 176–77. 187
Original Sin, 36, 43, 133–35,161, 219
Orthodox Church, 163
Otto, Rudolf, 254–55, 280

P

Pagan, 41, 129, 132, 139, 143, 175, 177, 188, 234, 238, 245–46, 253
Palestine, 65, 157, 221, 231, 248,
Pantheism, 8
Pantheon, 5, 42
Papal, 140, 193–95, 206, 209, 213–14, 216–17
Passover (Pesach), 50–51, 78
Pastor, 15, 20, 80, 134
Pastoral, 16, 272, 281
Patriarch, 28, 46–7, 51, 78, 81, 160, 266
Patristics, 20, 122
Paul (Apostle), 14–15, 20, 87, 96–7, 99, 110, 141, 149, 160, 171, 173, 179–80, 202, 211,
Pelagianism, 133–34, 150
Penance, 207, 216, 219, 145, 161–62, 182
Pentateuch, vii, 27, 85, 89–91, 94, 122, 275
Pentecost, 157, 171,
Persia, 34, 68–9, 73n108, 74, 76, 81, 221, 237–38
Peter (Apostle), 14–15, 87, 98–99, 101, 158, 171–73, 176–77, 180, 195, 208
Peter Lombard, 15, 140, 142–43
Pharaoh, 47–50, 58, 77, 189
Pharisees, 171
Philo of Alexandria, 89, 187
Piety, 135, 185, 197–98, 202, 211 [Roman Pietas], 174–75
Pilgrimage, 10, 203, 222, 228, 230–31, 234, 245–46, 264
Pious, 207
Plato, 22, 117, 129–31, 136–37, 142, 144

Plotinus, 130
Polygamy, 224
Polytheism, 5, 34, 2222, 227, 251
Pope, 113, 137, 140–41, 143, 147, 149–51, 158, 180, 187–90, 192–95, 200, 205–11, 213–14, 215n120, 217–18
Potiphar, 47
Predestination, 134, 145, 212
Preliterate, 253
Presbyter, 157, 216
Presbyterian, 21, 163
Priest, 8, 20–22, 62, 80, 91 130–31, 133, 158, 160, 162, 164, 182–83, 203–4, 206–11, 215n119, 216–17, 255, 260, 262, 268 [Priestly Source], 29, 33–4, 44, 93, 122
Primitive, 253, 257
Profane, 258
Prophecy/Prophets, vii, 11, 36, 40, 55, 59–79, 83–92, 97, 103, 114, 118, 141, 160, 170, 175, 179, 188, 220, 223, 225–37, 239, 242, 245–46, 264, 275–82
Proselytize, 250
Protestant, vii, 20–21, 24, 80, 83–4, 86–7, 93, 97, 137, 147, 150, 163–64, 167, 210, 212, 218, 278
Psychic, 62, 64, 260, 262
Puberty, 242, 259,
Purgatory, 210, 219
Puritan, 207

Q

Qur'an, vii, 8, 11–12, 35–8, 40, 44, 220, 223–28, 230, 232–34, 236–42, 244–46

R

Rabbi/Rabbinic, 118, 153, 170
Ramadan, 226, 230, 233, 236, 242–44, 247, 252
Reconciliation, 252
Redemption, 134, 163, 178
Reformation, viii, 19–20, 80, 87, 97, 128, 137, 157, 163–66, 191, 193–219, 278–80

Religion, vii, ix, 1–46, 62–63, 95,
    107, 109–10, 112, 131–32, 145,
    169–70, 173, 176–78, 181, 186,
    189, 196–97, 212, 220–22, 227,
    234, 236–39, 247–73, 279–82
Renaissance, 20, 122, 195–96
Repentance, 88, 102, 111, 244
Resurrection, 95–6, 101–2, 109,
    114–16, 124, 145, 159–60, 168,
    170, 202
Revelation, 14–19, 25, 67, 82, 87, 97,
    114, 125, 140, 142, 151, 166,
    201, 203, 208, 219, 224, 226–28,
    233–37, 240, 250
Ritual, 3, 9, 12, 33–4, 93, 97, 158, 222,
    239, 241, 246, 254, 256–57, 259,
    261, 263–64, 268, 276–78, 282

S

Sabbath, 12, 33, 37
Sacraments, 133, 145, 147, 158–59,
    161–62, 164–65, 168, 189, 199,
    207, 209, 212–13, 216
Sacred, 11, 17–19, 34, 81–2,
    84–85, 94, 110, 113, 115–17, 122,
    130–31, 140, 143, 145–46, 164,
    166–67, 197, 230, 245–46, 252,
    254–55, 258, 261, 265, 277–78
Sacrifice, 38, 86, 162, 174–75, 188,
    210, 246, 252, 256, 262, 265, 268,
    278
Salvation, viii, 13, 18–19, 71, 82, 85,
    95–6, 114, 116, 124, 128, 133–35,
    147, 152–67, 182, 207–8, 253
Satan (see Devil), 36–37
Schism, viii, 162, 191–219, 282
Schleiermacher, Friedrich, 105,
    120–21, 127
Scholastic(ism), 15–16, 19, 24, 136–
    37, 139n31, 143–45, 148–51, 210
Sect (sectarian), 95, 128, 130, 162,
    174, 179, 280
Shaman, 256, 262
Shavuot, 50
Shi'a/Shiite, 220, 229, 240, 263
Shinto, 8, 255
Sitz im Leben, 66

Society of Jesus, 218
Sorcerer (see Diviner), 228
Stonehenge, 262
Structuralism, 124
Sukkoth, 51
Sunni, 220, 240, 263
Superstition, 197–98, 204, 213, 230
Suzerain treaty, 52–3, 78
Symbol, 9–12, 43, 70, 143, 147, 150,
    157, 162, 165, 174, 188, 211, 231,
    244, 246, 254, 258–59, 261–62,
    268, 277, 281–82
Synagogue, 13, 170
Syncretism, 4
Synod, 215
Synoptic gospel, 95, 102–8, 122–23,
    126–27, 276–78, 280, 282

T

Taboo, 256–57, 265,277–78
Talmud, 111–12
Tanak, 46, 88–5, 88–90, 93, 97
Temple, 34, 53, 71, 75–6, 93, 100, 170,
    173, 251
Tertullian, 173, 176–77, 179, 187
Theism, 4
Theodicy, 130, 153
Theology, vii, 14–25, 40, 43,
    80–81, 93, 109, 122, 128, 135–38,
    140–45, 147, 149, 151, 155, 160,
    175, 187, 200–1, 208–9, 212, 276,
    278–81
Theriomorphism, 8
Torah, 27, 46, 55–6, 59, 83–84, 88–9,
    91, 94, 153, 238
Totem, 261
Transcendence, 6, 10, 251
Transubstantiation, 209
Trent, 20, 86, 140, 147, 215n120,
    218–19, 280
Tribal, ix, 92, 222–23, 249–50,
    253–62, 275
Trinity, 17, 145, 177, 187, 212, 278,
    282
Turner Victor, 259, 282
Tyndale, William, 215–17, 276

U

Ultimate, 2–3, 9–10, 12, 14–15, 17, 27,
    29, 81, 165, 178, 250, 252–53
Upanishad, 8, 251

V

Value, 11–12, 14, 28, 59, 110, 114,
    156, 167, 175, 196, 257, 260, 265,
    270–72, 278
Van Gennep, Arnold, 258–59, 282
Vatican, 119, 195, 281–82
Vulgate, 214–16

W

Westermann, 66, 282

Worship, 3, 8–9, 11–12, 33–4, 51, 55,
    70, 84, 92, 97–98, 131, 158, 165,
    170, 176, 181, 203, 221–22, 227,
    232, 234, 236, 239, 245–46, 255,
    257, 265, 267, 268
Wycliffe John, 193, 214–16

Y

Yom Kippur, 51, 252,

Z

Zipporah, 49,
Zoroaster/Zoroastrianism, 4, 237–38,
    250–51
Zealots, 173